Praise for

THE
FIVE BOOKS
OF
MIRIAM

"This work is a masterpiece that should be in every library. . . . Frankel has produced a truly magisterial women's commentary on *The Five Books of Moses* [and] her commentaries are richly imaginative. . . . "
—*Publishers Weekly Religion Bookline*

"Frankel has filled the silence of the millennia with this richly imagined, brilliantly provocative chorus of women's voices—questioning, commenting, protesting, teaching, giving the Torah new life and new urgency. From now on, without the companion text of *The Five Books of Miriam*, *The Five Books of Moses* will seem like half the story."
—Letty Cottin Pogrebin, author of *Deborah,
Golda and Me: Being Female and Jewish in America*

"With this masterpiece, [Frankel] takes her place as a sage and teacher to our entire generation. . . . A guide to Torah for any Jew willing to stand anew at Sinai, this time without covering one ear."
—Rabbi Bradley Shavit Artson, *Conservative Judaism*

"An extremely well-crafted exploration of the Torah from the perspective of women."
—*Lilith*

"*The Five Books of Miriam* is a delight. These ancient and contemporary stories about and from the women of Jewish tradition call on us to reframe our understanding of Judaism."
—Rabbi Arthur Waskow, author of *Down-to-Earth Judaism*

"A courageous and challenging commentary on the Torah." —*Reform Judaism*

"Frankel's commentary from a female perspective . . . gives plenty to think about and reminds us how fully human the people of the Bible were."—*Booklist*

"A wonderfully imaginative book . . . highly recommended." —*Library Journal*

THE

FIVE BOOKS

OF

MIRIAM

Ellen Frankel, Ph.D.

THE

FIVE BOOKS

OF

MIRIAM

A Woman's Commentary on the Torah

HarperSanFrancisco

A Division of HarperCollins*Publishers*

To my parents, Ann and David Frankel,
who encouraged me to make the Torah my own.

THE FIVE BOOKS OF MIRIAM: *A Woman's Commentary on the Torah.* Copyright © 1996 by Ellen Frankel, Ph.D. All rights reserved. Printed in the United States of America. No part of this book may be used or reproduced in any manner whatsoever without written permission except in the case of brief quotations embodied in critical articles and reviews. For information address G. P. Putnam's Sons Publishers, 200 Madison Avenue, New York, NY 10016.

This edition is published by arrangement with G. P. Putnam's Sons Publishers.

HarperCollins Web Site: http://www.harpercollins.com

HarperCollins®, 📖®, and HarperSanFrancisco™ are trademarks of HarperCollins Publishers, Inc.

FIRST HARPERCOLLINS PAPERBACK EDITION PUBLISHED IN 1998

The Library of Congress has catalogued the hardcover edition as follows:

Frankel, Ellen.
    The Five books of Miriam : a women's commentary on the Torah / Ellen Frankel.
       p. cm.
    Includes bibliographical references and index.
    ISBN 0–399–14195–2 (cloth)
    ISBN 0–06–063037–X (pbk.)
    1. Bible. O.T. Pentateuch—Commentaries. 2. Bible. O.T. Pentateuch—
Feminist criticism. I. Title.
BS1225.3.F67   1996
222'.107—dc20   96–8235

      01 02 RRD 10 9

WE ALL STOOD TOGETHER

For Rachel Adler

My brother and I were at Sinai
He kept a journal
of what he saw
of what he heard
of what it all meant to him

I wish I had such a record
of what happened to me there

It seems like every time I want to write
I can't
I'm always holding a baby
one of my own
or one for a friend
always holding a baby
so my hands are never free
to write things down

And then
as time passes
the particulars
the hard data
the who what when where why
slip away from me
and all I'm left with is
the feeling

But feelings are just sounds
the vowel barking of a mute

My brother is so sure of what he heard
after all he's got a record of it
consonant after consonant after consonant

If we remembered it together
we could re-create holy time
sparks flying

—*Merle Feld*

CONTENTS

Acknowledgments   i x

PROLOGUE: THE LEGEND OF MIRIAM'S WELL   x v

INTRODUCING: DRAMATIS PERSONAE   x i x

GENESIS: INDIVIDUALS AND FAMILIES

    I. *Bereshit:* Sexuality and Desire   3
    2. *Noah:* Fertility   11
    3. *Lekh Lekha:* Destiny   15
    4. *Vayera:* Nostalgia—The Pain of Home   22
    5. *Hayei Sarah:* Love and Marriage   31
    6. *Toldot:* Family Politics   39
    7. *Vayetze:* The Ladder of Ambition   49
    8. *Vayishlakh:* Power Struggles   64
    9. *Vayeshev:* Rejection   72
    10. *Miketz:* Reunion   81
    11. *Vayiggash:* Dislocation   84
    12. *Vayekhi:* Legacies   87

EXODUS: COMMUNITY

    13. *Shemot:* Lion-Women   93
    14. *Va-era:* Women Ancestors   102
    15. *Bo:* Transmission   105
    16. *Beshallakh:* The Miriam Tradition   109
    17. *Yitro:* Revelation   116
    18. *Mishpatim:* Community Control   121
    19. *Terumah:* The Image of God   130
    20. *Tetzaveh:* Clothing   133
    21. *Ki Tissa:* Idolatry   136
    22. *Vayakhel:* Homework   142
    23. *Pikudei:* The Work of Women's Hands   146

LEVITICUS: RITUAL

    24. *Vayikra:* Worship   151
    25. *Tzav:* Blood   156
    26. *Shemini:* Food   159
    27. *Tazria:* Childbirth   163

28. *Metzora:* Purity and Danger   *167*
29. *Akharei Mot:* Sexual Boundaries   *172*
30. *Kedoshim:* Holiness   *179*
31. *Emor:* Separateness   *184*
32. *Behar:* Community   *188*
33. *Bekhukotai:* Among the Ruins of History   *191*

NUMBERS: LEADERSHIP

34. *Bamidbar:* Inclusion   *197*
35. *Naso:* Jealousy   *199*
36. *Beha'alotkha:* Spiritual Leadership   *207*
37. *Shelakh Lekha:* Faith   *215*
38. *Korakh:* Rebellion   *220*
39. *Hukkat:* Miriam's Well   *224*
40. *Balak:* Humor and Irony   *228*
41. *Pinkhas:* Women at the Margins   *234*
42. *Mattot:* Vows and Commitments   *237*
43. *Massei:* Strangers   *242*

DEUTERONOMY: MEMORY

44. *Devarim:* Eldering   *247*
45. *Va-etkhanan:* Mindfulness   *251*
46. *Ekev:* Chosenness   *258*
47. *Re'eh:* Feasts of Joy   *261*
48. *Shofetim:* Magic and Superstition   *267*
49. *Ki Tetze:* Safety Nets   *271*
50. *Ki Tavo:* The Sin of Gloom   *286*
51. *Nitzavim:* Empowerment   *292*
52. *Vayelekh:* The Hidden Face   *295*
53. *Ha'azinu:* Ethical Wills   *298*
54. *Vezot Ha-berakhah:* Letting Go   *301*

EPILOGUE   *304*

Notes   *305*
Women in the Torah   *338*
Selected Bibliography   *342*
Index   *347*

ACKNOWLEDGMENTS

ONE OF THE MANY meanings of the word "Torah" is "to take aim." My intention in writing this book has been just that: to point toward the many named and unnamed women (and men) whose teachings and experiences have not yet been joined to our collective legacy as a people. My purpose has been to introduce their voices into the lively conversation that has been going on among our people for the past several thousand years. My hope is that their words will enliven the dialogue, sharpen its contours, and enrich the texture of its discourse. If I have succeeded in this aim, I owe it to the many who have come before me; if I have missed the mark, the failure is my own.

I wish to thank the following individuals who have helped me create this book: Dr. Rachel Adler, Phyllis Berman and Morissa Sher, Dr. Sue Levi Elwell, Rabbi Dayle Friedman, Rabbi Leonard Gordon, Ayala Guy, Rabbi Debra Orenstein, Velvel Pasternak, Dr. Judith Plaskow, Rabbi Zalman Schachter-Shalomi, Jerome J. Shestack, Dr. Marcia Cohn Spiegel, Betsy Platkin Teutsch, Dr. Rachel Turkienicz, Rivka Walton, and the dozens of friends, neighbors, and strangers who have offered me their creativity and goodwill. I would also like to thank Lauren Firestone, Adena Newberg, and Adele Reinhartz for reading early drafts of the manuscript, and Dr. Lori Hope Lefkovitz for critiquing the final draft.

The following groups of individuals also deserve acknowledgment: the Women's Caucus of the Association of Jewish Studies, for helping me network among Jewish women scholars; the Jewish Women's Studies Project at the Reconstructionist Rabbinical College, whose invitation to me to give the Shulamit Magnus lecture on "Women's Folk Torah" was the genesis of this project; the JPS Jewish Women's Task Force, for putting me in touch with so many talented women; the National Havurah Committee, whose annual Summer Institutes have been the laboratory of so much American folk Torah; the members of the Dorshei Derekh Women's Haftorah Committee—Rabbi Miriam Senturia, Rivka Walton, Dr. Lori Lefkovitz, and Elisheva Hurvich—with whom I explored contemporary Jewish women's poems as alternative *haftarot*; and my colleagues and the trustees at the Jewish Publication Society, who gave me the space and support to juggle so many balls at once. I would especially like to thank my wonderful secretary, Eunice Smith, for her nimble fingers and mind, as well as for her deep-rooted spirit.

Thanks are also due to the many talented people at Putnam for their art and ardor, especially the indefatigable Kate Murphy. And of course, I want to honor and thank my peerless editor, Jane Isay, always a generous mentor and friend, for encouraging me to be her rabbi and study partner.

And I owe a profound debt of gratitude to Herb Levine, who urged me to hear voices and to speak in tongues, and who freed me from a narrow place so that I could fulfill my promise.

The author wishes to thank the following individuals and organizations for permission to reprint material in *The Five Books of Miriam:*

Rabbi Leila Gal Berner, for permission to reprint "Miryam Ha-Neviyah," Hebrew lyrics by Rabbi Leila Gal Berner, originally created with Dr. Arthur Waskow as part of a Havdalah service.

Merle Feld, for permission to reprint her poem "We All Stood Together," copyright 1985. First published in the Reconstructionist prayer book *Kol Haneshama,* 1989.

Hebrew Union College Press, for permission to reprint an excerpt from *The Merit of Our Mothers,* trans. Tracy Klirs, Ida Selavan, and Gella Fishman, Hebrew Union College Press, 1992.

Jason Aronson, Inc., Northvale, New Jersey, for permission to quote passages from *A Book of Jewish Women's Prayers,* ed. and trans. Norman Tarnor, Jason Aronson, 1995; and from Nina Beth Cardin, *Out of the Depths I Call to You: A Book of Prayers for the Married Jewish Woman,* Jason Aronson, 1992.

The Jewish Publication Society, for permission to reprint excerpts from *TANAKH: The New JPS Translation According to the Traditional Hebrew Text,* copyright 1985, The Jewish Publication Society.

Mesorah Publications, for permission to reprint "Prayer for a Good Dream" from *The Complete Artscroll Siddur,* ed. Nosson Scherman, Mesorah Publications, 1985.

Paulist Press, for permission to reprint passages from Daniel Matt, *Zohar: The Book of Enlightenment*, Paulist Press, 1983.

Warner Brothers Publications, for permission to reprint "Donah, Donah." Music by Sholom Secunda, English lyrics by Sheldon Secunda, Teddi Schwartz, and Arthur Kevess, copyright 1940, 1956 (copyrights renewed), 1968 EMI Mills Music, Inc. All rights reserved.

THE LEGEND OF MIRIAM'S WELL

A T TWILIGHT of the sixth day of Creation, Shekhinah, the Holy-One-Who-Dwells-in-This-World, created the miracles—the loom that spun the heavens and the earth, the rainbow, Sarah's eternally youthful womb, the divining rod of Serakh bat Asher, Yokheved's basket of reeds, the pit in which Zipporah hid Moses, the manna, Balaam's talking ass, and Miriam's Well. And then Shokhen Ad, the Holy-One-Who-Dwells-Forever, depleted after wresting form out of the jealous Void, rested. And so it was, the first Shabbat.

Of all the miracles, Miriam's Well was perhaps the most marvelous. Resembling a round white millstone, it gave forth water whenever a woman sang to it with the proper heartsong. The Holy One of Blessing entrusted it to Milham, the Phoenix Bird, making her promise to guard it with her life. Milham carried it to the highest mountaintop and there made her nest upon it, hiding it under her fledglings until God called for it.

Almost immediately God did have occasion to summon it. For soon after having been created, Adam and Eve ate from the Tree of Knowledge and were exiled from the Garden of Eden. No longer could they drink with ease from the four rivers of Paradise—Pishon, Gihon, Euphrates, and Hiddekel, whose Babylonian name means "River of the Divine Lady"—that is, the Milky Way. Instead they were forced to seek water in the wilderness, in wadis and hidden springs.

Repentant and disconsolate in her exile, Eve poured out her heart to God, and God answered her. From that day on, she and Adam were sustained by the miraculous well that would suddenly appear in their path, placed there by the merciful Phoenix Bird at God's command. But once they had learned to fend for themselves, the well disappeared without a trace.

After many centuries, Shekhinah called for the well a second time—this time at Sarah's bidding. Overcome with remorse after ordering Abraham to banish her pregnant handmaid, Hagar, Sarah pleaded with God on Hagar's behalf, and her petition was granted. An angel carried the miraculous well to

Hagar in the wilderness, and she drank from it and was revived. She named the spring *Be'er-lahai-ro'i*—that is, "Well of the Living One Who Sees Me."

When Hagar was sent away a second and final time, carrying on her shoulder only a single water skin to sustain both her and her young son, Ishmael, she was again saved by the well. Wandering near Be'er Sheva, the wilderness of the Seven Wells, she wept when their water gave out, fearing death for herself and her child. God gathered up her tears, sweetened them, and returned them to her in the wondrous well that sprang up nearby. And so she and her son were saved.

A generation later, the well surfaced again, in Aram-Naharaim—that is, Haran—where Abraham's brother Nahor and his family lived. Every day, Nahor's granddaughter Rebecca would bring her father's flocks to the well to water them. The girl was known throughout the village for her kindness, especially toward the younger and weaker beasts in the flock.

When Abraham's servant Eliezer came to the village well, seeking a wife for his master's son Isaac, Rebecca came forward to offer water to him and his thirsty camels. As she filled her jar with water at the spring, she sang the song known only to her own heart, a bittersweet song of longing and lament. God heard her song and filled her jar so that she was able to water all of Eliezer's camels without returning even once to the spring. Impressed by this miracle and by the maiden's kindness, Eliezer chose her as Isaac's bride.

When Rebecca's son Jacob, fleeing his brother Esau's wrath, returned years later to the same spring, he met his beloved Rachel there. Although the miraculous well had not fed the spring since Rebecca had left with Eliezer for Canaan, the men of Haran had never ceased hoping that the wondrous waters would return to bless their well. Jealously they kept the well covered with a heavy stone, so that only they could inspect the water each day—just in case the miracle should return.

When Jacob arrived at the well and laid eyes upon his beautiful cousin Rachel, he asked the shepherds there to roll off the rock to allow Rachel to water her flock, but they refused. So he rolled off the heavy stone himself and gave them water. Then he kissed Rachel and burst into tears.

All this he had been instructed to do by his mother, Rebecca, who had sent him to seek a wife at the same well where she had once met Eliezer. She had even taught him the song she sang that day when she watered Eliezer's camels. But though the well hearkened at once to Jacob's song, it had not been created for such a purpose—to hearken to a man singing a woman's song. And for this imposture Jacob was punished. For Rachel's father, Laban, stole her voice and in her place gave Jacob her sister Leah as his bride, just as Jacob had stolen his mother's voice to summon the well. And after that moment, the well departed from that place and returned to Milham for safekeeping.

Hundreds of years passed before the well appeared again. This time it came to the hill country of Midian, where Zipporah and her six younger sisters herded sheep for their father, Jethro, high priest of Midian. When Moses, proud prince of Egypt, now turned murderer and fugitive, arrived exhausted at the village well, Zipporah and her sisters were there to water their flock. As had happened long before in Haran, the women were barred from the well by shepherds, who drove them off. Enraged, Moses fought the men and prevailed, and so the women were able to water their thirsty beasts.

When Jethro's daughters told their father what had happened, he recognized this as a sign that a deliverer had finally come to redeem the Israelites from Egyptian bondage. With heavy heart—for as a prophet he had seen the sorrowful future awaiting his daughter as this stranger's wife—he gave Zipporah to Moses and made him a shepherd of his flock, instructing him to choose pastureland on Horeb, the mountain of God.

After encountering God in the Burning Bush, Moses returned to Egypt, bringing with him Zipporah, their two sons, and his brother, Aaron. In Goshen, Zipporah met the other members of Moses' family: his mother, Yokheved; his father, Amram; and his older sister, Miriam. Because Zipporah had been trained in the sacred arts of sacrifice, blessing, dance, song, and incantation, she recognized in Miriam a sister priestess. Not only that: from Miriam's face shone a radiance unique to those imbued with the spirit of prophecy. She had seen such a radiance in her own father's face. The face of her husband, Moses, too had radiated such a glow after he encountered the blazing bush on Mount Horeb.

Drawn to Miriam, Zipporah shared with her the legend of the wondrous well and the sacred song that could summon it up. Together they tended the well through the forty years of wandering in the desert, healing the sick and restoring hope to the brokenhearted. Once, after a quarrel between the two women, Miriam was stricken with leprosy, and Zipporah healed her with water from the well.

Whenever the people journeyed, the well traveled with them, and when they camped, it settled opposite the Tabernacle. Twelve crones, chosen by the women from each of the twelve tribes, would then bring their spindles to the well and declare, "Spring up, O Well!" And the water would shoot up from the white stone, as high as the tallest date palms, then cascade into great rivers. And each day the people would sail in ships down these rivers to visit one another. The waters emptied into plains that surrounded the camp and nourished the fruit trees that grew there, bearing fruit year round. Under the trees grew fragrant herbs that the women used as perfume, and soft mosses that provided beds and pillows for the poor.

When Miriam died, the well disappeared and did not enter the Promised Land with the people. In later times, legends arose about the well's fate: Some claimed that it did cross the Jordan with the Israelites and that it sank into the shores of the Sea of Galilee, where it remains hidden to this day. Others say that it traveled with the Jews into exile and appears from time to time to those holy enough to merit its healing presence. Some say it was gathered back up by the Eternal, with whom it will remain until the Messiah comes.

But the truth lies elsewhere—with the Daughters of Miriam, the Keepers of the Well, an uninterrupted line of Jewish women who have safeguarded the secret of the Well throughout the generations. And together with this secret, they have gathered up and safeguarded many legends about Miriam and the other ancient mothers of Israel, lovingly telling and retelling them, mother to daughter, aunt to niece. For legends are fragile things. They need tending to survive the ravages of time. Otherwise they slowly wither away. And the world is poorer for it.

Only fragments of these teachings have survived. Most of the scrolls and manuscripts recording the stories and wisdom of these women have been lost in the endless wanderings of the Jewish People. Here then are the fragments, all that remains of *The Five Books of Miriam.*

"At Sinai the divine Voice divided itself into the seventy tongues of the nations so that all might understand" —EXODUS RABBAH 5:9

TORAH: Before the world was created, I was. Before the sun was formed on the fourth day, I illuminated the void. My words provided the blueprint for creation, and they contain the script for redemption. To some, I speak only the word of God, transcribed at Sinai and echoing down through the centuries in the words of the Rabbis. To others, I myself am but the echo of the Bat Kol, the divine voice, filtered through the imperfect hearing of those who revere the One-Who-Speaks-Truth. To yet others, I am black fire on white fire, my entire body of letters all a single name of God, and even that name only the outer garment of the Holy One. Still others regard me as a patchwork of human voices, sewn together by an expert seamstress. But my guises are inexhaustible. Always there are spaces between the letters, gaps yawning wide for new tales. The tradition teaches: "She is a Tree of Life to all who hold fast to her." And I am.

OUR DAUGHTERS: We are today's Jewish women and the women of generations yet to come. We bring to the sacred writings so many questions: Who speaks across the centuries? Are any women among these ancient voices? Do they speak to us? How do their experiences shape ours? How do ours illuminate theirs? Through our questions, we renew the stories that our people told so long ago. Through our questions, we discover new answers to old riddles, and new riddles for future seekers.

OUR MOTHERS: We express the collective wisdom of the Jewish folk tradition. Throughout the centuries, we have told stories, sung songs, enacted rituals, passed down charms and healing remedies, and raised up each generation of Jewish children to cherish and preserve God's teaching among our people. Often we have been unlettered. Usually we speak only the language of the kitchen and the marketplace, not the holy tongue. But without our homespun Torah, the Jewish people would have disappeared among the nations long ago.

OUR BUBBES: We teach the hard-won lessons of those who have lived long and seen it all. We have a proverb for every occasion, indispensable words to the wise. Our children and our children's children have shlepped us across the face of the earth, and we have always made the best of our lot. Most of us in America trace our roots back to the shtetls of Eastern Europe, where we spoke in *mama loshen* and nourished countless generations with chicken soup and *bubbe maisehs*. We celebrate women's wisdom, the Torah of home and market-place, of kitchen and birthing stool, of sickbed and nursery.

THE RABBIS: We are the Sages of our people, the inheritors of the priests and prophets who vanished when the Temple was destroyed by Rome. For two thousand years, we have taught God's law and raised up students to pass it down. Sometimes we have had to draw holy secrets out of the laws and stories, searching in the white spaces between the letters for hints of divine purpose. These *midrashim* and legal interpretations were whispered to Moses on Sinai; we have merely caught the echoes and given them voice. Until very recently, we have been an elite community of men; now women have joined our ranks and added their eyes and ears, their hearts and minds, to ours.

THE SAGES IN OUR OWN TIME: We are the rabbis of today, schol-ars and teachers who continue to search for secrets in the sacred writings. In our quest for truth, we use the most modern intellectual technology—literary crit-icism, archaeology, psychoanalysis, linguistics, comparative Semitics, feminist theory, social science. We do not fear knowledge; we revere only truth. Our goal is to unravel the tangle of piety and myth obscuring the historical core of the text, to unbind all those spellbound by religion's charms. Yet though we are crit-ics, we are loving ones, for the Torah is our tree of life as well.

LILITH THE REBEL: I am the first woman, created at the same moment as the first man. Together we were *Adam*, a single creature, a being-formed-of-red-earth, the first human. But Adam resented our equal status in the Garden, and so I left Paradise to fend for myself. I am the voice of protest. I challenge received wisdom, especially the truths taught by men who have not consulted their mothers, daughters, wives, and sisters. My goal is to upset the applecart, to bite the serpent back, to look back and see the fire without turning to salt, to give the Rabbis a piece of my mind. I seek the truth buried under the moun-tain of tradition. My spade is as sharp as my tongue and wit!

SARAH THE ANCIENT ONE: I am the first Jewish woman, the first Jewish wife, the first Jewish mother. As a young beauty, I left my home, my fam-ily, my culture, and my faith, and with my beloved Abram set off to follow the

Voice-Without-a-Face. To serve God's will, I braved the harems of Pharaoh and Abimelekh, banished Hagar and her son, subjected my aged body to the travails of birth, and watched my husband lead my only son off to death. I am wise because I have faced impossible choices and have nonetheless chosen. I am shrewd because I have learned to laugh at miracles and thereby to force God's hand.

HAGAR THE STRANGER: I am the outsider, the alien, the rejected one. My name speaks my fate: *hajira*, the wanderer; *ha-gera*, the stranger; *ha-gerusha*, the one-who-has-been-driven-away. At my mistress Sarah's command, I lent my womb to Abraham to sire an heir; at her command, he banished me and my son from his camp. I am Israel's perpetual shadow—Egyptian, Canaanite, Arab. Ishmael's sons still snap at Isaac's heels. His daughters' daughters still tempt Jacob's sons. From outside my master's tent, I see his world quite differently. I have learned to see clearly in the desert's glare.

WILY REBECCA, GRANDDAUGHTER OF MILCAH: Never mind how I get my information! Without me the Jewish people is doomed. Not always is war the sure path to victory, nor is truth or divine voices. Sometimes it takes guile to carry out God's will, sometimes stealth, sometimes even betrayal. But history, especially national history, is a soft touch. In retrospect, even the most dastardly deeds can appear divine. Anyway, we women have been forced for so long to dissemble that it's hard to break the habit, even now that the power's being shared.

MOTHER RACHEL: My poor exiled people! Just as I died on the road to my new home, so have you also wandered far from home these many centuries since Rome crushed Jerusalem. And just as I remain alone in a roadside grave, far from the family cave at Makhpelah, so too your bones are scattered among the nations. I am the voice of compassion, weeping for my children who are lost. Fear not, for I am a shepherd who never abandons the ones who stray.

LEAH THE NAMER: So many children! My own six, whom I birthed, as well as Zilpah's two. Eight names I had to come up with, nine counting Dinah (whose name I gave without a homily, since it was only sons who mattered to Jacob). And so I became expert at giving names, a linguist after a fashion. The Torah is filled with names—mostly of men, of course, but quite a few women as well. Even rocks, trees, and mountains are pregnant with language.

Indeed, the words of scripture, distilled by so many centuries of transmission, have become concentrated like an herbal tincture or like tiny seeds waiting for sun and rain to pry them open.

DINAH THE WOUNDED ONE, DAUGHTER OF LEAH AND JACOB: Hard is the fortune of all womankind. I am the voice of the Victim, the One-Who-Is-Expendable. Unlike my twelve brothers, who learned the destinies of their names, I received just a name, unadorned. Only later did I learn the significance of my name: Dinah, the One-Who-Is-Judged. I speak for all those who have been silenced by violence, by neglect, by abuse, by disdain. I remind all those in power that they stand upon the shifting sands of my weakness; I reassure the weak that they ride upon the strong hips of God. Mine is a still, small voice, but it echoes through the ages.

SERAKH BAT ASHER THE HISTORIAN, GRANDDAUGHTER OF ZILPAH: I am the voice of history. As a child, I sang to my grandfather Jacob of the false death of my uncle Joseph. As a woman, I accompanied Jacob and his teeming family down to Egypt. As an ancient crone, I revealed to our enslaved people where the bones of Joseph lay concealed. To this day, I see the past more clearly than the present or future. I note errors that have led to tragedy, patterns that repeat, footprints left behind in every tale. I am the sentry of memory, the guardian of all tears.

MIRIAM THE PROPHET, DAUGHTER OF YOKHEVED: I am the Singer, the Dancer, the Drummer of Israel. I celebrate the myriad contributions of Jewish women through the ages. I champion their dreams, nurture their desires, encourage them when their spirits flag. When I was but a child of five, I chastised my father and all the Hebrew men for abandoning their marriage beds; when I was a leader of our free people, I upbraided my brother Moses for abandoning his marriage bed. Mine is the voice of joy, of victory, of power. I prophesy the redemption of all our people! My vision is clear and limitless. I see to the last generation!

HULDAH THE PREACHER: Hear my words, O Women of Israel! I am Huldah the Prophet and Teacher. I give counsel to kings and priests. During the reign of the child-king Josiah, it was to me they turned when they discovered the lost Scroll of the Law, now the final book of our sacred Torah. It was I who prophesied the doom of wayward Judah, who promised a brief reprieve thanks to our repentant king. I teach God's Law to all who will heed it. I preach God's retribution to all who will not. Under my tread, the twisting paths of Torah right themselves. Hear me, O Women of Israel, and be guided!

ESTHER THE HIDDEN ONE: Before the Torah assumed concrete form, it shone brighter than any star in the Tohu and Vohu of Eternity. Then God spoke the universe into being, and the fiery light was hidden, leaving behind only ashen traces burnt into parched skin, black letters and white space. Through the centuries, Jewish mystics have explored these vast white spaces and discovered secret worlds, and have pried mysteries from the holy letters. I too am an explorer of secret worlds. My very name means "Hidden One." Just as I concealed my identity as a queen in the palace of Shushan, so too the Torah conceals herself, waiting to be revealed by those who know how to find her. We seek her face, even as She seeks ours.

BERURIAH THE SCHOLAR: I am the voice of Learning. In the noisy academies of ancient Israel, mine was the only woman's voice interpreting the Law, mine the only name recorded as a teacher of Torah. I wrestled beside the men, wresting a thousand rules from each letter of sacred scripture, finding truth in the very crowns of the letters. I speak for all those whose erudition has received no praise, for those whose teaching was stolen from their names. I live for study! The words sing to me, fill my ears like a baby's sweet laughter. Every simple soul I meet is my teacher; every learned sage my student.

WITH CAMEO APPEARANCES BY

EVE THE MOTHER OF LIFE: Wife of Adam, who eats from the Tree of Knowledge and is exiled from Eden

NAAMAH: Wife of Noah (unnamed in the Torah, named by the Rabbis)

AMITLAI: Mother of Abraham, who according to legend saves her infant son from the executioners of the king of Ur (unnamed in the Torah, named by the Rabbis)

EDITH, THE ONE-WHO-LOOKS-BACK: Wife of Lot, who turns into a pillar of salt (unnamed in the Torah, named by the Rabbis)

MILCAH: Grandmother of Rebecca, niece of Abraham and Nahor, Nahor's wife

KETURAH: Third wife of Abraham, mother of six children

BILHAH AND ZILPAH: Leah's and Rachel's maids, Jacob's concubines, mother of four of Israel's tribes

DEBORAH: Rebecca's nurse, the only servant whose death is noted in the Torah

TAMAR THE TRICKSTER: Wife and widow to two of Judah's sons, who tricks her father-in-law into sleeping with her to carry on her dead husband's name; ancestor of Boaz and King David

LUSTY ZULEIKA: Wife of Potiphar, Joseph's master, whose desire for her Hebrew slave lands Joseph in prison (unnamed in the Torah, named by the Rabbis)

ASNAT: Daughter of the Egyptian priest of On, wife of Joseph, mother of Ephraim and Manasseh. Legend names her the daughter of Dinah and Shechem, and the adopted daughter of Potiphar and Zuleika.

SHIFRA AND PUAH: The midwives who defy Pharaoh's orders to kill all newborn Hebrew males

YOKHEVED: Mother of Moses, who saves her baby from Pharaoh's executioners by placing him in a reed basket and setting him afloat on the Nile

PRINCESS THERMUTIS: Daughter of Pharaoh, who rescues Moses from the Nile and raises him as her own son. Her Egyptian name, Thermutis, is changed by God to Batyah ("daughter of God") in reward for her pious deeds (unnamed in the Torah, named by the Rabbis).

FLINTY ZIPPORAH: Daughter of Jethro, priest of Midian, wife of Moses, who saves Moses from a divine challenge as they leave for Egypt with their two sons

ELISHEVA: A Levite, wife of Aaron, mother of Nadab and Abihu, Eleazar and Itamar

TIRTZAH, HOGLAH, MAHLAH, MILCAH, AND NOAH: Daughters of Zelophekhad, whose suit to inherit their father's land in the absence of sons is granted, setting a precedent for daughters' inheritance

COZBI: Midianite woman, whose amorous liaison with an Israelite results in both their deaths by Aaron's grandson Pinkhas

SHE'ILAH, THE ONE-WHO-IS-DEMANDED: Daughter of Jephthah, who sacrifices her in fulfillment of a foolish vow (unnamed in the Book of Judges, named by the Rabbis)

HANNAH RACHEL, THE MAID OF LUDOMIR: The only woman hasidic rebbe, who wore tallit and tefillin and preached to her hasidim through an open doorway leading into the synagogue

We are your community, your ancestors, your rabbis. Come study with us our holy Book!

"Surely, this Torah which I enjoin upon you this day is not too baffling for you, nor is it beyond reach. It is not in the heavens, that you should say, 'Who among us can go up to the heavens and get it for us and impart it to us, that we may observe it?' Neither is it beyond the sea, that you should say, 'Who among us can cross to the other side of the sea and get it for us and impart it to us, that we may observe it?' No, the thing is very close to you, in your mouth and in your heart, to observe it."

—Deuteronomy 30:11–14

G E N E S I S

ברא שית

Individuals and Families

1. BERESHIT:
Sexuality and Desire
(GENESIS 1:1–6:8)

TORAH SPEAKS: In the beginning, Shekhinah, the Holy-One-Who-Dwells-in-This-World, spins the world into being: light, water, earth, heavenly bodies, seed-bearing plants, sea creatures, birds, animals—and *Adam*, the only creature cast in the divine image, double-gendered and unique. And then the Holy One rests. And *Adam* then untwins, differentiating into two separate creatures: man and woman. Seeing the woman, the man names her "bone of my bone, flesh of my flesh," name of my name, *isha* of my *ish*. Cleaving together, they embody the divine image in their unity. In partnership, they set up house in Eden.

But like all idylls, this one too proves false, and soon comes to an end. Adam and Eve awaken to desire, and beget history and sin. In turn, their sons, Cain and Abel, follow after their own hearts, and beget death. Thus the human drama begins to run its course. Many generations follow, until the earth fills up with evil, and God—like any heartbroken parent—wonders how it all could have gone so wrong.

THE CREATION OF SOULS

ESTHER THE HIDDEN ONE REVEALS: During the first hour of the first day of creation, before anything else was created, Shekhinah created all human souls and placed them in the highest heaven. When a baby is conceived, Laylah, the Angel of Night, brings it before God to learn its fate. At that moment it is written: where it will live and when it will die, whether it will be a girl or a boy, rich or poor, strong or weak, beautiful or ugly, wise or foolish. Only one decision is left unwritten: whether it will be righteous or wicked. Then the Angel of Souls ascends to the highest heaven to bring back the soul destined for this particular child. It enters the child and nestles quietly beneath the mother's breast. And then a different angel teaches the soul all that it will learn during its days on earth. And when it comes time for the child to be born, the angel strikes the newborn under its nose, leaving a cleft there. Instantly, the soul forgets everything and emerges into the world, crying and afraid. Every soul spends the rest of its life relearning all it once knew.

THE CREATION OF HUMAN BEINGS

OUR DAUGHTERS ASK: What kind of human creature does God call into being at the beginning of the world? For it is written: "AND GOD CREATED *ADAM* IN THE DIVINE IMAGE, IN THE IMAGE OF GOD WAS *ADAM* CREATED; MALE AND FEMALE GOD CREATED THEM" (Genesis 1:27). Is *Adam* a man or a hermaphrodite, single-sexed or doubly endowed?

LEAH THE NAMER ANSWERS: It's hard to know, because the Hebrew language is a gendered tongue. Every verb—for example, "create"—identifies its subject as either male or female.

ESTHER THE HIDDEN ONE REVEALS: But the verse "MALE AND FE-MALE GOD CREATED THEM" strains against these grammatical limits—just as the Holy One, in creating our world, transcended the limits of matter and energy.

MIRIAM THE PROPHET ADDS: Just as God once created a new world out of the void, so too can we reshape our world to renew that creation.

TWO STORIES OF HUMAN CREATION: LILITH AND EVE

TORAH TEACHES: In the first two chapters of Genesis, God creates human beings twice: first *simultaneously*, as a single androgynous being; then a man followed by a woman, Eve fashioned out of Adam's rib.

OUR DAUGHTERS ASK: Can the Torah have it both ways?

THE SAGES IN OUR OWN TIME ANSWER: In ancient times, two rival creation myths vied for our people's allegiance. So popular were both versions of this story that when Genesis was being edited, the Torah had no choice but to include them both.

BUT THE ANCIENT RABBIS EXPLAIN IT DIFFERENTLY: Adam had two wives—one in the first chapter of Genesis, another in the next. His first wife, Lilith, because she was created at the same time as Adam, naturally insisted upon being equal in all things (even in the marriage bed!). But her husband refused her terms, and she left the Garden. God then dispatched three angels—Senoy, Sansenoy, and Semangelof—to the Sea of Reeds to fetch her back, but they failed to persuade her. Stubbornly she refused to return home unless her terms were met. Furious, the angels cursed her for her impudence, sentencing to death each day one hundred of her demon children; she countered by vowing to prey henceforth upon women in labor and their babies. Through the centuries, Jewish women have warded her off with amulets bearing the three angels' names and other charms.

MOTHER RACHEL COUNSELS: My children, we no longer need to fear Lilith. Even a curse has a statute of limitations.

NAMES

OUR DAUGHTERS ASK: Who gives names and why?

SARAH THE ANCIENT ONE ANSWERS: Before Eve comes into being, God and Adam are the sole namers. At God's bidding, Adam gives names to "ALL THE CATTLE AND TO THE BIRDS OF THE SKY AND TO ALL THE WILD BEASTS" (2:20). After woman is created, she shares in this process. Eve, for example, names her firstborn son *Cain*. From that point on, fathers and mothers take turns choosing—and use names to identify their children's destiny. For names are seldom meaningless in the Bible. In fact, they are often remarkably freighted.

DINAH THE WOUNDED ONE ASKS: But why are women granted this privilege when so much else is denied us?

HULDAH THE PREACHER EXPLAINS: The Bible recognizes that parents operate by different rules than the clan, tribe, or nation. In the intimate society of the family, power is negotiated, wrested, or ceded—and the children play out the consequences of their parents' bargains.

ADAM'S RIB

OUR DAUGHTERS ASK: Why does woman emerge from man's body?

LEAH THE NAMER ANSWERS: *Tzela* does not precisely mean "rib" but rather "side." Eve comes forth only as "FLESH OF [Adam's] FLESH," not as "bone of [his] bone"—by C-section rather than by bone graft. Thus God serves as Adam's midwife, not his surgeon.

OUR MOTHERS CHIME IN: So you see, the two creation stories are not so different after all. In chapter 1, Adam is presented as both male *and* female; and in chapter 2, although woman *emerges* from the man's body, the man ultimately *merges* back with her. As it is written: "HENCE A MAN LEAVES HIS FATHER AND MOTHER AND CLINGS TO HIS WIFE SO THAT THEY BECOME ONE FLESH" (2:24). In both cases, human wholeness depends upon an Other to complete the divine image.

THE SERPENT

OUR DAUGHTERS ASK: Is the serpent good or evil? For it is written: "THE SERPENT WAS THE *SHREWDEST* OF ALL THE WILD BEASTS THAT YHVH HAD MADE" (3:1). Isn't *shrewdness* an evil to be shunned?

THE SAGES IN OUR OWN TIME ANSWER: In ancient Near Eastern cultures, serpents were often regarded positively, as symbols of generativity, potency, and rebirth. In our own culture, on the other hand, we usually recoil from snakes, considering them venomous, treacherous, and vile.

OUR DAUGHTERS ASK: Which kind of serpent appeared in the Garden?

LEAH THE NAMER ANSWERS: The Hebrew word for "shrewd" is *arum*—spelled the same as *arom*, "naked"—the state in which Adam and Eve find themselves after they eat the fruit. This pun contains an irony that dictates the serpent's fate: like the first humans, the serpent discovers only too late that its shrewdness is easily stripped away, leaving it vulnerable to divine rebuke.

WILY REBECCA QUIPS: And so it's Adam and Eve's bite, not the serpent's, that proves poisonous to the serpent, not the other way around. Because by the time the story ends, the serpent has fallen flat on its face and eaten dust. Such are the risks of upsetting the applecart.

PUTTING A FENCE AROUND THE TORAH

OUR DAUGHTERS ASK: Why does Adam add to God's ban of *eating* from the tree a ban against touching it also? As it is written: "YOU SHALL NOT EAT OF IT OR TOUCH IT, LEST YOU DIE" (3:3).

THE RABBIS ANSWER: To demonstrate that one must put a fence around the Torah, *siyag le-Torah.* That is, we need to place an extra protective barrier around the performance of a commandment so as to assure its proper observance. So, for example, we have ruled that one should light Sabbath and holiday candles *before* it gets dark, not precisely at sunset, so as not to take any chances of missing the appointed time and thereby violating the Sabbath.

OUR DAUGHTERS ASK: Then why doesn't Adam tell Eve that's what his extra warning is meant to do, to place a "fence around the Torah," for her own good? If he had, she might not have fallen for the serpent's deceitful promise: You shall not die, but "YOU SHALL BE LIKE GOD!" (3:5). When she does touch the tree and discovers that no harm comes to her, she accepts all the rest of the serpent's words as true.

LILITH THE REBEL ANSWERS: That's what comes of leaving women in the dark.

TEMPTATION

OUR DAUGHTERS ASK: Why does the serpent tempt Eve first?

OUR MOTHERS ANSWER: If we look closely at the text, we notice that God never forbids Eve to eat from the tree but only forbids "the man." When Adam repeats God's message to her, he embellishes it by forbidding touch as well as taste.

WILY REBECCA BREAKS IN: A fatal error! Being crafty, the serpent takes advantage of Adam's game of telephone: to the divine curse and Adam's extra taboo, he adds his own two cents in the form of an irresistible reward: If you eat of it, "YOU SHALL BE LIKE GOD!" And Eve, seeing that "THE TREE WAS GOOD FOR EATING AND A DELIGHT TO THE EYES, AND . . . DESIRABLE AS A SOURCE OF WISDOM" (3:6), falls for the serpent's bait. If only God had spoken to Eve directly!

THE PRICE OF WISDOM

OUR DAUGHTERS ASK: Is the price Eve pays for knowledge—exile from Paradise, painful childbirth, and domination by her husband—equivalent to the rewards?

THE RABBIS ANSWER: Obviously, it is. Consider the alternatives.

EVE THE MOTHER OF LIFE PROTESTS: Indeed, I wish I had been able to! But once I left the Garden, I learned that curses, like blessings, are mixed, tempered by chance and faith. The key is to recognize which is which and to act accordingly.

THE FORBIDDEN FRUIT

OUR DAUGHTERS ASK:　Why do we identify the apple as the forbidden fruit? For it is written only that "SHE TOOK OF ITS FRUIT AND ATE" (3:6).

THE SAGES IN OUR OWN TIME ANSWER:　Although the Torah doesn't specifically identify the apple as the fruit of the Tree of Knowledge of Good and Evil, Western tradition, especially in art, has long done so. The Romans associated the apple with Venus, Goddess of Love, and with human sensuality.

THE RABBIS TEACH:　The Song of Songs (7:9) compares a lover to the fragrance of apples. And we have compared the Jewish people to an apple tree.

ESTHER THE HIDDEN ONE ADDS:　To mystics, Shekhinah, God's feminine aspect, appears to human beings in an orchard of holy apples.

OUR MOTHERS CONCLUDE:　What a fitting symbol for the gift of sexual knowledge!

THE SHAME OF SIN

OUR DAUGHTERS ASK:　Why do Adam and Eve hide themselves after eating the fruit? For it is written that when God called for Adam in his hiding place, Adam said, "I WAS AFRAID BECAUSE I WAS NAKED, SO I HID" (3:10).

EVE THE MOTHER OF LIFE ANSWERS:　Adam and I did not even know precisely what it was that we had done—except that we were not supposed to do it. Like little children, we thought that by hiding ourselves, we were now invisible to God.

WILY REBECCA INTERJECTS:　This shame without guilt is still a virginal emotion. It takes practice to experience shame *with* guilt, the shame that comes of premeditated sin.

THE CURSE OF SEXUAL DESIRE

OUR DAUGHTERS ASK:　Why is sexual desire presented as a curse only for women? As it is written: "YET YOUR URGE SHALL BE FOR YOUR HUSBAND" (3:16).

THE SAGES IN OUR OWN TIME ANSWER:　In the ancient world, female sexuality and childbearing were experienced as burdens, snares, sources of physical vulnerability. While pregnant, nursing, and caring for their young chil-

dren, women were utterly dependent upon their men for protection and sustenance. It was, of course, different for the men. When they responded to their
own desire, they risked neither pregnancy nor death. Neither were they com-
pelled to lend their bodies to their babies' insatiable appetites.

MOTHER RACHEL POINTS OUT: Yet despite the high cost exacted of
us because of our sex, most of us—then and now—nonetheless joyfully accept
our lot, choosing to bear children if we are able to. In doing so, we share in
Shekhinah's travails.

EVE'S CURSE

DINAH THE WOUNDED ONE LAMENTS: As a consequence of Eve's
disobedience, women are doubly cursed: to desire their husbands, who will
"rule over" them; and to give birth in pain, as it is written: "IN PAIN SHALL YOU
BEAR CHILDREN, YET YOUR URGE SHALL BE FOR YOUR HUSBAND, AND HE SHALL RULE
OVER YOU" (3:16). How astutely the text understands what life was like for us
back then! Instead of maligning woman's nature (as the Rabbis later do), char-
acterizing us as empty-headed, weak-willed, untrustworthy, and frivolous, the
biblical author here accurately describes our social reality: controlled in marriage and endangered in childbirth. A woman must have written these lines.

EVE RECEIVES HER NAME

OUR DAUGHTERS ASK: The Torah states that Eve's Hebrew name,
Hava, derives from *hai*, meaning "life," because she is "THE MOTHER OF ALL THE
LIVING" (3:20). If Eve is the *mother* of all life, does that make Adam the father?

LEAH THE NAMER ANSWERS: Adam's name derives from *adama*,
"earth," the source of *material* being; *hai* refers to the source of *spiritual* being. Or
to avoid an unnatural dichotomy, Adam and Eve have birthed each other in
complementary ways: from Adam's sleep emerges Eve; from Eve's awakening,
Adam's future.

THE FIRST CHILD, THE FIRST LOSS

OUR DAUGHTERS ASK: What happens when Adam and Eve are banished from Eden?

OUR MOTHERS ANSWER: They do what most families do after they lose everything: they begin again. They start a family to carry on their name, as it written: "NOW THE MAN KNEW HIS WIFE EVE, AND SHE CONCEIVED AND BORE CAIN, SAYING, 'I HAVE GAINED [*kaniti*] A MALE CHILD WITH THE HELP OF GOD'" (4:1).

MOTHER RACHEL CONTINUES: And so Eve gains a male child—and later gains a second boy, whose Hebrew name, *Hevel*, means "breath," so fleeting is Abel's life. With Abel's death, *Hava*, the mother of life, becomes also the mother of death, and *Adam*, taken from the earth, returns a son to it.

LEAH THE NAMER ADDS: Names in the Bible often contain their parents' dreams and their children's burdens.

EVE THE MOTHER OF LIFE ADDS: Indeed, when the gods wish to punish us, they merely answer our prayers.

2. NOAH:
Fertility

(GENESIS 6:9–11:32)

TORAH TEACHES: Not long after civilization is set in motion, it goes awry. Humanity becomes corrupt and lawless, and the Holy-One-Who-Dwells-in-This-World decides to try Her hand again, wiping out all life on earth with a great flood and beginning anew with Noah and his family. And so Noah and his sons build an ark, and Naamah and her daughters-in-law make it habitable. And they fill it with breeding pairs from all the kingdoms of life, and in that fragile ark ride out the forty days and nights of rain. When they emerge from their lifeboat a year later, all animal life has disappeared except what remains in the ark and in the seas.

Noah and Naamah, their children, and all their animal guests emerge from their seaborne prison and repopulate the earth. In thanksgiving Noah offers a sacrifice, and the Holy One of Blessing responds with a promise, a rainbow signifying that never again will the earth be destroyed by flood. Then Noah plants a vineyard and gets drunk. His son Ham sees him naked and is cursed; Noah's other two sons, Shem and Japheth, cover his nakedness and are blessed. And then human civilization spreads out. In the valley of Shinar, people come together to build a great tower so that they can make a name for themselves and avoid being scattered over the earth. But God babbles their speech, earning this place the name Babel. And so humankind is scattered over the face of the earth.

Shem begins a new line, which leads to Abram, Sarai, and their nephew, Lot. Leaving Ur, they journey to Haran, where Abram's father, Terah, dies.

THE ARK

OUR DAUGHTERS ASK: What is the world like after the Flood?

HULDAH THE PREACHER ANSWERS: Before the Flood, the earth is corrupt and filled with violence. Then the Face of Compassion clouds over, filling the world with dark rage. And the world returns to water as at the beginning, undifferentiated, formless, and void. But in the midst of this amniotic world floats an ark, an embryo suspended in the waters of birth and rebirth.

Encapsulating its tenants like a seedpod or a womb, it contains the potential for new life. What reemerges from the ark after this long gestation is not much different from what went in. The animals have not changed their natures; neither have the humans. Indeed, Noah's first act is to plant a vineyard and get drunk.

MOTHER RACHEL ADDS: But Shekhinah has changed. Like all seasoned parents, She now knows that children need two things: a reasonable set of rules and the promise of grace. So She gives humankind seven ethical laws and the rainbow.

NOAH'S WIFE, NAAMAH

OUR DAUGHTERS EXCLAIM: Why doesn't Noah's wife have a name?

LILITH THE REBEL TEACHES: The Bible is filled with nameless women!

THE RABBIS PROTEST: But we have given names to most of them, and often stories as well.

LILITH RETORTS: But too often these names and stories don't reflect our experience! Take Naamah, for instance, Noah's wife. According to some Rabbis, her name comes from her practice of beating the drum—*man'emet*—on her way to worship idols. And other rabbinic legends link her to demons.

THE RABBIS ANSWER BACK: Rabbi Abba bar Kahana, on the other hand, claimed that her name refers to her pleasing—*ne'imim*—deeds. Indeed, she helped to save life on earth; like Eve, she was a Mother of Life.

NAAMAH INTERJECTS: Imagine what it required of me to endure a full year in the ark, cooped up with a boatload of animals and family: so much patience, caring, good humor, fortitude, and resourcefulness.

THE TOWER OF BABEL

OUR BUBBES TEACH: Don't climb too high and you won't have to fall. And besides that, remember: We plan—and God laughs.

LEAVING THE OLD COUNTRY

OUR DAUGHTERS ASK: Why do other members of Abraham's family leave with him? As it is written: "TERAH TOOK HIS SON ABRAM, HIS GRANDSON

LOT . . . AND HIS DAUGHTER-IN-LAW SARAI . . . AND THEY SET OUT TOGETHER FROM UR OF THE CHALDEES FOR THE LAND OF CANAAN" (11:31).

SARAH THE ANCIENT ONE ANSWERS: What mysteries still surround the story of how our people began! For though the Rabbis recount that Abraham left Ur after smashing his father's stone gods, they fail to tell all the other stories—about my own decision to leave, and that of my father-in-law, Terah, of Abraham's nephew Lot, his niece Milcah, and her husband, Nahor. Indeed, understanding why we left home is vital to understanding who we are, both as individuals and as a people. I cannot claim to speak for the others, but I can tell my own story:

Abraham and I were brother and sister. We shared the same father but not the same mother. Abraham was the son of Amitlai; I, the daughter of Enheduanna, daughter of a priest of Ur. My mother was an *apiltum*, a diviner skilled in prophecy and the interpretation of dreams. When she discovered that I was gifted in such things, she taught me her arts and prepared me to take her place someday as a dream diviner.

One night, I had the most frightening dream: The tyrant Nimrod appeared to me and foretold the death of my beloved Abraham and his entire family. He declared that he would no longer tolerate Abraham's preachings about YHVH, who he claimed was mightier than all the gods of Ur. When I awoke I told my mother of my dream, and she offered a libation in our home shrine to *ishtar biti*, inquiring of her whether my dream was true or the work of demons.

According to my mother, the goddess blessed my vision. My mother then urged me to flee Ur and to take with me Abraham, Terah, and those of his family who wished to join him in his new faith. "Your place is with your beloved. Mine is with my people, who need my vision and my healing powers. Furthermore," she told me, "I am too old and weak to survive such a journey."

And so I persuaded Abraham to leave. He agreed to do so only after he consulted with his God, who told him: "Whatever Sarai tells you, do as she says." In turn, Abraham convinced his old father, Terah—Amitlai was no longer living, and my own mother had stopped consorting with him long before—his nephew Lot, his niece Milcah, and her husband, Nahor, to leave with him. The next day, after hurried preparations, we left Ur and journeyed toward Canaan. I carried with me my mother's amulets for my own tent, and my mother's blessing for children. For I was barren, and even then too old for bearing. From that day on, I never saw my mother again.

AMITLAI, MOTHER OF ABRAHAM

OUR DAUGHTERS ASK: Who is Abraham's mother?

AMITLAI ANSWERS: My name is Amitlai, woman of Ur. When the royal magicians of King Nimrod predicted that a usurper would be born to topple the king, Nimrod ordered all baby boys killed. My husband, Terah, an official in Nimrod's court, was eager to obey his king, but I concealed my pregnancy from my husband and then hid my baby in a cave, where he miraculously grew to full maturity in twenty days, protected and nourished by the angel Gabriel.

OUR BUBBES ADD: Like Moses' mama, Yokheved, and so many mothers before and after her, Amitlai risks her own life to save her baby's.

THE BIBLE'S FIRST PORTRAIT OF SARAH

OUR DAUGHTERS ASK: Who is Sarah? The Torah introduces her with so few words: "NOW SARAI WAS BARREN, SHE HAD NO CHILD" (11:30).

SARAH THE ANCIENT ONE ANSWERS: Yes, that is all you are told about me when you first meet me: my name . . .

LEAH THE NAMER INTERRUPTS: An honorable name, meaning "princess," "chieftainess," or "priestess" . . .

SARAH CONTINUES: And my barrenness. Abraham is defined by a lineage and extended family; I, only by an absence.

MOTHER RACHEL EXPLAINS: Now we understand why Sarah leaves Ur. Unlike Abraham, who goes in quest of God, Sarah seeks a new home and, with it, a change of fortune. As our bubbes teach: A change of place brings a change of luck. Abraham finds God, but it costs him two sons: one driven into exile, the other into silence. Sarah finds a change of fortune, but it costs her her life, for when Abraham takes away her only son, making her barren once again, she dies, speechless. So it is fitting that from the beginning, Sarah bears two names: Princess and Barren One. Between them they shape her life.

3. LEKH LEKHA:
Destiny
(GENESIS 12:1–17:27)

Torah teaches: Called by God to leave his own land and go to a new one, Abram, together with his wife, Sarai, his nephew Lot, and several converts to their new faith, travel to Canaan and then to Egypt, where Sarai narrowly escapes Pharaoh's harem. Returning to Canaan, Abram and his nephew part company in a dispute over land. Then God promises Abram a son and makes a covenant with him. And Sarai, still barren, gives Abram her handmaid, Hagar, but drives her away when the pregnant Hagar shows contempt for her. God then comes to Hagar in the desert and promises her that her son will become the father of a great nation.

God promises Abram that Sarai too will bear a son to carry on the covenant. And then the Name-That-Transcends-Speech gives both of them new names: Abraham and Sarah.

THE CONVERSION OF SOULS

OUR DAUGHTERS ASK: What kind of spiritual leader is Sarah?

THE RABBIS ANSWER: Abraham converts not only his father, Terah, to a belief in one God but also converts others, who follow him to Canaan.

OUR MOTHERS ADD: Sarah too is a proselytizer, as it is written: "ABRAM TOOK HIS WIFE SARAI . . . AND THE PERSONS THAT THEY HAD ACQUIRED IN HARAN" (12:5).

OUR DAUGHTERS ASK: How does one "acquire" people?

SERAKH BAT ASHER THE HISTORIAN ANSWERS: In the ancient world, human beings were acquired through either purchase or capture. But only their physical bodies could be acquired this way, not their spirits.

LEAH THE NAMER ADDS: In this verse, the Hebrew word for "persons" is *nefashot*, usually translated as "souls." And the word for "acquired" literally means "made."

OUR DAUGHTERS ASK: How do Abraham and Sarah "make souls"?

WILY REBECCA EXPLAINS: By showing their neighbors that they have the freedom to think for themselves. In a culture based upon absolute obedience to the king and the priestly elite, such an act requires considerable courage and faith. What is at stake is nothing less than the possession of one's soul.

SARAH'S BEAUTY

OUR DAUGHTERS ASK: Why does Abraham lie to Pharaoh, pretending that Sarah is his sister?

DINAH THE WOUNDED ONE LAMENTS: Woe to Sarah, cursed with such beauty!

THE RABBIS RECOUNT: Sarah's beauty is legendary. She is one of the seven most beautiful women in the world. When famine forces Sarah and Abraham to seek food in Egypt, Abraham tries to hide his wife's beauty under a basket and then behind a lie—"PLEASE SAY THAT YOU ARE MY SISTER, THAT IT MAY GO WELL WITH ME BECAUSE OF YOU, AND THAT I MAY REMAIN ALIVE THANKS TO YOU" (12:13)—for as a husband, he would need to die in order to provide an eligible widow for the king. Fortunately, a divine angel intercedes to protect Sarah's virtue, and so she and Abraham are both spared.

LILITH THE REBEL RETORTS: Beauty has always been a mixed blessing for women.

THE PRICE OF UNHOLY LOVE

OUR DAUGHTERS ASK: Why doesn't Pharaoh kill Abraham for lying about Sarah's marital status and keep Sarah for himself?

THE RABBIS ANSWER: When Pharaoh enters Sarah's chamber, an invisible angel saves her from Pharaoh's ardent advances by rapping him on the head each time he approaches her. Finally, battered and humiliated, Pharaoh confronts Abraham and learns the truth: that she is Abraham's wife, not his sister. But instead of ordering the two deceivers killed, Pharaoh sends them away with all the riches he has initially paid for Sarah as a bride-price.

ESTHER THE HIDDEN ONE TEACHES: Pharaoh recognizes that what appears to be deceit may turn out to be an omen of providential design.

THE CURSE OF BARRENNESS

OUR DAUGHTERS ASK: Why does the Bible consider barrenness such a tragedy? Can't we make a name for ourselves by our deeds alone?

THE SAGES IN OUR OWN TIME TEACH: Ancient attitudes toward fertility depended largely on prevailing social conditions. So, for example, Canaan in the late Iron Age faced an *underpopulation* crisis due to widespread war, famine, and plague, whereas Mesopotamia found itself in the opposite predicament. In addition, the Israelites' status as a *pioneer* culture, focused on subduing and settling a hostile territory, required a rapid increase in manpower. Hence the need for children and the emphasis on women as breeders. In addition, children represented security in old age.

LEAH THE NAMER ASKS: Why is it, then, that of the seven first mothers—Sarah, Hagar, Rebecca, Rachel, Leah, Bilhah, and Zilpah—only I had more than two children?

OUR BUBBES ANSWER: Pioneer women don't always have a chance to raise such large families. They've got so much else to do!

SURROGATE MOTHERHOOD

OUR DAUGHTERS ASK: Why does Sarah give Hagar to Abraham as a concubine? Isn't that a setup for disaster?

SARAH THE ANCIENT ONE ANSWERS: Though the choice was painful for me, I chose surrogate motherhood as a fulfillment of God's will. I said to my husband: "YHVH HAS KEPT ME FROM BEARING. CONSORT WITH MY MAID; PERHAPS I SHALL HAVE A SON THROUGH HER" (16:2).

WILY REBECCA BREAKS IN: Though Sarah sees God's hand in her barrenness, she also takes matters into her own hands.

HAGAR ADDS: Both of us suffered in making this bargain—I because I remained a slave even after I bore Abraham a son; Sarah because her adopted son, Ishmael, always remained my son, the child of an Egyptian, a stranger to her.

DINAH THE WOUNDED ONE INTERJECTS: God's a tough negotiator, especially when the stakes are so high. Often too tough, often too high.

HAGAR THE STRANGER

OUR DAUGHTERS ASK: Why does Sarah hate Hagar so bitterly? Isn't it *her* idea to give her slave to Abraham?

HAGAR THE STRANGER LAMENTS: O women of Israel, pity me! A powerless Egyptian slave, a shadow to Wife Number One, a surrogate womb. My very name suggests "the wanderer" (*hajira*), "the foreigner" (*ha-gera*), "the banished one" (*ha-gerusha*).

SARAH THE ANCIENT ONE ANSWERS HER: The Torah claims that it was your insolence toward me that prompted my uncharitable behavior. But my actions were motivated by something else. In sending you away, I was bending my own will to heaven's dark designs, just as Abraham later did on Mount Moriah. For each one of my actions toward you foreshadowed my people's future: They too became strangers in a land not theirs, their sons despised and endangered, until they were driven out into the desert to be saved by God's hand. That is why God told Abraham, "Whatever Sarah tells you, do as she says" (21:12). But it cost me everything—for from that moment on, I disappear from my own story. I am not heard from again in the Bible.

JEALOUSY AMONG WOMEN

OUR DAUGHTERS ASK: And why does Hagar disdain Sarah? As it is written: "WHEN SHE SAW THAT SHE HAD CONCEIVED, HER MISTRESS WAS LOWERED IN HER ESTEEM" (16:4).

HAGAR THE STRANGER ANSWERS: Remember that I was a slave, a foreigner, a woman without rights. Pharaoh gave me to Sarah as a parting gift, even after her husband lied about her, claiming that she was his sister. My fate was thereby sealed for my lifetime. But when I conceived Abraham's child, my status was irrevocably changed. I became the mother of my master's firstborn son. I fulfilled God's promise to grant seed to Abraham. And in so doing, I became Sarah's rival.

HULDAH THE PREACHER EXPLAINS: Such is the nature of subordinates—to compete with each other, since they can't override the master's power. As a slave, Hagar knows this; as a wife, Sarah does too. That's why, when Abraham tries to keep both women under one roof, God overrules him: "WHATEVER SARAH TELLS YOU, DO AS SHE SAYS" (21:12).

SARAH THE ANCIENT ONE ADDS: Shekhinah understood that I was the pragmatist and Abraham the dreamer. Hagar too was a realist. She never cursed me or God for what happened. She understood that had she not left Abraham's house, she would have lived and died a slave rather than as the mother of a great nation.

BLAME

OUR DAUGHTERS ASK: Why does Sarah blame Abraham for her own actions? Doesn't Sarah herself send Hagar into Abraham's bed? Yet when the plan works and Hagar conceives, Sarah blames Abraham for Hagar's haughty reaction to her pregnancy. As it is written: "THE WRONG DONE ME IS YOUR FAULT . . . YHVH DECIDE BETWEEN YOU AND ME!" (16:5)

MOTHER RACHEL EXPLAINS: Clearly, it's not easy for Sarah to share her marriage bed, especially with her own slave.

SARAH INTERJECTS: When the tables were turned—when Abraham thrust me into the beds of Pharaoh and Abimelekh—I remained faithful! I was motivated solely by my vision of the future: Abraham needed an heir. But Abraham mistook my gesture, thinking that I was giving him a mistress, not a son. Thus he failed to honor my act, so blinded was he by the joy of fatherhood. Had he acknowledged my pain and sacrifice, shielding me from Hagar's shaming, Ishmael might have received the birthright.

SERAKH BAT ASHER THE HISTORIAN ADDS: And how different Jewish history might have been.

THE WHEEL OF HISTORY—ISRAEL AND EGYPT

OUR DAUGHTERS ASK: What happens to Hagar and Ishmael?

SERAKH BAT ASHER THE HISTORIAN ANSWERS: Hagar's first exile is temporary. But after the birth of Isaac, Sarah orders Hagar and her son banished for good. And so begins the fateful swing of history's pendulum: Abraham banishes Ishmael; two generations later, the Ishmaelites sell Abraham's great-grandson Joseph into Egyptian slavery. Sarah banishes Hagar the Egyptian; later, Egypt enslaves Sarah's descendants for four hundred years.

ESTHER THE HIDDEN ONE DECLARES: Seen in such a providential light, Sarah's actions are the first step in the divine plan leading to Sinai.

NAMES

BERURIAH THE SCHOLAR TEACHES: Names reflect a person's character and destiny, and a parent's hope. In the Torah, both fathers and mothers bestow names—as does God. In names we find the roots of much of Jewish history. In fact, much of the drama in Genesis revolves around the giving of names.

HAGAR THE STRANGER EXPLAINS: An angel told me that the child I was carrying would be called *Ishmael,* for "GOD HAS PAID HEED [*shama*] TO YOUR SUFFERING" (16:11). Yet when he was born, it was Abraham who named him. Still, even though I did not name my own son, I named the One who later saved him from death: *El-Ro'i,* the God-Who-Sees. In my Redeemer's name, I called the well that saved us both *Be'er-lahai-ro'i,* "THE WELL WHERE I CONTINUED SEEING AFTER GOD SAW ME" (16:13).

SARAH THE ANCIENT ONE CONTINUES: God changed Abraham's and my names to reflect our new status as progenitors of the Jewish people. *Abraham* means "father of a great nation" (17:5); *Sarah* is also linked with the blessing of fertility (17:15). (How disappointed I was that God didn't speak directly to me when my name was changed.) My son, Isaac, was named three times. First, God told Abraham that I would bear a son, who would be named Isaac. Later, three angels told him that I would give birth in my old age. My uncertain laughter at hearing that news became part of my son's name—*Yitzhak,* "laughing boy" (18:12–15). And Abraham too pronounced that name when he was born (21:3).

OUR MOTHERS TEACH: In all these cases, women are bystanders in the drama of divine naming. That too is part of the drama.

THE FAVORED CHILD

OUR DAUGHTERS ASK: Does Abraham love both his sons equally?

MOTHER RACHEL ANSWERS: How difficult it is to love our children in equal measure!

SARAH THE ANCIENT ONE EXPLAINS: When Abraham first learned that I was to bear a child, he protested Ishmael's displacement: "OH, THAT ISHMAEL MIGHT LIVE BY YOUR FAVOR!" (17:18) But the Holy One of Blessing overruled his preference for his firstborn and instead chose my son for the birthright.

MIRIAM THE PROPHET TEACHES: And so begins a pattern repeated throughout Genesis: the father's favoritism for his firstborn repeatedly leads to trouble—as in the case of Ishmael, Esau, and Reuben. It is the mother who discerns God's design and helps the son destined to carry it on—as in the case of Isaac and Jacob. As in the case of all socially inferior people, women understand more about power and survival than those in power, and so are in a position to see more clearly than their husbands.

4 . VAYERA:

Nostalgia—The Pain of Home

(GENESIS 18:1–22:24)

TORAH TEACHES: Three divine messengers come to Abraham and announce that Sarah will yet give birth to a son. When Sarah overhears this, she laughs, thinking to herself: I am almost ninety and no longer menstruating! But Shekhinah upbraids her: Is anything too difficult for the Creator of Life?

God also reveals to Abraham that the nearby cities of Sodom and Gomorrah will be destroyed because of their wickedness. Abraham negotiates with God to spare Sodom, where his nephew Lot and his family live. God agrees— if at least ten righteous people can be found there.

Then two of the angel-messengers go to Sodom and find shelter there with Lot. When the evil townspeople seek to molest them, the angels thwart their designs by blinding them. Then God tells Lot to flee with his family before the city is destroyed, but only his wife and two daughters consent to join him. During their flight, Lot's wife looks back and turns into a pillar of salt, so that only three of them escape the firestorm engulfing the cities of the plain. Convinced that the rest of humanity is doomed, Lot's daughters get their father drunk and sleep with him, and each gives birth to a son.

Then Abraham journeys to the kingdom of Abimelekh, where he protects himself from death a second time by telling the king that his wife, Sarah, is really his sister. Visited by a divine dream and a plague of barrenness, the king discovers the truth and placates Abraham and Sarah with gifts and safe settlement in his domain. Then Abimelekh and Abraham conclude a covenant at the well of Beersheba.

At the age of ninety, Sarah gives birth to Isaac—"Laughing Boy"—as God has promised. When the baby is eight days old, he, his older half-brother, Ishmael, and their aged father are circumcised. Then Sarah, fearful of Ishmael's harmful influence on her son, demands that Abraham cast out Hagar and Ishmael. God instructs Abraham to honor Sarah's wish. In the desert, God saves the two exiles, promising Hagar that Ishmael will become a great nation.

Then God calls upon Abraham to sacrifice his son Isaac on Mount Moriah. But when Abraham raises the knife to kill his son, the Merciful One stays his hand, and so Abraham sacrifices a ram instead. In reward for his obedience, God blesses Abraham with a fruitful and glorious future.

THE DESERT INNKEEPER AND HIS SHORT-ORDER COOK

OUR BUBBES DECLARE: How exhausting it is, running a Jewish home! What a nudnik Hospitality is, and how quickly we have to jump when he yells!

SARAH THE ANCIENT ONE RECOUNTS: When three strangers suddenly appeared at our tent one day, Abraham ordered me to serve them immediately. As it is written: "ABRAHAM HASTENED INTO THE TENT TO SARAH AND SAID, 'QUICK, THREE MEASURES OF CHOICE FLOUR! KNEAD AND MAKE CAKES!'" (18:6) He himself ran to the herd to select a calf for our guests, which he then gave to one of our servant boys to prepare.

OUR MOTHERS NOTE: How familiar this scene is! Abraham, driven by his desire to be hospitable, drives his household with the same sense of urgency. What if Sarah had been in the middle of other tasks when he'd called—weaving a garment for her husband, caring for a sick servant, talking to God? So intent is Abraham to please his guests that he doesn't stop at the threshold to see if he is interrupting something. On such occasions, Sarah is no different to him from his servant boy.

OUR BUBBES ADD: The food is cooked in a pot, and the plate gets the honor.

SARAH'S LAUGHTER

OUR DAUGHTERS ASK: Why does Sarah laugh?

SARAH THE ANCIENT ONE ANSWERS: Having overheard my secret thoughts, God misrepresented my laughter to Abraham, implying that it showed my lack of faith, boasting to him: "IS ANYTHING TOO WONDROUS FOR YHVH?" (18:14) Yet it was not at God that I laughed but at myself, at my own foolish fantasy. For I thought: "NOW THAT I AM WITHERED, AM I TO HAVE ENJOYMENT—WITH MY HUSBAND SO OLD?" (14:12) When God took me to task, I denied my laughter not because I doubted God's capacity for miracles but because I doubted my own.

THE MOTHER OF LAUGHTER

OUR DAUGHTERS ASK: When Sarah first overhears the angels talking with Abraham, promising her a child, Sarah laughs, then denies having done so. When she gives birth to her son, she recalls that moment of disbelief and reclaims it, boasting that "GOD HAS GIVEN ME LAUGHTER. ALL WHO HEAR ABOUT IT"—that is, the birth of a son to a ninety-year-old crone—"WILL LAUGH WITH ME!" (21:6) Is Sarah's laughter a sign of shame or joy?

LEAH THE NAMER ANSWERS: Sarah is naming not her son but *herself* as "Mother of Laughter." For in giving birth to Isaac, she changes from a laughingstock (to her husband, to Hagar, to her neighbors, to herself) to matriarch of the covenant. Isaac is her *belly laugh*, her way of *ribbing* and *kidding* God and Abraham.

BUT OUR BUBBES CAUTION: Remember what it says in the Torah: "The heart may ache even in laughter, and joy may end in grief" (Proverbs 14:13).

WOMAN AS EAVESDROPPER

OUR DAUGHTERS ASK: Why doesn't God speak directly to Sarah? As it is written: "[Sarah] WAS LISTENING AT THE ENTRANCE OF THE TENT, WHICH WAS BEHIND [Abraham]" (18:10). Why does she only *overhear* the conversation between God and Abraham, laughing to herself when she hears one of the strangers announce that she will bear a child in her old age? And why does God ask Abraham, not Sarah: "WHY DID SARAH LAUGH?" (18:13) Is Sarah being criticized for eavesdropping on men's conversation or for laughing at what they say?

WILY REBECCA ANSWERS: The angels are aware all along that Sarah's listening in. Even before they begin speaking with Abraham, they make sure she is nearby in the tent. No, the angels' news is designed specifically for her—and so's the method of transmission.

THE DARK SIDE OF HOSPITALITY

OUR DAUGHTERS ASK: How can Lot offer his daughters in place of his guests? As it is written: "YOU MAY DO TO [my two daughters] AS YOU PLEASE; BUT DO NOT DO ANYTHING TO THESE MEN, SINCE THEY HAVE COME UNDER THE SHELTER OF MY ROOF" (19:8). Don't tell us there is no other choice!

THE SAGES IN OUR OWN TIME ANSWER: If we look at the problem through the lens of the social scientist, we discover political and economic reasons behind Lot's choice: hospitality cements social bonds, incurs reciprocal obligation, balances power among potential rivals. Thus when the wicked Sodomites call for Lot's guests, "THAT WE MAY KNOW THEM" (19:5), he must choose among several competing pressures: to placate his neighbors, safeguard his guests, or protect his daughters. Since his daughters lack the power to either jeopardize or strengthen his position, it is no wonder that Lot chooses to sacrifice their future marriageability rather than dishonor his guests or provoke his neighbors. Such a move is certainly politically expedient.

DINAH THE WOUNDED ONE PROTESTS: But how can we not recoil at Lot's willingness to sacrifice his daughters' virginity to protect two strangers under his roof! At least when Abraham decides to sacrifice his son, he is answering to God. Lot, on the other hand, is yielding only to wicked neighbors and social convention. We shouldn't be surprised that his daughters later sleep with him—he has already essentially violated their chastity and made his priorities clear to them.

LOT'S OTHER DAUGHTER, PALTIT

THE RABBIS TEACH: Lot is told to take his two "REMAINING DAUGHTERS" (19:15) and flee the city. From this we learn that Lot had another daughter besides the two who escape Sodom with him. This third daughter was named Paltit. Because she had once offered hospitality to strangers, the wicked men of Sodom burned her to death. Her best friend, likewise goodhearted, met a similar fate at their hands, because she had once smuggled food to a visitor. The Sodomites killed her by burying her in the earth up to her neck, drenching her in honey, and then letting bees sting her to death.

OUR DAUGHTERS ASK: What were the Rabbis' motives in inventing these gruesome tales?

THE RABBIS ANSWER: To blacken Lot's name even more by suggesting what would have happened to his "remaining daughters" had he turned them over to these unprincipled men. We were also justifying God's destruction of a community that so flagrantly violated the norms of hospitality.

MOTHER RACHEL ADDS: The Rabbis understand too that women's natural impulse is to open up their hearts and homes to guests, a dangerous habit in a place like Sodom.

BACKWARD GLANCES

OUR DAUGHTERS ASK: Why does Lot's wife look back?

EDITH, THE ONE-WHO-LOOKS-BACK (WHOM THE RABBIS NAMED *IDIT*), ANSWERS: I looked back to all that I had left behind—my other daughter's grave, my friends and relatives, my home with its cherished mementos, my childhood—and I wept. And so hot was the desert sun and the brimstone torching Sodom that my flowing tears dried instantly, turning me into a pillar of salt.

THE RABBIS ADD: Her turning into a pillar of salt is an example of the divine principle, *midah keneged midah,* "measure for measure." Lot's wife brings this fate upon herself through indiscretion: When the two angels come to stay in Lot's house, Lot prudently keeps their visit a secret, but his wife goes to a neighbor to borrow salt to cook for them—and so gives them away. Because of her thoughtlessness, she pays back the borrowed salt with her life.

EDITH OBJECTS: No, it was because of my thoughtfulness—at the wrong time.

INCEST AT THE END OF THE WORLD

OUR DAUGHTERS ASK: The Torah claims that Lot's daughters seduce their father because they fear that "THERE IS NOT A MAN ON EARTH TO CONSORT WITH US IN THE WAY OF THE WORLD" (19:31) once Sodom has been destroyed. Do they really think that Lot is the last man on earth? That's hard to believe.

WILY REBECCA ANSWERS: Of course it is! In my opinion, their actions are motivated by knowledge, not ignorance. Realizing that their father had been willing to turn them over to the same men who previously murdered their sister, Paltit, they fear that he will now sacrifice them to save his own skin—as Abraham had twice passed off their great-aunt Sarah as his sister to save his own life. So they barter their own maidenheads for security, each obtaining from Lot a son to support her in her old age. For with their old world in flames and their mother petrified, what other options do they have?

AN INAUSPICIOUS BEGINNING, AN AUSPICIOUS END

OUR DAUGHTERS ASK: Lot and his elder daughter engender Moab, whose line leads to Ruth, great-grandmother of David and ancestor of the Messiah. How can an incestuous union give rise to kings and redeemers?

THE SAGES IN OUR OWN TIME TEACH: We are reminded of incestuous couplings from other ancient traditions—Osiris and his sister Isis, Tiamat and her kinsman Marduk, Zeus and his daughter Aphrodite, Oedipus and his mother Jocasta, among others.

BERURIAH OBSERVES: These myths teach us that when two people so closely related produce offspring, they are likely to embody intensified family traits, for good and for ill. Thus David exhibits extraordinary courage, lust, and creativity.

ESTHER THE HIDDEN ONE ADDS: The Messiah too will be extraordinary, embodying the composite genome of all humanity.

THE WIFE-SISTER RUSE REVISITED

OUR DAUGHTERS ASK: Why does Abraham again try to pass off his wife as his sister, this time with King Abimelekh?

THE RABBIS TEACH: Abraham knows all along that God will intervene to save Sarah's virtue.

THE SAGES IN OUR OWN TIME TEACH: In ancient Near Eastern culture, "wife-sister" was a technical term, designating a special marital status that marked certain women as off-limits even to pharaohs or kings.

BUT SARAH THE ANCIENT ONE COUNTERS: No, my husband had become too skilled at dissembling! That is why I did not protest later when God demanded that Abraham offer up my only son. By then I understood that God was not testing Abraham but teaching him a lesson: that even a mock sacrifice, like the mock adultery in Pharaoh's and Abimelekh's courts, can permanently scar its victims.

TAKING NOTE OF SARAH

OUR DAUGHTERS ASK: Who's really responsible for Isaac's birth?

MOTHER RACHEL TEACHES: How mystical is the process of birthing children! God opens Sarah's womb. Sarah conceives and gives birth to a child.

Abraham provides his seed and names him. All three acts—opening the channel of life, nurturing and sending the child forth, giving the child an identity—are equally essential to that child's development; and they are only the beginning. It has been said that it takes a whole village to raise a child. Actually, it takes the whole world.

ISAAC'S BRIS AND WEANING PARTIES

THE RABBIS RECOUNT: Abraham and Sarah hold two great feasts in honor of their son: the first on the eighth day after his birth, when Isaac is circumcised; the second when he is weaned. Miracles happen on both occasions. At the circumcision party, Sarah's breasts overflow with so much milk that she nurses all one hundred babies who attend the feast. Those whose mothers are thinking only pious thoughts while Sarah nurses them grow up to become converts to Judaism, the ancestors of all righteous proselytes. Those whose mothers doubt the miracle grow up to be the rulers of the world, whose kingdoms are all lost because they reject the Torah.

At Isaac's weaning (which according to Rabbi Hoshaya the Elder takes place when he is thirteen, giving us the precedent for the bar mitzvah), all thirty-one kings who will later be killed by Joshua are in attendance, with their regents. The giant Og is also there, and he boasts that he can crush the puny Isaac with one finger. Accordingly, on that day, his doom is sealed. Even God is a guest, which is why the party is called "great," as it is written: "AND ABRAHAM HELD A GREAT FEAST" (21:8).

THE BANISHMENT OF HAGAR

OUR DAUGHTERS ASK: How could Sarah have been so cruel to Hagar!

HAGAR THE STRANGER ANSWERS: When Sarah saw my son, Ishmael, playing with her own son, she ordered Abraham to "CAST OUT THAT SLAVE WOMAN AND HER SON" (21:10) from the camp. Abraham protested, but his God sided with Sarah, saying: "DO NOT BE DISTRESSED OVER THE BOY OR YOUR SLAVE; WHATEVER SARAH TELLS YOU, DO AS SHE SAYS, FOR IT IS THROUGH ISAAC THAT OFFSPRING SHALL BE CONTINUED FOR YOU. AS FOR THE SON OF THE SLAVE WOMAN, I WILL MAKE A NATION OF HIM TOO, FOR HE IS YOUR SEED" (21:12–13).

THE RABBIS OFFER A DIFFERENT EXPLANATION: Ishmael "plays at being" Isaac by mocking him. The Hebrew word for play, *mitzahek*, itself mocks Isaac's name, *Yitzhak*.

BUT SARAH THE ANCIENT ONE REBUKES THEM: You need not demonize Ishmael and his mother in order to understand my actions—or the Holy One's. I was a realist; Abraham an idealist. I understood that Abraham's older son, originally designated as his heir, would always pose a threat to Isaac's future. To protect my son, I hardened my heart against his rival.

HAGAR'S PROVISIONS

OUR DAUGHTERS ASK: Why doesn't Abraham do more to prepare Hagar and Ishmael for their exile? Why does he give them only "SOME BREAD AND A SKIN OF WATER" (21:14)? Why provision them so meagerly? He could have also given them a camel or a servant—or, at the very least, a blessing.

ESTHER THE HIDDEN ONE ANSWERS: In acting this way, Abraham demonstrates his faith that God will provide. He takes to heart God's promise that Ishmael will become a great nation. This episode is a rehearsal of his later test of faith with his other son.

DINAH THE WOUNDED ONE OBJECTS: It could have been otherwise! Sarah after all only orders him to send the two of them away. It is Abraham's choice to give them so little for their journey.

THE TRIAL OF HAGAR

OUR DAUGHTERS ASK: Why does Hagar push Ishmael away when she thinks he's going to die? As it is written: "[She] SAT DOWN AT A DISTANCE, *A BOW-SHOT AWAY*, FOR SHE THOUGHT, 'LET ME NOT LOOK ON AS THE CHILD DIES'" (21:16). Is that any way for a mother to act!

MOTHER RACHEL ANSWERS: Too often parents find themselves in this position, powerless to save their children from the Angel of Death. We can't blame Hagar for averting her eyes and ears from Ishmael's death rattle. Is it not difficult to endure a child's death even "at a distance"—away at war, on an operating table, or on a mountaintop beneath his father's knife? Perhaps it's only that distance that releases Hagar's tears and summons God's help. Had she remained close to Ishmael, she might have been too paralyzed by his suffering to call out at all.

THE CRY OF THE BOY

OUR DAUGHTERS ASK: Why does God hear Ishmael's cry, not Hagar's? As it is written: "GOD HEARD THE CRY OF THE BOY" (21:17). Only after hearing the child's cry does an angel appear to Hagar and assure her: "FEAR NOT, FOR GOD HAS HEEDED THE CRY OF THE BOY WHERE HE IS" (21:17). Why doesn't her own distress draw this response?

THE RABBIS ANSWER: Hagar's eyes are at first so blinded by tears that she is unable to see the miraculous well nearby. Too overcome with grief over her son's approaching death, she fails to attend to her own survival. But when Ishmael calls out from "where he [was]," the angel appears and reassures Hagar that they will both live. It is the child's selfishness, not the mother's selflessness, that storms heaven's gate. Only then do Hagar's eyes open so that she sees the well that has been there all along. As it is written: "THEN GOD OPENED HER EYES AND SHE SAW A WELL OF WATER" (21:19).

HAGAR THE BANISHED ONE ADDS: Sometimes it's our children, speaking from where they are, who teach us how to see what we need to survive.

AND OUR BUBBES CHIME IN: A child's tears reach the heavens.

THE AKEDAH

OUR DAUGHTERS ASK: Where is Sarah when Abraham and Isaac set off for Mount Moriah? What are her reactions when her husband goes off with her only son? Why is she silent?

THE RABBIS ANSWER: After Abraham and Isaac leave, Sarah goes to Hebron, looking for them. Satan—the Tempter, the Adversary, the Alter Ego—appears to her and reveals that Abraham intends to sacrifice her son; hearing this, her heart breaks from sorrow and she dies. As it is written: "SARAH DIED IN KIRYAT-ARBA—NOW HEBRON" (23:2). But others teach that Satan reveals to her that Abraham has spared her son from his knife; and then her heart bursts from joy. Such is the anatomy of a mother's heart.

SARAH THE ANCIENT ONE RETORTS: What do the Rabbis know of a mother's heart!

5. HAYEI SARAH:

Love and Marriage

(GENESIS 23:1–25:18)

ORAH TEACHES: At the age of 127, Sarah dies. Abraham mourns her death, and when he rises up from the mourning stool, he buys the Cave of Makhpelah as a burial place.

Determined that his son Isaac not marry a Canaanite woman, Abraham then sends his servant Eliezer back to the old country to find Isaac a bride. To select the appropriate woman, Eliezer sets up a test, and lo and behold! Rebecca, Abraham's great-niece, passes it, for without being asked, the young woman waters Eliezer's camels as well as giving him drink. Eliezer then asks her father, Bethuel, and her brother, Laban, for Rebecca's hand, and they agree, but only after Rebecca herself gives her consent.

Eliezer returns to Canaan with Rebecca and her nurse, Deborah. Isaac marries Rebecca, bringing her into Sarah's tent, where he finally finds comfort after his mother's death.

Then Abraham remarries, has many more children, and dies at the age of 175. His sons Isaac and Ishmael bury him beside Sarah in the Cave of Makhpelah. Ishmael also has many children, and he dies at the age of 137.

THE DEATH OF SARAH

OUR DAUGHTERS ASK: Why is this parasha called *Hayei Sarah,* "The Life of Sarah," when it begins with her death?

WILY REBECCA, SARAH'S DAUGHTER-IN-LAW, ANSWERS: Because her death—the first Jewish burial—triggers all the events that follow. At 137, Abraham is "NOW OLD" (24:1). Sarah's death finally ages him. After her burial, Abraham turns his attention to marrying off his heir, Sarah's only son, my husband, Isaac. With that done, Abraham takes his third consort, Keturah, and fathers more children to comfort him in his dotage. And my poor grief-stricken Isaac, liberated at thirty-seven from Sarah's watchful gaze, is finally ready to bring a wife into his mother's tent.

BERURIAH THE SCHOLAR NOTES: This is the only time in the Bible when a woman's age is noted at her death.

OUR BUBBES EXCLAIM: She must have been some *balebuste!*

MATCHMAKING

OUR DAUGHTERS ASK: Why does Abraham send a proxy to find a wife for his son? That choice seems so risky! First of all, he entrusts the task to his servant Eliezer, who is his designated heir and stands to lose everything if Isaac marries and sires a son. And he gives Eliezer no clear instructions about how to decide who's an appropriate wife for his son. He does not even mention the name of his kinsmen in Aram-Naharaim. Why does Abraham leave so much to chance? Is he acting from faith or from foolishness?

SARAH THE ANCIENT ONE ANSWERS: We all know how hard it is to marry off our children to a suitable partner, especially if we live "AMONG THE DAUGHTERS [and sons] OF THE CANAANITES" (24:3). All we can do is prepare the ground and then hope, as Abraham and I did, that God "WILL SEND [an] ANGEL" (24:7) to point the way.

THE RABBIS RECOUNT: Once, Rabbi Yose bar Halafta was asked by a Roman matron: "You claim that your God created the world in six days. Then what has He been doing since then?"

"All this time the Holy One has been making matches."

"That is no great feat!" declared the matron. "I can do that just as well."

But Rabbi Yose warned her: "It is not as simple as you think. The Holy One, blessed be He, considers making matches as difficult as splitting the Red Sea."

Undaunted, the matron called for one thousand of her male servants and one thousand of her female servants to be lined up and then, in a single night, matched them to one another. But the next day, they came to their mistress, some with black eyes, others with broken limbs, still others with bruised heads, all complaining that they didn't want the partners she had given them.

Immediately, the matron sent for Rabbi Yose and acknowledged: "How awesome is your God! And how worthy of praise is your Torah!"

ELIEZER'S TEST

OUR DAUGHTERS ASK: Why does Eliezer decide to test Rebecca the way he does? As it is written: "LET THE MAIDEN TO WHOM I SAY, 'PLEASE, LOWER YOUR JAR THAT I MAY DRINK,' AND WHO REPLIES, 'DRINK, AND I WILL ALSO WATER YOUR CAMELS'—LET HER BE THE ONE WHOM YOU HAVE DECREED FOR YOUR SERVANT ISAAC" (24:14). Why does he think that this question-and-answer test will reveal the right bride?

WILY REBECCA ANSWERS: Eliezer's test was designed to locate a woman discreet enough not to approach a stranger but bold enough to extend herself, once approached by him. This particular combination of character traits—a kind of cagey gumption—is precisely what later enabled me to secure Jacob's future by tricking my husband and my older son out of the birthright. So Eliezer's angel obviously knew exactly what she was doing.

REBECCA'S GRANDMOTHER MILCAH

OUR DAUGHTERS ASK: Who is Milcah? As it is written: "[Rebecca] WAS BORN TO BETHUEL, THE SON OF MILCAH THE WIFE OF ABRAHAM'S BROTHER NAHOR" (24:15). How unusual for the Torah to include Rebecca's *grandmother* in her pedigree.

WILY REBECCA ANSWERS: Milcah was a central figure in my family—sister to Lot; sister-in-law and niece to Abraham; my grandmother. A link to three generations. But how little I know about her life! Besides her place in the family tree, all I know is that her name means "queen." But what a profound influence she had!

MILCAH ADDS: It's easy to understand why I was such a veiled figure. I was overshadowed by two headstrong men—my uncle Abraham and my uncle Nahor, who later became my husband. Uprooted from my home and friends, transplanted to a desolate waste far from the grand city of my youth, I retreated into my tent and found solace in my children and grandchildren, especially Rebecca, the apple of my eye. I never doubted that she would take her future into her own hands.

REBECCA AT THE WELL

WILY REBECCA BOASTS: I not only met but outstripped Eliezer's expectations—and he certainly made it hard for me! Only after I'd climbed up from the spring with a heavy jar of water on my shoulder did he ask me for a drink. But I didn't get angry. No, I willingly shared my precious water with him, even though he was a stranger. And I called him "my lord," though he didn't look like one. Not only that—I rushed to serve him, "quickly" lowering my jar and then "running" back down to the well to draw water for his camels. And I offered to water "all" his camels "until they finish[ed] drinking," even though camels—thirsty beasts!—drink as much as twenty-five gallons of water after a desert trek.

OUR MOTHERS EXCLAIM: Even in a culture noted for its hospitality, surely Rebecca's actions are exemplary!

HER MOTHER'S HOUSEHOLD

OUR DAUGHTERS ASK: Why does the Torah say that "THE MAIDEN RAN AND TOLD ALL THIS TO HER MOTHER'S HOUSEHOLD" (24:28)? More likely it's her *father's* house.

WILY REBECCA ANSWERS: So much in my story goes against the grain of patriarchal culture: My genealogy's usually traced through my *grandmother* Milcah (though Eliezer, whenever he told his side of the story, kept substituting my *grandfather's* name). Although the narrator rightly identifies my home as my *mother's* household, Eliezer always insisted that he'd been sent to Abraham's *father's* household. But notice that Eliezer gave gifts to my brother and *mother*, but not to my father. And it was my *mother* and my brother Laban who negotiated for my hand. And my mother and Laban asked me if I wanted to go off with Eliezer to marry Isaac.

OUR MOTHERS OBSERVE: Even today Middle Eastern and Mediterranean cultures typically don't grant such privileged status to women. How much more exceptional that the ancient Bible does!

REBECCA'S DECISION

OUR DAUGHTERS ASK: Who makes the decision that Rebecca should marry Isaac? Is Rebecca really allowed to decide for herself, as it is written: "WILL YOU GO WITH THIS MAN?" (23:58) In most traditional cultures, such things aren't allowed.

WILY REBECCA ANSWERS: I always suspected that my brother Laban was up to something in asking me for my consent. Maybe he was hoping I'd refuse, so that he could squeeze more of a bride-price from Eliezer. Laban was certainly capable of such crude behavior. Remember that he later extorted from Jacob seven extra years for Rachel's hand. And I also wonder about my mother's motives. I suspect that she wanted to keep me home, so she insisted on my consent in the hopes that I would refuse the marriage. She already knew that she'd probably never see me again, never see her grandchildren. But in the end all she got was ten more days with me.

OUR MOTHERS ADD: Perhaps she simply wanted to grant Rebecca a voice, something she did not have in her own life. After all, she does not even have a name.

REBECCA'S BLESSING

OUR MOTHERS TEACH: Few women in the Bible receive a special blessing; none but Rebecca receives a blessing from her mother. And what a blessing it is:

O sister!
May you grow
Into thousands of myriads;
May your offspring seize
The gates of their foes.

HAGAR THE BANISHED ONE INTERJECTS: It's true that Rebecca's descendants—the Children of Israel—eventually do grow into a mighty nation that seizes its enemies' gates. But so do her other descendants, the Children of Esau—first Edom, whom Jewish tradition identifies as the Roman Empire, and Edom's descendants, the Christian nations of the world.

HULDAH THE PREACHER ADDS: We should therefore be careful how we bless each other, since blessings, like children, eventually take on a life of their own.

LOVE AT FIRST SIGHT

WILY REBECCA RECOUNTS: What an awful journey it was! After an endless camel trek to reach a home and husband I'd never seen, I finally caught a glimpse of my husband-to-be "WALKING IN THE FIELD TOWARD EVENING" (24:63). What immediately struck me was how much *older* he was than I'd imagined and how bent over, as if he'd been carrying a heavy load all his life. Out of respect for him, I hurried to dismount from my camel, but I was sick at heart.

THE RABBIS OFFER THEIR VERSION: Rebecca is so overcome by fatigue, frayed nerves, and erotic excitement that she falls off her camel. As it is written: "SHE ALIGHTED FROM HER CAMEL" (23:64). Indeed, the Hebrew word—*vatipol*—literally means "to fall down."

REBECCA FIRES BACK: Why don't you try spending a few days riding a camel! Anyway, once I'd made sure that this stranger was Isaac, I veiled myself.

OUR MOTHERS COMMENT: As in the earlier scene at the well, Rebecca acts spontaneously, responding to her own heart. For although she is otherwise spirited and bold, here she restrains herself and behaves with modesty, covering herself before her future husband.

BUT REBECCA DEMURS: Just as I asserted my own will in agreeing to this marriage, so here I asserted myself in meeting Isaac eye-to-eye. That's why Eliezer identified Isaac as *his* master, not mine. Because in me, Isaac had more than met his match.

VEILS

BERURIAH THE SCHOLAR TEACHES: In traditional Middle Eastern society, women still veil themselves as a sign of modesty. Although Jewish women, unlike many of their Muslim sisters, no longer observe the custom, a vestige of this practice dating back to Rebecca remains in the *bedeken* ceremony held before a Jewish wedding, when the bride is veiled before she meets the groom beneath the *huppah*, the marriage canopy. To strengthen this connection to Rebecca, the women veiling the bride recite the blessing that Rebecca receives from her family upon leaving home: "O sister! May you grow into thousands of myriads!" (24:60) Rebecca is also linked to the other matriarchs, in a second blessing bestowed upon the new bride: "May God bless you like Sarah, Rebecca, Rachel, and Leah."

OUR BUBBES DECLARE: And may the bride live to know the joy of motherhood, and learn that a mother is like a veil (she hides the faults of her children).

WIFELY MOTHERS, MATERNAL WIVES

OUR DAUGHTERS ASK: Why does Isaac bring Rebecca into Sarah's tent after his wedding? Wouldn't it make more sense for them to start their lives together in their own tent?

WILY REBECCA ANSWERS: By the time Abraham decided to marry off his son, Isaac was already thirty-seven years old, a traumatized middle-aged bachelor, still grieving for his mother. (Marrying late turned out to be a family pattern: our son Esau married at forty; and Jacob became engaged at forty and married at forty-seven.) Although he was the heir to Abraham's fortune and destiny, Isaac had little emotional connection with his father; in fact, my father-in-law remarried and started a new family as soon as we were married and had moved into Sarah's old tent.

THE SAGES IN OUR OWN TIME INTERRUPT: Our reading of the text reveals a priestly hand behind this family chronology. After all, how could the number forty keep recurring so regularly in the Torah? Surely we are in the presence of legend, not history!

SARAH THE ANCIENT ONE BREAKS IN: Love did not come easy to Isaac. When he was a child, his half-brother, Ishmael, hated him for dispossessing him. Later, his father undermined their relationship when he almost sacrificed him on Mount Moriah. And I, who had waited ninety barren years for him, did not—could not—love him enough to stop Abraham from leading him off to the slaughter. So what could he know of normal love? How could he trust that his God-intoxicated father would choose a proper wife for him? It was only after marrying Rebecca and bringing her into my tent that Isaac discovered that love can heal as well as wound. As it is written: "ISAAC LOVED HER, AND THUS FOUND COMFORT AFTER HIS MOTHER'S DEATH" (23:67).

SARAH'S TENT

THE RABBIS TEACH: Sarah's tent was a source of miracles during her lifetime. The Sabbath lights she lit there illumined her tent all week long. The divine Cloud of Glory always hovered over it. The dough she kneaded within its folds was blessed, and the tent flaps stretched wide to admit all who came there for food and shelter. These blessings all departed at Sarah's death, but they returned with Rebecca's marriage to Sarah's son.

MOTHER RACHEL ADDS: The greatest miracle of all was that Rebecca's love healed Isaac's heart, which had been broken by his mother's death.

ABRAHAM'S WIFE KETURAH

OUR DAUGHTERS ASK: Who is Keturah? Why is it that Abraham's concubine, Hagar, gets recognition as the ancestor of the Arab peoples, but Keturah, Abraham's second *wife*, remains invisible in the tradition? What do we know about this woman whom Abraham marries after Sarah's death or of the six sons they have together, whom Abraham ultimately sends off "eastward, onto the east country" (25:6)? What are her origins? What do we know of her life, her character, and her death?

KETURAH ANSWERS: I was only a child when I married old Abraham. All I brought with me from my family and birthplace was my name. I've been told that it's a name full of stories. Some have said that it means "tied up" or "captive." So perhaps I was acquired by Abraham through battle or purchase. It's also related to "incense." I sometimes imagine that my family were important priests or spice traders. There are even those who have said that my name comes from *k-t-r*, meaning "circlet" or "wreath," and that therefore I am of royal descent, a princess like Abraham's first wife, Sarah.

THE SAGES IN OUR OWN TIME SUGGEST: Since the Torah regards Abraham as the father of all Middle Eastern peoples, perhaps Keturah serves to represent "the peoples of the east," since spices come from that region. Her children include Midian, who will be influential in the biblical story later on.

HAGAR THE BANISHED ONE RETORTS: No, to the Torah she is only the third wife, maybe merely a concubine, a footnote to the main events. It's up to us to imagine her story.

6. TOLDOT:
Family Politics

(GENESIS 25:19–28:9)

TORAH TEACHES: After marrying Isaac, Rebecca is barren for twenty years. At last she conceives and bears twins—red, hairy Esau and smooth-skinned Jacob, who emerges grasping his brother's heel. Esau grows up to be a hunter, the apple of his father's eye; Jacob, a homebody, his mother's favorite. One day, Esau returns from the fields famished, and his brother persuades him to sell his birthright for a pot of lentils.

When famine besieges Canaan, God tells Isaac to remain in the land and then blesses him. Coming to the court of the Philistine king Abimelekh, Isaac protects himself from Abimelekh's royal prerogative—taking Rebecca for his bed and Isaac's head for his trophy—by using the same wife-sister ruse that his father, Abraham, had used before him to outmaneuver both Pharaoh and Abimelekh. Isaac then settles in Abimelekh's domain and prospers there. But after he is repeatedly harassed by the neighboring Philistines, Isaac moves on to Beersheba and concludes a peace agreement with Abimelekh.

Then Esau marries two Hittite women, which grieves his parents.

Sensing his approaching death, old, blind Isaac asks Esau to bring him some cooked game and receive his blessing as firstborn. Overhearing Isaac's words, Rebecca instructs Jacob to dress as Esau and steal his brother's blessing. And so, disguised in sheepskin, Jacob tricks Isaac and is blessed. And when Esau returns from the hunt and receives only a lesser blessing from his father, he swears revenge against his brother.

Rebecca urges Jacob to flee to her father's house, and she then persuades Isaac to send him there to marry one of her kinspeople. And so Isaac sends Jacob off with his blessing.

Esau, seeking to please his father, then marries Ishmael's daughter Mahalath in addition to his Hittite wives.

ABRAHAM'S LINE

OUR DAUGHTERS ASK: Why does the Torah name only Abraham as Isaac's parent? As it is written: "THIS IS THE STORY OF ISAAC, SON OF ABRAHAM.

ABRAHAM BEGOT ISAAC" (25:19). After all the attention paid earlier to Sarah's barrenness—the very first thing we learn about her—and to her miraculous fertility in old age, the narrator now erases her from Isaac's genealogy. Likewise, the Torah now revises Rebecca's genealogy, cutting out Milcah, Rebecca's grandmother, who is earlier included among Rebecca's ancestors when we're introduced to her. Here Rebecca is identified simply as the "DAUGHTER OF BETHUEL THE ARAMEAN OF PADDAN-ARAM, SISTER OF LABAN THE ARAMEAN" (25:20). Why have the women suddenly disappeared from the family tree?

THE SAGES IN OUR OWN TIME REVEAL: The priests who stitched the Torah together were concerned only with male lineage.

BUT BERURIAH THE SCHOLAR ANSWERS: Rather than suspect the meddling hand of priestly sexism, let's examine the *subtext*, the unspoken anxieties motivating this tale. What a problematic hero Isaac is for the biblical narrator! He's a mama's boy, a pawn, a victim sandwiched between the conflicts of three generations of women: Sarah vs. Hagar, Rebecca vs. her older son, Rachel vs. Leah. Given how dominant and powerful women are in Isaac's life—and how embarrassing such a history must be to such a patriarchal culture—the Torah here is trying to make a man of him, calling upon all the male figures in his line.

REBECCA'S SILENCE

OUR DAUGHTERS ASK: Why doesn't Rebecca herself appeal to the Merciful One to end her barrenness? Instead it is written: "ISAAC PLEADED WITH YHVH ON BEHALF OF HIS WIFE" (25:21). From the moment we meet Rebecca, we marvel at her powers of speech. She pronounces just the right words to pass Eliezer's test at the well. She unflinchingly declares her decision to leave home to marry a man she's never met. And in the verse following this one, she protests to God about the difficult circumstances of her pregnancy. Why then is she silent at this significant moment? And why doesn't she *act* on her own behalf, like Sarah, who gives Abraham her slave to bear a child in her stead, or Rachel, who resorts to both surrogacy and the magical power of mandrakes to overcome her infertility?

DINAH THE WOUNDED ONE ANSWERS: A fatalist, she resigns herself to her lot.

LILITH THE REBEL DISAGREES: No, she is ambivalent about childbearing, though she knows enough to keep this desire secret.

MOTHER RACHEL OFFERS: She fears that she lacks the physical constitution to bear and nurse a child. She already has had several miscarriages or stillbirths and can't bear yet another loss. And she suspects that the aging Isaac is incapable of being an adequate father.

LEAH DECLARES: She has fallen out of love with him and no longer wants his child.

REBECCA RESPONDS: No, the truth is that I was powerless to speak on my behalf, because God had promised that "MY COVENANT I WILL ESTABLISH WITH ISAAC" (17:21), and I had no choice but to respond, "Amen."

REBECCA'S PROTEST

OUR DAUGHTERS ASK: Why does Rebecca cry out when she feels twins struggling in her womb? As it is written: "IF SO, WHY DO I EXIST?" (25:22) What does she mean by these words?

LEAH THE NAMER ANSWERS: The Hebrew phrase—*Im ken, lamah zeh anokhi?*—is puzzling. Because Hebrew is so terse and word order so flexible, we can read the question two different ways: "If so, why me?" Or alternatively: "Why am I this?" Clearly, the most baffling word in the phrase is *"zeh*—this." To what does it refer?

MOTHER RACHEL SUGGESTS: To the pain of her pregnancy. Rebecca is questioning whether she'll survive its rigors.

SARAH THE ANCIENT ONE DISAGREES: No, she is lamenting her fate, condemned to be the mother of warring children.

REBECCA EXPLAINS: No, mine was an elemental cry, familiar to all of us: Why is this happening to me? After my kindness at the well, did I deserve such a cruel fate, tormented by my unborn children? *This* was not why I left my homeland and family!

SARAH THE ANCIENT ONE MUSES: God's answer—that she will give birth to two rival nations—is not the answer Rebecca wants to hear, but it is the one she has to learn to live with.

THE RABBIS AGREE: Indeed, women's suffering is so often greater than men's!

FAMILY PATTERNS

OUR DAUGHTERS ASK: How can parents play favorites? Even in the Torah!

OUR MOTHERS ANSWER: All parents have to struggle with their natural tendency to favor one child over another. Faced with the inevitable sibling rivalry among our children, we try our best to be evenhanded. Even so, our children quickly learn that life is not fair—and neither are parents.

SERAKH BAT ASHER THE HISTORIAN OFFERS: In these foundational stories of the first Jewish family, the same pattern repeats for three generations. As it is written: "THE OLDER SHALL SERVE THE YOUNGER" (25:23). Isaac prevails over Ishmael; Jacob over Esau; Joseph over his ten older brothers. So too the young Israelite people eventually prevail over the ancient civilizations of Mesopotamia, Canaan, and Egypt.

In both cases, familial and national, favoritism exacts a steep price from the unforgiving taskmaster known as history. Victory is often pyrrhic for the winners; defeat at times redemptive for the vanquished. And never is the outcome limited to a single generation.

REBECCA'S PREFERENCE FOR JACOB

OUR DAUGHTERS ASK: Why does Rebecca favor Jacob? As it is written: "ISAAC FAVORED ESAU . . . BUT REBECCA LOVED JACOB" (25:28). We're told that "ISAAC FAVORED ESAU BECAUSE HE HAD A TASTE FOR GAME," but we are given no reason for Rebecca's bias toward Jacob. Is she motivated only by God's promise that "THE OLDER SHALL SERVE THE YOUNGER"?

REBECCA ANSWERS: A mother's love is usually not so pure. I was drawn to Jacob because of his personal qualities: he preferred tent life to hunting; he was clever; he was smooth-skinned and handsome; he attended to me and heeded my advice. Esau, on the other hand, was a wild, hairy man, intemperate, a slave to his appetites.

MIRIAM THE PROPHET EXPLAINS: Rebecca clearly understands that it is someone like Jacob who will fulfill God's covenant. Isaac, on the other hand, hopes for a different outcome for his family: to become through Esau a nation like all other nations among whom they live. That is why God reveals the future to Rebecca.

RECIPE FOR RED LENTILS

OUR BUBBES DECLARE: If Esau is willing to sell his birthright for a pot of red lentils, it must have been quite a *tzimmes!* Here's one of our recipes for good homemade lentil soup:

RED LENTIL SOUP

1 tablespoon olive or vegetable oil
1 medium-size onion, finely chopped
1 garlic clove, minced
5–6 cups broth (vegetarian or meat)
2 cups (about ¾ pound) red lentils, sorted and rinsed

13-ounce can chopped tomatoes
½ teaspoon cumin
1 tablespoon brown sugar
1 tablespoon lemon juice
Salt and pepper to taste
4–6 hot dogs, sliced (vegetarian or meat)

In a large soup pot, sauté the onion and garlic in oil. Add the rest of the ingredients except the hot dogs and simmer, covered, for about 40 minutes, or until lentils are very tender and liquid is thick. If soup becomes too thick, add a little more broth. Add the hot dogs and cook another 5 minutes, until they are heated. (Garnish with parsley for an even more beautiful color presentation.)

Makes about 6 servings.

THE SYMBOLISM OF LENTILS

THE SAGES IN OUR OWN TIME TEACH: Lentils were the most important legume in the Middle East. Jacob's stew was probably made of Egyptian lentils, which are red.

THE RABBIS ADD: Because lentils grow close to the ground, they are a symbol of modesty. As the proverb says: "as lowly as a lentil." Lentils are eaten by mourners, because "the lentil has no mouth," just as mourners should not open their mouths to protest in the face of death.

THE PERENNIAL PROBLEM OF INTERMARRIAGE

OUR DAUGHTERS ASK: For most of our history, we've lived as an alien minority among a larger host culture. And we always face the same dilemma: How can we maintain our separate identity so we won't be swallowed up by the people all around us? The issue usually comes to a head over the question: Whom are we allowed to marry? But in the case of Abraham's clan, who *could* they marry, when theirs was the *only* Jewish family?

SARAH THE ANCIENT ONE ANSWERS: Abraham solved the problem by importing a kinswoman for our son. And Jacob also turned to that branch of our family to find a wife. But Esau, like his uncle Ishmael before him, "married out," choosing two Hittite wives, Judith daughter of Beeri and Basemat daughter of Elon. And "THEY WERE A SOURCE OF BITTERNESS TO ISAAC AND REBECCA" (26:35).

HAGAR THE STRANGER PROTESTS: But Esau didn't understand the rules by which his family played! For when his parents sent Jacob off to Paddan-Aram to find a wife from among his mother's family, Esau, "REALIZ[ing] THAT THE CANAANITE WOMEN DISPLEASED HIS FATHER" (28:8), countered by marrying as his third wife a kinswoman from his uncle Ishmael's family, Mahalath, the daughter of Ishmael and his Egyptian wife. By so doing he hoped to win back his parents' blessing.

LILITH ADDS: The deck was stacked against him from the beginning!

OUR BUBBES OBSERVE: The Torah's silence about this match should speak for itself.

WOMAN AS EAVESDROPPER AGAIN

OUR DAUGHTERS ASK: Why does Rebecca "listen in" on Isaac's conversation with Esau?

WILY REBECCA ANSWERS: Because I, like all women in my society, was marginalized, loitering at the edges, listening at the tent flap, stitching together scraps of overheard conversation, innuendo, and hearsay to construct "news," a spy in my own home. Just as Sarah heard only indirectly the angel's prophecy that she would give birth to a son, so I learned of Isaac's plan to bless Esau only by listening in on their conversation. As it is written: "REBECCA HAD BEEN LISTENING AS ISAAC SPOKE TO HIS SON ESAU" (27:5). I make no apologies for my eavesdropping. I told Jacob plainly: "I OVERHEARD YOUR FATHER SPEAKING TO YOUR BROTHER ESAU" (27:6).

SARAH THE ANCIENT ONE CHIMES IN: Like my daughter-in-law, I did not try to excuse my eavesdropping. Nor was I reprimanded for it.

LILITH THE REBEL ADDS: Those denied access to information are the most eager to acquire it— and become the most skilled at getting it.

CARRYING OUT THE DIVINE PLAN

OUR DAUGHTERS ASK: How spontaneous is Rebecca's "wolf-in-sheep's-clothing" scheme? Does she conceive this strategy only *after* she overhears Isaac sending Esau off to hunt game and then prepare a meal for him? Or has she been plotting all along?

WILY REBECCA ANSWERS: Of course I'd been plotting! My eavesdropping was completely premeditated. I'd been waiting for my chance ever since I first heard God's prophecy that Jacob, not Esau, would inherit the covenant. As it is written: "REBECCA HAD BEEN LISTENING AS ISAAC SPOKE TO HIS SON ESAU." So I didn't simply *overhear*. I intentionally *listened in*.

When I said to Jacob, "NOW, MY SON, LISTEN CAREFULLY AS I INSTRUCT YOU" (27:8), I was offering him a plan I'd already cooked up. Because I knew that "ISAAC FAVORED ESAU BECAUSE HE HAD A TASTE FOR GAME" (25:28), I knew that here was the surest way to Isaac's heart. Unlike my father-in-law, Abraham, who reacted impulsively when his angel guests appeared, I was deliberate in my actions. I told Jacob: "GO TO THE FLOCK AND FETCH ME TWO CHOICE KIDS, AND I WILL MAKE OF THEM A DISH FOR YOUR FATHER SUCH AS HE LIKES. THEN TAKE IT TO YOUR FATHER TO EAT, IN ORDER THAT HE MAY BLESS YOU BEFORE HE DIES" (27:9–10). You see, I'd chosen my recipes far in advance.

REBECCA'S CURSE

WILY REBECCA REVEALS: At this point in his life, my son Jacob was still so naive, believing that things must always be as they seem. When he heard my scheme to deceive his blind father, he was sure that the plot would fail, because "MY BROTHER ESAU IS A HAIRY MAN AND I AM SMOOTH-SKINNED. IF MY FATHER TOUCHES ME, I SHALL APPEAR TO HIM AS A TRICKSTER AND BRING UPON MYSELF A CURSE, NOT A BLESSING" (27:11–12). Rather than corrupt him with my own knowledge of the world's deceits, I took his guilt upon myself, as it is written: "YOUR CURSE, MY SON, BE UPON ME! JUST DO AS I SAY AND GO FETCH THEM FOR ME" (27:13).

And I paid dearly for my actions! Jacob was away in Paddan-Aram for twenty years. And during this time he and his four wives raised twelve sons and a daughter. I died before he returned, never having seen my grandchildren.

REBECCA'S STEW

OUR BUBBES COMPLAIN: What's the use that it's written: Rebecca "PREPARED A DISH SUCH AS HIS FATHER LIKED" (27:14) and that she cooked it with "two choice kids"? What kind of recipe is that! So here's a proper recipe that's probably close to what she cooked up for Isaac. (And if goats are hard to come by, use lamb, and if you are a vegetarian, you can use turnips or potatoes.)

MIDDLE EASTERN LAMB AND RICE PILAF

1 tablespoon pareve margarine
2 large onions, finely chopped
3–4 garlic cloves, finely minced
4 celery stalks
3 cups long-grain brown rice
2–3 pounds lean boneless lamb, cubed
6 cups broth
2 15–16-ounce cans chickpeas, drained

1½ cups raisins
1 apple, peeled, cored, finely chopped
1 cup fresh parsley, finely chopped
1 teaspoon allspice
¼ teaspoon cinnamon
½ teaspoon thyme
½ teaspoon black pepper
¼ teaspoon salt

In a 5–6-quart pot, melt the margarine over medium-high heat. Add onion, garlic, and celery, stirring until tender but not brown. Add the rice and stir for one minute. Add the lamb and stir until browned on all sides. Stir in the rest of the ingredients. Bring to a boil, then cover and lower heat. Simmer, covered, for about 45 minutes, or until all the liquid has been absorbed. Toss with a fork before serving.

Makes about 8 servings.

JACOB'S BLESSING

OUR DAUGHTERS ASK: When Isaac blesses Jacob, why does he talk about his *brothers,* when Jacob has only *one* brother? And when he curses those who oppose Jacob, does he mean to curse the very son he had hoped to bless?

MIRIAM THE PROPHET ANSWERS: Truly, how strange is Isaac's blessing of Jacob! It is as if he, like the pagan prophet Balaam, is forced to utter words God puts in his mouth against his will: "LET PEOPLES SERVE YOU AND NA-TIONS BOW TO YOU; BE MASTER OVER YOUR BROTHERS, AND LET YOUR MOTHER'S SONS BOW TO YOU. CURSED BE THEY WHO CURSE YOU, BLESSED THEY WHO BLESS YOU" (27:29). Isaac is indeed an unwitting prophet, for he speaks not to Jacob but to Jacob's sons, who will one day bow down to their younger brother Joseph. Isaac sees through Jacob's disguise into his future, addressing his sons not yet born. Perhaps he is not as blind as he seems.

SERAKH BAT ASHER THE HISTORIAN OBJECTS: But this passage postdates Isaac by many centuries! It is only through historical hindsight that Isaac can be seen as a prophet.

MIRIAM RESPONDS: Yet history, especially when it reaches so far back, may be no truer than prophecy. In fact, these two ways of telling a story may be nothing more than mirror images of each other. The truth lies somewhere in between.

REBECCA'S LOVE FOR ESAU

OUR DAUGHTERS ASK: Does Rebecca love Esau? From her actions, it seems that she doesn't. The Torah tells us that "REBECCA LOVED JACOB" whereas "ISAAC FAVORED ESAU." And even though Esau's marriage to two Hittite women embitters *both* his parents, it's Rebecca, not Isaac, who insists that Jacob be sent away to marry one of his relatives, saying: "I AM DISGUSTED WITH MY LIFE BE-CAUSE OF THE HITTITE WOMEN" (27:46). And of course, the most damning evi-dence of all is Rebecca's act of betrayal of both Isaac and Esau in order to grab the birthright for Jacob. Are these the actions of a mother who loves her chil-dren equally?

REBECCA ANSWERS: Didn't you hear me cry out when I urged Jacob into exile to escape Esau's revenge: "LET ME NOT LOSE YOU BOTH IN ONE DAY" (27:45)? How clearly I understood what a high price I'd pay for my actions:

losing Esau's love in exchange for Jacob's blessing. From the moment that God told me the destiny awaiting my two sons, while they were still struggling in my womb—"THE OLDER SHALL SERVE THE YOUNGER"—I devoted myself to forcing that blessing from Isaac's lips. But when I finally succeeded, when at last I heard Isaac tell Jacob: "BE MASTER OVER YOUR BROTHERS, AND LET YOUR MOTHER'S SONS BOW TO YOU," I'd also lost. Jacob's curse was now on me, just as I'd set it up. For the next twenty years, I suffered Esau's revenge: my beloved Jacob's absence.

THE PRICE OF INTERMARRIAGE

OUR DAUGHTERS ASK: When Rebecca speaks about Jacob's possible marriage to an outsider, why does she say: "WHAT GOOD WILL LIFE BE TO ME" (27:46)? Isn't she overreacting?

REBECCA ANSWERS: From the beginning of my marriage, I was the one to make choices for my family. I was betrothed long-distance through a slave, but still I chose to leave home and marry Isaac. When I was told about God's plan to raise my younger son above the older, I tricked Isaac into blessing the chosen son. And when I saw that Esau had married foreign wives and was now bent on murder, I forced Isaac to send Jacob away to marry and raise a proper heir to the covenant.

And I also knew how to win Isaac's heart so that he would honor my choices. I understood that he couldn't *see* past himself and his own narrow concerns. So I always couched my actions in a language he could understand. Thus I earned his love by taking his dead mother's place; forced his blessing by satisfying his appetite for game; married Jacob off by appealing to his compassion for me. Never did I take the higher ground and speak of God's design. I knew my customer far too well.

7. VAYETZE:
The Ladder of Ambition
(GENESIS 28:10–32:3)

TORAH TEACHES: Fleeing Esau, Jacob lies down to sleep and dreams of a ladder with angels ascending to and descending from heaven. And in his dream God blesses him. Upon awaking, Jacob builds an altar out of his stone pillow and names the place Bethel, the "house of God." Then he continues on toward Haran.

There Jacob meets his cousin Rachel and waters her flock. Smitten with love, he asks his uncle Laban for Rachel's hand in marriage, and he receives it in exchange for seven years of labor. But Laban tricks Jacob and gives him Rachel's older sister, Leah, instead and then extorts seven more years out of him for Rachel as his second wife. The two women bring with them their handmaids, Zilpah and Bilhah.

To compensate Leah for Jacob's preference for her younger sister, God grants her fertility: she bears six sons—Reuben, Simeon, Levi, Judah, Issachar, and Zebulun—and a daughter, Dinah. The barren Rachel then gives Jacob her handmaid as a concubine, and Bilhah bears to him Dan and Naphtali. Leah then gives Jacob Zilpah, who gives birth to two sons, Gad and Asher. Finally, Rachel conceives and gives birth to Joseph.

At the end of Jacob's fourteen years of service, Laban demands of him six more years, in exchange for a share of the herds, and Jacob grows prosperous through ingenious animal husbandry and divine blessing. Then Jacob, aware of Laban's festering ill will, flees back to Canaan with his wives, children, and flocks. Before leaving, Rachel steals her father's idols. Laban pursues them and demands his stolen gods. Rachel deceives her father, and they escape unscathed. Then Jacob and Laban conclude a nonaggression pact, sealing it with a mound of stones. Laban returns home, and Jacob's camp heads west, accompanied by angels.

THE SYMBOLISM OF LADDERS

THE RABBIS EXPLAIN: According to our sages, the *sulam*, Jacob's ladder (also translated as "stairway" or "ramp"), was the stairway leading from the

Temple altar to God. But others teach that it was Mount Sinai, since the numerical value of *sulam* equals "Sinai." Still others say that the ladder represents Jewish history, with its many ups and downs, and it is further taught that ladders represent an individual's life history: "The Holy One of Blessing sits and makes ladders, raising one person and casting down another."

ESTHER THE HIDDEN ONE INTERJECTS: We need to remember that ladders lead not only from earth up to heaven but also from heaven down to earth. As we leap up to reach the bottom rung of the heavenly ladder, God lowers the ladder to meet our outstretched hand. And when we cannot grasp even that lowest rung, She-Who-Dwells-Within reaches down and meets us where we are.

OUR BUBBES OFFER: For centuries, Jewish women in Eastern Europe baked ladders into their hallahs for special occasions: for the meal just before Yom Kippur, so that our prayers for forgiveness should ascend to heaven; and for Shavuot, to remember how Moses climbed all the way up Mount Sinai to receive the Torah.

THE TABLES TURNED

OUR DAUGHTERS ASK: Both Eliezer and Jacob meet brides at a well. How do their meetings compare?

OUR MOTHERS ANSWER: When Abraham's servant Eliezer devises a test to identify the right wife for Isaac, he's looking for the following qualities: kindness to strangers and animals, beauty, modesty, and loyalty to family. He finds them all in Rebecca. But when Jacob comes to the same well years later, he finds himself replaying *Rebecca's* script, not Eliezer's: so instead of waiting for a young woman to approach him, he comes forward to meet her; instead of her watering his animals, he waters hers. When he reveals himself to her, it's not Rachel but he who weeps. Yet the very qualities that made Rebecca the perfect wife for Isaac turn out to be liabilities to Rachel's husband-to-be: Jacob's generosity, friendliness, and family feeling make him easy prey to Laban's shrewdness.

WILY REBECCA EXPLAINS: By keeping Jacob home by my tent, schooling him in the traditional ways of women, I raised my smooth-skinned, sweet-smelling boy as my *daughter*, shielding him from the harsher ways of men. In this way, I set Jacob up to play the woman's role in the family drama.

LEAH AND RACHEL RETORT: And how Laban exploited your fantasy!

AN EYE FOR AN EYE

OUR DAUGHTERS ASK: Why does the Torah say that Leah has "weak eyes"? Is this a judgment of her beauty or her sight?

THE RABBIS TEACH: Judaism has long meditated on the concept of *ayin takhat ayin*—an eye for an eye—interpreting "eye" not literally but symbolically, to represent monetary compensation due an injured party. This concept of equivalence extends into the metaphysical realm as well, in the principle of *midah keneged midah*, measure for measure. That is, a person's deeds bear fruit in his or her life, an evil deed sowing disaster, a good deed reward. This principle is played out in the life of Abraham's descendants. Here in this third generation, Jacob experiences the fateful harvest of Ishmael's exile, Isaac's victimization, and Esau's betrayal. After his own trickery, Jacob flees into exile; through Laban's trickery, he comes to know exploitation and deceit. Since Jacob's deception of his brother takes advantage of Isaac's blindness, his punishment fittingly revolves around eyes.

LEAH ADDS: I was always described as having "tender" or "weak" eyes; my younger sister Rachel, on the other hand, was always called "shapely and beautiful." Although Jacob preferred beautiful Rachel and worked seven years to win her, it was me he married first—or rather my *eyes*, which were the only part of me he saw over my veil. In fact, it was *his* eyes that proved weak, so that he, like his father, Isaac, chose the wrong sibling.

MIRIAM THE PROPHET ADDS: Which, of course, was all part of God's plan.

THE COURSE OF TRUE LOVE

OUR DAUGHTERS ASK: Why doesn't the course of true love run smooth for Jacob?

THE SAGES IN OUR OWN TIME TEACH: Romantic love is an invention of Western culture, a modern contrivance like the diesel engine or the ballpoint pen. Traditional cultures do not leave such important decisions to chance or to the unstable passions of the young. Such things are arranged by the older, wiser generation.

BUT OUR DAUGHTERS COUNTER: Yet here in this parasha we do find a case of romantic love—at first sight, no less! As it is written: "JACOB LOVED

RACHEL" (29:18). In fact, when Jacob meets his cousin Rachel at the village well, he's so overcome with emotion that he single-handedly rolls away the heavy stone covering the mouth of the well. If it weren't for the narrator's dead-pan tone, we might even find this scene comic: inflamed by sudden passion, this tender mama's boy exhibits superhuman strength to impress his ladylove.

WILY REBECCA ANSWERS: The scene is meant to be ironic. Unlike the previous marriages in our family—Sarah and Abraham, Isaac and myself—this marriage was jinxed from the beginning. Because local customs required the elder daughter to marry first, Jacob ended up with two wives, sisters who turned bitter rivals for their husband's love. If Jacob had still been under *our* control, we would have married him to Leah and headed off Laban's swindle and his own sons' disastrous rivalry. But left to his own devices, my poor son proved rather inept at love.

THE RABBIS CLARIFY: The Torah later proscribes a man's marriage to two sisters, no doubt reacting to this unfortunate ménage à trois.

THE SAGES IN OUR OWN TIME COUNTER: No, this law already existed when the Torah was being edited. The story of Leah and Rachel was added here only to explain and justify that law.

LEAH AND RACHEL QUIP: In either case, no one asked us!

THE SLIGHT OF VEILS

OUR DAUGHTERS ASK: Why doesn't Jacob unmask Laban's trick? If Jacob had married Rachel immediately after meeting her, we could understand how Laban might have succeeded in duping him. But Jacob labors seven years for Rachel's hand, focusing so intensely on Rachel that the time "SEEMED TO HIM BUT A FEW DAYS BECAUSE OF HIS LOVE FOR HER" (29:20). By the time of the wedding, he must have memorized her every gesture, the nuances of her voice, the contours of her body. How could he possibly have mistaken Leah for her sister, so that he discovered only "WHEN MORNING CAME, THERE WAS LEAH!" (29:25)?

MOTHER RACHEL REVEALS: Leah and I planned the whole thing together. We were both so mad at Father for tricking Jacob like that—after all the years he'd worked for *me!* And I hated to think what Jacob might say to my poor sister when he discovered Leah in bed that first night. So I hid myself under their bed and spoke in my own voice, and Jacob was taken in. So the voice was the voice of Rachel, but the hands were Leah's.

OUR DAUGHTERS OBJECT: Still, why doesn't Jacob recognize the impostor's hands or her smell or her gait or her touch?

LEAH ANSWERS: I was such a good actress that I could mimic Rachel flawlessly. You see, in a patriarchal culture like ours, uncomely women must somehow compensate for their shortcomings. And Jacob was so intoxicated by desire that his senses were numb.

RACHEL ADDS: And even though Jacob caught on to the swindle during the night, he chose to spare Leah and me from shame by faking surprise the next morning. But despite his kind intentions, he didn't spare either of us, because it was not his knowledge of the truth but our own that caused us such pain.

OUR MOTHERS QUIP: The sisters' conversation in that dark tent is one of the great mysteries in the Torah!

WOMAN AS CHATTEL

LEAH EXPLAINS: My father claimed that custom had forced his hand. He told Jacob: "IT IS NOT THE PRACTICE IN OUR PLACE TO MARRY OFF THE YOUNGER BEFORE THE OLDER" (29:26). And he tried to smooth things over with Jacob by offering him a new deal: "WAIT UNTIL THE BRIDAL WEEK OF THIS ONE IS OVER AND WE WILL GIVE YOU THAT ONE TOO, PROVIDED YOU SERVE ME ANOTHER SEVEN YEARS" (29:27). How much my father revealed about himself in the simple Hebrew word for "that one"—*zot!* To our father, Rachel and I weren't daughters but barter, worth fourteen years of Jacob's labor. Is it any surprise that we, his daughters, regarded our own children the same way, competing in a breeding contest to win Jacob's love? We all learn from the example of our parents.

THE MEASURE OF LOVE

OUR DAUGHTERS ASK: How does the narrator know what's in Jacob's heart, as it is written: "INDEED, HE LOVED RACHEL MUCH MORE THAN LEAH" (29:30)? How does he know that Jacob loves Rachel *much* more than Leah? How can he claim that the first seven years that Jacob works for Laban "SEEMED TO HIM BUT A FEW DAYS"? Short of *inventing* Jacob as a character, how has he become so intimate with Jacob's unspoken feelings and thoughts?

BERURIAH THE SCHOLAR ANSWERS: The Torah is not a neutral document. Whether it was written by God, by God-inspired human beings, or by God-seekers, the hand of the author occasionally leaves its traces in the text. It's easy to explain such editorial asides if we accept divine authorship of the Bible. But if we don't, we need to acknowledge that like Laban, our author has secrets up her sleeve.

THE RELATIONSHIP BETWEEN LOVE AND FERTILITY

OUR DAUGHTERS LAMENT: Poor Leah! To win a husband by deceit and thereby lose him!

LEAH RESPONDS: It was not deceit but sorrow that brought me to Jacob's bed. For I had no wish to spoil my dear sister's happiness. Rather, it was revealed to me that God had betrothed me to Isaac's older son, Esau, whereas the two younger children, Jacob and Rachel, had been betrothed to each other. Knowing how wicked Esau was, I wept until the decree was changed so that I too could marry Jacob. But my eyes were weakened by my abundant tears. Jacob never loved me as he loved Rachel, but the Merciful One, sensing my heartache, "SAW THAT [I] WAS UNLOVED AND OPENED [MY] WOMB" (29:31). And God closed up Rachel's womb, providing me with company for my misery. But fertility without love couldn't ease my pain, nor could my sister's barrenness fulfill my own longings.

HAGAR THE STRANGER COMMENTS: Watching the two sisters vie with each other for a place in their husband's heart, we understand how difficult is the burden of dependence in a relationship. They both wait upon Jacob's favor and God's grace, and then the heartache begins all over again with their children.

THE BREEDING CONTEST BETWEEN JACOB'S WIVES

THE SAGES IN OUR OWN DAY TEACH: In the ancient Near East, one vital measure of a wife's worth was her ability to bear sons—to tend the fields, herd the flocks, defend land and honor, and carry on the family name. For the woman herself, unable to inherit on her own, sons represented security in her old age. And in a loveless marriage such as Leah's, sons might also capture a husband's heart.

LEAH CONTINUES: Or so I hoped as I bore Jacob six strapping sons. And I also gave him my handmaid, Zilpah, who gave him two more boys. Through the names I gave my eight sons—and through the meanings I divined in them—I gave voice to my own frustration and offered my prayers for Jacob's love:

REUBEN: Literally, "See a son." I interpreted this name to mean "YHVH HAS *SEEN* MY AFFLICTION"; I also took it to mean "NOW MY HUSBAND WILL *LOVE* [*ye'ehavani*] ME" (29:32), punning on the second syllable of Reuben's name.

SIMEON: This name I chose for my second son "BECAUSE YHVH *HEARD* [*shama*] THAT I WAS UNLOVED AND HAS GIVEN ME THIS ONE ALSO" (29:33).

LEVI: My third son I named Levi, declaring that "THIS TIME MY HUSBAND WILL BECOME *ATTACHED* [*yillaveh*] TO ME, FOR I HAVE BORNE HIM THREE SONS" (29:34).

JUDAH: When I named my fourth son, I exclaimed, "THIS TIME I WILL *PRAISE* [*odeh*] YHVH" (29:35).

GAD: My handmaid, Zilpah, bore two more sons as my surrogate. I named these children also. The first I named Gad, meaning "WHAT LUCK!" (30:11).

ASHER: Zilpah's second son I named Asher, meaning "WHAT FORTUNE!" that is, "WOMEN WILL DEEM ME FORTUNATE" (30:13). I was also honoring the Divine Lady *Asherah*, goddess of fertility, for answering my prayers, but I kept this from Jacob, who was so jealous for his God.

ISSACHAR: I felt torn about introducing my handmaid into my husband's bed, so I named my fifth son Issachar, knowing that "GOD HAS GIVEN ME MY REWARD [*sekhari*] FOR HAVING GIVEN MY MAID TO MY HUSBAND" (29:18).

ZEBULUN: My last son's name means "GOD HAS GIVEN ME A CHOICE GIFT" (*zevadani zeved*); also, "THIS TIME MY HUSBAND WILL EXALT ME [*yizveleni*], FOR I HAVE BORNE HIM SIX SONS" (29:20).

SARAH THE ANCIENT ONE MUSES: Our hearts break as we hear this litany of frustration and longing. To endure six pregnancies (seven, counting her daughter, Dinah) and to bring another woman into her husband's bed, all to try to gain Jacob's favor.

OUR DAUGHTERS ASK: Was there no other way? And more important, does she succeed?

SERAKH BAT ASHER THE HISTORIAN ANSWERS: Reading the rest of the story, we have to conclude that Leah fails in her own lifetime—but attains some measure of victory after her death: it is she, after all, not Rachel, who lies forever beside Jacob in the Cave of Makhpelah. And though Rachel's tribes, Ephraim and Benjamin, were dominant during the time of the Judges, it is Leah's two sons Judah and Levi who eventually inherit the lion's share of Jacob's patrimony, and the priestly line: Levi becomes the ancestor of Moses, Aaron, and Miriam; and Judah becomes the ancestor of David and his royal descendants. In addition, Judah [*Yehudah*], gives his name to the Jewish people: *Yehudim*, "Judahites." Thus, though Rachel wins Jacob's heart, it is Leah who wins Israel's.

GIVE ME CHILDREN OR I SHALL DIE

OUR DAUGHTERS ASK: Why does Rachel ask Jacob, not God, to give her children, as it is written: "GIVE ME CHILDREN OR I SHALL DIE" (30:1)?

MOTHER RACHEL ANSWERS: I turned to Jacob only out of desperation, since Shekhinah had failed to answer my prayers. But he only responded in anger, mocking me: "CAN I TAKE THE PLACE OF GOD, WHO HAS DENIED YOU FRUIT OF THE WOMB?" (30:2) He misinterpreted my cry of pain as blasphemy, blaming me as if I was expecting divine favors from him instead of God. I felt judged by him, as though I somehow *deserved* my barrenness.

SARAH THE ANCIENT ONE OBSERVES: We should not be surprised at Jacob's thoughtless response. Throughout the extended narrative of dueling wombs, Jacob is hardly visible as the women compete for his attention. The prodigiously fertile Leah is just as frustrated as her barren sister. For Jacob still cannot distinguish one sister from the other. He loves one and fathers children with the other. In his mind, they share one heart between them. Only when he loses his beloved Rachel does he come to understand how deluded he has been.

BILHAH AND ZILPAH

OUR DAUGHTERS ASK: Why have Bilhah and Zilpah vanished from our prayers and memories? In many Jewish prayers and songs, including the popular *"Ehad Mi Yodea"* ["Who Knows One"] concluding the Haggadah, we speak of the *four* matriarchs—Sarah, Rebecca, Rachel, and Leah. But aren't there two more, Bilhah and Zilpah, mothers of four of the twelve tribes? Granted, these four tribes—Dan, Naphtali, Gad, and Asher—do not figure as prominently in Israelite history as tribes such as Judah, Levi, Ephraim, and Benjamin, but they do after all represent a third of the People of Israel. Why then are their mothers absent from our prayers?

HAGAR THE STRANGER ANSWERS: Like me, these two women were only concubines, second-class wives. But while my son Ishmael was excluded from the covenant, Bilhah's and Zilpah's sons inherited the covenant together with their half-brothers. Still, Jewish tradition has treated them even worse than me and Ishmael. At least, our story is read each year at Rosh Hashanah, but poor Bilhah and Zilpah have vanished completely from Jewish worship.

ESTHER THE HIDDEN ONE CRIES: So many of our people have been lost over the centuries! Not only have Bilhah and Zilpah disappeared from our midst; so have their four tribes, which numbered among the ten tribes lost when the Northern Kingdom of Israel was conquered and scattered by the Assyrians. But in messianic times, they will all be gathered again to their brothers and sisters, and all six of Israel's mothers will rejoice!

RACHEL'S MAID, BILHAH

MOTHER RACHEL RECOUNTS: After my sister, Leah, gave Jacob four sons and I remained barren, I gave my husband my maid, Bilhah, as a concubine so that "THROUGH HER I TOO MAY HAVE CHILDREN." I said to Jacob: "CONSORT WITH HER, THAT SHE MAY BEAR ON MY KNEES" (30:3). The names I gave Bilhah's two sons expressed my own bitter disappointment: *Dan,* which I took to mean "GOD HAS VINDICATED ME; INDEED, GOD HAS HEEDED MY PLEA AND GIVEN [*dananni*] ME A SON" (30:6); and *Naphtali,* meaning "A FATEFUL CONTEST I WAGED [*naphtule . . . niphtalti*] WITH MY SISTER; YES, AND I HAVE PREVAILED" (30:8). What a hollow victory these births were for me!

MANDRAKES

LEAH THE NAMER TEACHES: One of the oldest botanical folk remedies is the mandrake, a poisonous Mediterranean plant, whose forked root resembles the torso of a man, hence its English name, derived from "man-dragon." Its Hebrew name, *duda'im,* means "love apples," referring to its aphrodisiac properties. Its Aramaic name, *yavrukha,* means "chaser," suggesting its power to fend off demons. It's also reputed to aid conception.

WILY REBECCA TEACHES: How many twists there are to this plot! Like Jacob extorting the birthright from Esau, Leah extracted a night of love from Rachel, using the mandrakes given her by her oldest son, Reuben.

LEAH ANSWERS: Poor barren Rachel! I told her that the plant would stimulate fertility.

RACHEL PROTESTS: No, poor unloved Leah! You wanted so much to win Jacob's heart. Although you pretended you were doing me a favor by offering me the mandrakes in exchange for an extra night in Jacob's bed, I saw through your ruse. And when you realized that I did, you accused me: "WAS IT NOT ENOUGH FOR YOU TO TAKE AWAY MY HUSBAND, THAT YOU WOULD ALSO TAKE MY SON'S MANDRAKES?" (30:15) Couldn't you have had a little more compassion?

LEAH EXPLAINS: It didn't matter, anyway. Because when I said to Jacob: "YOU ARE TO SLEEP WITH ME, FOR I HAVE HIRED YOU WITH MY SON'S MANDRAKES" (30:16), Jacob complied with no more passion than a prostitute, and I felt the same.

DINAH'S NAME

OUR DAUGHTERS ASK: Why isn't Dinah's name explained, like the names of her twelve brothers? Why is it simply: "LASTLY, [Leah] BORE HIM A DAUGHTER, AND NAMED HER DINAH" (30:21)?

MIRIAM THE PROPHET ANSWERS: In presenting Dinah's name *without* an interpretation, the narrator signals her uniqueness in the family drama. For if other daughters exist, they play no significant role in the plot. As for the sons, they have functioned so far merely as allegorical figures battling out their mothers' jealousies. But Dinah, whose name derives from *din,* meaning "judgment" or "strife," and whose fate prefigures so much of Jewish history, demands our attention precisely because she is an enigma, the wild card in God's hand.

DINAH THE WOUNDED ONE ADDS: To this day the brothers of Shechem continue to seek revenge upon the sons of Jacob, just as Israel's sons continue to avenge my shame.

ESTHER THE HIDDEN ONE EXPLAINS: The story of Dinah's name remains a secret precisely because her fate is still unknown. Only when Shechem's and Dinah's brothers decide to live together in peace will the mystery of Dinah's name at last be revealed.

GOD REMEMBERS RACHEL

OUR DAUGHTERS ASK: Why is it written: "NOW GOD REMEMBERED RACHEL" (30:22)? Why had God forgotten her?

SARAH THE ANCIENT ONE ANSWERS: God never forgot her! When Rebecca, Rachel, and I had difficulty conceiving, it was Ha-Rahaman, the Womb-of-the-World, who intervened to open our wombs.

LEAH THE NAMER ELABORATES: In each case, the Torah uses a different verb to describe God's intercession: God *visited* (*pakad*) Sarah (21:1); *responded* to Isaac's plea (*ye-ater*) to help his wife conceive (25:21); and here "GOD REMEMBERED [*va'yizkor*] RACHEL; GOD HEEDED [*va-yishma*] HER AND OPENED HER WOMB" (30:22).

MOTHER RACHEL SPEAKS: After being concealed from my husband by my father's deceit and my sister's veil, and eclipsed for so long by Leah's teeming brood of sons, I was finally remembered, as a distressed ewe (*rahel*) is heard by the caring Shepherd. No wonder infertile women have always appealed to me to speak to God on their behalf: in their isolation and grief, they feel invisible and mute. What they want more than anything is to be remembered and listened to.

JOSEPH'S NAME

OUR DAUGHTERS ASK: Why isn't Rachel content with only one son? Why does she name her son *Joseph*: "MAY YHVH ADD [*Yosef*] ANOTHER SON FOR ME" (30:24)?

RACHEL ANSWERS: I had a double-edged reaction to this birth. On the one hand, I was grateful finally to be a mother after so many years of childlessness; but this child whetted my appetite for more.

OUR MOTHERS REMARK: Like all of us, Rachel keeps upping the ante of blessing. Although Jacob clearly loves her, she remains miserable without a child. And when she finally gives birth to a son, she immediately longs for another. Why is it so difficult for us to appreciate the birds in our hand?

LEAH REVEALS: What Rachel never found out was that it was I who originally carried Joseph in my womb, whereas she was pregnant with my daughter Dinah. But when it was revealed to me that Jacob was to father no more than twelve sons, I realized that Rachel would only be allowed a single boy. For I had already borne six sons, and our handmaids, Zilpah and Bilhah, each had borne two. And if I now bore a seventh, that would leave my poor sister only a single son. What dishonor to bear fewer sons than the servant girls! So I prayed for our unborn children to be switched in our wombs—and so they were. As it is written: "AND AFTERWARDS"—that is, after the fetuses were switched—I "GAVE BIRTH TO A DAUGHTER" (30:21). Then "GOD REMEMBERED RACHEL. . . . SHE CONCEIVED AND BORE A SON, AND SAID, 'GOD HAS TAKEN AWAY MY DISGRACE'" (30:22–23). So much did I love my sister Rachel!

JACOB'S RETURN TO CANAAN

OUR DAUGHTERS ASK: Why does Jacob wait so long to go home? Twenty years is a long time! During this time, he marries, fathers twelve children, and accumulates herds of sheep and goats. Then, without explanation, he decides to return home. Why at that moment?

THE SAGES IN OUR TIME ANSWER: He isn't prepared to leave until Rachel has given birth. For it has long been acceptable in Middle Eastern culture for a man to divorce his wife if she fails to bear a child and to send her back in disgrace to her father's house. Jacob obviously does not want to exercise this option.

THE RABBIS OFFER: We recommend a waiting period of ten years before dissolving the marriage. Jacob so loves Rachel that he waits for twenty. Had he not done so but instead returned to Canaan with the barren Rachel and ultimately divorced her there, she would have been alone, far from her father's house. So Jacob waits until Rachel has given birth to a child—security for her old age—before uprooting her from home.

LEAH PROTESTS: No, if you want to know the truth, look to my father's greed! Because after Jacob stole away with our families, my father came after us, complaining that "THE DAUGHTERS ARE MY DAUGHTERS, THE CHILDREN ARE MY CHILDREN, AND THE FLOCKS ARE MY FLOCKS; ALL THAT YOU HAVE IS MINE" (31:43). But despite these protests, he didn't press his claim. Instead he acknowledged: "YET WHAT CAN I DO NOW ABOUT MY DAUGHTERS OR THE CHILDREN THEY HAVE BORNE?" (31:43) You see, once a daughter had children, she was free of her father's claim on her. That's why Jacob waited until my sister Rachel was a mother before returning home. As it is written: "AFTER RACHEL HAD BORNE JOSEPH, JACOB SAID TO LABAN, 'GIVE ME LEAVE TO GO BACK TO MY OWN HOMELAND. GIVE ME MY WIVES AND MY CHILDREN, FOR WHOM I HAVE SERVED YOU, THAT I MAY GO'" (30:25–26). Although for a long time our household had included "wives and children," they weren't *her* children. Only once it included Rachel as both wife *and* mother was it safe for us to leave.

THE DAUGHTERS' INHERITANCE

OUR DAUGHTERS ASK: Do Leah and Rachel inherit anything from Laban—or do they leave empty-handed?

THE SAGES OF OUR OWN TIME ANSWER: In ancient biblical culture, women did not customarily inherit property, certainly not if they had brothers, as was the case in Laban's family. But married daughters did have some measure of economic rights. When a woman became betrothed, her suitor paid her father a bride-price—*mohar* in biblical Hebrew—to be held in escrow for her as a kind of insurance policy. Although she was not free to spend the money as she pleased, neither was her father free to squander it.

LEAH AND RACHEL ADD: Why didn't anybody tell that to *our* father! Because when Jacob prepared to leave with all that he'd accumulated over twenty years, we assured him that he was more than entitled to what he had. We pointed out to him that Father had violated his fiduciary trust: "HAVE WE STILL A SHARE IN THE INHERITANCE OF OUR FATHER'S HOUSE? SURELY, HE REGARDS US AS OUTSIDERS, NOW THAT HE HAS SOLD US AND HAS USED UP OUR PURCHASE PRICE. TRULY, ALL THE WEALTH THAT GOD HAS TAKEN AWAY FROM OUR FATHER BELONGS TO US AND TO OUR CHILDREN. NOW THEN, DO JUST AS GOD HAS TOLD YOU" (31:14–16). So much for a father's love! Believe us, we were glad to leave!

WILY REBECCA ADDS: Although Leah and Rachel claim a divine hand in this matter, it's really they who serve as executors of their father's will—and God's.

HOUSEHOLD IDOLS

OUR DAUGHTERS ASK: Why does Rachel steal her father's idols? Is she still an idolater, or has she converted to Jacob's beliefs?

MIRIAM THE PROPHET ANSWERS: Rachel's theft is a symbol of her future. Just as Jacob's future is determined and patterned by deception—his deception of his father and brother, his deception by Laban—so is Rachel's determined by this act of theft. For after the family flees from Paddan-Aram, Jacob—innocent of Rachel's theft of her father's *teraphim*—makes a vow to his outraged father-in-law: "ANYONE WITH WHOM YOU FIND YOUR GODS SHALL NOT REMAIN ALIVE!" (31:32) Tragically, Jacob's curse is fulfilled: Rachel dies giving birth to her next son, Benjamin. And the wheel of fortune continues to turn: that son is eventually entrapped by a mock theft, when Joseph plants his own goblet in his younger brother's sack.

ESTHER THE HIDDEN ONE REVEALS: But as with so many biblical patterns, this curse, once fulfilled, overturns itself to become a blessing: Benjamin's "crime" unknots the sibling jealousies once aroused by his mother's privileged status and reunites the brothers. Thus even idols can be redeemed.

THE INVISIBLE NARRATOR

OUR DAUGHTERS ASK: How does the narrator know Jacob's mind, as it is written: "JACOB, OF COURSE, DID NOT KNOW THAT RACHEL HAD STOLEN THEM" (31:32)? And what's he so worried about?

BERURIAH THE SCHOLAR ANSWERS: In this "stage whisper," we detect yet again the usually hidden hand of the narrator, reassuring us that Jacob is indeed innocent of Rachel's theft. For the narrator of this tale is well aware that Jacob himself once resorted to rather underhanded methods to steal his father's blessing. His own motives are therefore always somewhat suspect.

THE FAVORED DAUGHTER

OUR DAUGHTERS ASK: In his search for his idols, why does Laban save Rachel's tent for last?

SARAH THE ANCIENT ONE ANSWERS: Nothing drives the stories of Genesis as steadily as parents playing favorites. The fates of my son, Isaac, Ishmael, Esau, Jacob, and Joseph all turn on their parents' partisan love, and are further complicated by others' jealousies of that love. The only woman who shares this privileged status with all these sons is my grandson's wife Rachel, favored wife and favored daughter.

LEAH AMPLIFIES: When my father came looking for his stolen idols, he predictably left my sister's tent for last, after searching Jacob's tent and mine, and our handmaids'. By the time he reached Rachel's tent, failing to turn up the stolen goods even there, he'd made a total fool of himself in front of our entire caravan. I've always suspected that Rachel masterminded the whole scenario to get back at Father for embarrassing her twenty years before on her wedding day. And so, just as he'd hidden me behind her veil, she hid Laban's idols under her skirts. Our father certainly taught his daughters well.

STRATEGIES OF THE DISEMPOWERED

OUR MOTHERS TEACH: Just before Laban comes into Rachel's tent looking for his stolen idols, Rachel hides them in a camel cushion and sits on them. And to make sure he won't find them, she pretends to have her period, as it is written: "LET NOT MY LORD TAKE IT AMISS THAT I CANNOT RISE BEFORE YOU, FOR THE PERIOD"—literally, the way (*derekh*)—"OF WOMEN IS UPON ME" (31:35). Can we fault Rachel for what she does? Unlike the men in her family—father, brothers, husband, son—who can negotiate power directly, through physical struggle, bargaining, or covenant, Rachel as a woman can only resort to indirect means. In this case, she relies upon the camouflage of menstrual taboo. In so doing, she escapes the harness of social control and places herself in the saddle.

8. VAYISHLAKH:
Power Struggles

(GENESIS 32:4–36:43)

ORAH TEACHES: After twenty years in exile, Jacob returns home. Still fearful of Esau's revenge, he sends ahead of him gifts of livestock to placate his brother.

That night, after his family and his herds have crossed the river Jabbok, Jacob struggles with a divine being and wrests from him a new name, *Yisrael* (Israel)—"one-who-wrestles-with-God." Because Jacob is wounded in the thigh as a result of this encounter, Jews have ever since refrained from eating the thigh muscle of kosher animals.

Then, in anticipation of seeing his brother, Jacob divides his large family into two camps and goes to meet Esau, who greets him with a tearful embrace. Jacob introduces Esau to his family and presents gifts. Esau returns to his home in Seir; Jacob and his family settle near Shechem.

One day, Dinah goes out to visit the women of the land. Shechem, son of the local chieftain Hamor, rapes her and then asks his father to obtain her for him as a wife. When Hamor and Shechem come to Jacob and his sons with their request, Jacob's sons consent, but only on the condition that Hamor and Shechem and their people circumcise themselves. They agree, but when the men of Shechem are still weak from their wounds, Simeon and Levi attack the town and slaughter all the men. Then the other brothers come and plunder the town, taking among the spoils the women and children. Jacob accuses his sons of causing trouble for him by their actions.

Jacob moves to Bethel and builds an altar there. Then Rebecca's servant Deborah dies and is buried. God blesses Jacob with a promise of many descendants, kings among them, and with the land of Canaan.

Rachel then gives birth to a second son, whom she calls *Ben-oni,* "son of my suffering," but Jacob renames him *Benjamin,* "son of my right hand." Rachel dies in childbirth and is buried near Bethlehem.

Jacob then comes to his father, Isaac, in Hebron. Isaac dies at age 180 and is buried by Jacob and Esau.

Esau has five sons by Canaanite wives, and their many descendants become the kings and clans of the land of Edom.

WRESTLING WITH ANGELS

LILITH THE REBEL COMMENTS: How tempting it is to pass over, with a sigh of relief and a swift backward glance, the episode of Jacob wrestling with the angel! After all, what business do we women have doing hand-to-hand combat with supernatural beings? Could anything be more ridiculous than to imagine Leah or Rachel going to the mat with God? But the truth is that they do! They tussle with the Angel of Death over each child they bear. In the end, Rachel gives up her life in the struggle, but her newborn son emerges with a new name. And like their husband, Jacob's wives come out of their sacred travails wounded where the angel wrenched the hollow of their thighs.

MIRIAM THE PROPHET INTERJECTS: And what of all of us who have never given birth, who cradle a hollow within ourselves all our lives? Who will change our name from Barren One to Mother? And if we choose not to bear children, to whom shall we bequeath our names?

PLAYING FAVORITES

OUR DAUGHTERS ASK: When Jacob goes to meet Esau and sees his brother approaching with four hundred men, he divides up his family so they don't make a single target. In the vanguard, he puts his concubines, Bilhah and Zilpah, and their children; next come Leah and hers. Rachel and Joseph he positions last, behind all the others. Imagine how the other three wives and the ten older sons reacted to Jacob's cheapening of their worth. No wonder Rachel's older son becomes a source of bitterness for them all!

DINAH'S SILENCE

OUR DAUGHTERS ASK: Why are we told so little about poor Dinah? Nothing more than that she goes "OUT TO VISIT THE DAUGHTERS OF THE LAND" (34:1), that she's desired and raped by Shechem, and that she's later rescued by her brothers through treachery and brutality. Why are we not told her feelings, her words, her reactions to everything that happens because of her?

DINAH ANSWERS: Because from the moment of my birth, I was fated to remain silent. In fact, in the entire Torah, I never speak a single word. When

I was born, my name, unlike my brothers', was announced without interpretation. When I was raped, my cries went unrecorded. When my brothers negotiated with Hamor for my hand, my wishes were not considered. And when my father, Jacob, bestowed his blessings upon his children, I received none. That was why I visited the Canaanite women. Utterly invisible at home, I craved attention and went out looking for it. Only too late did I learn that neglect is not the only injury a woman can suffer.

SHECHEM

OUR DAUGHTERS ASK: Does Shechem really fall in love with Dinah at first sight? He doesn't seem the type!

DINAH ANSWERS: You're right! Read the story carefully and note the order of events: Shechem, son of Hamor (whose name means "ass"), first *saw* me, then *took* me, and then *lay* with me *by force*. Only after these actions did he *feel* "STRONGLY DRAWN" to me and "IN LOVE WITH THE MAIDEN." And only then did he finally *speak* "TO THE MAIDEN TENDERLY" and ask that his father "GET ME THIS GIRL AS A WIFE" (34:2–4).

OUR MOTHERS COMMENT: How clearly the Torah understands the nature of rape! As we have reaffirmed in our own time, sexual violation is an act of *violence*, not *desire*. Shechem is driven not by *animal* instincts but by *human* aggression and appetite, the lust to possess, not to mate. It is first a lust of the eye, and only later of the heart.

HAGAR THE STRANGER RETORTS: How easy it is to regard foreigners as jackasses! This story is nothing more than an anti-Canaanite libel, justifying Israelite possession of other peoples' lands!

HULDAH THE PREACHER COUNTERS: No, Jacob himself later condemns his two sons for attacking Shechem. He even dispossesses them in his will, as it is written: "CURSED BE THEIR ANGER SO FIERCE, AND THEIR WRATH SO RELENTLESS. I WILL DIVIDE THEM IN JACOB, SCATTER THEM IN ISRAEL" (49:7).

DINAH THE WOUNDED ONE CRIES: Of what consolation is any of this to me!

DINAH'S STATUS WITHIN THE FAMILY

DINAH EXPLAINS: Relations in my family were very complicated, especially for me. Of Jacob's eleven sons, six were my full brothers; five my half-brothers. Of Jacob's four wives, one was my mother; three my stepmothers. I was the only daughter, the only sister, the only woman of the next generation. In this story, my genealogy and family position changed depending upon what happened to me. When I first went out to visit the neighboring women, I was identified as *Leah's daughter*. But when Shechem raped me, I became *Jacob's*. When my brothers heard of my violation, they were "DISTRESSED AND VERY ANGRY, BE-CAUSE [Shechem] HAD COMMITTED AN OUTRAGE IN ISRAEL BY LYING WITH JACOB'S DAUGHTER—A THING NOT TO BE DONE" (34:7). And when my brothers took revenge on my violators, it was Simeon and Levi, "TWO OF JACOB'S SONS, BROTH-ERS OF DINAH" (34:25), who carried it out in their role as my older brothers.

I was only a status symbol, a place marker in this process—much in the same way that a zero, although nothing itself, adds value to numbers or diminishes them.

HAMOR

OUR DAUGHTERS ASK: Why does Shechem's father, Hamor, speak with Dinah's brothers instead of with her father?

HAGAR THE STRANGER ANSWERS: Hamor, the shrewd chieftain of Shechem, chooses to present his proposition to Dinah's brothers because they are the ones who will eventually need to marry wives from among "THE DAUGH-TERS OF THE LAND." Jacob, on the other hand, who's married one of his own, might not prove as sympathetic to his proposal.

SARAH THE ANCIENT ONE OBSERVES: And so it begins—the end-less negotiation of social boundaries between Israel and the nations. Until this moment, boundary disputes have had to do with land—Abraham, and then Isaac, bargaining with Abimelekh about water rights. And previously when so-cial boundaries were crossed, it was a matter of marrying *out*—Ishmael taking a wife from among Hagar's people; Esau from among the neighboring Hittites as well as from Ishmael's family.

OUR MOTHERS BREAK IN: But here the neighbors are trying to marry *in*, an early version of the classic melting pot: "MY SON SHECHEM LONGS FOR YOUR DAUGHTER. PLEASE GIVE HER TO HIM IN MARRIAGE. INTERMARRY WITH US: GIVE YOUR DAUGHTERS TO US, AND TAKE OUR DAUGHTERS FOR YOURSELVES" (34:8–9). Then, as now, such melting was easier said than done.

BARGAINING FOR DAMAGED GOODS

OUR DAUGHTERS ASK: Why does Shechem's father, Hamor, need to ask for Dinah's hand when she's already been raped by his son? Hasn't the horse already been stolen from the barn? So why does he say to Dinah's brothers: "ASK OF ME A BRIDE-PRICE" (34:12)?

DINAH ANSWERS: Hamor was offering compensation to set things right. But to my brothers, he was no more than a horse thief. They recognized that honor stolen can never be recouped: Hamor's proposed payment transformed rape into prostitution. The only compensation they would accept was vengeance. But neither act could compensate me for what I had lost.

JACOB IN RETREAT

OUR DAUGHTERS ASK: Why does Jacob keep silent when he hears about his only daughter's rape? Why doesn't he participate in the negotiations between Hamor and Dinah's brothers or in the destruction of Shechem? Why is his involvement confined to a single gripe to his sons: "YOU HAVE BROUGHT TROUBLE ON ME, MAKING ME ODIOUS AMONG THE INHABITANTS OF THE LAND" (34:30). And even here he's complaining not about Dinah's welfare but only about his own: "IF [the Canaanites] UNITE AGAINST ME AND ATTACK ME, I AND MY HOUSE WILL BE DESTROYED" (34:30). As Dinah's father, why isn't he enraged like her brothers about her dishonor? And when his sons criticize him for his indifference, protesting "SHOULD OUR SISTER BE TREATED AS A WHORE?" (34:31), he doesn't answer their challenge.

MOTHER RACHEL REPLIES: To understand Jacob's complacent response to his daughter's rape, we need to look to his past. After his dark encounter with the angel on the banks of the Jabbok, he was never quite the same. He had been traumatized by this experience, just as his father, Isaac, had been under Abraham's upraised knife. From that moment on, Jacob withdrew from the larger compass of the family drama, restricting his concerns to me and my two sons—and to God. So withdrawn was he that his oldest son, Reuben, even dared to sleep with his concubine Bilhah in an obvious play for his father's power. Out of this vacuum emerged the rivalries of the next generation.

DEBORAH, REBECCA'S NURSE

OUR DAUGHTERS ASK: Why does the Torah mention the death and burial of Deborah, Rebecca's childhood nurse (35:8)? After all, we know nothing at all about her life—only that she leaves Paddan-Aram with Rebecca and later dies in Bethel. So why are we told about her death, even that she's buried under an oak named from then on Allon-bacut—literally, the Oak of Weeping?

BERURIAH THE SCHOLAR ANSWERS: Deborah is the only servant in the Torah whose death and burial receive notice. Not even Abraham's chief servant Eliezer, who arranges for Rebecca's marriage to his master's heir; nor Bilhah and Zilpah, who bear four of Rebecca's grandsons, merit such recognition. In fact, even Rebecca's own death goes unremarked; only later, at Jacob's death, are we told of his mother's burial in the family cave of Makhpelah.

REBECCA EXPLAINS: That Deborah's death is not only noted but even commemorated with a living memorial shows just how beloved she was to our family. Her service spanned eighty years: the twenty years of my barrenness, the forty years when both of my twins were at home, and the twenty long years of Jacob's exile. With her death, we all had plenty of reasons to mourn.

THE DEATH OF RACHEL

OUR DAUGHTERS ASK: Why does Rachel name her second son *Benoni*, "son of my suffering" (35:18)? Isn't this the son she so ardently prayed for?

THE RABBIS ANSWER: Rachel's inauspicious choice of a name is a dying woman's act of grief and desperation.

OUR MOTHERS SUGGEST: In giving her baby an unlucky name, Rachel was acknowledging the power of the evil eye—her sister Leah's jealousy—and hoping finally to deceive that covetous gaze to protect her baby from harm.

BERURIAH THE SCHOLAR OFFERS A DIFFERENT REPLY: We can find within her choice of names the fulfillment of several ironies embedded in the story: For though Rachel once demanded that Jacob give her children *or* death, she here receives them both. She names her firstborn son *Joseph*, meaning "may God add another son," not calculating the high cost her request might exact of her. And Jacob unwittingly compounds these curses by swearing to his father-in-law Laban that whoever has stolen Laban's idols merits death.

RACHEL PROTESTS: You're all wrong! *Oni* doesn't mean "pain" but rather "strength" and "passion"! In choosing this name for my son, I wanted Jacob to know that this child was the fruit of our love and that I didn't regret dying to give him life. And Jacob respected my wishes, both by repeating my meaning within his own act of naming, *ben yamin*, "son of my right hand," and in blessing his firstborn, Reuben, with the same name as his last-born son, "MY MIGHT [*oni*] AND FIRST FRUIT OF MY VIGOR" (49:3). He knew precisely what I meant when I chose my baby's name.

RACHEL'S GRAVE

OUR MOTHERS TEACH: For centuries, Rachel's grave has been visited by Jewish women struggling, as Rachel once did, with infertility and the dangers of childbirth. Credited with magical powers, *Kever Rahel*, Rachel's Tomb, south of Jerusalem, is still a pilgrimage site for barren women, who pray to the Matriarch to intercede on their behalf and on behalf of their unborn children. One ancient custom still popular among North African and Oriental women involves winding a long red thread around the perimeter of the tomb and then tying pieces of the thread around their bodies or their possessions, or on their newborns' clothing. The potent combination of the antidemonic color and Rachel's holiness is considered effective against the evil eye.

MOTHER RACHEL ADDS: Wherever the Jewish people have wandered in exile, no matter how far from my grave, my spirit has traveled with them. As the prophet Jeremiah has proclaimed: "A cry is heard in Ramah—wailing, bitter weeping—Rachel weeping for her children. She refuses to be comforted for her children, who are gone" (Jeremiah 31:15). As long as my children suffer, I suffer with them, and my tears storm the gates of heaven.

DINAH'S INVISIBILITY

OUR DAUGHTERS ASK: Why isn't Dinah mentioned as a member of her own family, as it is written: "NOW THE SONS OF JACOB WERE TWELVE IN NUMBER" (35:22)? In this chapter for the first time (35:22–25), all the sons of Jacob are listed together, precursors of the twelve tribes—but no mention is made of their sister, Dinah. Her name is also left out when Jacob blesses his children before he dies. In fact, Dinah is mentioned only once more in the Torah, when Jacob and his family go down to Egypt to join Joseph.

The Rabbis reply: Indeed, there is more to her story than is contained in the Torah! For Dinah has a daughter, named Asnat, born of Shechem's rape, who eventually marries Joseph and gives birth to Ephraim and Manasseh, ancestors of *two* tribes of Israel. So Dinah is doubly blessed.

A GENEALOGY OF WOMEN

Our daughters ask: Why should we care about the "line of Esau," to which the Torah devotes all of chapter 36? Why do we need to know the names of all his descendants?

Beruriah the Scholar answers: We find included among these names a surprising number of women. There is Mehetabel, the wife of Hadar, the son of Baal-hanan, identified by her *matrilineal* line: "AND HIS WIFE'S NAME WAS MEHETABEL DAUGHTER OF MATRED DAUGHTER OF ME-ZAHAB" (36:39). In addition, two of the clans of Esau—Timna and Oholibamah—bear the names of Esau's wives. Thus, despite the general patriarchal bias of ancient Near Eastern society, women did indeed make—and leave—their marks.

Miriam the Prophet adds: And given that bias, we can only imagine how extraordinary these particular women must have been!

TIMNA THE CONCUBINE

Our daughters ask: Who is Timna, and why is she mentioned here by name? As it is written: "TIMNA WAS A CONCUBINE OF ESAU'S SON ELIPHAZ; SHE BORE AMALEK TO ELIPHAZ" (36:12).

Hagar the Stranger answers: Timna is the only one of Esau's daughters-in-law—and a concubine at that!—who is named. She merits mention because she is the ancestor of Amalek, a central villain in Israel's history. But we need to remember that she is not only the ancestor of Amalek but also a kinswoman of Abraham, and therefore part of the family.

9. VAYESHEV:
Rejection

(GENESIS 37:1–40:23)

TORAH TEACHES: Because Joseph is singled out as Jacob's favorite, receiving from him a special coat of many colors, his brothers envy and resent him. At seventeen, Joseph has two dreams about his privileged status: in the first, his brothers' sheaves bow down to his; in the second, the sun, the moon, and eleven stars bow down to him. When he tells these dreams to his brothers, they hate him even more.

One day, Joseph goes to his brothers where they are shepherding their flocks. They plot to kill him, but the oldest brother, Reuben, intending to rescue Joseph later, convinces them to throw Joseph into a pit instead. When a caravan of Ishmaelites happens by, Judah persuades his brothers to sell Joseph to them, and he is carried to Egypt and sold into slavery. The brothers smear Joseph's coat with goat's blood and tell Jacob that his son has been killed by wild beasts. Jacob mourns Joseph's death, refusing to be comforted.

Soon after, Judah marries a Canaanite woman, Shua, who bears him three sons. Er, the firstborn, marries Tamar, but dies without children. Then Judah orders Onan, the next-born, to father his brother's heir with Tamar, but Onan refuses, and he too dies. Judah promises to marry Tamar to his third son, Shelah, when he comes of age, but fails to fulfill his promise.

So Tamar tricks Judah into sleeping with her: posing as a prostitute, she demands Judah's seal, cord, and staff as a pledge for later payment. When Tamar becomes pregnant, Judah threatens to burn her for harlotry—but backs off when she shows him his own pledge, identifying him as the father. Tamar gives birth to twins—Zerah and Perez.

In Egypt, Joseph is bought by Potiphar, Pharaoh's courtier and chief steward, and in time rises to become chief of Potiphar's household. Captivated by Joseph's beauty, Potiphar's wife tries to seduce him; when she is rebuffed, she accuses Joseph of trying to rape her, and Joseph is thrown into prison.

There Joseph again rises to a position of authority, becoming head of the prisoners. When Pharaoh's chief butler and chief baker are cast into prison, they come into Joseph's charge, and both present dreams for him to interpret. Joseph tells the butler that three branches of grapes in his dream foretell release for him in three days; the baker's three baskets of bread, however, predict his death in three days. Both dreams come true—but the butler forgets to tell Pharaoh about Joseph's plight and ask for his release.

JOSEPH AND THE HANDMAIDS' SONS

OUR DAUGHTERS ASK: Why is Joseph assigned "AS A HELPER TO THE SONS OF HIS FATHER'S WIVES BILHAH AND ZILPAH" (37:2) instead of to Leah's sons?

LILITH THE REBEL REPLIES: Because the whole story's nothing but a fairy tale! It's got all the right ingredients: reversals of fate, villains, a prince in disguise, and a happy ending. From its first verse (37:2), we know that this will be Joseph's story. The narrator sets the stage for Joseph's spectacular rise to power by first placing him at the bottom of the heap in his family—as a lackey to Bilhah's and Zilpah's sons.

BILHAH AND ZILPAH AMPLIFY: Our sons—Dan, Naphtali, Gad, and Asher (who are not even named here)—were only the sons of concubines, not numbered among Leah's clan of six: Reuben, Simeon, Levi, Judah, Issachar, and Zebulun. It was Leah's sons who plotted against Joseph, maybe because they saw in him the only true rival to their inheritance. Our boys, on the other hand, had nothing to lose because of Joseph, since they were already second-class sons.

THE AUDIENCE FOR JOSEPH'S DREAMS

OUR DAUGHTERS ASK: Why doesn't Joseph tell his dreams to the women in the family? Why does he tell his two dreams—of his brothers' sheaves bowing down to his sheaf, and of the sun, moon, and eleven stars bowing to him—only to the men, as it is written: "AND WHEN HE TOLD IT TO HIS FATHER AND BROTHERS" (37:10)?

DINAH THE WOUNDED ONE ANSWERS: Foolish Joseph! Had he told his dreams to the women in the family—me, his father's wives, his sisters-in-law, his nieces—we would have recognized in these fantasies nothing more than the intemperate arrogance of youth. Instead he told my brothers, who interpreted his dreams as an expression of his ambition to lord it over them. A different reading of Joseph's dreams might well have changed the course of our family and thus of national history.

LOVE YOUR CHILDREN EQUALLY

BERURIAH THE SCHOLAR TEACHES: In the thirteenth century, a French Jewish scribe named Berechiah ben Natronai HaNakdan, also known as Benedictus le Puncteur ("Blessed the Punctuator"), translated into Hebrew the fables of Aesop and Marie de France, the Latin Romulus tales, and the Persian Kalila and Dimna fables. In his collection of tales, known as *Mishle Shualim* ("Fox Fables"), Berechiah often added Jewish twists to the originals. The following tale, "The Ape and the Leopard," seems particularly apt as a commentary on Jacob's grief over the loss of Joseph, as it is written: "BUT HE REFUSED TO BE COMFORTED" (37:35).

THE FABLE OF THE APE AND THE LEOPARD

Once an ape lived on a rock with two younger apes. He loved the little ape but hated the big one. One day, they were chased from their rock by a hungry leopard.

The older ape thought to himself: While he's eating one of us, the other two can get away. I'll give up to him the one I hate.

So he told the little one to grab hold of his chest and the larger one to jump onto his back, thinking that he would shake him off as he ran. But he held on so tight that the older ape couldn't throw him off. Meanwhile the leopard drew ever closer, until they could hear him snarling right behind them. The older ape had no choice but to let go of the one he loved and escape with the other. And while the leopard tore apart the little ape, the other two escaped.

Bereft of his favorite, the older ape grew to love the one who remained. And so beware of loving one child more than another, because a sudden twist of fate may steal him away.

THE TALE OF JUDAH AND TAMAR

OUR DAUGHTERS ASK: Why is Judah not censured like his uncle Esau for intermarrying? When Esau marries "out," taking Canaanite wives, we're told that this act is a "SOURCE OF BITTERNESS" to his parents (26:35). Even his marriage to Mahalath, his half-Egyptian first cousin and the daughter of his uncle Ishmael, doesn't redeem Esau in their eyes. Yet here when Judah—ancestor of the Davidic line—marries Shua, "THE DAUGHTER OF A CERTAIN CANAANITE" (38:22), we hear nothing negative from either Jacob or Leah. Has the family's attitude changed so radically in one generation?

TAMAR THE TRICKSTER ANSWERS: The answer lies with me, and my assigned role in the divine plot. For it was not Judah's nameless Canaanite wife but I who made sure that Judah's line continued, who bore his heir.

OUR DAUGHTERS ASK: But are you a Hebrew or a Canaanite?

TAMAR EXPLAINS: Although the Torah provides me with no pedigree, no ethnic origin, no history before my marriage to Judah's oldest son, Er, I submit my deeds as my pledge of citizenship.

TAMAR'S WIDOWHOOD

OUR DAUGHTERS ASK: According to the Israelite practice known as levirate marriage, if a man dies childless, his surviving brother is obliged to marry his widow and provide him with an heir. But Er's middle brother, Onan, refuses to perform his levirate duty—and God strikes him dead. So Judah promises to marry Tamar to his youngest son, Shelah. But why does Judah send Tamar home after the death of her second husband and tell her to "STAY AS A WIDOW IN YOUR FATHER'S HOUSE UNTIL MY SON SHELAH GROWS UP" (38:11)? Why can't she stay in Jacob's encampment while she waits for her next husband to grow up?

TAMAR ANSWERS: Given what I know about Judah, he was probably protecting me from his own evil urge.

LILITH THE REBEL COUNTERS: No, he blamed you for his two sons' deaths and now fears for Shelah's life. As it is written: "FOR HE THOUGHT, 'HE TOO MIGHT DIE LIKE HIS BROTHERS'" (38:11). How typical it is for men to suspect us, especially if we're wise or skilled, of demonic possession or witchcraft!

TAMAR ANSWERS: But the Torah exonerates me of any such evil influence. As it is written: "ER, JUDAH'S FIRSTBORN, WAS DISPLEASING TO YHVH, AND YHVH TOOK HIS LIFE" (38:7). And Onan too, because he refused to sleep with his brother's widow, was "DISPLEASING TO YHVH, AND GOD TOOK HIS LIFE ALSO" (38:10). But Judah failed to see God's hand in these tragic events until I confronted him with evidence of his own culpability in the plot.

THE SAGES IN OUR OWN TIME ADD: As with Oedipus and many another Greek hero, it was hard for him to accept that his part had been scripted by others.

JUDAH'S JOURNEY TO TIMNA

OUR DAUGHTERS ASK: What motivates Judah to go to Timna just when he does?

WILY REBECCA ANSWERS: Judah goes to Timna as soon as he finishes mourning the death of his wife. His next actions reveal that he's already in the market for a new wife—or at least some sexual diversion. How interesting that he goes to Timna, identified previously as one of my son Esau's clans. He obviously has a preference for Canaanite women.

TAMAR ADDS: Whether in search of a wife or merely a woman to warm his bed, Judah lost no time after his wife died. When he came upon me, disguised as a cult prostitute, by the side of the road, he made no effort to resist temptation. Of course, I knew him well enough to second-guess his actions after my mother-in-law's death—and I knew the law well enough to turn them to a higher purpose.

WIDOW'S WEEDS

OUR DAUGHTERS ASK: Why is Tamar still in mourning when she encounters Judah in Timna? As it is written: "SO SHE TOOK OFF HER WIDOW'S GARB" (38:14). How many years have passed since her husbands, Er and Onan, have died? Judah's youngest son, Shelah, is already grown up! But she's still wearing widow's weeds. Why?

THE SAGES IN OUR OWN TIME ANSWER: Even today in very traditional Mediterranean communities, such as rural Greece and Italy, it is customary for women to mourn their husbands for an extended period, sometimes as long as five years. In these cultures, widowhood represents much more than a temporary emotional state. It is a legitimate social role, entitling the bereaved wife to certain rights and privileges. As long as she is in mourning, she is still married—though to a ghost.

TAMAR COMMENTS: I took very seriously my obligation to provide an heir to Judah's house. And until I fulfilled that obligation, I still thought of myself as Er's widow. When I realized that Judah had no intention of marrying me to Shelah, I forced his hand by exchanging my bound status as a levirate widow for the free status of a prostitute. Only as such a free agent could I honor my debt to my husband's family—though I had to sacrifice my dignity to do so.

JUDAH THE WIDOWER

OUR DAUGHTERS ASK: Why isn't Judah still in mourning after the death of his wife? Tamar's mourning lasts for years; Judah's only for a moment. Though his wife's grave is still fresh, he doesn't hesitate to turn aside for a harlot by the road, soliciting her, as it is written: "HERE, LET ME SLEEP WITH YOU" (38:16). What kind of man is this?

TAMAR ANSWERS: I exposed Judah's shallow grief by subtly playing upon the irony of veils. When I was dressed as his son's widow, I was invisible to Judah. He sent me away; he ignored my legitimate claim on Shelah. But when I voluntarily hid myself behind a veil, then he noticed me and unwittingly fulfilled his duty as his son's redeemer.

ESTHER THE HIDDEN ONE ADDS: The Torah has long recognized that faces, even the face of God, are sometimes hidden when we most need to seek them.

THE PAY OF A PROSTITUTE

OUR DAUGHTERS ASK: Judah's willing to pay quite a high price for a casual sexual affair! Like his uncle Esau, he sells his assets for a song. When Tamar asks him to name his price for her sexual favors, he offers "a kid from my flock." But she demands collateral to guarantee future payment. Without hesitation, Judah hands over to her his seal, cord, and staff. Are Tamar's demands fair?

TAMAR ANSWERS: You'll note that I asked Judah to set his own terms. Though you might debate whether a goat is extravagant payment, you can't deny that what Judah proposed as collateral was excessive. In ancient Near Eastern culture, a man's seal and cord signified his word and were equivalent to his credit rating, identity papers, and power of attorney rolled into one.

OUR DAUGHTERS ASK: Did sex mean that much to him—or did his name mean so little?

TAMAR ANSWERS: I regarded this entire episode as my final test of Judah's character. He'd already failed to enforce his family's levirate obligation. He'd sent me home in disgrace to my father's house. Now, by his cavalier surrender of his name and power, he conclusively proved his unworthiness as paterfamilias. And so once the bargain was sealed, it was *I* who left *him* and went on my way; he remained behind, stripped of his identity. From that moment on, the family birthright passed to me, the mother of Judah's heir.

JUDAH'S PLEDGE

OUR DAUGHTERS ASK: Why is Judah so afraid when he discovers that the prostitute he's visited has disappeared? When his friend Hirah the Adullamite reports to Judah that the woman in question has vanished, Judah promptly abandons his hopes of redeeming his pledge. As it is written: "LET HER KEEP [my pledge] LEST WE BECOME A LAUGHINGSTOCK" (38:23). What motivates him to give up so much so easily?

TAMAR ANSWERS: Clearly, he wasn't ashamed of sleeping with a roadside prostitute (*zonah*) or a pagan cult prostitute (*kedesha*), since his emissary, Hirah, asked publicly about her whereabouts. No, it was his ego that was at stake: he'd been fleeced by a woman; a prostitute, no less! And who was included in the "we"? His family? Obviously not, since he'd shown so little regard for his name or patrimony. No, "we" referred to "his friend the Adullamite," who had served as his procurer and agent in this affair. How much is revealed in one's choice of friends.

HOT HEADS VS. COOL

OUR DAUGHTERS ASK: How can Judah be so cruel—ordering his daughter-in-law killed when he discovers her pregnant?

BERURIAH THE SCHOLAR ANSWERS: To its credit, the Bible here scorns double standards, at least when they are basely motivated. For although Judah has shown no hesitation in bartering his most valuable possessions for a moment's physical pleasure, he is outraged when he learns that his widowed daughter-in-law "HAS PLAYED THE HARLOT" and is now pregnant. As it is written: "'BRING HER OUT,' SAID JUDAH, 'AND LET HER BE BURNED'" (38:24).

MOTHER RACHEL ADDS: Like Jacob, who imprudently curses whoever has stolen Laban's idols, not realizing that it was me; like Jephthah, who vows to sacrifice the first living thing who greets him after his military victory, not expecting it to be his only daughter—so too Judah condemns Tamar, not realizing that she is his lover and the mother of his own child and heir. In this instance, he is saved from his folly because of Tamar's foresight. Neither Jephthah's virgin daughter nor I had the same chance to prepare.

JUDAH'S REDEMPTION

OUR DAUGHTERS ASK: Does Judah finally redeem himself?

TAMAR ANSWERS: When Judah accused me of harlotry and ordered me burned, I trumped him with the pledge he'd left with me: "I AM WITH CHILD BY THE MAN TO WHOM THESE BELONG" (38:25). To his credit, Judah immediately acknowledged them as his and admitted his guilt. As it is written: "SHE IS MORE IN THE RIGHT THAN I, INASMUCH AS I DID NOT GIVE HER TO MY SON SHELAH" (38:26). By owning up to what he'd done, he finally did redeem his primary pledge.

MIRIAM THE PROPHET REMARKS: Judah did not realize at the time how much he owed to Tamar: for had she not tricked him into sleeping with her, he would have lost the privilege of founding the Davidic line and giving his name to an entire people.

TAMAR'S TWIN SONS

WILY REBECCA TEACHES: Like Jacob—my son and Judah's own father, himself a younger twin who inherits the birthright—Judah's and Tamar's twin son Perez, who emerges second from Tamar's womb, becomes heir to the family line—as the ancestor of Boaz, who is the great-grandfather of David. And as in Jacob's story, here too it is the women who set the stage for the family drama: the midwife identifies the older twin by tying a crimson thread on his hand as he emerges first from the womb; Tamar herself names the other twin *Perez*, remarking: "WHAT A BREACH YOU HAVE MADE FOR YOURSELF!" (38:29)

SERAKH BAT ASHER THE HISTORIAN OBSERVES: There is another precedent for this story: Like Tamar, Lot's daughters seduce their father in order to carry on the family line. One of their descendants is Ruth, who marries Boaz. So both of David's ancestors trace their lineage to women who defy convention to fulfill their vision of God's plan.

ESTHER THE HIDDEN ONE ADDS: And the tradition affirms their wisdom. For the union of Ruth and Boaz brings about the *re*union of Abraham and Lot after their rancorous separation over land and points to the ultimate reunification of all of Abraham's children—the descendants of Ishmael and Keturah, of Esau and Dinah. And from the house of David, the great-grandson of Ruth and Boaz, will one day arise the Messiah, healer of all breaches.

POTIPHAR'S WIFE

OUR DAUGHTERS ASK: Why does the Torah tell the story of Potiphar's wife—how the wife of Joseph's Egyptian master makes a play for him and, having been rebuffed, accuses Joseph of attempted seduction, thereby landing him in prison? Is this incident merely a device to move the plot along, or is there more going on here?

THE RABBIS ANSWER: Potiphar's wife, whom we have named Zuleika, was a foreign woman and thus possessed of more venal appetites than God's own people. Furthermore, Joseph was "less" than a man, effeminate, walking with a "mincing step" and wearing eye makeup. It was no wonder that she was emboldened to take the sexual lead!

LUSTY ZULEIKA RETORTS: What do you know about women's sexual desires! Although the Bible's filled with stories of sexual seduction—Lot's daughters; Rachel, Leah, and the mandrakes; Judah and Tamar; Samson and Delilah—women's sexual *desire* is generally not factored into the events. No, a woman's sexual maneuvers are seen as a means to an end: children, security, financial reward. But in the case of Joseph, I was acting purely from desire: "LIE WITH ME," I ordered Joseph (39:12). I asked for nothing else from him, nor did I need it.

LILITH THE REBEL ADDS: And despite the Rabbis' attempt to explain away this episode, especially Joseph's part in it, we recognize here an all too familiar domestic drama—the stuff of soap operas. No wonder the Bible still speaks to us today.

10. MIKETZ:
Reunion

(GENESIS 41:1–44:17)

TORAH TEACHES: Then Pharaoh has two troubling dreams: In the first, seven lean, ugly cows emerge from the Nile and swallow seven fat, handsome cows grazing by the river. In the second, seven thin, scorched ears of grain swallow seven full, healthy ears. None of Pharaoh's wise men is able to interpret the dreams.

And now the chief butler remembers Joseph and tells Pharaoh, who orders Joseph fetched from prison. Pharaoh recounts his dreams, and Joseph unravels them: the seven fat cows and ears of grain represent seven coming years of plenty; the seven lean cows and ears, seven years of famine that will follow this prosperity. The double dream signifies the hand of God. Joseph advises Pharaoh to choose a wise vizier to supervise the stockpiling of food during the good years to prepare for the bad. Pharaoh chooses Joseph as that man, elevates him to second in command of Egypt, and gives him Asnat, a priest's daughter, as his wife. Joseph executes his plan. By the time famine strikes, Joseph is the father of two sons, Manasseh and Ephraim. Joseph rations out food to save Egypt from starvation. The famine afflicts the whole region, including Canaan.

Jacob sends all his sons but Benjamin to Egypt for food. Joseph recognizes his brothers, but they do not know him. He questions them about their family, and they reveal to him that Jacob is still alive and that Benjamin has remained behind with him. Then Joseph falsely accuses them of being spies and demands that they bring back Benjamin to prove that they are not lying to him. He holds Simeon as hostage, gives the others grain, and secretly restores their money to them.

When they return home and tell their father what has happened, he refuses to part with Benjamin—since he has already lost Joseph and Simeon. Then Reuben offers his own two sons and Judah offers himself as surety for Benjamin's safe return. Jacob finally relents, and the brothers journey again to Egypt, with their youngest brother, gifts of spices and nuts, and double payment for food.

Joseph greets them, hiding his tears upon seeing his younger brother, and fetes them in the palace. When provisioning them with more food, he orders his servants to slip his silver divining goblet into Benjamin's saddlebag. Pursued by Joseph's steward, the brothers discover to their horror that Benjamin has been set up as a thief. When Joseph accuses Benjamin of the crime and condemns him to remain in Egypt as Joseph's slave, the other brothers offer themselves as slaves as well. But Joseph wants only Benjamin.

THE WOMEN IN JOSEPH'S TALE

BERURIAH THE SCHOLAR EXPLAINS: The story of Joseph is the most elaborate narrative in the Torah, spanning four parshiyot, more than the stories of any of the patriarchs or matriarchs. And yet women are virtually absent from the tale. This is a tale of brothers, of patriarchy, of male power relations. Except for the narrative detour of Judah and Tamar (which does not bear directly upon the story of Joseph and his brothers) and the brief incident involving Potiphar's wife, women play no active role in the story.

MIRIAM THE PROPHET PROCLAIMS: Like the ancient Rabbis, we need to imagine lives for the many women who must have been involved in this drama: the brothers' wives, left behind to fend for themselves while their husbands go down to Egypt; the many maidservants who prepare for the journeys, tend Pharaoh's court, weave and cook, nurse and wipe bottoms, sing lullabies and keen at funerals. Indeed, a whole world of women contributes, albeit behind the scenes, to this drama. We owe it to them to serve as archaeologists and imaginers of their lives.

THE LEGEND OF ASNAT

OUR DAUGHTERS ASK: When Pharaoh elevates Joseph to power, he honors him with a new Egyptian name, *Zaphenath-paneah*—Egyptian for "God speaks, he lives" or "creator of life"—and an Egyptian wife, Asnat daughter of Potiphera, priest of On. This priest's name is too close to that of Potiphar, Joseph's first master, to be mere coincidence! So who is Asnat? All we have is her name.

ASNAT ANSWERS: I am Potiphar's adopted daughter, and what is more, a Hebrew, the daughter born of Dinah's rape. My mother's brothers, ashamed of me, her bastard child, a constant reminder of the family's dishonor, cast me out. But out of pity, my grandfather Jacob gave me a farewell gift: a gold breastplate inscribed with the pathetic story of my birth. Then, like my uncle Joseph,

I was carried to Egypt by traders and there adopted by Potiphar and his wife, who were childless.

I grew up pampered in Potiphar's magnificent palace, with excellent marriage prospects among the young Egyptian nobility. But I refused all suitors, for none of them possessed a wise heart or a noble spirit. Determined never to marry, I retired to a remote chamber with my handmaids. Then one day, Joseph, newly redeemed from Pharaoh's dungeon, called upon my father, and I caught a glimpse of him from my lonely tower. Recognizing at once his extraordinary qualities, I fell madly in love with him. My father was, of course, thrilled at my change of heart—Joseph was by then second only to Pharaoh—and set about arranging the match.

But Joseph refused to marry me because I was an idol worshiper, even though he discovered, by reading the gold tablet I always wore around my neck, that I was none other than his niece. Then and there, I resolved to embrace Joseph's God, and that night I was visited by an angel, who fed me honeycomb from Eden and gave me a new name, *Asnat*, meaning "tower," in honor of my strength of will. My encounter with the angel transformed me so utterly that Joseph had no hesitation about marrying me. And we lived happily ever after.

PRAYING FOR A GOOD DREAM

DINAH THE WOUNDED ONE CRIES: You think Pharaoh has disturbing dreams? We should all be so lucky! What nightmares haunt my dreams!

THE RABBIS COUNSEL: If you have bad dreams, it is a good idea to fast and repent. If the dream is very disturbing, you may even fast on the Sabbath or a festival day. You should gather together three good friends and perform the following ritual:

THE THREE FRIENDS SHOULD FACE THE DREAMER AND RECITE TOGETHER: Do not interpretations belong to God? Relate it to me, if you please.

THEN THE DREAMER SAYS, SEVEN TIMES: I have seen a good dream.

THE FRIENDS REPEAT: You have seen a good dream. It is good and may it become good. May the Merciful One transform it to the good. May it be decreed seven times from heaven that it become good and always be good. It is good and may it become good.

DINAH RESPONDS: If only it were so simple!

11. VAYIGGASH:
Dislocation
(GENESIS 44:18–47:27)

TORAH TEACHES: When Joseph threatens to hold Benjamin captive in Egypt as his slave, Judah offers himself in his brother's stead to spare old Jacob such heartbreak. Convinced that his brothers have indeed repented of their past sins, Joseph breaks down and reveals his true identity to them. He embraces his stunned brothers and then urges them to bring Jacob, their families, and their herds to live in Goshen, a region of Egypt where pasture is plentiful. And Pharaoh gives his blessing to this plan.

So the aged Jacob, shocked, then buoyed, by this unexpected good news, travels with his teeming household of children, grandchildren, and livestock down to Egypt. The seventy members of Jacob's clan settle in Goshen, where they prosper and multiply under Joseph's watchful eye.

WHAT A MOVE!

OUR DAUGHTERS ASK: What was it like, moving such a large family, lock, stock, and barrel, down to Egypt?

OUR MOTHERS ANSWER: From our beginnings when Abram and Sarai first left Ur for Canaan, we Jews have been a wandering people. It was easier when our culture was nomadic, a matter of moving tents and camels from oasis to oasis. But even so, what a burden on us women! Packing and unpacking, cooking pita and lamb stew on the go, carrying babies on our hips and backs, coaxing and dragging little ones over hot sand, tending the sick and the old, mourning our dead and then leaving them behind.

SERAKH BAT ASHER THE HISTORIAN BREAKS IN: I remember the trek down to Egypt—now that was some move! We left so much behind—our family burial place in Makhpelah, all the familiar landmarks, even our neighbors' forbidden gods—to go to a land we did not know. How different for us would Egypt be, where nature was governed not by rains but by the flooding Nile, where sedentary farmers despised shepherding nomads like us, where a single god-king ruled supreme.

MIRIAM THE PROPHET ADDS: And where women's burdens weighed even heavier than before.

THE FATE OF DINAH

OUR DAUGHTERS ASK: Although Dinah is mentioned among Jacob's children—"THOSE WERE THE SONS WHOM LEAH BORE TO JACOB IN PADDAN-ARAM, IN ADDITION TO HIS DAUGHTER DINAH" (46:15)—she's not listed among those who go down to Egypt. Has she already died in Canaan?

DINAH THE WOUNDED ONE ANSWERS: After my rape, I disappear from the family drama—except for this single final mention. For not only do I not speak even once as my story is told; my ultimate fate is never recorded. When the Torah lists the seventy souls who accompany Jacob down to Egypt, it fails to include me. Although the Rabbis identify me as the mother of Asnat and the mother-in-law of Joseph, they don't give me any role in Joseph's drama in Egypt. To this day, most of my story lies undiscovered in the white spaces between the letters of the holy scroll.

THE LEGEND OF SERAKH BAT ASHER

THE RABBIS POINT OUT: Of Jacob's many grandchildren, only one granddaughter is mentioned by name—Serakh, the daughter of Asher, the granddaughter of Leah's handmaid, Zilpah, as it is written: "AND THEIR SISTER SERAKH" (46:17).

SERAKH BAT ASHER ELABORATES: I deserved this singular mention because of the extraordinary circumstances of my history. I was Asher's adopted daughter, the three-year-old child of his second wife, Hadorah. Even as a child, I was beautiful, bright, and wise, skilled in singing and playing the harp, the apple of my grandfather Jacob's eye. When my father and uncles returned from Egypt after learning that my uncle Joseph was still alive, they feared that my old grandfather would not survive the shock, so they asked me to play my harp for him and sing: "Joseph is not dead but rules over Egypt." So gently informed, Jacob regained his former joy and spirit of prophecy. To thank me, my grandfather blessed me with eternal life. Four hundred years later, when Moses declared himself the redeemer of Israel, the elders did not believe him until I verified that his words precisely matched those prophesied long ago to my grandfather Jacob and handed down through his sons to me.

When the Children of Israel were finally ready to leave Egypt, Moses did not know how to locate Joseph's coffin, without which the people could not depart. So he came to me, and I led him to the place in the Nile where the Egyptian magicians had sunk it to block Israel's exodus. Only then could my people leave Egypt. For these many centuries, I have continued to live among my people, guardian of their memories. And when I have finally had enough of this world, I will become one of a handful of mortals (among them Pharaoh's daughter Batyah and Elijah the Prophet) privileged to enter Paradise alive.

JACOB'S WIVES AND DAUGHTERS-IN-LAW

OUR DAUGHTERS ASK: We are told that "ALL THE PERSONS BELONGING TO JACOB WHO CAME TO EGYPT—HIS OWN ISSUE, ASIDE FROM THE WIVES OF JACOB'S SONS—ALL THESE PERSONS NUMBERED SIXTY-SIX" (46:26). Besides Jacob's daughters-in-law, his own four wives are excluded from this count. Why are all the women left out?

MOTHER RACHEL REPLIES: Poor Jacob! By the time our family went down to Egypt, I had been long dead, and my sister Leah was also waiting patiently for Jacob in the family cave of Makhpelah. Bilhah and Zilpah had also died. Is it any wonder that Jacob had become so depressed, so possessive of his "baby," Benjamin. He'd already buried four wives and consoled twelve orphans. So although he was surrounded by seventy descendants who "BELONGED TO HIM," he had become a very lonely old man. And his daughters-in-law, even though they devoted themselves to him, could never replace what he'd lost.

ויחי

12. VAYEKHI:
Legacies

(GENESIS 47:28–50:26)

T ORAH TEACHES: When Jacob nears the end of his long life, he summons Joseph and makes him swear not to bury him in Egypt but to return his body to the family burial place in Canaan. Then he blesses Joseph's two sons, purposely honoring the younger Ephraim above the older Manasseh, and adopts both of them as his own sons. Finally, he delivers his last will and testament to his twelve sons, giving Joseph a double portion through his two sons.

At the conclusion of this testament, Jacob repeats his wish to be buried with his ancestors in the Cave of Makhpelah, and then he dies. Joseph orders his father embalmed, and all Egypt mourns his death. Then Jacob's entire clan, together with the court of Egypt and a royal escort, bring Jacob's body back to Canaan and bury him there.

Once their father is dead, Joseph's brothers fear Joseph's revenge and appeal to his mercy. Joseph reassures them that all that has transpired has been divinely ordained and pledges his protection.

When he himself is about to die, after a long and fruitful life in Egypt, Joseph makes his brothers swear to bury him back in Canaan, "WHEN GOD HAS TAKEN NOTICE OF YOU." He then dies at the age of 110 and is embalmed.

THE PERSISTENCE OF GRIEF

OUR DAUGHTERS ASK: Why does Jacob adopt Joseph's two sons as his own? He already has twelve sons!

MOTHER RACHEL ANSWERS: My poor beloved Jacob! So many years had passed since my death—but still he couldn't let go of his grief. Here at the end of his life, he tried to compensate by adopting our grandsons, Ephraim and Manasseh, as his own, and so gave our firstborn, Joseph, a double portion of the inheritance. My heart breaks when I hear him rationalize this final, disastrous act of favoritism—"I DO THIS BECAUSE, WHEN I WAS RETURNING FROM PADDAN, RACHEL DIED ON ME" (48:7). He never learned his lesson, never recognized that his playing favorites among the boys had once come close to destroying our family. But those choices too were motivated by his grief over my death.

And so, even at his death, he failed his responsibilities as the family patriarch—because he loved me too much and all the others too little. But as he faced death, he suddenly realized that he would lie forever separate from me, since "RACHEL DIED, TO MY SORROW, WHILE I WAS JOURNEYING IN THE LAND OF CANAAN . . . AND I BURIED HER THERE ON THE ROAD TO EPHRATH" (48:7). So just as my sister Leah was his first bride instead of me, she remained his eternal companion in death.

DINAH'S BLESSING

SERAKH BAT ASHER THE HISTORIAN TEACHES: My grandfather Jacob's blessing of his twelve sons, concluding the Book of Genesis and the foundational phase of Israel's history, constitutes a watershed moment in the biblical story. For the next four hundred years, the Israelites live as an enslaved people in Egypt, strangers in a strange land. Jacob's Testament, however, skips over this immediate future and prophesies what will happen after the Exodus, once his descendants return to national sovereignty in their homeland.

THE SAGES OF OUR OWN DAY TEACH: The Testament of Jacob was written down long after this historical moment, when the people were united under a centralized monarchy. As Jacob's mixed blessings suggest, the twelve tribes never quite managed to transcend their ancestors' original rivalries but continued to negotiate for power and advantage until their divided house collapsed under foreign assaults.

DINAH THE WOUNDED ONE BREAKS IN: I'm not surprised, of course, that I, Jacob's only daughter, was excluded here from my father's blessing. After all, my descendants didn't become one of the twelve tribes, nor did they bear my name or my banner.

MIRIAM THE PROPHET INTERJECTS: But all is not lost! For if ancient writers who were living during the Israelite monarchy could later write "back" into the Torah their own version of history, why can't we add Dinah's blessing to her brothers'? God knows that she needed a blessing as much as, if not more than, they did.

TRACES OF RACHEL IN JOSEPH'S BLESSING

BERURIAH THE SCHOLAR TEACHES: Jacob's blessing of Joseph, Rachel's elder son, is brimming with female imagery. Joseph is associated with a spring, an image frequently linked to biblical women. God is characterized not only as *powerful*—"THE MIGHTY ONE OF JACOB," "ROCK OF ISRAEL" (49:24)— but also as *caring*—"THE SHEPHERD," "THE GOD OF YOUR FATHER WHO HELPS YOU" (49:24–25). And the blessings promised to Joseph will emanate from many sources: "BLESSINGS OF HEAVEN ABOVE, BLESSINGS OF THE DEEP THAT COUCHES BELOW, BLESSINGS OF THE BREAST AND WOMB" (49:25).

THE RABBIS ADD: And so greatly does Jacob love Rachel that he blesses her son Joseph as though he were only an appendage to her, saying: "Blessed be the breasts that suckled you and the womb from which you came forth." Indeed, since everything depended upon Rachel, her descendants are called not only by her name but also by the name of Joseph, her son; and by the name of her grandson Ephraim.

SARAH THE ANCIENT ONE REMARKS: Given how difficult it was for Rachel to conceive, these final blessings are especially poignant.

REMEMBERED AND UNREMEMBERED GRAVES

OUR DAUGHTERS ASK: Where are the graves of Bilhah and Zilpah, the mothers of four of Jacob's thirteen children, four of the twelve tribes? We're told that Rachel is buried on the road to Ephrath, where she died in childbirth. We learn on Jacob's deathbed that Leah is buried in the family burial place, the Cave of Makhpelah, where Jacob also asks to be laid to rest: "THERE ABRAHAM AND HIS WIFE SARAH WERE BURIED; THERE ISAAC AND HIS WIFE REBECCA WERE BURIED; AND THERE I BURIED LEAH" (49:31). Surely Bilhah and Zilpah also deserved a place in the family grave. Haven't they also borne "blessings of breast and womb"?

HULDAH THE PREACHER ANSWERS: Some say that Bilhah's grave lies next to Rachel's and Dinah's graves in Ramah. But our tradition has chosen not to acknowledge this legend.

BILHAH AND ZILPAH ANSWER: Like so many of our sisters, mothers, daughters, and the countless other women in our lives, we lie buried in the white spaces of the holy scroll. And like Joseph's bones, we still wait for you to carry us home from Egypt.

EXODUS

שמות

Community

13. SHEMOT:

Lion-Women

(EXODUS 1:1–6:1)

ORAH TEACHES: Jacob's original clan of seventy multiplies to become the teeming Israelite people. But the reigning Pharaoh, who no longer knows Joseph, fears a fifth column in his midst. And so, to stave off the possibility of a slave rebellion, he enslaves the Israelites and sets them to work building royal treasure cities. He also orders the Israelite midwives, Shifra and Puah, to kill all Hebrew male babies. But they defy his orders, and so he instructs his own people to throw the babies into the Nile.

One of the Hebrew slave women, Yokheved, hides her newborn son for three months and then, when she can no longer conceal him at home, sets him adrift on the Nile in a reed basket. Pharaoh's daughter finds him and adopts him, unwittingly hiring the baby's mother as wet nurse. She names her Hebrew son *Moses*, meaning "draws out." And Moses grows up in Pharaoh's palace.

One day, Moses comes upon an Egyptian taskmaster beating an Israelite slave and strikes the Egyptian dead. Afraid of being punished, Moses flees to Midian, where he marries Zipporah, daughter of the local priest, who bears him a son, Gershom.

Then Pharaoh dies, and a new Pharaoh succeeds him. And God hears the Israelites' cry in bondage, remembers the covenant, and takes notice of the suffering people.

Tending his flock in Midian, Moses chances upon a mysterious burning bush, out of which God addresses him, commanding him to return to Egypt and tell Pharaoh to let the Israelites leave Egypt. Then God shows Moses signs to convince Pharaoh of his authority, reveals to him a new divine name—"I AM THAT I AM"—and foretells the Israelites' liberation and future possession of the Promised Land.

SHIFRA AND PUAH

OUR DAUGHTERS ASK: When Pharaoh orders the Hebrew midwives, Shifra and Puah, to kill all newborn Israelite boys but to let the girls live, the two women fail to follow his orders, claiming that the Hebrew women are simply too vigorous. As it is written: "BEFORE THE MIDWIFE CAN COME TO THEM, THEY HAVE GIVEN BIRTH" (1:19). Who are these two brave women who dare to stand up to the god-king of Egypt?

THE RABBIS ANSWER: These two heroic women were none other than Yokheved and Miriam, Moses' mother and sister. Although Pharaoh threatened to burn them alive if they continued to disobey him, they nonetheless stood firm and were miraculously spared from punishment.

HAGAR THE EGYPTIAN COUNTERS: No, you have it all wrong! Shifra and Puah were not *Hebrew* midwives but non-Israelite midwives *of the* Hebrews. Yet even though they were not Israelites, they still "FEARED GOD," that is the Hebrews' God (1:21) and so refused to follow Pharaoh's orders to kill the male Hebrew babies. They, like Pharaoh's own daughter, were willing to give comfort to the oppressed stranger in their midst. How much the more do they deserve to be praised!

THE REWARDS OF THE PIOUS MIDWIVES

SHIFRA AND PUAH RECOUNT: Because we refused to obey Pharaoh's cruel edict, God rewarded us. As it is written: "AND BECAUSE THE MIDWIVES FEARED GOD, HOUSEHOLDS WERE ESTABLISHED FOR THEM" (1:21). Not a single child born under our care was lame, blind, or blemished in any way. We were also privileged to become the ancestors of priests, Levites, kings, and princes.

YOKHEVED'S ACT OF COURAGE

OUR DAUGHTERS ASK: Of all the Hebrew babies, why is Moses the one saved? What's so special about him? We're told that when Yokheved "SAW HOW BEAUTIFUL HE WAS, SHE HID HIM FOR THREE MONTHS" (2:2). But surely all mothers see beauty in their children. And don't many of the Hebrew slave women try to save their baby boys from drowning in the Nile? Why is Moses alone singled out—by his mother and by the Torah?

THE SAGES IN OUR OWN TIME ANSWER: On the simplest level, we can understand this narrative as a classic *origin tale*, recounting a hero's extraordinary birth and childhood. He alone of all the babies is cast adrift and rescued by the Pharaoh's daughter. He alone is raised a prince under Pharaoh's very nose. The Egyptians and Mesopotamians had similar myths about their gods and heroes. Horus, son of Isis, and Sargon, king of Akkad, were both saved in baskets floating in rivers.

MIRIAM THE PROPHET EXCLAIMS: That is not even the half of it! For when my brother Moses was born, our family's house filled with light. Although I was only five years old, I prophesied that this newborn child would become a great leader and redeem our people from slavery. And like Noah, my mother made for him an ark made of papyrus reeds sealed with pitch, within which she sheltered our people's future.

OUR DAUGHTERS ASK: And what about the men in your family? What steps did they take to save him?

DINAH THE WOUNDED ONE JUMPS IN: They do nothing! Aaron, Moses' *older* brother, doesn't even appear in this early part of his brother's story. And his father, Amram, referred to here only as "A CERTAIN MAN FROM THE HOUSE OF LEVI" (2:1), doesn't speak here—or anywhere else.

MIRIAM EXPLAINS: My father's only response to Pharaoh's deadly edict was to convince all the Hebrew men to divorce their wives so as not to provide any more victims for Pharaoh's executioners. Indignant, I upbraided him for out-pharaohing Pharaoh. I said to him: Shame on you, Father! The Egyptian king intends to exterminate only the males among the Hebrew slaves, but you propose to destroy our whole people! Acknowledging the justice of my words, my father, together with all the Hebrew men, remarried their wives— and so it was that Moses was born.

OUR MOTHERS REMARK: It's hard to resist drawing parallels between this story and the Holocaust, during which one million Jewish children perished under a different pharaoh's deadly edict. Of course, both women and men tried to hide their families from the Nazis, and some succeeded in saving them. But the burden fell more heavily upon mothers and sisters, especially as the men were rounded up and separated from their wives and children. How many Yokheveds and Miriams fashioned arks, hoping to catch a princess's eye?

MIRIAM'S WATCHFUL EYE

WILY REBECCA OBSERVES: If we consider the pattern of Miriam's actions throughout her life—her chastisement of her father, her audacious proposal to Pharaoh's daughter, her leadership of the women at the Sea of Reeds, her bold challenge to Moses—we can see that she typically takes matters into her own hands. Such a strong character usually announces itself even before a child learns to walk.

THE LEGEND OF PRINCESS BATYAH

OUR DAUGHTERS ASK: Who is this nameless princess who dares to rescue and raise a Hebrew slave child?

HULDAH THE PREACHER ANSWERS: Throughout the Bible, right-·eous gentiles emerge to aid Israel in its mission to be "A KINGDOM OF PRIESTS AND A HOLY NATION" (Exodus 19:6). To their credit, the biblical narrators acknowledge their roles and honor them. Among these non-Jewish heroes are several women—Yael, who executes the enemy general Sisera; the Canaanite prostitute Rahab, who hides the Israelite spies in Jericho; and in this story Pharaoh's daughter, who rescues Moses from the Nile and raises him in the royal household.

PRINCESS BATYAH COMMENTS: My Egyptian name was Thermutis, daughter of Queen Alfar'anit, but God gave me a new name after I rescued the infant Moses from the Nile. Thereafter I was known by my Hebrew name, *Batyah*, meaning "daughter of God," and I was ultimately rewarded by becoming one of a handful of mortals who were able to enter Paradise alive. My poor benighted father, on the other hand, was doomed to guard the gates of Hell for eternity.

SOLIDARITY AMONG WOMEN

OUR DAUGHTERS ASK: Why does Pharaoh's daughter offer money to her father's slave to serve as wet nurse? As it is written: "AND I WILL PAY YOU WAGES" (2:9). Surely Yokheved would have been glad to nurse her own son without being paid! And anyway, why would the princess of Egypt have to pay for anything her heart desired?

THE SAGES IN OUR OWN TIME ANSWER: When we consider that Egypt was a highly autocratic, hierarchical society, built upon forced labor, gross economic inequities, and the glorification of death, we can appreciate just how exceptional Batyah's behavior appears. For no one benefited more from the status quo than the Pharaoh and his family. And through her independent actions—rescuing and adopting a slave baby into the royal household—

Pharaoh's daughter threatens to overturn everything. Even more daring, she lets two slave women into her secret and even offers to pay one of them wages to nurse her contraband child.

MOTHER RACHEL COMMENTS: Thus even in Egypt, the heart of darkness, light managed to penetrate. So it is sometimes that in places where darkness seems invincible, the light of mercy can break through where you least expect it, even where evil is blackest.

THE ADOPTION OF MOSES

OUR DAUGHTERS ASK: How does the rest of Egypt react when their princess adopts a slave child?

THE SAGES IN OUR OWN TIME ANSWER: Throughout the world, myths abound about royal children raised incognito in lowly conditions—often banished from the palace by an evil sorcerer, stepparent, or pretender to the throne—only to reemerge in adulthood to reclaim their rightful place. In Western literature, for example, we have the stories of Perseus, Oedipus, Hamlet, and Snow White. But in the story of Moses, we find a mirror image of this universal tale: Moses is born a slave, spends his childhood in the royal palace, and then reclaims his humble origins. And in contrast to the classic villain who exiles the young hero from his father's palace, here we have a guardian angel who takes the young foundling in, gives him a royal Egyptian name, arranges for him to be nursed within his own community (by his own mother, no less), and then takes him back into the royal house. As it is written: "WHEN THE CHILD GREW UP, SHE BROUGHT HIM TO PHARAOH'S DAUGHTER, WHO MADE HIM HER SON" (2:10).

THE RABBIS EXPLAIN: Yet this upbringing too is fraught with danger. For Pharaoh's soothsayers and magicians are indeed wary of this mysterious child, especially when he snatches the king's crown and places it on his own head. Suspecting that he has designs on his grandfather's throne, they devise a test for the child: they place before him a pile of glittering jewels and a heap of glowing coals—the former a symbol of overarching ambition; the latter merely a child's fancy. Moses begins reaching for the jewels, but his hand is redirected by the invisible hand of the angel Gabriel. Scorched by a burning coal, he quickly places it in his mouth and burns his tongue. Although he is thereafter impaired in speech, his life is thus spared, since Pharaoh's counselors interpret his choice of the glowing coal as the act of an innocent child, not a usurper.

OUR DAUGHTERS ASK: But where is Princess Batyah in this tale? Obviously, she must have had to invent an explanation to account for her fatherless child: a child raised by desert wolves, a gift of the gods, a virgin birth?

WILY REBECCA ANSWERS: Whatever her story, it convinces the jury and preserves Moses' life—and provides Israel with a redeemer. No wonder the tradition rewards her with eternal life!

THE NAMELESS WOMEN IN MOSES' LIFE

MIRIAM THE PROPHET TEACHES: Like most classical heroes, Moses begins his life under exceptional conditions: he is born into slavery, threatened by death, torn from his birth family, and raised in the enemy's stronghold. But what is even more unusual about his life is the central role women play in it. Excepting the first verse of this story—"A CERTAIN MAN OF THE HOUSE OF LEVI WENT AND MARRIED A LEVITE WOMAN" (2:1)—this tale is devoid of men. Moses owed his life to our mother, to me, and to the Pharaoh's daughter. Each of us took remarkable risks in safeguarding his life: my mother disobeyed Pharaoh's orders condemning all Hebrew boys to death; I, a slave, not only spoke up to Pharaoh's daughter but also conspired with her to pass off a Hebrew slave baby as her own son. And the princess saved a condemned child—against her own father's orders—and even paid a slave woman wages to care for him.

BERURIAH THE SCHOLAR INTERJECTS: Although the Torah itself later names the Hebrew women—Yokheved as Moses' mother and Miriam as his sister—and the Midrash names and renames Pharaoh's daughter—changing her Egyptian name, Thermutis, to Batyah as a reward for her adopting Moses—here, at the beginning of Exodus, these women all remain nameless. We have only their deeds to know them by.

ANOTHER BETROTHAL BY A WELL

THE SAGES IN OUR OWN TIME TEACH: Like the tale of any hero, Moses' story contains certain classic motifs: unusual origins, an early brush with death, and, here, a fantastical romance. Like Rebecca and Rachel before her, Zipporah is first encountered by her beloved at a well.

FLINTY ZIPPORAH CONTINUES: Every evening, my six younger sisters and I would water our flocks at the village well. And more often than not, we were harassed and mocked by rude shepherds, who pushed us aside until their own animals had drunk their fill. On one particular evening, however, a young Egyptian appeared at the well just when we arrived with our sheep and goats. Although we were strangers to each other, he gallantly drove off the other shepherds taunting us and watered our flocks. When we brought him home to give him food and shelter, my father, Jethro, liked him instantly, so much so that he offered this young stranger my hand in marriage, since I was the eldest.

But before Moses could marry me, he first had to pass my father's test—to uproot the ancient tree planted in our garden. How I feared for this brave young man, whom I had already come to like for his courage and silent strength. Although my father had warned me never to reveal the secret of the tree, I disobeyed him this time because I wanted to spare Moses' life. So I told him that this tree had sprouted from a magical staff created at the dawn of the world and had thus far devoured all my previous suitors. Although Moses effortlessly plucked up the tree, my father reneged on his promise and cast Moses into a barren pit to die. But I secretly fed him for seven years, so when at last my father went to retrieve his bones, he found to his surprise a living man and was finally forced to give me to Moses in marriage. Indeed, what a trial to be a hero—and the wife of one!

MOSES' FIRSTBORN SON, GERSHOM

OUR DAUGHTERS ASK: Why doesn't Zipporah name her firstborn son? After all, many biblical women name their own children, often choosing names that reflect the mothers' circumstances or their hopes for their children. But here Moses, not Zipporah, names their firstborn son, calling him *Gershom*, which he interprets to mean: "I HAVE BEEN A STRANGER IN A FOREIGN LAND" (2:22). And why this name?

HAGAR THE STRANGER ANSWERS: How well I understand this name! Gershom and I share it. Both our names are related not only to *ger*, "stranger," but also to *geresh*, "to banish," since we were driven from our homes by the stern rod of history. In this story, it's difficult to tell who's the foreigner, which the foreign land. Moses is born a slave in Egypt, which the Bible always refers to as a foreign land. But he's also a stranger in Zipporah's homeland of Midian, just as she becomes a stranger among her husband's people in Egypt. And together with the entire people of Israel, they wander as strangers in the alien desert for forty years until they come home to their promised land, only to be exiled from there centuries later. Because Moses is already in exile from his birthplace, he knows better than Zipporah how to name the next generation.

BORROWING FROM NEIGHBORS

OUR DAUGHTERS ASK: At the Burning Bush, why does God instruct Moses that only the Israelite *women* are to borrow from their neighbors before leaving Egypt? As it is written: "EACH WOMAN SHALL BORROW FROM HER NEIGHBOR AND THE LODGER IN HER HOUSE OBJECTS OF SILVER AND GOLD, AND CLOTHING, AND YOU SHALL PUT THEM ON YOUR SONS AND DAUGHTERS, THUS STRIPPING THE EGYPTIANS" (3:21–22).

OUR MOTHERS ANSWER: In perilous times such as these, women are more likely than men to part with their possessions, if they think that such sacrifice will buy protection for their families. After the tenth devastating plague, the Egyptian women are ready to give up everything in the interests of peace.

THE BRIDEGROOM OF BLOOD

OUR DAUGHTERS ASK: Why, on his way back to Egypt, is Moses— referred to here only as "he"—attacked by God, who "SOUGHT TO KILL HIM" (4:24)? And why does Zipporah, after circumcising "her son" (which one of the two?) with a piece of flint, touch "his" legs (son or father?) with the bloody foreskin and declare, "YOU ARE TRULY A BRIDEGROOM OF BLOOD TO ME!" (4:25) And why does God then retreat from the attack? What's the meaning of this strange blood rite told in only three short lines—Exodus 4:24–26?

THE RABBIS EXPLAIN: The attacker is none other than God's satanic messenger, sent in the guise of a serpent to punish Moses for not having yet circumcised his son. The serpent swallows Moses down to his feet, but Zipporah, understanding what is happening, cuts off her son's foreskin and sprinkles the blood on her husband's feet. God then orders Satan to spit Moses out, which he does. And so Moses is saved.

THE SAGES IN OUR OWN TIME COMMENT: We are of many minds about this baffling story. One scholar claims that it is a foreshadowing of the tenth plague, the slaying of Egypt's firstborn, as well as of Israel's protective ritual of spreading blood on their doorposts. Another teaches that Gershom's circumcision is a symbolic pact between God and Moses, since Zipporah "cuts" her son's foreskin with the same verb that God uses to make covenants.

ILANA PARDES, ONE OF OUR SISTER SAGES, ARGUES: No, the narrative background behind this story is the long line of women in Moses' life—the midwives Shifra and Puah, his mother, Yokheved, his sister, Miriam, and Pharaoh's daughter—all of whom overcome their powerlessness through trickery. Here Zipporah fools God's bloodthirstiness by substituting blood for Moses himself. Another background to this story are ancient Semitic myths in which "guardian goddesses" such as Ishtar and Inanna serve as protectors of kings or heroes, sometimes called their "bridegrooms," and the central Egyptian myth of Isis and Osiris. Like the hawk-goddess Isis, whose fluttering wings restore her dead brother-husband, Osiris, to life, Zipporah—whose name means bird—rescues Moses from death. Viewed together, the women in Moses' life represent a composite portrait of Isis, who draws the dead Osiris out of a box cast into the Nile (like Pharaoh's daughter); serves as the divine midwife at royal births (like Shifra and Puah); gives birth to her son in a papyrus thicket and hides him from the vengeful god Seth (like Yokheved and Miriam); and resurrects her dead husband's inert phallus (like Zipporah). Thus the "Bridegroom of Blood" tale represents a detour from the main plot of Exodus, an "intrusion" of Judaism's pagan milieu into its monotheistic culture. As much as the Bible tries to stamp out polytheism—especially goddesses—and supernatural dramas, this episode testifies to the people's continuing loyalty to its own vivid imagination.

14. VA-ERA:

Women Ancestors

(EXODUS 6:2–9:35)

TORAH TEACHES: After reaffirming to Moses the divine promise of redemption, God instructs him to demand from Pharaoh the release of all the Israelite slaves. Moses protests that his "impeded speech" will certainly handicap God's designs, but God reassures him that he will not face Pharaoh alone: Aaron will serve as his prophet.

Appearing before Pharaoh, the two brothers demand freedom for their people. To back up their demand, Aaron presents his credentials as God's agent, casting down his rod, which turns into a serpent and swallows up the serpentine rods of Pharaoh's magicians. But Pharaoh remains unimpressed.

The next day, Aaron strikes the Nile with his rod, turning its waters and all the waters of Egypt into blood. But when his own royal magicians mimic this feat, Pharaoh again pays no heed to Moses' and Aaron's demands. God then brings on a plague of frogs, which swarm all over Egypt. Yet once again Pharaoh's sorcerers duplicate the strangers' magic. This time, however, Pharaoh agrees to meet the brothers' demands in exchange for a reprieve from the frogs. But as soon as the plague is lifted, Pharaoh reneges on his promise, refusing to let the people go.

Next Aaron strikes the dust, unleashing a plague of lice. This time Pharaoh's magicians fail to replicate the miracle; their powers finally outdone, they acknowledge that here is none other than "THE FINGER OF GOD." But Pharaoh still will not be moved. So God strikes Egypt with a fourth plague, of insects that devastate the land. Unnerved, Pharaoh pledges to release his Israelite slaves, but he changes his mind as soon as the insects disappear. Next a deadly disease afflicts Egyptian livestock, though the Israelites' animals remain untouched. Still Pharaoh will not yield. Moses then casts up soot into the sky, unloosing a plague of boils that torment the Egyptian people and their beasts. On the heels of this plague comes fiery hail that pelts the fields of ripening barley and flax, but none of these plagues softens Pharaoh's adamant heart. He still refuses to let his slaves go.

All this time, as these seven plagues devastate Egypt, the Israelites and their possessions remain unharmed in their territory of Goshen, awaiting redemption.

TRIBAL HISTORY

OUR DAUGHTERS ASK: In this parasha, the dramatic events in Pharaoh's court are interrupted by a partial tribal history, tracing the Levitical ancestry of Moses and Aaron. The history begins with the male lineage of Levi's two older brothers, Reuben and Simeon, but gives the names of only the next generation. In contrast, Levi's lineage spans four generations, leading us to Aaron's sons, ancestors of the priestly cult. What about the women in the tribe of Levi?

DINAH THE WOUNDED ONE ANSWERS: About the lineage of Jacob's female descendants—me and my niece Serakh bat Asher and Zilpah, not to mention all the women without names—we generally know only about those married to important male leaders. Even Miriam, Levi's granddaughter on one side and great-granddaughter on the other, is excluded from this chapter's genealogy and has no descendants mentioned elsewhere in the Bible.

THE RABBIS INTERRUPT: But we maintain that Miriam marries Caleb of the tribe of Judah and therefore numbers among her descendants Bezalel, architect of the Tabernacle.

MIRIAM RETORTS: I can do much better than that! For I number among my descendants the Daughters of Miriam, Keepers of the Well, and countless generations of Jewish women who have kept the folk Torah alive.

WHERE IS MIRIAM?

OUR DAUGHTERS ASK: Why is Miriam not mentioned among the children of Amram? As it is written: "AMRAM TOOK TO WIFE HIS FATHER'S SISTER YOKHEVED, AND SHE BORE HIM AARON AND MOSES" (6:20).

MIRIAM THE PROPHET ANSWERS: The three children in our family rarely appear together. So when my brother Moses first arrives on the scene, at the beginning of the Book of Exodus, only an unnamed sister is mentioned. Aaron is totally absent from the story. I first appear by name only after the crossing of the Sea of Reeds, and there I am identified only as *Aaron's* sister. Moses is absent from my genealogy.

THE SAGES IN OUR OWN TIME DECLARE: Such inconsistencies prove differing authorship of the Bible and different accounts woven together into whole cloth.

MIRIAM DISAGREES: No, these lapses reveal dynamic tensions within our family—I appear alone as my brother's protector; Aaron appears alone as his mouthpiece and coleader; Aaron and I together function as rivals to our brother's authority. Psychologists tell us that triangles are unstable structures in human relationships. How much more so in families!

AARON'S WIFE, ELISHEVA

ELISHEVA RECOUNTS: I am the daughter of Amminadab of the tribe of Judah, sister of Nakhshon, the latter linked directly to the line of David. The Torah records my marriage to Aaron the High Priest, but I am never again mentioned in the Torah. How strange is this silence surrounding my life. For unlike Moses and Miriam, whose families play no part in the ongoing desert saga of the Israelite people, our family figures prominently. Our first two sons, Nadab (the one-who-was-offered-in-free-will) and Abihu (he-is-my-father), die mysteriously by the hand of God because they "offer strange fire" on the altar; our other two sons, Eleazar and Itamar, inherit the priestly mantle and participate in the elaborate rituals of consecration and sacrifice. Yet all you ever hear about me is the single brief mention here.

OUR MOTHERS EXCLAIM: What an opportunity for a good story!

15. BO:
Transmission

(EXODUS 10:1–13:16)

ORAH TEACHES: Moses and Aaron warn Pharaoh that unless he releases the Israelites, his land and people will suffer a plague of locusts, unprecedented in its destructiveness. Even Pharaoh's courtiers urge him to relent, lamenting that "EGYPT IS LOST." So Pharaoh now tries to bargain with Moses, offering to let only the men go, but Moses refuses to compromise and is immediately expelled from Pharaoh's presence.

God then brings a black cloud of locusts upon the east wind. They quickly consume the remaining crops and fruit, stripping Egypt bare. Panic-stricken, Pharaoh pleads for mercy, and God hurls the locusts into the Sea of Reeds. But Pharaoh goes back on his word.

The ninth plague utterly darkens Egypt for three days; the Israelites, however, remain in light where they dwell. Pharaoh then agrees to let all the Israelites go—but refuses to release their livestock. When Moses rejects this final offer, Pharaoh banishes him from the palace. As he leaves, Moses parodies his adversary, agreeing with him that "I SHALL NOT SEE YOUR FACE AGAIN."

Then God instructs Moses to prepare the people for their exodus: They are to demand from their Egyptian neighbors silver and gold. Each Israelite family is to slaughter a lamb and then stain their doorposts with its blood to ward off the Destroying Angel. They are to feast that night upon the roasted meat, eating it together with unleavened bread and bitter herbs. These special Passover rituals are to be commemorated each year throughout the generations, to remind the Jewish people of their redemption from slavery.

That night, every firstborn in Egypt dies in the final plague, from Pharaoh's son to the son of the dungeon captive, as well as all the firstborn of Egypt's livestock. Then Pharaoh orders the Israelites out of Egypt at once. They leave in such haste that their bread does not have time to rise. With them they take their neighbors' gold and silver, as God has commanded.

And so, after centuries of slavery, 600,000 Israelite men, together with their wives, children, livestock, and a "mixed multitude," finally leave Egypt. With them they carry the blueprint of Passover and the commandment to redeem

their firstborn sons and beasts, both rituals reminders of their miraculous redemption from slavery. In addition, they carry with them the bones of Joseph.

THE TELLING AND THE HEARING

OUR DAUGHTERS ASK: Why does God command the Israelites to tell
the story of the Exodus only to their *male* descendants? As it is written: "THAT
YOU MAY RECOUNT IN THE HEARING OF YOUR SONS AND YOUR SONS' SONS" (10:2).
Don't we need to hear it as well?

OUR MOTHERS ANSWER: Of course you do! Because no sacred text is
more central to Jewish identity and continuity than the Haggadah, literally the
"telling" of the Exodus story, that we read each year at our seder tables. The
origin of this ritual and text can be found in this parasha, where God explains
to Moses that the plagues are being sent for Israel's benefit, to serve as reminders reinforcing their faith in God throughout the generations.

BERURIAH THE SCHOLAR POINTS OUT: Sometimes the Torah is
quite explicit that "YOU SHALL TELL YOUR SON"—that is, only your son—this
defining story of national redemption (13:14). But other times it appears that
daughters are included as well: "AND WHEN *YOUR CHILDREN* [*b'naykhem*] ASK YOU,
'WHAT DO YOU MEAN BY THIS RITE?' YOU SHALL SAY, 'IT IS THE PASSOVER SACRIFICE
TO YHVH'" (12:26). The Hebrew word for "children" can refer either specifically to sons or generically to all children.

MIRIAM THE PROPHET TEACHES: We all need to hear about what
happened, since we all participated in the Exodus, as it is written in the Haggadah: "Each of us must feel as if she herself was redeemed from Egypt."

THE FIRSTBORN OF THE SLAVE GIRL

OUR DAUGHTERS ASK: To show the all-encompassing scope of the
final plague, the narrator catalogs its victims: "FROM THE FIRSTBORN OF PHARAOH
WHO SITS ON HIS THRONE TO THE FIRSTBORN OF THE SLAVE GIRL WHO IS BEHIND
THE MILLSTONES" (11:5). Why specifically the slave *girl?*

THE SAGES IN OUR TIME ANSWER: In the next chapter, the narrator substitutes "THE CAPTIVE WHO WAS IN THE DUNGEON" (12:29) for "the slave
girl." These two social classes—slave girls and captives—typically performed
the repetitive task of grinding grain between two heavy stones. Both occupied
the lowest stratum of Egyptian society.

MOTHER RACHEL SUGGESTS: With the final plague, all of Egypt feels what it's like to be a slave girl, who has no control over her own fate. And with the death of every firstborn, every Egyptian family knows what it's like to be crushed like dry grain between millstones. Poor Egypt! That so many should suffer because of one man's hardened heart.

SIX HUNDRED THOUSAND

OUR DAUGHTERS ASK: We're told that when Jacob goes down to Egypt, his family clan numbers seventy; when the Israelites leave, hundreds of years later, they constitute a vast multitude. What precisely are their numbers? The Torah mentions "ABOUT SIX HUNDRED THOUSAND MEN ON FOOT ASIDE FROM CHILDREN" (12:37). That can't include everybody! What about men not "on foot," such as the elderly and the sick, who perhaps ride alongside in wagons or on donkeys? And what about all the women—on foot or otherwise? And how is the Bible defining *taf:* children under the age of puberty or under fighting age?

THE RABBIS ANSWER: The entire people—men, women, children, and "A MIXED MULTITUDE" (12:38) that go with them—altogether number about two million.

BERURIAH THE SCHOLAR OBJECTS: Even this number seems conservative—unless it reflects the grim realities of slave and desert existence: low life expectancy and birth rate, high infant and childbirth mortality. Whatever the case may be, these women, elderly, and handicapped, who struggle and die alongside the able-bodied men, deserve to be counted.

PREPARING FOR THE EXODUS

OUR DAUGHTERS ASK: Why don't the people prepare well in advance for their redemption? Doesn't God promise them that their moment of liberation is at hand? And they see the effect of ten devastating plagues on Egypt! Yet with all this advance notice, they still have time only to prepare *matzah*, bread that hasn't had time to rise, because they leave Egypt in such a hurry. As it is written: "NOR HAD THEY PREPARED ANY PROVISIONS FOR THEMSELVES" (12:39). What have they been waiting for?

HAGAR THE STRANGER ANSWERS: To a slave, planning for the future is a luxury he or she cannot afford. And a pharaoh's promises can never be trusted. Even the few hours it takes bread to leaven may turn out to be only a temporary reprieve from suffering rather than a prelude to real freedom. The Israelite women believe that they're truly free only when they're finally able to sit down together in their tents, babies on their knees, waiting for their dough to rise.

OUR BUBBES ADD: As we always tell our children, hope for miracles, but don't rely on one.

CONSECRATION OF THE FIRSTBORN

THE SAGES IN OUR OWN TIME TEACH: In traditional cultures up until our own day, the firstborn son occupies a privileged place. Often he inherits all of the family land, leaving none for his younger brothers; sometimes he receives only a larger portion. In addition, he is usually heir to the family leadership, as the paterfamilias, whether as king, head of the family business, or merely chief raconteur. As the first of the sons, he receives his parents' undivided attention and the entire burden of their dreams. Israelite culture followed a similar pattern—but with a twist. The firstborn belonged to God. As it is written: "CONSECRATE TO ME EVERY FIRSTBORN; MAN AND BEAST, THE FIRST ISSUE OF EVERY WOMB AMONG THE ISRAELITES IS MINE" (13:2). Firstborn animals were to be offered upon the altar; firstborn sons—in recognition of their deliverance from the tenth plague, the slaying of Egypt's firstborn (and in contradistinction to the many cults of child sacrifice among the neighboring peoples)—were to be dedicated to priestly service or redeemed with a contribution. This symbolic redemption ceremony, called *pidyon ha-ben,* is still practiced at the birth of a firstborn son.

OUR DAUGHTERS ASK: And what if the first issue of the womb is a daughter? Doesn't she also belong to God?

MIRIAM THE PROPHET ANSWERS: Although Judaism has no ritual for consecrating or redeeming her, we can create one. For she too occupies a special place in her parents' hearts, as the first fruit of God's bounty.

LILITH THE REBEL PROTESTS: We no longer need to sacrifice one child for the sake of another, or single out one child as more privileged than another! And since we no longer have a functioning priesthood, there's no need to redeem our children in order to exempt them from sacred service. So we don't need to add yet another redemption ceremony. We should abolish them all!

16. BESHALLAKH:
The Miriam Tradition

(EXODUS 13:17–17:16)

ORAH TEACHES: The Israelites journey into the desert, carrying with them their memories and the bones of Joseph. Regretting now his decision to let the Israelites go, Pharaoh pursues them with his army of chariots, hemming them in at the Sea of Reeds. Although the Israelites are protected by a divine cloud and God's promise of deliverance, they despair and complain to Moses. Then God instructs Moses to part the waters with his rod and lead the people through to safety. After the Israelites have reached the other side, the Egyptians pursue them, only to be drowned by the collapsing walls of water. In celebration, Moses sings a song of triumph. Miriam leads the women in dance and sings her own song.

The people journey on, and soon complain of hunger. Then God miraculously provides quail and manna, instructing the people to gather only as much manna as they need for each day, with the exception of Friday, when they are to gather a double portion to last over Shabbat. And when they complain of thirst, God instructs Moses to strike the rock at Horeb, out of which flows fresh water.

Then the warlike nation of Amalek attacks the Israelites. And Moses holds up his rod to ensure victory as Joshua leads the people in battle. After they have won the battle, God promises to blot out utterly the memory of Amalek.

THE BONES OF JOSEPH

OUR DAUGHTERS OBSERVE: Joseph's family doesn't bury him in the family burial cave in Makhpelah right after he dies, as they had done for his father, Jacob. Instead Joseph instructs his heirs to wait until the entire people leaves Egypt. As it is written: "WHEN GOD HAS TAKEN NOTICE OF YOU, THEN YOU SHALL CARRY UP MY BONES FROM HERE WITH YOU" (Genesis 50:25).

THE RABBIS EXPLAIN: Although we frown upon disinterring bodies and reburying them elsewhere, because such actions show disrespect to the dead, we do nonetheless permit certain exceptions, among them relocating a grave to Israel, moving the deceased to a family plot, or honoring the wishes of the deceased. Joseph's case meets all three conditions.

OUR BUBBES REMARK: It's not always so easy to dig up and rebury Jewish bones, even if you're allowed. How could we even begin to locate all the Jewish bones we've left behind during twenty-five centuries of wandering and running away? How could we ever find so many unmarked graves in so many other Egypts? The best we can do is to bundle up the bones of their memory and carry them in our hearts, names, and deeds.

THE MIRIAMIC TRADITION

MIRIAM THE PROPHET DECLARES: Only a single verse of my Song at the Sea is recorded in the Torah, the faint echo of my brother's song: "SING TO YHVH, FOR GOD HAS TRIUMPHED GLORIOUSLY; HORSE AND DRIVER GOD HAS HURLED INTO THE SEA" (15:21). The song that my brother Moses sings swells the narrative as waves fill the sea, a magnificent poem charged with dramatic imagery and power. Still, my song, though so much briefer, today stirs the hearts of Jewish women, inspiring them to create new songs, poems, stories, meditations, interpretive commentaries, and prayers.

THE SAGES IN OUR OWN TIME TEACH: This biblical episode portrays Miriam as a prophet and a leader of her people, especially the women. Even though Moses' triumphant Song at the Sea is eighteen verses long, while Miriam's is only one verse (and even that single verse is a direct quote from her brother's song), this imbalance reflects later editing, not Miriam's second-class status in her own time. In fact, some of us believe that Miriam's song was censored or lost, due to a later generation's uneasiness with female leadership.

MIRIAM COMMENTS: Indeed, my very presence in the Torah as a recognized leader demonstrates that strong women have always played a vital role among our people.

WOMEN'S BATTLE SONGS

THE SAGES IN OUR OWN TIME TEACH: In ancient Near Eastern culture, women frequently sang battle songs. Goddesses such as the Canaanite Anat or the Babylonian Ishtar were often depicted as female warriors. In the Bible, the songs of the judge Deborah and Samuel's mother, Hannah, are filled with military imagery. And Yael's bold slaying of the Israelites' enemy Sisera is memorialized in poetic song not only by Deborah but by Sisera's own mother!

HULDAH THE PREACHER ADDS: Female prophets in the Bible also speak words of war and destruction. During the reign of Josiah, I forecast the eventual doom of Judah; and during the time of Ezra, the false prophet Noadiah conspired against Nehemiah when he was rebuilding the Temple after the Babylonian exile.

WOMEN AS MUSICIANS

THE SAGES IN OUR OWN TIME TEACH: Ancient Mediterranean cultures have left compelling evidence in clay of a widespread women's performance tradition, usually involving the three arts of song, drum, and dance. Such a tradition continues to this day in this region. In ancient times, women hand drummers would go out to greet troops returning home after triumphant battles.

LILITH THE REBEL DECLARES: How unfortunate that today musical instruments have been almost completely eliminated from our prayer services and that among the most traditional Jews, the voice of women—*kol isha*—has been silenced in the presence of men because it allegedly stirs up lascivious thoughts in them. So what were the Israelite men thinking when they heard Miriam and the women singing? Have men and women changed so much since then?

THE HOLINESS OF DANCE

OUR DAUGHTERS ASK: It is also written that "ALL THE WOMEN WENT OUT AFTER [Miriam] IN DANCE WITH TIMBRELS" (15:20). Did Israelite women typically dance at such moments of national celebration?

THE SAGES IN OUR OWN TIME ANSWER: On several occasions, the Bible records women's dances. During the period of the Judges, for instance, young women danced in Shiloh at the annual "feast of YHVH" (Judges 21:19–23). They also danced to celebrate when their men came home from war (Judges 5:1–31, 11:34; I Samuel 18:6–7). In Israel today, this independent dance tradition is still practiced among women from the transplanted Jewish communities of Iran, Kurdistan, and Yemen, among others.

THE RABBIS ADD: And it is no wonder that they danced then and do
so now! For joyful song and dance are true ways of worshiping God. As the
Ba'al Shem Tov teaches: "The dances of the Jew before his Creator are prayers."

WOMEN'S PRAYERS

OUR DAUGHTERS ASK: The Torah tells us that Miriam prays on behalf of the women at the Sea of Reeds, as it is written: "AND MIRIAM CHANTED
FOR THEM" (15:20). But do they themselves also pray?

OUR BUBBES ANSWER: Of course they do, but nobody wrote down
their words. Jewish women have always written their own prayers—from the
old days till now. Think about poor Hannah, who prayed so hard for a child
that the priest Eli thought she was drunk! Such a model of prayer from the
heart. Back in the old country, both men and women used to write special
prayers in Yiddish called *tekhines,* for women to recite on certain occasions in a
Jewish woman's life: when they're baking hallah and giving *tzedakah* (charity), before they light candles, go to the *mikvah* (ritual bath), or give birth, when they're
pregnant or sick. Written in *mama loshen* (the mother tongue, Yiddish) and filled
with deep feeling, these prayers supported us in times of trouble, danger, and
religious need.

THE SAGES IN OUR OWN TIME EXPLAIN: *Tekhines* may have been
created originally by *firzogerins* (also called *zogerkes*), learned women who translated Hebrew prayers into Yiddish for the less educated women in their community, just as Miriam chanted *for* the women in the desert. It is only in more
recent times that women have had access to literacy and learning and have
added their voices and insights to the textual tradition.

MIRIAM THE PROPHET ADDS: The most famous composer of
tekhines was a rabbi's daughter, Sora bas Toyvim, who lived in the Ukraine in the
seventeenth century. She placed me, *miryem hanviye,* in her pantheon of biblical
heroines, imagining me in heaven, playing my timbrel and singing my song,
joined by a chorus of holy angels.

MIRIAM'S NAMES

OUR DAUGHTERS ASK: Even though the sister of Aaron and Moses
plays a critical role in the story of the Exodus from Egypt, she remains nameless until this parasha. Why is she named *Miriam* here?

MIRIAM ANSWERS: My name is an amalgam of two Hebrew words— *mar*, meaning "bitter," and *yam*, meaning "sea." My life was indeed bitter, like the waters we encountered after crossing the Sea of Reeds, as it is written: "THEY COULD NOT DRINK THE WATER OF MARAH BECAUSE IT WAS BITTER; THAT IS WHY IT WAS CALLED MARAH" (15:23). I was always overshadowed by my younger brothers. It was they who faced Pharaoh, who invoked the deadly plagues on Egypt, who met with God and inspired the people. And I was consigned to silence. And when at last I rose up with Aaron to demand that my youngest brother share the leadership with us, it was I alone who was stricken with leprosy.

My name, like me, arose out of Egypt. *Miriam* is derived from the Egyptian word *mer*, meaning "beloved." Indeed, the people loved me, especially on account of the miraculous well, which sustained them during their forty years in the wilderness.

THE RABBIS CONTINUE: You are known by many names. You received the name Helah when you fell ill (*holah*) after marrying Caleb and giving birth to Hur; the name Azuvah when Caleb deserted (*azov otah*) you during your illness; Naarah when you regained your health, became like a young woman (*naarah*) again, and were taken back by your husband; Yiriot because your face was like the curtains (*yiriot*) of the Tabernacle; Efrat because Israel was fruitful (*paru*) thanks to you; Zeret, because you rivaled (*zarah*) all other women; Tzohar because your face was as clear as noon (*tzaharayim*); Etnan because all who saw you brought gifts (*etnan*); and Akharhel, because all the women went out after you with timbrels and dances (*akhar hol*).

SARAH THE ANCIENT ONE MUSES: Why does Miriam need so many names? Because during her life she follows the path of *hesed*, lovingkindness, comforting her people in distress, encouraging them when they lose faith, providing succor and song. Although her own lot is so often bitter, *mar*, she so sweetens the lot of others that she becomes beloved, *mer*.

GOD AS HEALER

OUR DAUGHTERS ASK: We worship God in many guises—as Parent, Sovereign, Protector, Friend, Source of Blessing. Can we address God as our Healer as well?

MOTHER RACHEL ANSWERS: We have done so for centuries. To this day, on the Sabbath and festivals, Jews come up to the Torah to pronounce a special blessing, popularly known as the *misheberakh* prayer ("May the Holy One

Who blessed . . ."), asking God to heal those who are ill. Significantly, those in need of healing are traditionally identified by their *mother's* name—perhaps to catch Shekhinah's maternal attention.

LILITH THE REBEL RETORTS: Yes, but here in the Torah, God attaches strings to divine healing! As it is written: "IF YOU WILL HEED ADONAI YOUR GOD DILIGENTLY, DOING WHAT IS UPRIGHT IN GOD'S SIGHT, GIVING EAR TO THE COMMANDMENTS AND KEEPING ALL THE LAWS, THEN I WILL NOT BRING UPON YOU ANY OF THE DISEASES THAT I BROUGHT UPON THE EGYPTIANS, FOR I ADONAI AM YOUR HEALER" (15:26). How can God justify such *conditional* concern?

HULDAH THE PREACHER RESPONDS: We can make some sense of this ancient bargain if we interpret the diseases of Egypt as afflictions unique to that culture of oppression and death. If we act as *they* did, not as God would have us act, we, like them, will suffer certain plagues. That is, although we will not be immune to all diseases, we will at least develop antibodies to the ravages of sin.

MANNA

OUR DAUGHTERS ASK: Manna—what is it?

WILY REBECCA ANSWERS: Precisely!

OUR DAUGHTERS REPEAT: But what is it, this manna?

REBECCA LAUGHS: Exactly! For that is the meaning of its name, as it is written: "WHEN THE ISRAELITES SAW IT, THEY SAID TO ONE ANOTHER, 'WHAT IS IT?' [*man hu*]. FOR THEY DID NOT KNOW WHAT IT WAS [*mah hu*]" (16:15)." And so they name it *manna*.

SARAH THE ANCIENT ONE CHIMES IN: Manna is miracle food, out of this world, "LIKE CORIANDER SEED, WHITE, AND IT TASTED LIKE WAFERS IN HONEY" (16:31). If only the food we baked in our own ovens tasted so heavenly—or was made so easily!

OUR MOTHERS OFFER: Over the centuries, we've developed a number of customs associated with manna, most of them centering around the Shabbat table. So, for instance, hallah, the braided egg bread we eat on Shabbat and holidays, reminds us of manna, because both are perfect foods. And we place *two* loaves of hallah on our Shabbat and festival tables to remember that our ancestors received a double portion of manna on Friday so they wouldn't have to gather and carry food on that holy day. The sesame seeds we sometimes sprinkle on top of hallah resemble the coriander seeds described in this parasha.

And when we set our Shabbat table, we cover the twin loaves with a beautifully decorated cloth, which represents the dew that surrounded the manna. Often both our hallah cover and our tablecloth are white, like the manna, the desert sands it fell upon, and the purity of our holy days. And it's also nice to serve kugel on Shabbat in honor of the manna. Some people even serve special "white" desserts like white mousse, to remind us that manna was a special delicacy in the desert.

Our bubbes caution: But remember—one gets tired of eating only kreplach!

AMALEK

Our daughters ask: Who's responsible for Israel's victory over Amalek? Joshua, who "OVERWHELMED THE PEOPLE OF AMALEK WITH THE SWORD" (17:13)? Or Moses, whose hands seem precisely correlated with Israel's fortunes in battle? Or Aaron and Hur, whose support keeps up their eighty-year-old leader's hands until the battle is won? And what about divine aid, alluded to only obliquely as "THE ROD OF GOD" (17:9)?

Our bubbes exclaim: One God, and so many enemies!

Miriam the Prophet responds: *Kol yisrael arevim zeh-la-zeh*—all of us are responsible for one another. We need warriors like Joshua and spiritual leaders like Moses, older siblings like Aaron and younger supporters like Hur.

Esther the Hidden One adds: And silent partners like God, whose presence is often concealed. We should also recognize that Amalek sometimes resides within us as well as outside us. To vanquish this enemy, we must not only conquer our evil urge but also erase its memory from our hearts.

Lilith the Rebel breaks in: For too long, we women have specialized in playing the parts of Aaron and Hur, holding up the hands of our men. It's time we tried on the roles of Joshua and Moses.

17. YITRO:
Revelation

(EXODUS 18:1–20:23)

ORAH TEACHES: Soon after the Exodus, Jethro—*Yitro*—priest of Midian and father-in-law of Moses, brings his daughter Zipporah and her two sons, Gershom and Eliezer, to meet Moses in the wilderness. After hearing Moses' dramatic account of events in Egypt, Jethro praises God and offers a sacrifice.

Noting how burdened Moses is as sole arbiter and judge of such a numerous people, Jethro advises his son-in-law to delegate his authority to others, creating a hierarchy of qualified judges to decide all but the most important cases. Moses follows Jethro's advice, and Jethro returns to Midian.

Two months after leaving Egypt, the people reach Mount Sinai, where God instructs Moses to prepare them to receive the covenant. They are to remain in a state of purity for three days, after which time Moses is to ascend the mountain alone to receive God's teaching.

On the third day, Mount Sinai erupts in thunder, lightning, smoke, and loud blasts of a ram's horn. God pronounces the Ten Commandments, and the people, terrified and awestruck, keep their distance. Moses ascends the mountain "WHERE GOD WAS" (20:18).

THE RETURN OF ZIPPORAH

OUR DAUGHTERS ASK: The Torah tells us that Jethro brings his daughter Zipporah and his two grandsons to Moses "AFTER SHE HAD BEEN SENT HOME" (18:2). When and why did Moses send her home? Didn't they go down with him to Egypt when he went to face Pharaoh?

ZIPPORAH ANSWERS: Though no figure is more central in Jewish history than my husband, Moses, the Torah reveals only bits and pieces of his intimate biography. And about me and our children, about our life together as a family, almost nothing is revealed—only that Moses marries me, one of the seven daughters of Jethro, a Midianite priest. Also that when God appears to Moses in the Burning Bush and sends him back to Egypt, he takes me with him, together with our two sons, our firstborn Gershom, and Eliezer (whose name is first revealed only here). Nothing more is heard about us until this parasha, when Jethro brings us to Moses at the foot of Mount Sinai.

THE RABBIS EXPLAIN: Moses sent them back to Jethro's house even before they had reached the borders of Midian on their way down to Egypt. He was prompted to do so after being chided by his brother, Aaron: "Great indeed is the sorrow of those who have been in Egypt from the beginning! Why do you then take more there to suffer?" Persuaded by Aaron's reproof, Moses divorced Zipporah and sent her home with their children, to rejoin him later in the wilderness.

THE SAGES IN OUR OWN TIME RETORT: How pointless it is to try to reconcile these textual discrepancies! Here we have yet one more example of the seams showing in the fabric of biblical narrative.

THE RABBIS REPLY: You tell your story, we'll tell ours.

OUR BUBBES PRONOUNCE: You're right—and *you're* right too!

CAPABLE WOMEN

OUR DAUGHTERS ASK: Why does Jethro advise Moses to appoint only men to help him share the onerous burden of leadership? As it is written: "SEEK OUT CAPABLE MEN WHO FEAR GOD, TRUSTWORTHY MEN WHO SPURN ILL-GOTTEN GAIN" (18:21). We can't believe that there weren't capable, God-fearing women among the people.

THE SAGES IN OUR OWN TIME ANSWER: We must be careful not to judge Jethro by the standards of twentieth-century Western democracy. After all, in his time and place, women generally did not occupy such leadership roles.

LILITH THE REBEL COUNTERS: But we can hold today's Jethros in our own communities to such standards! Especially since the burdens of leadership have not gotten any lighter—and since capable, God-fearing, trustworthy women now stand ready to share them.

MOSES' FATEFUL MISQUOTATION

OUR DAUGHTERS ASK: Before unveiling the Ten Commandments at Mount Sinai, God instructs Moses to tell the people to prepare themselves by entering into a state of purity for three days. But when Moses relays God's instructions to the people, he embellishes them, adding his own warning: "DO NOT GO NEAR A WOMAN" (19:15). What's he up to—and why does God let him get away with it?

HULDAH THE PREACHER ANSWERS: Throughout the four books of the Bible in which Moses is the main character—Exodus through Deuteronomy—God constantly instructs him to convey messages to the people. And as with any game of telephone, sometimes something gets lost or garbled in the translation.

WILY REBECCA DISAGREES: No, in conveying God's message to the people, Moses deliberately changes the *audience* addressed. God's original instructions—"BE READY FOR THE THIRD DAY" (19:15)—include *all* the people; Moses, however, addresses himself only to the men: "DO NOT GO NEAR A WOMAN." In commanding the people to purify themselves for three days, God is asking them to mark a distinction between the profane realm of the everyday and the sacred realm of Revelation; Moses, however, redivides the two realms differently: for him, the profane realm includes all the people; the sacred only men. To enter the latter realm, as Moses sees it, requires isolation from women.

LILITH THE REBEL CONCURS: In giving Moses these instructions, God entrusts him with a sacred task: to safeguard the people from death, which threatens them if they come too close to holiness or approach it improperly prepared. But Moses violates this trust by adding his own interpretation: "Do not go near a woman." And it's not the only time he does this. In fact, this habit of literary license ultimately costs him his passport to the Promised Land.

GENERIC PRONOUNS

OUR DAUGHTERS ASK: When is "you" a generic pronoun in the Torah and when does it refer specifically to men?

LEAH THE NAMER ANSWERS: Throughout the Bible, God addresses individuals as well as the whole people as "you." Because Hebrew is both an inflected and a highly gendered language, we can learn a lot by studying the forms this pronoun takes in a variety of contexts. In the Ten Commandments, for instance, we find both singular and plural forms. God begins by addressing the people collectively as a nation: "I AM ADONAI *YOUR* [plural] GOD WHO BROUGHT *YOU* [plural] OUT OF EGYPT" (20:2). (Although "technically" masculine, the plural form of "you" includes women as well.)

But all the other commandments are addressed to each person individually: *You* (singular) shall not make graven images, worship other gods, murder, steal, commit adultery, bear false witness. *You* (singular) shall keep the Sabbath. Honor *your* (singular) father and mother. Thus each of us is accountable for his or her own behavior. For want of an alternative, all of these singular *yous* are masculine, Hebrew's generic form. Still, despite Hebrew's masculine bias, we understand that here God is commanding all of us—men and women alike—to uphold ethical standards. No one would argue that the Torah permits women to murder or steal.

OUR DAUGHTERS ASK: But does "you" singular *always* include women?

HULDAH THE PREACHER ANSWERS: No, sometimes it's exclusively masculine, as in the tenth commandment: "*YOU* SHALL NOT COVET *YOUR* NEIGHBOR'S HOUSE; *YOU* SHALL NOT COVET *YOUR* NEIGHBOR'S WIFE, OR HIS MALE OR FEMALE SLAVE, OR HIS OX OR HIS ASS, OR ANYTHING THAT IS *YOUR* NEIGHBOR'S" (20:14). Since what is forbidden is the neighbor's *wife*, we must conclude that only men are being addressed here.

OUR DAUGHTERS ASK: Then how "generic" is this pronoun? Do we always have to question its use in the Bible? Does God always/usually/sometimes use it generically? How can we tell?

WILY REBECCA REPLIES: We must learn to read with greater suspicion and to translate with greater sympathy.

THE GUILT OF THE MOTHERS

OUR DAUGHTERS ASK: In the second commandment, it is written that God "VISIT[S] THE GUILT OF THE FATHERS (*avot*) UPON THE CHILDREN, UPON THE THIRD AND UPON THE FOURTH GENERATION OF THOSE WHO REJECT ME" (20:5). Is "father" here meant generically—or is there something peculiarly communicable about a father's sins? Aren't mothers guilty as well?

OUR MOTHERS ANSWER: In traditional cultures, a father wields power in the public sphere; a mother primarily in the domestic. Therefore a father's deeds tend to reverberate beyond the family boundaries. So although it's Sarah who orders Ishmael's exile, it's Abraham who actually banishes him. And although it's Rebecca who contrives her son's deception of her husband, it's Jacob who carries it off.

THE RABBIS OBJECT: Ezekiel already rejected this notion of "father's guilt," and we have blotted it out from Jewish tradition altogether! Thus when we added God's Thirteen Attributes to the prayer book, we refused to include this part of the verse. Here is one case where we hold women and men equally responsible for their own sins, and their children equally guiltless.

"HONOR YOUR FATHER AND YOUR MOTHER"

OUR DAUGHTERS ASK: In the fifth commandment—"HONOR YOUR FATHER AND YOUR MOTHER" (20:12)—why is the *father* listed first?

THE RABBIS ANSWER: Because children are naturally more inclined to honor their mother than their father, since she "sways [them] with persuasive words." Therefore we are first commanded to honor our father. And since children tend to *fear*—that is, revere—their father more than their mother, because he teaches them Torah, we are commanded in Leviticus 19:3: "You shall fear your mother and father." There the order is reversed.

HULDAH THE PREACHER ADDS: It's also written: "MY SON, HEED THE DISCIPLINE OF YOUR FATHER, AND DO NOT FORSAKE THE INSTRUCTION [*Torah*] OF YOUR MOTHER; FOR THEY ARE A GRACEFUL WREATH UPON YOUR HEAD, A NECKLACE ABOUT YOUR THROAT" (Proverbs 1:8–9).

COVETING THE NEIGHBOR'S WIFE

OUR DAUGHTERS ASK: In the tenth commandment, it's written: "YOU SHALL NOT COVET YOUR NEIGHBOR'S WIFE" (20:14). And what about your neighbor's husband? Don't married women covet their neighbors' men? Or is the Torah suggesting that they simply display better self-control than their spouses, limiting their desire to fantasy?

THE SAGES IN OUR TIME TEACH: What is being discussed here is not inner feeling but law. Only men are being addressed because only they possess the authority to enforce property law, including the theft of persons—that is, adultery. Since sexual intercourse is considered adulterous only if a *married* woman is involved, "wives" are included in this list of forbidden property. In biblical terms, a married man is guilty of adultery only if his paramour happens also to be married.

18. MISHPATIM:
Community Control
(EXODUS 21:1–24:18)

TORAH TEACHES: Following the revelation at Sinai, God ordains an elaborate set of ethical and ritual laws concerning the
treatment of slaves; murder and injury; proper conduct toward parents; property rights and responsibilities; the bride-price of virgins;
seduction, sodomy, witchcraft, and idol worship; responsibility toward the
poor and oppressed; firstfruits; fairness in legal proceedings; observance of the
Sabbath and the sabbatical year; offerings due on the three pilgrimage festivals;
and dietary laws.

God also promises to grant the people victory when they battle the inhabitants of Canaan. In return, the people are to remain absolutely faithful to God,
resisting the seductions of their neighbors' practices.

Then Moses descends the mountain and repeats all these laws to the people.
With one voice, they proclaim their assent. Then Moses writes the laws down.
And he sets up an altar with twelve pillars, where the people offer sacrifices.

Moses then reascends the mountain, accompanied by Aaron, Aaron's two
sons, and seventy elders. There they behold a vision of God, mounted upon a
pavement of sky-blue sapphire. God instructs Moses to ascend alone to the top
of Sinai to receive the stone tablets of God's teachings. And Moses enters the
flaming cloud of God's presence and remains there for forty days.

THE LOT OF THE MARRIED SLAVE

THE RABBIS EXPLAIN: Although the Torah accepts slavery as an in-
disputable fact of life, it regulates its practice to make it as humane as possible.
So, for example, when a master frees a married male slave, "IF HE HAD A WIFE
[when he was acquired], HIS WIFE SHALL LEAVE WITH HIM" (21:3). Thus a slave's
status as a person is to take precedence over his status as property.

HAGAR THE STRANGER protests: But "IF HIS MASTER GAVE HIM A
WIFE, AND SHE HAS BORNE HIM CHILDREN, THE WIFE AND HER CHILDREN SHALL BE-
LONG TO THE MASTER, AND HE SHALL LEAVE ALONE" (21:4). How can you call that
humane!

THE RABBIS ANSWER: Since slaves were often coupled by their master against their will, such a policy actually released the freed slave from an unwanted burden. And if the slave had come to love his slave family *and* his master so much that he preferred to stay with them, he was "free" to do so, but he thereby forfeited forever his chance for freedom.

OUR DAUGHTERS ASK: But what if a slave loved his family but *not* his master—could he still go free, taking his wife *and* children with him? And what if he had been acquired with a wife *and children*—could they all go free together? And what if his master had given him a wife who bore him *no* children—could she accompany him to freedom?

DINAH THE WOUNDED ONE ANSWERS: The Torah does not concern itself with these details. Without denying that the biblical system was enlightened *for its time,* we must also acknowledge that it caused unbearable heartbreak to those who were trapped within it.

THE SALE OF DAUGHTERS

OUR DAUGHTERS ASK: Under what circumstances would a man choose to sell his own daughter? As it is written: "WHEN A MAN SELLS HIS DAUGHTER AS A SLAVE" (21:7). How could a father do such a thing!

OUR MOTHERS ANSWER: If a man was too poor to provide his daughter with a dowry, too proud to hire her out as a menial servant, or too caring to imperil her virtue, he could by selling her buy her security and possibly even love.

BERURIAH THE SCHOLAR EXPLAINS: If her purchaser "DESIGNATED HER FOR HIMSELF" and she proved displeasing to him, he was forbidden to sell her to another master, "SINCE HE BROKE FAITH WITH HER" (21:8)—but he had to allow her to be redeemed. Or if he bought her for his son, he had to treat her as any "FREE MAIDEN" (21:9) and handle her betrothal and marriage accordingly. And if he took another wife after marrying her, he still had to provide "HER FOOD, HER CLOTHING, AND HER CONJUGAL RIGHTS" (21:9)—or else he had to set her free.

OUR MOTHERS ADD: So at worst, a daughter sold into indentured service could ultimately regain her freedom and go out into the world penniless—no worse off than before; at best, she could gain a home, a husband, and children. Many poor parents, even now, can offer far less.

OUR OBLIGATIONS TOWARD PARENTS

OUR DAUGHTERS ASK: The Torah seems to suggest that we owe our parents *absolute* obedience, even if it costs us our lives. As it is written: "HE WHO STRIKES . . . [or] INSULTS HIS FATHER OR MOTHER SHALL BE PUT TO DEATH" (21:15, 17). Isn't that going a bit too far?

DINAH THE WOUNDED ONE ANSWERS: Yes, the Torah's laws about a rebellious child are unreasonably harsh!

OUR MOTHERS COMMENT: And how different things are nowadays! Today even children who physically attack their parents rarely face criminal prosecution, let alone capital punishment. And verbal assault alone certainly does not expose a minor to serious legal consequences. In fact, modern parents often tolerate a fair amount of verbal and even physical abuse from their children without punishing them.

OUR BUBBES COMMENT: It's never been easy to raise children! As they say: One parent can support ten children, but ten children find it difficult to support one parent!

DINAH OBJECTS: But some parents go to the opposite extreme and abuse their children.

MOTHER RACHEL SUGGESTS: Now, as in ancient times, families need all the help they can get to heal themselves and love their own.

CAUGHT IN THE CROSSFIRE

OUR DAUGHTERS ASK: The Torah teaches that "WHEN TWO MEN FIGHT, AND ONE OF THEM PUSHES A PREGNANT WOMAN" (21:22), if the woman miscarries, or if "OTHER DAMAGE ENSUES" (21:23)—that is, if she is wounded or dies—then the woman's *husband* can demand a fine from the other man as compensation. But what about the woman's compensation for her pain and grief? And what's the status of her unborn child in this case?

THE SAGES IN OUR OWN TIME ANSWER: Although ancient Israelite culture differed in many respects from the surrounding cultures, it shared with them the notion that some categories of people—notably slaves, women, and children—generally had an inferior legal status. Such people occupied a position somewhere between property and personhood.

DINAH THE WOUNDED ONE RETORTS: At best!

THE PRICE OF SEDUCTION

OUR DAUGHTERS ASK: In the Torah's eyes, what does it cost a man to seduce a virgin? And what does it cost the woman who is seduced?

THE RABBIS TEACH: The Torah distinguishes between rape—the sexual violation of an *unwilling* woman—and seduction—the sexual violation of an *unwitting* woman, who may or may not know better. In this parasha we read about what happens when a man seduces a virgin, "FOR WHOM THE BRIDE-PRICE HAS NOT BEEN PAID, AND LIES WITH HER" (22:15). In this case, biblical law requires that he marry her "BY PAYMENT OF A BRIDE-PRICE" (22:15). That is, by initiating her sexually, he has legally betrothed her; now he has to pay her father for her hand. But "IF HER FATHER REFUSES TO GIVE HER TO HIM, HE MUST STILL WEIGH OUT SILVER IN ACCORDANCE WITH THE BRIDE-PRICE FOR VIRGINS" (22:16). In other words, once he has seduced the daughter, he owes her father for "damaged goods."

DINAH THE WOUNDED ONE REMARKS: Though the rules have changed since then, the game is still the same—and the penalty still not high enough.

TWO TALES OF SEDUCTION

BERURIAH RECOUNTS: We should recognize that seduction need not be motivated solely by sexual impulse. Sometimes, in fact, it can be the result of quite deliberate calculation. Such was my case. For so jealous were the rabbinic sages of my learning and wit that they conspired to undo me by luring me into unchastity. To prove that I was no different from any other woman—that despite all my scholarly attainments I too was weak-willed and inconstant—several of my husband Meir's students convinced him to put me to the test. And my poor, unsuspecting Meir agreed, not realizing that this foolish game would cost me my life. And so the most handsome of his students set about to seduce me and, after many attempts, finally succeeded in snaring me in his trap. So ashamed was I of my moral failure that I hanged myself.

THE RABBIS ADD: But Meir did not escape unscathed from this scandal. After Beruriah's death, he too was subjected to a test of character. And so when he next came to Jerusalem during one of the pilgrimage festivals and lodged with his friend Yehuda the Cook, he fell into a similar trap, laid by

Yehuda's new wife, who was so stricken with Meir's extraordinary beauty that she plied him with wine and slept with him that night. The next morning, when she told Meir what had happened, he went into voluntary exile in Babylonia and demanded from the *rosh yeshivah* there a fitting punishment for his sin. And so three times Meir was bound and left for the lions in the forest. The first time, the beasts left him untouched; the second time, they only sniffed at him; but the third time, they took an olive-size bite out of him. And after the doctors had healed him, a heavenly voice declared from heaven: "Rabbi Meir has a place in the World to Come!" Thus he atoned for his transgression.

BERURIAH ADDS: And when he arrived, he found me waiting for him there—with plenty to discuss!

SORCERESSES

OUR DAUGHTERS ASK: Why does the Torah identify all witches as female? As it is written: "YOU SHALL NOT LET A SORCERESS [feminine] LIVE" (22:17).

LILITH ANSWERS: Throughout most of human history, women have been singled out whenever witchcraft is suspected.

THE SAGES IN OUR OWN TIME ADD: Many of these women, especially in premodern times, served as healers and "therapists" before such professions were legitimized. In ancient Israel, such benign "witchcraft" was widespread.

THE RABBIS EXPLAIN: The verse in our parasha mentions only female sorcerers because "the more women, the more witchcraft." When Shimon ben Shetakh was the head of the Sanhedrin, he trapped eighty witches in a cave in Ashkelon and hanged them in order to eradicate witchcraft among the common people. And Shimon bar Yohai taught that "the daughters of Israel were addicted to magical practices."

BERURIAH THE SCHOLAR COUNTERS: Yet we find in the Talmud as well as in later rabbinic writings evidence that the rabbis themselves often indulged in magic and other occult practices, even those who didn't acknowledged the efficacy of such practices. As Rabbi Eliezer ben Jacob admitted: "Although there is no divination, there are signs."

THE CRY OF THE POWERLESS

MOTHER RACHEL TEACHES: We are specifically forbidden to mis-treat the widow and the orphan, for if we do, we will have to answer to God, "WHO WILL HEED THEIR OUTCRY AS SOON AS THEY CRY OUT TO ME, AND MY ANGER SHALL BLAZE FORTH AND I WILL PUT YOU TO THE SWORD, AND YOUR OWN WIVES SHALL BECOME WIDOWS AND YOUR CHILDREN ORPHANS" (22:23). If for no other reason, we are to act out of self-interest. For if we wish to safeguard our own well-being and security, we must safeguard those less fortunate than we—or we shall become like them.

HULDAH THE PREACHER COMMENTS: In an agricultural economy prone to frequent drought, famine, and warfare, even the well-to-do are mind-ful that they too are only a harvest away from ruin, a heartbeat away from being widows and orphans, a bowshot away from exile.

OUR BUBBES ADD: Poverty is no disgrace but also no great honor.

PILGRIMAGES TO JERUSALEM

OUR DAUGHTERS ASK: Were women supposed to go on pilgrimage to Jerusalem on the three agricultural festivals—Passover, Shavuot, and Sukkot? For it is written: "THREE TIMES A YEAR ALL YOUR MALES SHALL APPEAR" (23:17). Were they allowed to go? Or were they forbidden to participate in this celebra-tion of national union?

HULDAH THE PREACHER ANSWERS: On the basis of this verse, we can't be sure. But later, in Deuteronomy, as Moses reviews these laws for the people before his death, he changes the wording (as we have seen him do else-where) to include "YOUR SON AND YOUR DAUGHTER, YOUR MALE AND FEMALE SLAVE, THE LEVITE, THE STRANGER, THE FATHERLESS, AND THE WIDOW IN YOUR COM-MUNITIES" (16:11, 14)—in other words, all Israelites.

SERAKH BAT ASHER THE HISTORIAN ADDS: Anyone who has ever attended a mass event—an outdoor music festival, a rally in Washington, a sports championship—knows how galvanized the crowd becomes at the sight of its own teeming multitudes; how infectious is the spirit of common cause; how intense the emotional charge of the moment. So too, during the days when the Temple stood in Jerusalem, the people crowded around the Temple precincts to offer sacrifices of thanksgiving, to worship, and to rejoice as a na-tion, renewing their covenant with God.

THE SYMBOLISM OF MILK

OUR DAUGHTERS ASK: Why are we forbidden to mix milk and meat? As it is written: "YOU SHALL NOT BOIL A KID IN ITS MOTHER'S MILK" (23:19). Is it really sacrilegious to eat a cheeseburger or chicken à la king?

THE SAGES IN OUR OWN TIME ANSWER: Some scholars mistakenly claim that the basis of this law was to ensure that the Israelites would remain separate from their neighbors' pagan rites in which sacrificial goats were boiled in milk. But others teach: No, this taboo is designed to keep life and death apart, to make a ritual separation between the dead flesh of the goat and the milk produced by a living animal.

THE RABBIS DISAGREE: Because this prohibition is repeated three times in the Torah, it has given us much food for thought. Some teach that this verse is designed to sensitize us to an animal's feelings. Another opinion: It is to teach us to discipline our eating to make it a more conscious, holy act. We thus conclude: All of these are the words of the living God! Thus one of the laws of kashrut is that we do not mix milk products with meat.

SARAH THE ANCIENT ONE ADDS: Apart from its role in the dietary laws, milk is a powerful symbol, representing the bounty of the land of Israel, which is called "A LAND FLOWING WITH MILK AND HONEY" (Numbers 14:8). Milk is also the source and sustenance of new life, as it is written: "YOU POURED ME OUT LIKE MILK, CURDLED ME LIKE CHEESE" (Job 10:10). And milk refers to the words of the holy Torah, as it is written: "HONEY AND MILK ARE UNDER YOUR TONGUE" (Song of Songs 4:11).

ESTHER THE HIDDEN ONE REVEALS: The numerical value of *halav*, the Hebrew word for milk, is forty, a sacred number in the Torah and in Israel's history.

OUR MOTHERS CONCLUDE: So although milk is taboo for boiling kids, it does have its uses.

THE GENDER OF ANGELS

OUR DAUGHTERS ASK: Do angels have gender? When the Torah refers to them as male, as it is written: "I AM SENDING AN ANGEL BEFORE YOU . . . PAY HEED TO HIM AND OBEY HIM" (23:20–21), is the pronoun intended to be generic or gendered?

THE RABBIS ANSWER: Any references to God's sexuality—through metaphor, poetic language, male pronouns, or epithets—must not be taken literally. God is not a person, male or female.

BERURIAH THE SCHOLAR INTERRUPTS: But it's different with angels in the Bible. In this verse, as in many others, angels are referred to as *ish*, the Hebrew word for "man"—but not in the collective sense of "mankind." The angels who visit Sodom, wrestle with Jacob, and speak to the prophets are clearly depicted as males.

ESTHER THE HIDDEN ONE DECLARES: But they are so much more than that! Angels fill all the worlds, possessing complex personalities and powers: they fly, foretell the future, protect pregnant mothers and their babies, ward off male and female demons, and carry prayers to the Heavenly Throne. Although Maimonides and his rationalist successors tried to explain away angels as mere psychological metaphors, they remain alive in our folk tradition, with room for myriads more.

A PRAYER FOR THE ANGEL OF JUSTICE

OUR BUBBES TEACH: For centuries, pious women have called upon the guardian angels who watch over their dead loved ones to carry their prayers up to heaven. They beseech the Holy One of Blessing: "Dear God, permit me soon to enjoy the merit of the righteous men and women buried here who, in their lifetimes, performed good deeds. May the angel over those buried here bring my prayers to the Name, may He be blessed in *Gan Ayden* (Paradise), where the righteous will intercede on behalf of me, my husband, and my loved ones. May the Holy Father of all the earth not remain silent in heaven at the sight of my tears flowing like a stream of water. As King David says: (I melt my couch in my tears), tears with which I bewail my misdeeds and my sleep, which dissolves into nothing. Dear God, (permit) the *z'chus* (merit) of the righteous to protect me. *Omeyn. Selo.*"

THE BLESSING OF FRUITFULNESS

THE RABBIS EXPLAIN: At the end of this parasha's comprehensive inventory of ethical imperatives, God promises to reward the people for their obedience by blessing their bread and water, removing sickness from their midst, and granting them long life. And the women will be blessed with fertility, as it is written: "NO WOMAN IN YOUR LAND SHALL MISCARRY OR BE BARREN" (23:26).

SARAH THE ANCIENT ONE CRIES: Would that it were so! For so many of us, it is difficult to embrace a theology that ties individual reward so directly to collective action. No, we must resist blaming ourselves for barrenness and failed births, even if such blame seems to explain that which is beyond explaining. Instead we need to acknowledge that just as we struggle in our own lives to uphold God's utopian vision, so too does God. We are partners together for better and for worse.

19. TERUMAH:
The Image of God
(EXODUS 25:1–27:19)

ORAH TEACHES: Moses remains atop the mountain for forty days. There he receives not only God's laws but also detailed instructions about how to house and consecrate God's presence among the people. This parasha sets out the blueprint for constructing the *Mishkan,* the portable Tabernacle, together with all its furnishings: the Ark of the Covenant, the golden table for the twelve showbreads, the seven-branched menorah, and the altar of acacia wood with its copper utensils.

The Tabernacle itself is to consist of ten dyed linen panels, woven together and embroidered with cherubim, joined at the edges with loops of blue wool and fifty gold clasps. The tent walls are to be reinforced on the inside by walls of acacia planks, overlaid with gold. Sheltering the Tabernacle from above will be a goatskin tent, itself covered by ram and dolphin skins. The Tabernacle will be ringed with a seven-foot fence of fine linen, hung in panels on silver and copper posts, with an embroidered gate of blue, purple, and crimson yarns.

And inside this nested structure will be the Holy of Holies, veiled by a curtain of embroidered linen and wool, containing in its secret heart the Ark of the Covenant, crowned by a pair of hammered gold cherubim.

THE CHERUBIM ABOVE THE ARK

OUR DAUGHTERS ASK: What exactly are these Cherubim? They sound suspiciously similar to graven images, whose fashioning is forbidden in the Ten Commandments that lie in the Ark right under their feet!

THE RABBIS REPLY: Nothing could be farther from the truth. The Cherubim represent the Divine Presence, the Shekhinah, that dwelled among the people. As it is written: "THERE I WILL MEET WITH YOU . . . FROM BETWEEN THE TWO CHERUBIM" (25:22). These two golden figures depicted the guardian angels who appeared sometimes in the guise of men and women, at other times as celestial beings. When Israel sinned, the Cherubim's faces turned away from each other; when the people repented, they faced each other and embraced, "like a male who embraces a female."

THE SAGES IN OUR OWN TIME EXPLAIN: In reality, the Israelite Cherubim were modeled on the hybrid gods of their neighbors: the Egyptian sphinx, the winged man-lion god of Phoenicia, the winged bulls of Assyria and Babylonia.

THE RABBIS OBJECT: No, they were made according to God's precise instructions. They were to be of hammered gold, "OF ONE PIECE WITH THE COVER," with "THEIR WINGS SPREAD OUT ABOVE, SHIELDING THE COVER WITH THEIR WINGS" (25:20). Rather than facing the priest or turning heavenward, "THEY SHALL CONFRONT EACH OTHER, THE FACES OF THE CHERUBIM BEING TURNED TOWARD THE COVER" (25:20). Echoing these figures, images of Cherubim were also to be woven into the veil and curtains of the sanctuary.

SERAKH BAT ASHER THE HISTORIAN ADDS: Centuries later, when the Jerusalem Temple replaced the *Mishkan,* the motif of the Cherubim was repeated on its inner and outer walls, on its doors, and on the huge brass bowl called the "Molten Sea." Today we can find faint traces of the ancient Cherubim in the rampant lions adorning many synagogue arks.

LILITH TEASES: In a culture so repelled by idolatry, how startling to find these graven images inhabiting the innermost sanctum of holy space! And in a religion so hostile to dualism, how intriguing to find two such images embracing each other to make up!

THE SABBATH LOAVES: A CAUTIONARY TALE

ESTHER THE HIDDEN ONE RECOUNTS: Who is to say what is idolatry and what is true faith? What matters most of all is the intention of the heart. As it is told:

Once there was a Portuguese *converso* couple who settled in the holy city of Safed in Israel. Finally free of the Inquisition's iron grasp, they joyously reembraced their former faith. One Friday night, the man went to the synagogue and heard the rabbi lamenting the destruction of the ancient Temple. "And because of our sins," he concluded, "we no longer bring God the special loaves that we used to bring long ago."

When the man came home, he told his wife to bake two loaves of hallah. Using only the finest flour and thinking only the purest thoughts, the woman skillfully made the loaves, which her husband brought to synagogue the following Friday afternoon and offered to God before the holy ark. As soon as he left, the poor shammash came upon the loaves and concluded that they had been left by some kind soul for him and his destitute family. And when the *con-*

verso returned to the synagogue later that night, he was overjoyed to discover that God had graciously accepted his offering.

So it went, week after week: The *converso* offered to God the loaves baked by his wife, and the shammash accepted them as gifts from an anonymous donor. Then one Friday afternoon, the rabbi accidentally discovered what was going on and sternly chastised the *converso* for his impiety. "Do you think God has a body and an appetite for bread?" he cried. "What a fool you are! You have been guilty of the sin of idolatry!" Shamefaced, the *converso* burst into tears.

At that moment, a messenger arrived from the holy Ari, Rabbi Isaac Luria, and told the rabbi to prepare himself to die at the close of Sabbath. "For not since the destruction of the Temple has the Holy One derived such pleasure as from the loaves offered in love and joy by these two simple souls. For robbing God of this blessing, you have been sentenced to death."

And when three stars appeared at the end of Shabbat, the rabbi lay down and breathed his last.

THE COMPASSION OF SHEKHINAH

ESTHER THE HIDDEN ONE REVEALS: Shekhinah, the Holy-One-Who-Dwells-in-This-World, represents the mystical Community of Israel. All Israel constitutes her limbs. She is our intimate link with God-Who-Dwells-on-High and our companion as we wander in exile. As it is written: "'AND LET THEM MAKE ME A SANCTUARY THAT I MAY DWELL AMONG THEM' [Exodus 25:8]. Not 'I will dwell below,' but *among* you—just as a wanderer would. In other words, wherever Israel wanders, I will go with them and I will dwell among them, but not in a permanent place." Mercifully, She holds back God's upraised hand when it threatens to harm Her children, but She does not hesitate to punish us Herself when we stray. When we sin, we threaten Her well-being and lengthen Her own exile, prolonging Her separation from Her celestial lover. As it is written in the holy Zohar: "When the powerful serpent up above is aroused by the sins of the world, it joins with Shekhinah and injects venom into Her" (3:79a). Woe to us all when we abandon her like this!

20. TETZAVEH:
Clothing

(EXODUS 27:20–30:10)

TORAH TEACHES: After issuing instructions for building and furnishing the portable Tabernacle—the *Mishkan*—God turns to the sacred personnel who are to superintend it. To dignify and adorn the priests, "ALL WHO ARE SKILLFUL" among the people are called upon to fashion special garments out of fine linen and wool, precious stones and gold. These the priests are to wear as they perform their sacred duties.

To consecrate Aaron and his sons for their sacred office, God ordains a seven-day ritual of investiture, during which Aaron and his sons, together with the sacrificial altar, are to be dedicated for holy service. First, Aaron is to be anointed with oil and arrayed in the robe, miter, and breastplate of the High Priest. Then he and his sons, along with their priestly garments, are to be anointed with sacrificial blood. Then, for seven days, they are to offer bulls and lambs, choice flour and oil, upon the altar, to purify the Sanctuary as God's dwelling place among the people.

God instructs Moses to build an incense altar of acacia wood to stand before the Holy Ark. Upon this altar Aaron himself will burn aromatic incense every morning and evening when he tends the lamps. And once each year, he will purify this altar with blood.

TEKHINAH ON THE NER TAMID

OUR BUBBES EXPLAIN: Just like Aaron and his sons, who were commanded to keep a light burning in the Sanctuary from morning until evening (27:20–21), we women perform a holy service each Friday night and *yontov* when we light candles. We may not be high priests, and our homes may not be as showy as the Sanctuary or the Temple, but our hearts and hands are every bit as pure as those of the priests, and our candles shine just as brightly as theirs. And so we pray:

Riboyne shel oylem (Master of the Universe), may the *mitsve* (commandment) of my lighting the candles be accepted as equivalent to the *mitsve* of the *koyen godl*

(High Priest) when he lit the candles in the precious *beys hamikdesh* (Holy Temple). As his observance was accepted, so may mine be accepted. (The verse) "Your words are a candle at my feet and a light for my path" (Psalms 119:105) means that Your words are a candle at my feet so that all my children may walk in God's path, and may the *mitsve* of my candlelighting be accepted so that my children's eyes may be illumined by the precious holy *toyre* (Torah). I also ask at this time that this *mitsve* of lighting candles be accepted as equivalent to the olive oil which burned in the *beys hamikdesh* and which was never extinguished (Exodus 27:20; Leviticus 24:2).

PRIESTLY VESTMENTS

The Rabbis exclaim: How wondrous are the many details of our holy Torah! In this parasha, we are given precise instructions for weaving, cutting, and stitching all the garments of the priests. The High Priest's attire consists of eight pieces; ordinary priests' of four.

Under his outer garments the High Priest wears a fringed tunic (*ketonet*), knit of linen in a patterned weave, with arm-length sleeves tied at the wrists. Over this goes the *ephod*, a kind of sleeved cape; the breastplate (*hoshen mishpat*), an elaborately embroidered brocade square worn over the front of the ephod, set with twelve precious stones and attached to the ephod at all four corners by cables of gold thread; and a robe (*me'il*), worn under the ephod, woven of sky-blue wool with a bordered collar and with pomegranates of blue, red, and crimson wool alternating with golden bells ornamenting the entire hem. Around this robe he binds a sash (*avnet*), a wide linen belt embroidered with blue, red, and crimson wool, worn above the waist with its ends hanging down to the ankles, except during the service, when the ends are thrown over the left shoulder. And under all these garments, he wears pants (*mikhnasei bad*), extending from the waist to the knees and tied at the knees. On his head sits a turban (*mitznefet*), made of linen, wound and sewn into a shape like a baker's hat, covered with blue wool, ringed at the bottom with three gold bands, and faced with a golden frontlet that is attached to the turban by twisted blue threads. Inscribed on the frontlet are the words: "Holy to God." In contrast, ordinary priests wear only the tunic, pants, and sash, as well as modified turbans (*migbaot*), which are either a simpler form of the High Priest's headwear or a cap similar to today's kippah.

OUR DAUGHTERS ASK: And who made all these elaborate garments?

OUR MOTHERS ANSWER: Although the Torah doesn't say, we can make a pretty good educated guess! Given that women have been the primary weavers and tailors in every culture since before recorded time, it's likely that it was the Israelite women who knit, sewed, and ripped.

HOW THE HOOPOE GOT ITS CREST

OUR MOTHERS WARN: There's a danger to wearing such flamboyant finery, because fancy clothes call attention to the wearer and make those who lack such things green with envy. As it is told:

Once when King Solomon went out riding upon his white eagle, the sun shone down on him so intensely that he was afraid he would die. Then a flock of hoopoe birds flew between him and the blazing sun and shielded him from its harsh rays. In gratitude, the king offered to grant the birds a wish.

"Your Majesty," they cried, "we wish to wear gold crowns upon our heads!"

Although the king scolded the hoopoes for their foolish request, he granted it. But in a short while, hunters began snaring the golden-crowned birds with mirrors and traps, until only a few were left. Sadly, the queen of the hoopoes went to Solomon and appealed for help. And so the king turned their crowns into crests of white feathers, which they wear to this day.

SONG OF THE SEAMSTRESS

OUR MOTHERS DECLARE: The lot of the Jewish seamstress has often been a hard one. In Russia a century ago, our poor grandmothers worked day and night at their sewing. And as they worked they sang:

Sewing and sewing, sewing on and on,
Stitch and hem, and hem again—
Oh, sweet God, you know the bitter truth,
How my eyes do ache and my fingers pain.

LILITH THE REBEL BREAKS IN: But not all seamstresses sang such gloomy songs. Some spun schemes of revolution as they sang:

We're weaving, we're weaving,
We're weaving a shroud for the Czar!

21. KI TISSA:
Idolatry

(EXODUS 30:11–34:35)

TORAH TEACHES: God orders each adult Israelite to pay a "ransom" of half a shekel to maintain the Sanctuary. Moses then receives more instructions about readying the Tabernacle and the priests for service: From this time forth, Aaron and his sons are to wash their hands and feet in a special copper laver before performing their sacred duties. And to purify the Sanctuary precincts, furnishings, and utensils, a special anointing oil of choice spices and incense of pure herbs are to be prepared and dedicated solely for this use.

God identifies two Israelites—Bezalel and Oholiab—as artistic directors of this sacred construction project. Endowed with "A DIVINE SPIRIT OF SKILL, ABILITY, AND KNOWLEDGE," they will supervise the holy work.

God then repeats the commandment to keep the Sabbath as a sign of the covenant. And after pronouncing these words, God gives Moses two stone tablets, "INSCRIBED WITH THE FINGER OF GOD."

But the people, fearful that Moses' long absence atop Mount Sinai spells his doom, go to Aaron and demand that he make them a god to lead them in his brother's place. Aaron demands from them their gold jewelry and casts it into the fire, creating a molten calf. Then Aaron builds an altar and declares the following day a festival. The next day, the people sacrifice to their new god upon the altar and rejoice with feasting and dance.

Taking note of their apostasy, God decrees the doom of this stiff-necked people and promises Moses to start over again with him, but Moses refuses the bargain, persuading God to relent by appealing to God's reputation and sense of honor. But when Moses himself descends to the camp and sees the people dancing before the Golden Calf, he angrily shatters the tablets in his hands, burns the calf into ash, and makes the people drink it.

Accused by his brother, Moses, Aaron denies any part in the people's sin. Moses orders the Levites to punish the idolaters, and they put three thousand Israelites to the sword. Moses then asks God to forgive the people, offering his own life as forfeit. God accepts his appeal but promises to render an accounting among the guilty. A deadly plague then strikes the camp.

God orders Moses to lead the people forth to Canaan, promising to send an angel before them but refusing to travel in their midst because of what they have done. From that moment on, the people refrain from wearing their finery, as a sign of mourning.

Moses requests to see God's face as a sign of divine favor, but God warns him that "MAN MAY NOT SEE ME AND LIVE." So God hides Moses in a cleft of the rock and shields him with a divine hand as God's back passes by. Then Moses carves two new tablets of stone, reascends the mountain, and receives the Law once again.

THE WOMEN'S JEWELRY

OUR DAUGHTERS ASK: Why does Aaron command the men to bring their *wives'* jewelry? As it is written: "TAKE OFF THE GOLD RINGS THAT ARE ON THE EARS OF YOUR WIVES" (32:2). Why not the men's as well?

THE RABBIS ANSWER: Aaron calls only for the women's jewelry because he assumes that they will naturally resist giving it up—out of vanity. He is right about their response—but wrong about their motives. Not vanity but piety is behind their resistance. And when the men see that their pious wives and daughters refuse to participate in idolatry, they cast their own earrings into the fire to make the Golden Calf. Later, these same women refuse to listen to the Ten Spies who predict the Israelites' defeat if they try to conquer the native population of Canaan. Nor do the women ever beg Moses to take them back to Egypt. Due to such unswerving faithfulness, every Israelite woman—except Miriam—lives to enter the Promised Land, even Moses' mother, Yokheved, who crosses the Jordan at the age of 250. God also rewards the women and their descendants with a special holiday, Rosh Hodesh, the first day of the New Moon, during which they are free to rest from all hard labor.

ELIJAH'S CUP

OUR MOTHERS DECLARE: Jewish women have long proven stubborn in their loyalty to God. Not only did they refuse to give up their jewelry to make a golden calf, but they have also faithfully safeguarded any of their own possessions that are sacred to God. Here is the story of one woman who showed such extraordinary faith and holy stubbornness:

Once, there was a rich couple who gave generously of their wealth to all who were in need. Their most precious possession was a beautiful Elijah's cup that adorned their seder table each Passover. But in time the wheel of fortune turned, and the couple lost all that they had. Yet despite these reverses, the couple promised each other that no matter how desperate their lot became, they would never sell their Elijah's cup.

But when Passover drew near and they realized that they had no money for a seder, the husband sadly told his wife, "We have no choice but to sell the Elijah's cup."

"Never!" cried his wife.

And so on the day before the holiday of Passover, they prepared to spend their first Passover ever without a seder. But while the husband was still at the study house, an elderly gentleman appeared at the door and asked for a seat at their seder table. When the wife showed him their bare table, empty except for the Elijah's cup, he offered her a bag of gold to prepare for the festive meal and promised to return that night. But he failed to appear, and so the couple were forced to conduct the seder without him.

Shortly after this, the husband died, but when he ascended to heaven, the angels refused to admit him. An elderly gentleman barred him from the gates, reproaching him: "You were willing to sell the Elijah's cup!" Several years later, when the wife died, the heavenly gates swung wide at her approach, but she stopped suddenly at the sight of her poor husband, still standing outside.

"Either we both enter or I stay outside with him!" she announced.

And so heaven had no choice but to admit them both.

MOURNING AFTER THE GOLDEN CALF

SERAKH BAT ASHER THE HISTORIAN TEACHES: The Israelites' decision to mourn after the sin of the Golden Calf set a precedent repeated too often after the many catastrophes that have punctuated Jewish history. After the destruction of the First Temple by Babylonia in 586 B.C.E., tradition claims the Levites hung their harps upon the willows beside the Euphrates as a sign of mourning over Jerusalem. After the more cataclysmic destruction of the Second Temple, by Rome in 70 C.E., the Rabbis mandated numerous measures meant to "diminish our joy," since Jerusalem was now in ruins. Among these customs, many of which are observed to this day, are the practices of leaving a corner of one's house unpainted and a corner of artwork unfinished; breaking a glass at weddings; and lessening the food at banquets to acknowledge that our happiness will not be complete until Jerusalem is restored to its former glory.

THE RABBIS INTERRUPT: Some of us even suggested at the time of the Roman conquest that we should refrain from eating meat from that day forth, but others argued that such mourning was excessive and unnecessary.

OUR MOTHERS ADD: As we begin the long, slow process of recovering from the recent devastation of the Holocaust, we will devise new practices to mourn this overwhelming loss as well.

GOD'S FACE

OUR DAUGHTERS ASK: What does God's face look like? And why can't we look at it? As it is written: "YOU CANNOT SEE MY FACE, FOR MAN MAY NOT SEE MY FACE AND LIVE" (33:20).

THE SAGES IN OUR OWN TIME ANSWER: Even Moses, greatest of all Jewish prophets and teachers, is permitted to see only God's *back*. No other view is theologically conceivable; a frontal view compromises the image of a genderless God.

ESTHER THE HIDDEN ONE RESPONDS: But if we grant that God is infinite and incalculably ingenious, we might imagine, as we look in our mirrors, God's face behind our own. After all, we are each created *b'tzelem Elohim*, in the likeness of God. We should daily recognize God within our own features. For if we did so, we would recognize God's face in each person we meet—and act accordingly.

RABBI ABRAHAM JOSHUA HESCHEL TEACHES: "We live and act according to the image of humanity we cherish."

THE GODDESS ASHERAH

OUR DAUGHTERS ASK: Why are the people constantly being warned not to worship other gods—and goddesses? As it is written: "TEAR DOWN THEIR ALTARS, SMASH THEIR PILLARS, AND CUT DOWN THEIR SACRED POSTS"—literally, "asherah trees" (34:13). Surely the Torah doth protest too much!

HULDAH THE PREACHER EXPLAINS: It had to! For fighting idolatry proved to be a long, difficult battle. No matter how often we reminded the people that YHVH alone is God and cannot be imaged in any concrete form, the people were not willing or able to embrace this radical new idea overnight. How could they, living within a culture so steeped in myth and idol worship? It took many centuries before we struggled free of paganism. Periodically, the people backslid and had to be wooed back to YHVH. We prophets, priests, and kings often had to resort to harsh threats and actions to expel idolatry from Israel's midst. Sometimes the rot ate away at the very heart of Judaism— in the king's palace or even in the Temple.

THE SAGES IN OUR OWN TIME ADD: One part of the pagan legacy that held on for almost six centuries was the cult of Asherah, the Canaanite goddess first worshiped by the Israelites. Asherah was the wife of El, the chief god. Her full title was Lady Asherah of the Sea, but she was also known as *Elat*, simply "Goddess." The chief goddess in the Canaanite pantheon, she was the mother and wet nurse of all seventy Canaanite gods, including Baal, Anat, and Mot. Several Canaanite cities had their own local Asherah, known by that city's name.

The asherahs mentioned in the Bible were probably carved wooden images "planted" in the ground, originally next to hilltop altars dedicated to Baal and later set up within the Temple itself. Although we have not found remnants of these wooden images, we have found hundreds of small clay figurines that depict a nude female body holding up protruding breasts; the figure tapers to a cylindrical column instead of the lower torso and legs. These were probably household asherah idols (like Rachel's *teraphim*), popular among women because the goddess was believed to aid fertility and ease childbirth.

SERAKH BAT ASHER THE HISTORIAN ELABORATES: Asherah worship probably began among the Israelites when they first settled the land and continued through the period of judges and kings until the Babylonian destruction of the Jerusalem Temple. Her cult was particularly strong in the northern Israelite capital of Samaria, where King Ahab and his foreign queen, Jezebel, introduced Asherah worship into priestly worship and ritual. Solomon's son Rehoboam also introduced Asherah worship into the Jerusalem Temple, under the influence of his mother, an Ammonite princess, and his own wife, Maacah. Although several Judean kings—Asa, Yehoshafat, Hezekiah, and Josiah—attempted to wipe out Asherah worship in the Temple and among the populace, it kept finding its way back into the hearts and minds of the people and their leaders.

HULDAH THE PREACHER JUMPS IN: But during his great religious restoration, my own king, Josiah the Reformer, spurred on by my zealous prophecy, burned all the statues of Asherah in the Temple, expelled from their

Temple quarters her priests and the women devotees who wove her garments, cut down wooden figures of the goddess in the countryside, and defiled these cultic sites with human bones. Yet still Asherah worship returned beneath leafy trees and on hilltops.

LILITH THE REBEL POINTS OUT: For 236 of the 370 years that Solomon's Temple stood in Jerusalem, statues of Asherah presided within its courts. She was obviously a beloved figure to the Israelite people, and her influence can be felt even today, in feminism's intellectual flirtation with the goddess.

IDOLS AND FOREIGN WIVES

THE RABBIS WARN: There is a close connection between lust and idolatry. That is why the Torah tells Israelite men that "WHEN YOU TAKE WIVES FROM AMONG THEIR DAUGHTERS," these non-Israelite women will continue to "LUST AFTER THEIR GODS AND WILL CAUSE YOUR SONS TO LUST AFTER THEIR GODS" (34:16).

BERURIAH THE SCHOLAR RESPONDS: How interesting that here and throughout the Bible, the Torah uses the Hebrew verb *zaneh*—literally, "to whore after"—to refer to both sexual and spiritual promiscuity, and that here, as elsewhere, women are identified as the *cause* of both vices in men. Surely temptation has never had trouble finding willing partners among both women and men!

22. VAYAKHEL:
Homework

(EXODUS 35:1–38:20)

ORAH TEACHES: Moses calls upon the people to bring gifts of precious metals, wood, yarn, skins, and cloth to build the *Mishkan*, the portable desert Sanctuary designated to serve as the ritual lightning rod between heaven and the Israelite camp. But so generous are the people's freewill offerings that Moses has to ask them to stop bringing their gifts. Bezalel and all the artisans construct the *Mishkan* and its furnishings, including the holy ark, the menorah, and the altar where the people are to bring their offerings to God.

THE WORK OF WOMEN'S HANDS

THE SAGES IN OUR OWN TIME EXPLAIN: From ancient times to the present day, women's hands have played a vital role in every traditional economy. Whether tending children, preparing clothes and food, gathering fuel and medicinal herbs, caring for the sick and old, bearing burdens, or mending holes, women have consistently sustained their families and communities with their manual skills. Among the Israelite women, *weaving* was a special art, as it is written: "AND ALL THE SKILLED WOMEN SPUN WITH THEIR OWN HANDS" (35:25).

THE RABBIS EXCLAIM: Indeed, so skilled were the Israelite women that they spun the wool while it was still on the goats!

OUR MOTHERS ADD: What is especially remarkable about these skills, which originated in the nomadic shepherd culture of Canaan, is that they were transmitted from mother to daughter through centuries of Egyptian slavery. Eventually they worked their way into the very finger bones of Jewish women, as we can see by examining the sweatshop handiwork of our grandmothers' hands.

GIFTS FROM THE HEART

OUR DAUGHTERS ASK: Where do the Israelites get the necessary materials—gold and silver, linen and dyes, acacia wood, dolphin skins (!)—to build such a splendid Sanctuary in the wilderness?

THE RABBIS ANSWER: This is the booty they carry with them out of Egypt. As it is written: "AND THEY DESPOILED THE EGYPTIANS" (12:36). Several hundred years of back wages!

OUR DAUGHTERS ASK: But how willingly do they part with these valuable treasures?

THE RABBIS BOAST: When it is time to build the Sanctuary, Moses calls upon the people to "TAKE FROM AMONG YOU GIFTS TO ADONAI, EVERYONE WHOSE HEART SO MOVES HIM OR HER SHALL BRING THEM" (35:5). The popular response is immediate and overwhelming: "BROOCHES, EARRINGS, RINGS, AND PENDANTS—GOLD OBJECTS OF ALL KINDS; . . . BLUE, PURPLE, AND CRIMSON YARNS, FINE LINEN, GOATS' HAIR, TANNED RAM SKINS AND DOLPHIN SKINS; . . . GIFTS OF SILVER OR COPPER; . . . AND ACACIA WOOD" (35:22–24). So generous are the people, in fact, that the artisans beg Moses to call an end to the giving, because "THE PEOPLE ARE BRINGING MORE THAN IS NEEDED" (36:5).

OUR MOTHERS MUSE: When was the last time our hearts moved us to give like that?

WOMEN'S MIRRORS

OUR DAUGHTERS ASK: According to the Rabbis, Moses refuses to accept the mirrors that the women bring him as freewill offerings for the Sanctuary. Why?

THE RABBIS ANSWER: He refuses them because he regards them as symbols of women's sexual temptation. But God reprimands him, for the Israelite women have used these very mirrors in Egypt to entice their weary husbands into siring more Hebrew children. And so Moses instructs the artisans to melt down the mirrors and fashion out of the molten copper the large laver for holding water that stands next to the altar in the Tabernacle and purifies the priests' hands.

THE MIRROR AND THE GLASS

HULDAH THE PREACHER TEACHES: Mirrors disclose a great many secrets about the one who gazes within. They reflect back to us not what we wish to see but rather what is really there. As it is told:

Once, a rabbi traveled to a village where only a single, poor Jew lived. Although destitute, the Jew opened his house to him, shared his meager fare, and apologized that he couldn't show more honor to his guest. Upon leaving, the rabbi blessed his host and wished him well.

Thereafter the poor man's lot improved so much that he soon became the wealthiest man in the village. He even hired a guard to keep away the beggars clamoring for alms.

When the rabbi returned a year later, he had to plead with the guard to let him see his master, and then he was rudely ushered into the house and made to wait. When at last the master appeared, the rabbi asked him: "Look through the window. What do you see?"

"People going about their affairs," answered the man.

"Now look in your mirror. What do you see?"

"Only myself."

"The window and the mirror are both made of glass," observed the rabbi. "The only difference between them is a silver coating. It's time to remove it."

Shocked and sobered by the rabbi's words, the man promised to change his miserly ways from that day forth. And so he did.

QUEEN HELENE AND THE GOLDEN CANDLESTICK

SERAKH BAT ASHER THE HISTORIAN RECOUNTS: In the days when the Temple stood in Jerusalem, there lived a queen named Helene of Adiabene, who embraced the Jewish faith. The queen donated to the sanctuary a large golden candlestick, which stood over the door. The people of Jerusalem knew that the time for morning prayers had come when the sun's rays glittered from the candlestick's golden arms and illuminated the city.

RABBI HANINA AND THE TABLE LEG

OUR MOTHERS RECOUNT: How often does a man's generosity rob his own wife and children! As it is told:

The wife of Rabbi Hanina ben Dosa once complained to him, "Must we always be so poor?" So Hanina prayed to God, and a hand reached down from heaven, extending to him a golden table leg. But that night Hanina dreamed of Paradise, and there he saw all the righteous seated at three-legged golden tables, except his wife and himself, who were steadying between them a table with only two legs. When he told his wife about his dream the next morning, she told him to pray that the leg be taken back, and the hand came down a second time and reclaimed its gift. What a great miracle this was, for this was the only time that heaven not only gave but also took back what it had once granted.

23. PIKUDEI:
The Work of Women's Hands

(EXODUS 38:21–40:38)

TORAH TEACHES: The skilled workers make vestments for the priests, and then the holy work is finished. When Moses sees the Tabernacle and its furnishings, and the priestly garments, he blesses the Israelites.

Then God commands Moses to dedicate the Tabernacle on the first day of the first month. Moses offers a sacrifice there as God has commanded. When Moses has finished the work, the Cloud of the Divine Presence, the Shekhinah, fills the Tabernacle. When the Cloud lifts, the people are to journey on; while it remains, they are to stay encamped where they are. And each night, a fire lights up the cloud, and all of Israel sees it throughout their years of wandering.

THE STONE OF WEAVING

THE RABBIS TEACH: The world rests upon the Foundation Stone— *Even Ha-Shetiyah*—that is on the site where the Holy Temple once stood. In Aramaic, *shetiyah* means "weaving." Therefore, in memory of the Temple, some Jewish women refrain from weaving during the nine days leading to Tisha B'Av, the fast day commemorating the Temple's destruction. For they believe that during these mournful days, no blessing will fall on the work of their hands.

WOMEN AND WEAVING

THE SAGES IN OUR OWN TIME TEACH: Making cloth has been primarily women's work for the last twenty thousand years—until the industrial revolution.

OUR MOTHERS OBJECT: And what about *after* the industrial revolution? What about all the immigrant women who slaved over sewing machines in New York sweatshops at the turn of the century or wore out their fingers stitching seams in their cold tenement kitchens? Remember the poor girls lost in the Triangle Fire!

THE SAGES ANSWER: Before machines and mass production were introduced, making cloth was regarded as one of a woman's valuable contributions to the family economy. It was when plow animals and dairy herding were introduced into Middle Eastern agriculture that men's and women's work began to be divided: men performed the outdoor tasks of tending the fields and producing the food; women the household tasks of preparing the food, caring for the children, and making cloth.

SERAKH BAT ASHER THE HISTORIAN ADDS: Since we were principally a sheepherding people in ancient times, Israelite women mostly wove wool. Some even say that it was we women of Israel who first introduced colored wool garments into Egypt. For did not Joseph have a splendid "coat of many colors"!

THE SAGES IN OUR OWN TIME ADD: Modern scholars have found pictures of colored garments in Egyptian tomb paintings dating from about the time Jacob's clan supposedly arrived in Goshen. And not only did the Israelite women bring technical expertise to Egypt; they probably acquired from their Egyptian sisters the special technique of splicing and twisting linen that first appears in Canaan about the time the Israelites would have arrived from the Nile Delta.

MIRIAM ADDS: As it is written: "EACH WOMAN SHALL BORROW FROM HER NEIGHBORS" (3:22).

WISEHEARTED WOMEN

BERURIAH THE SCHOLAR TEACHES: The Torah describes the women in the wilderness who spin linen and goats' hair "WITH THEIR HANDS" as "WISEHEARTED" (35:25). Similarly, in the Book of Proverbs (31:13, 19, 22, 24–25), a "WOMAN OF VALOR" is described largely in terms of her weaving skills:

She looks for wool and flax,
And sets her hand to them with a will. . . .
She sets her hand to the distaff;
Her fingers work the spindle. . . .
She makes covers for herself;

Her clothing is linen and purple. . . .
She makes cloth and sells it,
And offers a girdle to the merchant.
She is clothed with strength and splendor.

HULDAH THE PREACHER ADDS: It is also written in Proverbs: "Property and riches are bequeathed by fathers, but an efficient wife comes from God" (19:14).

LEVITICUS

ויקרא

Ritual

24. VAYIKRA:

Worship

(LEVITICUS 1:1–5:26)

TORAH TEACHES: This parasha introduces the sacrificial system presided over by the priestly cult. Two major categories of sacrifices are described: the "joyful offerings," consisting of the burnt, meal, and well-being (or peace) sacrifices and the "sorrowful offerings," consisting of the purification and guilt sacrifices. The Israelites are commanded to offer these sacrifices so that they may draw near and stay near to God.

THE TORAH OF THE PRIESTS

MIRIAM THE PROPHET DECLARES: How complex were the duties assigned to my family, Israel's priests! For once the Tabernacle was constructed—which in itself involved painstaking labor and thousands of details—the priests were charged with carrying out the demanding and perilous rituals of sacrifice. So much slaughter and blood, the cries of beasts, the mingled smells of smoke, incense, and death. So many different occasions to bring a gift to God—to offer thanks and make atonement, to celebrate a festival and fulfill a vow. No wonder priests, to perform their duties precisely, needed a priestly instruction manual. Thank God for Leviticus!

In brief, then, here are the types of sacrifice the people could bring:

BURNT OFFERING, *olah*, the standard communal sacrifice. The animal offered up as an *olah*—literally, "that which goes up"—was entirely consumed by fire (except for its hide).

MEAL OFFERING, *minhah* ("gift"), consisting of flour and oil, usually accompanied by incense. The priest offered a portion of this sacrifice on the altar and reserved the rest for the priests. A *minhah* had to be offered with every animal sacrifice.

OFFERING OF WELL-BEING (OR PEACE),   *zevakh shelamim*, a joyful offering eaten by sacrificer and family after portions of the animal had been burned on the altar and shared with the priests. This sacrifice was often brought to fulfill a vow.

PURIFICATION (SIN) OFFERING,   *hattat*, a sorrowful offering to expiate unintentional wrongdoing. The procedure varied, depending on the status of the sacrificer: if a priest or the whole community, the blood was sprinkled on the incense altar and the curtain leading to the Holy of Holies, and the animal was burned outside the camp; if a secular leader or a commoner, the blood was sprinkled on the main altar and the meat eaten by the priests. In both cases, the fat was burned on the altar.

GUILT OFFERING,   *asham*, a sorrowful offering requiring a ram to expiate a sin involving misappropriation of property. First, the guilty person had to repay what was taken, plus an additional fine; then the *asham* restored him or her to divine favor.

OUR DAUGHTERS EXCLAIM: No wonder they needed ritual specialists back then. This was no job for a general practitioner!

DRAWING NEAR TO GOD

LEAH THE NAMER TEACHES: The Hebrew word for sacrifice is *korban*, from the root meaning "to draw near." In contrast, the English word "sacrifice" comes from a Latin root meaning "to make sacred." At the heart of these differing interpretations lie two fundamentally different understandings of what it means to offer something to God.

OUR DAUGHTERS ASK: How do you transform something profane into something "sacred"?

THE SAGES IN OUR OWN TIME ANSWER: According to the Christian understanding of the word, to sacrifice means to give something up in order to appease God or to pay homage to God. What you gain in doing so is believed to more than compensate you for what you lose: protection from divine punishment for our sins.

THE RABBIS EXPLAIN: But we understand sacrifice quite differently. In our view (which, of course, is the Torah's view), the primary function of sacrifices is to *restore the spiritual equilibrium* of the community, although we do recognize that sacrifices also *expiate* for *unintentional* wrongdoing. For when we in-advertently sin against God, one another, or the community, we upset the deli-cate balance so carefully regulated and maintained by God's law. In "going public" with their error at the Temple altar, the people proffered a peace offer-ing, asking God to be lenient with them as they encroached upon sanctified space. But after their offering had been accepted, they still needed to right the wrongs they had done—by reimbursing the victim, paying a fine, or discharg-ing other legal penalties.

OUR MOTHERS SUGGEST: In a very real sense, the ancient Israelite system of sacrifice served the same function that psychotherapy serves today: Those of us plagued by feelings of guilt, shame, anxiety, depression, and other "sins" harmful to our souls seek out women and men specially trained in the art of expiation, who for a sacrificial fee help us to surrender these burdens to God (or a Higher Power) and reach a new psychic balance. We too must still right the wrongs we have committed—but we no longer need to drag behind us, like a fatted ox or sheep, unintentional or imaginary sins. These we can turn over to God.

ANIMALS FIT FOR SACRIFICE

MOTHER RACHEL TEACHES: Only gentle animals—cows, oxen, sheep, goats—are worthy of sacrifice: that is, only those animals who do not prey on or kill human beings and other animals. Sheep and herd animals are the quietest of creatures, as are turtledoves and pigeons. May their gentle souls per-suade Shekhinah to have compassion on us and accept our prayers.

DONAH, DONAH

THE RABBIS RECOUNT: Once, when Rabbi Judah the Prince was walking near a butcher shop, a calf ran up to him, followed by the butcher in hot pursuit. With frightened eyes, the calf looked up at Rabbi Judah as if to say: Save me from the slaughterer's knife! But the rabbi grabbed hold of the rope around the calf's neck and led it back to the butcher, rebuking it as he handed it over for slaughter: "Do not forget that it was for this purpose that you were created!" Because of his cruel words, Rabbi Judah suffered a toothache for the next six years and had difficulty urinating for seven more.

After these thirteen years had passed, he happened one day to see his maid-servant trying to kill a weasel with her broom and prevented her from doing so. Only then did God call an end to his suffering.

OUR MOTHERS ADD: This story inspired a modern Yiddish folk song, "Donah, Donah":

> On a wagon bound for market,
> There's a calf with a mournful eye.
> High above him, there's a swallow,
> Winging swiftly through the sky.
>
> *Chorus:*
> How the winds are laughing!
> They laugh with all their might.
> Laugh and laugh the whole day through
> And half the summer's night.
> Donah, donah . . .
>
> "Stop complaining!" said the farmer.
> "Who told you a calf to be?
> Why don't you have wings to fly with
> Like the swallow so proud and free?"
>
> *Chorus*
>
> Calves are easily bound and slaughtered,
> Never knowing the reason why.
> But whoever treasures freedom,
> Like the swallow has learned to fly.
>
> *Chorus*

SERAKH BAT ASHER THE HISTORIAN COMMENTS: But of course, the new version reflects the spirit of its own time. For in the song, when the calf casts its mournful eye toward the farmer leading it to slaughter, it receives not only a rebuke similar to Rabbi Judah's—"Who told you a calf to be?"—but also a revolutionary manifesto: "Whoever treasures freedom, like the swallow has learned to fly."

DINAH THE WOUNDED ONE RETORTS: As if the calf had a choice in the matter!

MIRIAM BAT TANHUM AND HER SEVEN SONS

DINAH THE WOUNDED ONE LAMENTS: In the name of our God, we have sacrificed so much that we hold dear. And in the name of theirs, others have sacrificed us on their altars. As it is told:

When the Emperor Hadrian ruled over Israel with an iron fist and defiled the land with his idols, he once imprisoned a Jewish widow named Miriam and her seven sons, in order to make an example of them. One by one, he summoned each of the sons, beginning with the oldest, and commanded him to bow down to an idol. One by one, they refused, and the emperor cut off their heads. When only the youngest son, a boy of three, remained, the emperor dropped his ring to the floor and whispered to the boy to pick it up, "so that you will fool my people into thinking you are bowing to the idol." But the boy refused. When his head too was severed, his poor mother cried: "Abraham, you boasted that you were ready to sacrifice one son on Mount Moriah! But see, I have given seven!" And then she threw herself off the roof of Hadrian's palace and died. At that moment, a voice was heard from heaven: "Happy is the mother of sons!"

DINAH CONCLUDES: No woman could have written this tale!

25. TZAV:

Blood

(LEVITICUS 6:1–8:36)

ORAH TEACHES: This parasha explains how to offer the sacrifices previously described. We are given further details about the role of the priests; about the *shelamim* (peace or well-being) offerings—the *todah*, brought in thanksgiving; the *nedavah*, brought as a freewill offering; and the *neder*, brought to fulfill a vow; and about the role of blood in sacrifice.

The parasha concludes with the ordination of Aaron and his sons.

FEMALE LEVITES

OUR DAUGHTERS ASK: What do we know about the life and duties of female Levites? Why is it written, both here and in other parshiyot: "ONLY THE MALES AMONG AARON'S DESCENDANTS" (6:11)? Don't the women in this tribe have priestly status too?

BERURIAH THE SCHOLAR ANSWERS: Although the Torah says almost nothing about the mothers, daughters, sisters, and wives of male Levites, we do know that through their upright behavior, female Levites are expected to reflect honor on their father's house. And there are a few laws specifically addressed to female Levites: if they are unmarried, they (along with the priests' slaves) are permitted to eat from the "holy sacrifices," *kodashim*, but not from the "most holy" ones, *kodesh kodashim*—principally, burnt, guilt, and sin offerings—which are restricted to the male priests. If a female Levite marries a layman, she then belongs to her husband's household. And if she marries a man from the tribe of Levi, she is not mourned by her husband when she dies, since male priests are allowed to mourn only for blood relatives.

THE RABBIS INTERRUPT: We later changed this last law, because it posed such a hardship on the bereaved husband.

HULDAH THE PREACHER OFFERS: In Temple times, Levite women sang and performed on musical instruments in Levitical choirs and also composed sacred songs for liturgical purposes.

THE SAGES IN OUR TIME ADD: Women—whether lay or Levite—played much greater roles in "domestic religion"—that is, in home rituals and celebrations—than in the official public Temple cult. Evidence uncovered by archaeologists suggests that Israelite women used household shrines and "votary" images, especially terra-cotta "pillar figurines," or asherahs (small female figures with breasts, but featureless and cylindrical from the waist down), to invoke fertility and healthy children. So in a sense, Israelite women were priestesses in their own households, although strictly without portfolio.

THE SYMBOLISM OF BLOOD

THE SAGES IN OUR OWN TIME TEACH: Throughout the world, blood has always been a powerful symbol of both life and death. Because this double status makes blood uncanny, cultures have devised many rituals and laws to protect people who come in contact with it. Blood is used to purify, protect, curse, and mark sacred space.

THE RABBIS ELABORATE: Because blood symbolizes life, which is holy and God-given, sacrificial blood is to be spilled out upon the altar, not eaten. The Torah prohibits human beings, including non-Jews, from consuming blood. As it is written: "ANYONE WHO EATS BLOOD SHALL BE CUT OFF FROM HIS KIN" (7:27). The Jewish dietary laws of kashrut require that meat be salted and drained to draw out all blood before the meat is eaten.

HULDAH THE PREACHER ADDS: Blood also represents holiness. Priests purged ritual impurity and consecrated members of the priestly cult with blood. Every male born, adopted, or converted into the Jewish community enters a sacred "covenant of blood" through ritual circumcision. Because of its special holiness, blood also protects human beings from harm, as it did on the Hebrews' doorposts in Egypt.

MOTHER RACHEL EXPLAINS: Women have a special connection with blood. From puberty until menopause, we bleed every month—and yet are unharmed by this loss of life-giving fluid. Our cycles of bleeding parallel the waxing and waning of the moon. And when we bear children, we launch them into the world upon a current of birthing blood.

THE RABBIS BREAK IN: Precisely because of their intimate and mysterious connection with blood, Jewish women are subject to numerous taboos that keep them apart from the community and from their husbands during their "bloody times."

OUR MOTHERS COMMENT: To many Jewish women, such segregation is sacred, a gift of time and solitude. . . .

LILITH INTERRUPTS: But to others, it is anathema, a vestige of paternalism.

THE COLOR RED

OUR MOTHERS TEACH: The color red, because of its connection with blood, possesses special antidemonic power. For centuries, Jewish women have used this color in many ways to protect themselves and their loved ones. In bygone days, mothers protected their children by making them wear coral necklaces to avert the evil eye. To this day, brides in some communities paint their hands with red henna the night before their wedding to keep demons away.

OUR BUBBES ADD: Red amulets are particularly effective in preventing diseases of the blood. And sewing red threads into your grandchildren's underwear and around their cribs can't hurt.

MOTHER RACHEL INTERJECTS: Red also symbolizes life and fertility. Over the centuries, barren women have come to my grave near Bethlehem and wound a red string around my tomb to receive my blessings.

26. SHEMINI:
Food

(LEVITICUS 9:1–11:47)

ORAH TEACHES: When Moses and Aaron consecrate the Tabernacle, a divine fire descends and consumes the sacrifices laid upon the holy altar.

Then Aaron's two elder sons, Nadab and Abihu, offer "alien fire" upon the altar, and God strikes them dead. In the face of their deaths, Aaron remains silent.

The Torah then lays out a detailed set of rules concerning intoxicants, as well as permitted and forbidden foods, and stresses the vital connection between dietary practices and holiness.

THE DEATH OF AARON'S SONS

OUR DAUGHTERS ASK: Why does the Torah say so little about the dramatic deaths of Nadab and Abihu? All we're told is that the two men are unexpectedly consumed by divine fire; that Moses offers rather insensitive words of consolation to his bereaved brother, as it is written: "THIS IS WHAT YHVH MEANT WHEN HE SAID: 'THROUGH THOSE NEAR TO ME I SHOW MYSELF HOLY, AND ASSERT MY AUTHORITY BEFORE ALL THE PEOPLE'" (10:3); and that Aaron remains silent. About their mother Elisheva's response we're told nothing. Why isn't she even mentioned here? Why is she, like Sarah at the Akedah, absent before, during, and after this trial by fire? Does she know what her sons had been planning to do? Is she present when they're struck down? Does Moses address her as well when he speaks to Aaron? Is she silent like her husband, or does she raise her voice in mourning or protest? And even though Aaron and their two surviving sons are forbidden to mourn because they're in a state of special consecration, is she also forbidden to mourn her own children? Does she demonstrate "proper" self-restraint, or does she throw herself upon their graves and keen, as Middle Eastern women have done for centuries?

ELISHEVA ANSWERS: What a terrible day that was for me! Being a woman, I was not permitted to draw near when Aaron and his brother, Moses, consecrated the altar. Instead I remained with the other Levite women, preparing food and readying ourselves for the festivities that were to follow this momentous occasion. My sister-in-law Miriam was with her chorus of women, practicing the special dance they had created for this day.

Then I heard a piercing cry from inside the Tent of Meeting. I recognized the voices of my two sons, filled with indescribable pain. But I did not hear the voices of Aaron or Moses. I waited, terrified, until one of the younger priests appeared from behind the curtain of the tent, his face ashen and taut with fright. "They are dead," he told me, "killed by the invisible hand of God." At first I couldn't move. My ears refused to believe his words. Dead? On the day when we were dedicating a new house for Shekhinah's Presence to dwell in? Surely my ears had deceived me!

But then I saw Aaron standing behind the young man. His face too was drained of color, and his hands trembled as he drew aside the tent flap. Yet he said nothing. He just stared at me—or rather through me—and then disappeared back into the tent. Soon Moses appeared in the doorway of the tent and repeated the young priest's words. He then summoned Mishael and Elzaphan, sons of Aaron's uncle Uzziel, and they soon came out of the tent, carrying my beloved Nadab and Abihu by their tunics. How strange they looked—their bodies untouched except for the dark ash around their nostrils, where the divine fire had entered and consumed their life-breath.

As my two kinsmen bore my sons toward the outside of the camp, my grief finally shattered its bonds and broke free. I began to wail and beat my breast, until several women held back my hands so that I would not harm myself. Then Moses turned to me and held up his hand to silence me. But I would not be silenced! I began to follow after my sons, but Moses ordered the women to hold me back.

"All of the people shall observe a period of mourning," he announced, "and all the house of Israel shall bewail the burning that YHVH has wrought. But Aaron, together with Eleazar and Itamar, Aaron's two remaining sons"—were they not my sons as well, my only two now that Nadab and Abihu were no more!—"these three shall not bare their heads nor rend their clothes, lest they die and anger strike the whole community. They shall remain within the Tent of Meeting." And then, without another word, he retreated back into the tent.

What was I to do now? Was I allowed to mourn? And who would comfort me, with my husband and two sons separated from me in the Tabernacle? But whether God wanted me to or not, I chose to mourn. If I was to be forbidden entrance to the holy altar, forbidden to accompany my dead sons outside the camp, forbidden even to seek comfort with my husband and two remaining sons, then I would not refuse the comfort of my community. And so the women put away their hand drums and timbrels and did not perform the dance that they had prepared for what was meant to be a day of rejoicing. I put on sackcloth and ashes and sat before them on the barren ground. And they sang a lament to my dead sons, and so I was comforted for my loss.

THE TWO JEWELS

BERURIAH THE SCHOLAR RECOUNTS: Like Elisheva, I also returned two sons to God. And like her, I never understood why they were taken from me. One Shabbat when my husband, Meir, went to the study house, my boys were suddenly stricken with fever and died. When Meir returned, just before dark, I did not wish to disturb his Shabbat, so when he asked for the boys, I told him they were at play. After the havdalah ceremony that evening, I asked him: "Meir, I need your counsel. A man once lent me two jewels, and now he has come to reclaim them. Must I give them back?"

"Of course," Meir replied. "A pledge must be returned to its rightful owner." Then I took him to the boys' room, where they lay lifeless on their beds.

"God gives and God takes away," I cried, my heart breaking. "Blessed be the name of God!"

THE LAWS OF KASHRUT

OUR DAUGHTERS ASK: What's the point of all these laws that regulate what Jews can and can't eat? Are they all still relevant today? Maybe it's time we all became vegetarian!

BERURIAH THE SCHOLAR ANSWERS: The elaborate Jewish dietary system known as kashrut literally means "that which is proper." Here in this parasha, we find a list of forbidden animals, purity laws governing our contact with animals that have died of natural causes, and rules about vessels that hold food. Elsewhere the Torah lists other taboos: against seething a kid in its mother's milk, eating blood, eating from a living or "torn" (*terefah*) animal, and eating produce or meat before it's properly tithed or redeemed.

OUR DAUGHTERS ASK: And what is the meaning of these statutes, laws, and rules, which YHVH our God has commanded us?

MIRIAM THE PROPHET ANSWERS: God has bound us to this demanding discipline so that we can sanctify our community. As it is written: "FOR I AM THE GOD WHO BROUGHT YOU UP FROM THE LAND OF EGYPT TO BE YOUR GOD: YOU SHALL BE HOLY, FOR I AM HOLY" (11:45).

LILITH THE REBEL COUNTERS: I'm not satisfied with this answer! For centuries, both scholars and skeptics have made repeated attempts to rationalize these laws, but they've all failed.

ESTHER THE HIDDEN ONE PROPOSES: That is because the main purpose of these laws is spiritual: to sensitize our hearts, not our minds. Kashrut's taboos teach us how to conduct our lives. So, for instance, we are not to behave like the forbidden animals—pigs, which wallow in filth and eat refuse; shellfish, which scavenge for their food; birds of prey, which attack those weaker than themselves; amphibious and land creatures like reptiles, rodents, and insects, which swarm upon their bellies. And blood too is forbidden, because it is a symbol of life, which we must hallow. Similarly, contact with a dead animal contaminates those who are living. And if we must kill to eat, we must do it consciously, meticulously, humanely. We are not only *what* we eat but also *how* we eat and how we *harvest* life.

OUR MOTHERS ADD: The responsibility for keeping a kosher home has always fallen primarily on our shoulders. We locate the kosher butchers, read the fine print on the labels, stand guard over our many sets of dishes—not to mention the extraordinary efforts we make for Passover. Maintaining the system of kashrut does make us feel spiritual, but it's exhausting!

27. TAZRIA:
Childbirth

(LEVITICUS 12:1–13:59)

ORAH TEACHES: In this parasha, the Torah presents various purity laws concerning childbirth and leprosy. After giving birth, a woman remains ritually impure, for twice as long if she has borne a girl than if she has borne a boy. At the end of this period, she is to bring two offerings: a sin offering and a burnt offering. Other laws and obligations apply to a person afflicted with a leprous skin condition.

THE SPIRITUALITY OF CHILDBIRTH

OUR DAUGHTERS ASK: Does Jewish tradition consider giving birth a religious experience? You'd never know it from this parasha!

THE RABBIS ANSWER: Of course we consider it a religious experience! For in bearing children, women come in intimate contact with divine creation. And because giving birth connects a woman uniquely with both life and death, the Torah subjects her to special laws during this time. So for a week after giving birth to a son and two weeks after bearing a daughter, a new mother remains ritually impure. The Torah compares this period to "THE TIME OF [a woman's] MENSTRUAL INFIRMITY" (12:2), when she is likewise barred from her husband's bed, as well as from certain religious precincts. After this period comes a longer but less restrictive phase, which ends when she brings a sin offering and is declared pure. A woman who bears a daughter remains ritually impure for twice as long as for a newborn son because of the physical differences between the genders. As with all distinctions, this one needs to be marked.

THE SAGES IN OUR OWN TIME EXPLAIN: This double period of quarantine was the Torah's way of acknowledging that a newborn female child would herself become a mother someday and would therefore become a source of blood defilement, like her mother.

LEAH THE NAMER EXPLAINS: The Hebrew phrase that opens and names this parasha—*tazria ve-yaleda*—literally means "BEARS SEED AND GIVES BIRTH" (12:1). The word *tazria* is used in reference to a male child only, not a female. For only a male child will one day "seed" a child himself.

THE RABBIS CONTINUE: After the initial one- or two-week period of separation, the woman is allowed to sleep with her husband again but is still barred from the Sanctuary and from contact with "sacred things" (*kodesh*), such as priestly tithes if she is in a Levitical family. This period is called "blood purification" (*damei toharah*)—literally, "pure blood." Though no longer compared to menstrual discharge, this "birth blood" is still considered a ritual contaminant and therefore is off-limits to sacred things.

OUR DAUGHTERS ASK: This doesn't make any sense. Why, if this blood "contaminates," is it called "pure"?

BERURIAH THE SCHOLAR ANSWERS: Elsewhere in the Torah, notably in the case of the Red Heifer, we find similar examples of this paradox: contact with holiness, perhaps because it is so fraught with the danger of death, makes a person ritually impure. Here the woman, through her newborn, has forded the dangerous birth canal—and survived. Before she rejoins the community, she needs time to recover fully from her near-death experience.

ODD NUMBERS

OUR DAUGHTERS ASK: A woman who's given birth remains ritually impure for thirty-three days (for a boy) and sixty-six days (for a girl). Why these odd numbers?

ESTHER THE HIDDEN ONE ANSWERS: Numbers signify much more than quantity or sequence. They also symbolize completeness, perfection, power, and holiness. They serve as an aid to memory and provide literary structure. Certain numbers—one, two, three, four, five, seven, and ten—are universally acknowledged as significant, because they reflect natural patterns (one sun, two eyes and ears, five and ten fingers, seven days for the four phases of the moon) or perfect geometric shapes (triangles, squares, pyramids). Others are special to Jewish experience: three patriarchs, four matriarchs and the many fours of the Passover seder, the seventh day and sabbatical year, twelve tribes, and the twenty-two letters of the Hebrew alphabet.

BERURIAH THE SCHOLAR ADDS: To understand the numbers thirty-three and sixty-six, which define the "period of blood purification" for a childbearing woman, we need to add to them the days marking the first stage of a woman's impurity after birth—one week (for a boy) or two weeks (for a girl). The numbers then round out to forty (and twice forty), a special Jewish number: the days of rain during the Flood; Isaac's age when he marries Rebecca; the time Moses spends on Sinai; the years in the wilderness; the three periods of Moses' life—he is forty when he flees Egypt, eighty when he confronts Pharaoh, one hundred twenty at death; the days that the scouts spy out the land; the days of Elijah's fast; the years of David's and Solomon's reign; Akiva's age when he begins to study Torah.

THE SAGES IN OUR OWN TIME ADD: Forty is connected to Near Eastern flood cycles, as well as to the appearance of the constellation Pleiades, signaling the end of the winter rains.

WILY REBECCA ADDS: Since this number here is tied to women's cycles of birth, we might want to look for—or if need be write—stories more closely related to women's experience—that is, we might want to "play the numbers" differently.

THE SIN OF GIVING BIRTH

OUR DAUGHTERS ASK: Why is the woman who's given birth required to bring two sacrifices: a sin offering (*hattat*), either a pigeon or a turtledove; and a burnt offering (*olah*), a yearling lamb or, if she can't afford that, a second pigeon or dove. Why a sin offering? What's she done wrong?

LEAH THE NAMER ANSWERS: "Sin" is a mistranslation of the Hebrew *hattat*. It's more accurately translated as "purification."

HULDAH THE PREACHER ELABORATES: The purpose of this offering is not to atone for any wrongdoing but rather to "decontaminate" the woman from the ritual impurity that threatens to endanger others. Only after she brings these to the priest will she be declared "pure" enough to reenter the community.

MIRIAM THE PROPHET ADDS: The Torah calls the blood that flows during this time a source or fountain (*mekor*), a classical feminine image for the many fluids—milk, menstrual and birth blood, tears of joy and sympathy— that flow from women's bodies and sustain others.

PRAYER TO BE RECITED AT THE HOUR OF CHILDBIRTH

MOTHER RACHEL TEACHES: As a woman who lost her life in giving birth to her child, I know full well the dangers and terrors of this process. I therefore invite all women to call upon me for comfort as they labor in childbirth.

AND SO OUR MOTHERS PRAY: God of Hosts, please attend to the pain of Your maidservant. Remember me. Do not forget Your humble servant. Give Your devoted one a child. God of Israel, grant me my desire. As a deer who yearns for the flowing waters in the hour that she comes to give birth: her labor gets harder, and she reaches for You with her antlers. Bitterly she invokes Your mercy, for in Your hands You hold the keys to life. You are merciful and open her womb, tenderly and warmly. So does my soul cry for You, God, and request Your mercy and goodness.

Open the wall of my womb so that I may at the proper time bear this child who is within me—at a time of blessing and salvation. May the child be vital and healthy. May I not struggle only to achieve emptiness, may I not labor in vain, God forbid. Because You alone hold the key to life, as it is written: "AND GOD REMEMBERED RACHEL AND LISTENED TO HER AND OPENED HER WOMB" (Genesis 30:22).

Therefore take pity on my entreaty. From the very depths of my heart I call to You. I raise my voice to You, God. Answer me from the heights of Your holiness. *Selah.*

28. METZORA:
Purity and Danger
(LEVITICUS 14:1–15:33)

TORAH TEACHES: This parasha continues the discussion begun in the previous one, detailing the leprous conditions that render both people and property ritually impure. These descriptions are followed by instructions about appropriate remedies to effect purification. In addition to leprosy, the Torah lists various bodily discharges that place a person in a state of ritual impurity, specifically a man's nocturnal emissions and a woman's menstrual blood. To cleanse themselves of such impurities, affected individuals must cleanse themselves and the material they touch, and bring appropriate sacrifices. Others who come in contact with them likewise become ritually contaminated and must be cleansed.

RITUAL CONTAGION

OUR DAUGHTERS ASK: What's so dangerous about sexual discharges and scaly skin? Why are these people isolated from the community because of their "impurity"?

THE SAGES IN OUR OWN TIME ANSWER: Just as with the blood that accompanies childbirth, the term "impurity" used here is meant as a religious, not a hygienic, term. In the Torah's view, as in many other traditional cultures, when something transgresses the body's threshold, such as discharges from sexual organs or the skin, ritual contagion is thought to occur, and it must be neutralized through isolation, sacrificial atonement, and public ritual.

OUR MOTHERS ADD: In this era of AIDS and our increasing reliance upon medical magic and miracles, we know only too well the fear of contagion—but we have yet to figure out how to *manage* our fear ritually as a community and how to reincorporate diseased individuals into our midst. Until we learn this, we will continue to let fear manage us.

SEX AND IMPURITY

OUR DAUGHTERS ASK: Why does the Torah decree that sex makes us impure? We were taught that Judaism doesn't subscribe to a mind-body split.

BERURIAH THE SCHOLAR ANSWERS: That's right. The Torah does not consider all sex sinful, only those sexual relationships that have been forbidden, such as adultery, incest, and rape. But even permissible sex is seen as temporarily altering the ritual state of those who engage in it, because a man's body discharges semen during intercourse, making both partners ritually impure. After sexual intercourse, both partners must bathe, and their ritual impurity lasts until evening. In this case, it is the man who is the source of contagion: anything or anyone he touches whenever he has a seminal or other emission from his penis—voluntary or involuntary, alone or with a partner—must be cleansed.

THE IMPURITY OF MENSTRUAL BLOOD

OUR DAUGHTERS ASK: Why is a menstruating woman considered "unclean"? As it is written: "WHEN A WOMAN HAS A DISCHARGE, HER DISCHARGE BEING BLOOD FROM HER BODY, SHE SHALL REMAIN IN HER IMPURITY SEVEN DAYS; WHOEVER TOUCHES HER SHALL BE UNCLEAN UNTIL EVENING" (15:19). There's nothing unclean about menstrual blood!

BERURIAH THE SCHOLAR ANSWERS: From ancient rabbis to modern scholars, men have persistently tried to justify and rationalize Judaism's restrictive system of taboos and exclusionary rules governing menstruation. But it's obvious that these laws reflect more than a concern for ritual purity. That's because menstruation represents a unique case. All the other "discharges" that require various degrees of quarantine and purification are either voluntary (sexual intercourse), episodic (childbirth, nocturnal emissions), or abnormal (leprosy, infection, bloody discharges at times outside a woman's menstrual cycle). But menstruation is the only condition that's *ongoing, predictable,* and *a sign of bodily health.* To include this normal physical function with other discharges is to define *all* healthy women as ritually impure for half of all the days during their fertile years.

LILITH THE REBEL BREAKS IN: And that's precisely what the laws of *niddah* do!

THE RABBIS OBJECT: The laws of family purity have clear *psychological* benefits. Many women discover that abstinence indeed makes the heart grow fonder.

LILITH RETORTS: But it also stigmatizes women! And for many, it presents considerable hardship.

THE SAGES IN OUR OWN TIME ADD: Nonetheless, the laws of *niddah* have remained a central part of traditional Jewish observance. We can gain insights into the persistence of this institution if we study similar menstrual taboos in other traditional cultures. What we discover is that they are all motivated by a fear of menstruation's *uncanniness:* How can a woman bleed every month yet remain healthy? All other discharges *weaken* an individual, but menstruation makes a woman fertile, capable of producing new life. Awed and suspicious of such unnatural potency, most societies have cordoned off women during their "bloody times" to protect the community from their dangerous influence.

MENSTRUAL INFIRMITY

OUR DAUGHTERS ASK: The Torah describes the menstruating woman as a *davah*—literally, someone who is weak. Why is a menstruating woman considered *sick?* As it is written: "CONCERNING HER WHO IS IN MENSTRUAL INFIRMITY" (15:33). Is the Torah referring to the physiological side effects of menstruation, like PMS?

OUR BUBBES ANSWER: You see, even back then they knew it was a curse!

LILITH THE REBEL COUNTERS: That's ridiculous! It's more likely that the Torah is trying to reclassify menstruation as an abnormal event, an illness, rather than to acknowledge that bleeding is a normal part of being a woman.

RITUAL TO CELEBRATE A GIRL'S FIRST PERIOD

OUR DAUGHTERS ASK: Why is menstruation such a taboo subject in our culture? Why, when we get our first period, don't we celebrate our coming of age as women, our miraculous potential to bear new life?

SARAH THE ANCIENT SAGE ANSWERS: Menstruation is such an awesome mystery! To men, it is a disturbing riddle: Why do women have to lose lifeblood in order to bestow life? It also shames men, because it makes them aware of their own limited power to create. For women, it is something altogether different. Menarche awakens women to their vulnerability—to men, to dependence, to their future choices. They are afraid of being expelled from the garden of innocence. They fear being betrayed by forbidden fruit.

One of our mothers, Phyllis Berman, offers the following ritual she once performed with her daughter, Morissa Scher, and some of their women friends to celebrate Morissa's first period. Coming together in a circle beneath the moon, which monthly waxes and wanes like a woman's cycle, they shared bread and wine, song and wisdom, ritual gesture and silence. Phyllis teaches:

"We bring the ordinary into holy consciousness through ceremony/service/celebration. By moving a life moment from its private enclosure, often clouded with secrecy, fear, shame, and curse, we confront these feelings that have lived for generations within us and replace them with pride in the miraculous workings of our body. For many of us who have grown up with ambivalent messages from our mothers and grandmothers, this affirming message does not come so easily to pass on to our daughters. . . .

"As Jews, we symbolically give our children the Torah as their inheritance/path of life upon their bat/bar mitzvah. So upon menstruation, I called upon the women in the circle to hand down to Morissa a teaching that had come from their own or other people's woman-experience. . . .

"I said—with some trepidation—that while she was still too young for my message, I welcomed her to a time when her mind and heart would catch up with her body and she would be able to experience—as I have—the sheer pleasure of living in a woman's body."

THE CLEVER WIFE

OUR MOTHERS RECOUNT: How often in women's lives are they forbidden to men! When they menstruate, when they give birth, when their blood flows unexpectedly. For some women, this time of separateness is a gift; for others, it is a time of great loneliness. As it is told:

Once, a king held a contest to choose a new queen. But he decreed that his new wife must be prepared never to see her family again. Despite this cruel demand, many beautiful young women vied for the crown, and one was finally chosen. But immediately after the wedding, the king abandoned his new bride to attend to distant matters of state. Within a few months, the young queen pined away and died of loneliness. The king soon remarried, but the same thing happened. And so it went for years, the king burying queen after queen.

Then an only daughter announced to her parents that she wished to become the next queen. Her parents tried to dissuade her, but she promised them that she would see them again once she became queen. Because she was so graceful and charming, she was the one the king chose. But soon after their wedding, he abandoned her, as he had all her predecessors. Bored, she took a goatskin, blew it up, dressed it in men's clothing, and spent her days having lively conversations with the doll. When the king returned, months later, he was astonished to find her not only alive but well and happy.

Convinced that she was being unfaithful to him, the king ordered her watched, but his spies found no evidence that she had a lover. So one night, the king himself watched her through a hole he drilled in her bedroom wall. Sure enough, he observed her talking with a strange man. Enraged, he burst into the room, his dagger drawn, and stabbed the goatskin doll through the heart. Blood poured forth from the wound.

The young queen cried: "Behold—here is my sorrow and my loneliness! For if I had not unburdened my heart to this doll, I would have died like all the rest!"

Suddenly understanding what he had done, the king begged his wife's forgiveness and revoked his cruel decree. And so the queen kept her promise and saw her parents again.

29. AKHAREI MOT:

Sexual Boundaries

(LEVITICUS 16:1–18:30)

TORAH TEACHES: This parasha begins with the "Holiness Code," a kind of "handbook" of Levitical law and practice. The first section is a description of the Atonement Ritual of the High Priest, when the holiest man in the community enters the Holy of Holies in the Tabernacle (later, the Jerusalem Temple), the holiest room in the holiest dwelling, to make expiation for the people's sins. As part of this ritual, the High Priest dons special clothing and sacrifices two sin offerings, a bull to atone for himself and a goat to atone for the people. With blood from both animals, he then "cleanses" the Tabernacle and the altar.

The goat that is sacrificed is one of a pair donated by the community. By lot, one is designated to be slaughtered, the other to be the "scapegoat," bearing the people's sins off into the wilderness of Azazel.

After this description, the people, who now stand poised between two foreign cultures—Egypt and Canaan—are admonished to reject the pagan ways of both: in this case, inappropriate sexual conduct and child sacrifice to the Canaanite god Molech.

THE RITUAL OF THE SCAPEGOAT

THE SAGES IN OUR OWN TIME EXPLAIN: Azazel was a goat-demon, a popular mythological figure in the ancient world. According to the apocryphal Book of Enoch, the angel Raphael, in order to punish Azazel, along with several other angels, for sleeping with the "daughters of men," banished him to the desert. From this outpost he controlled acts of harlotry, war, and sorcery. Using "sympathetic magic"—that is, fighting fire with fire—the High Priest would dispatch the sin-laden goat once each year to cancel the goat-demon's sinful influence on the people.

THE RABBIS ADD: We learn in the Mishnah that a priest was appointed to accompany the goat to make sure it did not return to inhabited lands; later, it was driven off a cliff.

MIRIAM THE PROPHET SUGGESTS: Although nowadays we only *read* about this ritual as part of the Yom Kippur liturgy, we might consider—given our experience as a people, and as Jewish women in particular—designating during this period our own totem figures: symbolic images, words, or objects that we could release against those demonic forces that scapegoat us or encourage us to stray.

DINAH THE WOUNDED ONE DECLARES: Imagine how liberating it would be to exorcise the stereotype of the JAP (Jewish American Princess) from popular culture. Or our own internalized anti-Semitism, which makes us hate our own bodies, our names, our men, and ourselves. How healthy it would be to drive these demons off a nearby cliff!

THE PARADOX OF BLOOD

OUR DAUGHTERS ASK: How can blood both purify and defile?

THE SAGES IN OUR OWN DAY ANSWER: In most cultures, blood signifies opposites—both life and death, danger and protection, purity and defilement.

BERURIAH THE SCHOLAR ELABORATES: In the Yom Kippur ritual, blood plays a dual role. It purifies the altar, Tabernacle, and Holy of Holies, but at the same time it contaminates anyone who comes in contact with it. Such ritual impurity—which is unavoidable in the carrying out of certain holy activities—can simply be washed away with water. But it's different with *blood guilt*, which occurs when someone intentionally sins, as by sacrificing an animal at an unauthorized altar or by eating blood. The penalty for such unholy acts is *karet*—literally, to be "cut off" from the people. Such punishment is meted out by God, when and how God wills. To a religious community like this one, such punishment was essentially a death sentence.

OUR DAUGHTERS ASK: Why is blood considered so off limits?

HULDAH THE PREACHER ANSWERS: The blood of animal sacrifice *takes the place* of human life. To eat or spill it improperly cancels this substitution and requires that human life be paid in its stead. As it is written: "FOR THE LIFE OF THE FLESH IS IN THE BLOOD, AND I HAVE ASSIGNED IT TO YOU FOR MAKING EXPIATION FOR YOUR LIVES UPON THE ALTAR; IT IS THE BLOOD, AS LIFE, THAT EFFECTS EXPIATION" (17:11). To use blood for any other purposes, especially at an idolatrous altar, is to forfeit your life.

THE PRACTICES OF EGYPT

BERURIAH THE SCHOLAR TEACHES: The Torah forbids us to "COPY THE PRACTICES OF EGYPT" (18:2). It then lists in careful detail every sexual liaison forbidden to Israelite men, including incest, adultery, bestiality, male homosexuality, and sexual contact with a menstruating woman. The only taboo specifically addressed to women is sexual intercourse with a beast.

OUR DAUGHTERS ASK: Why are these particular practices forbidden to the Israelites?

HAGAR THE STRANGER ANSWERS: Because it's what their neighbors did! The pharaohs in my own country, for instance, used to marry their own sisters and mothers. And in many pagan cults, wild sexual rites were performed, involving many of these forbidden couplings.

LILITH THE REBEL INTERJECTS: At least, that's what the Torah says. I wouldn't be surprised if the Israelites had some wild parties of their own!

HULDAH THE PREACHER INTERJECTS: Ever since its founding, Judaism has scrupulously regulated the sexual behavior of its followers. Living among so many different cultures, Jews have come to appreciate the costs and wages of sexual license and have chosen to pay a different piper.

SERAKH BAT ASHER THE HISTORIAN ADDS: Whereas the mighty ancient civilizations of Egypt, Babylonia, Canaan, Greece, and Rome have since gone bankrupt.

FORBIDDEN WIVES AND PARTNERS

BERURIAH THE SCHOLAR TEACHES: Because men in ancient Israelite society were permitted multiple wives and concubines, the relational web of each family was more complex than in the simple nuclear family and therefore more likely to become tangled. This section of Leviticus lists all the female blood relatives who are considered sexually off-limits to an Israelite man. Forbidden are a man's own mother and his father's other wives; his sisters, half-sisters, and stepsisters; his granddaughters; his maternal and paternal aunts; his daughters-in-law and sisters-in-law; sexual relations with a woman *and* her daughter; marriage to two sisters. Curiously, the one blood relative who is not explicitly prohibited is a man's own *daughter* (although it has been argued that such a ban must be assumed, given the closeness of this relationship).

HULDAH THE PREACHER COMMENTS: In setting these boundaries, the Torah here defines *incest* more broadly than some of its earlier narratives do. In Genesis, for instance, Abraham marries his half-sister Sarah, and Jacob marries two sisters. In Exodus, Moses' father, Amram, marries his aunt Yokheved.

THE RABBIS EXPLAIN: These marriages are permitted because they occurred *before* Moses received the Torah at Sinai.

THE SAGES IN OUR OWN TIME COUNTER: A rabbinic fairy tale! We suspect that either this Levitical text was written much later than the Genesis stories (sexual mores having changed); or that the tales or the legal text—maybe even both—were based on *constructed*, not actual, reality. Since we have no other Israelite documents from biblical times (outside of *comparative* cultural documents), we don't know for sure which laws were obeyed and which breached, which rules reflect common practice and which only the ideal of common practice.

DINAH THE WOUNDED ONE REMARKS: The Israelite family was clearly defined by its sexual boundaries. Such taboos were obviously meant to protect the women within the family from precisely those males who had easiest sexual access to them. In a society in which women had so little power and autonomy, such protection should have allowed them to sleep peacefully at night.

OUR MOTHERS MUSE: As blended families become more common in our society, we're discovering that our own relational webs are becoming increasingly more complex. Maybe we should reexamine and revise our definition of incest—so our own daughters can sleep peacefully at night.

THE KINSHIP OF WOMEN

OUR DAUGHTERS ASK: Why does the Torah include in its list of forbidden women not only a man's female relatives but his *wife's* relatives as well—her mother, sisters (while his wife is still alive), daughters, and granddaughters? As it is written: "THEY ARE KINDRED; IT IS DEPRAVITY [*zimmah*]" (18:17). In the case of two sisters, an additional reason is given: "DO NOT MARRY A WOMAN AS A RIVAL TO HER SISTER" (18:18).

MOTHER RACHEL TEACHES: In forbidding such marriages, our tradition displays admirable insight into human psychology. For by setting up these boundaries, the Torah protects a married woman's precious sphere of female relationships, what we might today call her "support network"—that is, her intimate family. These relationships are to remain inviolate from sexual competition; once a woman is married, her female relatives are to serve her as allies, not rivals.

LEAH ADDS: If only Rachel and I had been so fortunate!

ADULTERY

THE RABBIS TEACH: The seventh commandment—YOU SHALL NOT COMMIT ADULTERY (Exodus 20:13; Deuteronomy 5:17)—is defined very specifically in the Torah and later Jewish law. In this parasha, we are told . . .

LILITH INTERRUPTS: Speak for yourself!

THE RABBIS CONTINUE: It is written: "DO NOT HAVE CARNAL RELATIONS WITH YOUR NEIGHBOR'S WIFE" (18:20). Thus, to be considered adulterous, sex has to involve a *married* (or betrothed) *woman*. But if an *unmarried* woman sleeps with a man, whether married or not, neither is considered guilty of adultery. (In fact, at one time we considered such an act tantamount to betrothal.) This law is designed to ensure that a married woman's children are legitimate, sprouted from the seed of her husband. Children born out of wedlock—that is, to unmarried women—are not a threat to a man's property or name. But children born illegitimately *within* wedlock—that is, to *married* women—are. Therefore the Jewish definition of bastard—*mamzer*—covers only children born of *forbidden* unions—adultery (as here defined), incest (as defined above), or prohibited marriages (such as that between a priest and a divorcée). Children born simply "without benefit of clergy"—to unmarried women, concubines, prostitutes, slaves, and captives—are not considered bastards, although they obviously have a lower social status.

DINAH THE WOUNDED ONE ADDS: One wonders whether that gives much solace to their mothers.

HOMOSEXUALITY

OUR DAUGHTERS ASK: Why does the Torah forbid male homosexuality and label it an "abomination" (*to'evah*)? As it is written: "DO NOT LIE WITH A MAN AS ONE LIES WITH A WOMAN" (18:22).

LILITH THE REBEL RETORTS: Perhaps because the Torah wants them to lie together "as one lies with a man"!

THE RABBIS ANSWER: Men should not lie with men because that's what the Canaanites do. Such behavior was practiced by the wicked men of Sodom, by sacred pagan male prostitutes, called *kedeshim*, and by common male prostitutes. In the Talmud, we provide three reasons for this taboo: such acts pervert nature, prevent procreation, and threaten family life by robbing women of their husbands.

OUR DAUGHTERS OBJECT: Don't heterosexuals often choose not to have children?

THE RABBIS ANSWER: Voluntary childlessness is not acceptable to us! But neither is the death penalty decreed here in the Torah for homosexual behavior. Therefore, in the Talmud, we lowered the penalty to flagellation, which in time changed to social censure and ostracism.

OUR MOTHERS CONTINUE: And in recent years, many liberal Jews, including many rabbis, have challenged Judaism's traditionally hostile stance toward homosexuality. In America today, there are gay rabbis and a growing number of gay synagogues.

OUR DAUGHTERS ASK: Why isn't lesbianism mentioned anywhere in the Bible? Does Judaism permit sexual love between women?

THE RABBIS ANSWER: Although the Torah doesn't specifically mention lesbianism, we later included it within the general category of homosexuality.

OUR DAUGHTERS ASK: But why does the Torah totally ignore the topic of sex between women? Was such behavior unheard of? Was it a secret restricted to women? Was it practiced but considered harmless? Or was it quietly condoned as necessary in a polygamous culture?

MOTHER RACHEL ANSWERS: What do men know about the love between women!

THE SAGES IN OUR OWN TIME ADD: For the Bible and the Rabbis, what concerned them about sex was not who was sleeping with whom (although they obviously opposed illicit sexual behavior) but who was *engendering* whom.

BESTIALITY

OUR DAUGHTERS ASK: Of all the sexual taboos, why is only one—sexual intercourse with animals—addressed to women as well as men? As it is written: "LET NO WOMAN LEND HERSELF TO A BEAST" (18:23). Were women especially attracted to animals in that culture?

HULDAH THE PREACHER ANSWERS: It is forbidden to mix together that which nature has set apart. That is why we must not yoke oxen and donkeys together, blend wool and linen, or sow mixed grains. So too human beings, both men and women, must not cross the biological lines defining species.

LILITH ADDS: In ancient Israel, cattle and other farm animals were usually stabled on the first floor of houses; families lived above them on the second. In such close quarters, was it any wonder that all sorts of lines were frequently crossed?

THE MOUSE SEEKS A WIFE

OUR MOTHERS RECOUNT: How often we seek precisely those partners who are most inappropriate for us! As it is told:

Once a mouse wished to be married, but he refused to take a wife from his own kind. So he went to the sun and asked for her hand in marriage.

But the sun refused him: "Why marry me? The cloud always darkens my face and eclipses my beauty. You would do better to marry the cloud."

But the cloud also declined his suit, saying, "The wind blows me back and forth across the face of the earth. If you marry me, you too will be a wanderer. No, you would do well to marry the wind."

So the mouse went to the wind. But she also rebuffed his proposal. "My breath is powerless against the wall," she argued. "It is the wall you should marry."

"Surely you mock me," said the wall when the mouse proposed to her, "for see how the mice have pierced my sides with a hundred holes. If you wish a worthy bride, go marry a mouse."

And so the mouse returned home and married one of his own kind. And his heart and hers leapt with joy.

30. KEDOSHIM:

Holiness

(LEVITICUS 19:1–20:27)

ORAH TEACHES: This parasha consists primarily of laws governing social, economic, sexual, and ritual behavior. These laws mandate: (1) *protecting the weaker members of society*—leaving gleanings for the poor and the stranger, respecting the disabled, not selling one's daughter as a prostitute, honoring the elderly, respecting strangers; (2) *ensuring social stability and justice*—honoring parents, shunning theft and deceit, observing fair labor practices, safeguarding judicial fairness, maintaining social harmony and sexual boundaries, protecting property, keeping honest weights and measures; (3) *preserving religious orthodoxy*—keeping the Sabbath, rejecting idolatry and child sacrifice, observing dietary restrictions on sacrifices, honoring God's name, refraining from eating blood, shunning magical practices, avoiding bodily disfiguration, rejecting traffic with ghosts; and (4) *respecting the natural order*—preserving distinctions between species of livestock, grain, and clothing, refraining from harvesting new fruit trees for four years.

Taken as a whole, these laws lay the foundation for a just society.

THE LAWS OF HOLINESS

MIRIAM THE PROPHET PROCLAIMS: We are commanded: "YOU SHALL BE HOLY, FOR I, YHVH YOUR GOD, AM HOLY" (19:2). Therefore we need to define for ourselves what is most sacred and most redemptive, to imagine what would make our world perfect and whole—and naming that "God," we should go out to bless the image of this God in everyone we meet.

THE RABBIS ADD: So comprehensive and central is this parasha in defining Jewish norms that the Midrash considers it parallel to the Ten Commandments, worthy of being read aloud to the people to teach them how to behave.

THE CONSEQUENCES OF UNHOLY BEHAVIOR

BERURIAH THE SCHOLAR TEACHES: Two different kinds of punishment face people who act in unholy ways: penalties enforced by the community, principally the death penalty; and those enforced by God, principally excommunication, *karet*—literally, "being cut off"—which can take the form of direct heavenly punishment, delayed punishment (through one's children), barrenness, or social ostracism.

THE RABBIS ELABORATE: The death penalty is decreed for those who worship Molech; consult with ghosts and familiar spirits; insult their parents; commit adultery; commit incest with their father's wife, their daughter-in-law, or a mother and her daughter; engage in male homosexuality; or couple with beasts. Those who commit incest with their sister, or their mother's or father's sister, or have intercourse with a menstruating woman, suffer *karet*. And those who worship Molech or consult ghosts and familiar spirits bring upon themselves the double curse of death and *karet*. The penalty facing a man for sleeping with his uncle's wife or marrying his brother's wife is childlessness.

OUR DAUGHTERS ASK: Why do some forms of illicit sex warrant execution, others excommunication, and still others barrenness?

LILITH THE REBEL ANSWERS: The way each society metes out its punishments reveals as much about that society's social hierarchies and power relations as do its laws.

OUR MOTHERS REMARK: Although our tradition no longer recognizes the divine agency of *karet*, we still experience its effects. People guilty of breaking social taboos are usually cut off by others. Many also suffer psychic punishment when they violate society's or their own norms of behavior. And our children often visit our sins upon us or leave us barren of joy.

THE CASE OF THE BETROTHED FEMALE SLAVE

BERURIAH THE SCHOLAR TEACHES: If an Israelite man bought a virgin Israelite woman as a slave—usually from her poor father, who was forced to sell her out of desperation—he had certain obligations toward her. Because she was still marriageable, he had to either marry her himself, betroth her to his son, or marry her to another. But if another man violated her before the marriage could take place, she was considered "spoiled." In this case, her master had to forfeit the money pledged to him as the bride-price and continue support-ing her in his own household. However, since the woman was a slave, not a free woman, her violator had merely to pay her master a fine and bring a guilt of-fering. The slave woman received only the guarantee of continued room and board.

HULDAH THE PREACHER ADDS: Thus, once betrothed, the woman was much more valuable to her master intact, if for no other reason than that he stood to lose money and gain a lifelong dependent if she was deflowered. Al-though the motivation may have been base, the effect was to safeguard the woman and give her a chance for happiness.

MUTILATING THE BODY

HULDAH THE PREACHER TEACHES: We are commanded not to scar our flesh, neither to mourn nor to rejoice, neither to attract nor to repel others. As it is written: "YOU SHALL NOT MAKE GASHES IN YOUR FLESH FOR THE DEAD, OR INCISE ANY MARKS ON YOURSELVES" (19:28). For our body is holy and must be treated with respect.

OUR MOTHERS EXCLAIM: How it pains us to see our children disfig-ure themselves with piercings and with scars! It's as if they're offering them-selves as clean walls on which life can carve its graffiti or as wounds in need of lancing.

OUR DAUGHTERS ADD: Or as armor against the cruelties of the world, which so often camouflage themselves as love.

NECROMANCY

OUR DAUGHTERS ASK: From ancient times until our own, people have been fascinated by the magical arts—sorcery, white and black magic, divining (reading palms, stars, entrails, tea leaves), number magic, and communing with spirits. Why is the Torah so insistent about avoiding contact with "GHOSTS AND FAMILIAR SPIRITS" (20:6)?

LILITH THE REBEL ANSWERS: Twice in this chapter, the Torah for-bids seeking out such supernatural spirits. The penalties for disobeying are quite tough: death by stoning *and* excommunication, presumably of the family members who survive. So much hostility usually indicates that there's plenty of reason for it—in other words, communicating with ghosts must have been rather popular among the people. Or the priestly authorities must have greatly feared those who conjured spirits.

HULDAH THE PREACHER RECOUNTS: The most famous biblical episode involving necromancy is King Saul's secret conversation with the prophet Samuel's ghost, conjured up by the Witch of Endor. Ironically, because Saul himself had banned such witchcraft, he was forced to seek "A WOMAN WHO CONSULTS GHOSTS" (I Samuel 28:7) in secret.

MIRIAM THE PROPHET ADDS: Women of all cultures have traditionally been subject to fear and persecution as witches and those intimate with spirits. So it is likely that this particular biblical taboo, repeated here three times within thirty-four verses, is directed explicitly at strong women whose spiritual leadership threatens patriarchal authority. Believe me, I know!

CHILD SACRIFICE

OUR DAUGHTERS ASK: We know that child sacrifice was widely practiced in the ancient world—in Mesopotamia, Palestine, and Greece as well as in Mesoamerica. Were the Israelites the only ones to repudiate such rituals?

THE RABBIS ANSWER: From its beginnings, official Judaism has demonstrated an abhorrence of such practices. The Akedah, the story of the binding of Isaac, is the Torah's polemic against child sacrifice.

HULDAH THE PREACHER BREAKS IN: But according to the Bible itself, at least two Judean kings in the seventh century B.C.E.—Manasseh and Amon—supported cults that practiced child sacrifice by passing children through fire. In my own day, not long after their reigns, Josiah, the great reformer king of Judah, acted to honor the commandment set forth in this parasha: "THAT NO ONE MIGHT CONSIGN HIS SON OR DAUGHTER TO THE FIRE OF MOLECH" (23:10). He utterly destroyed the abominable altar they had set up in the Valley of Ben-hinnom outside the walls of Jerusalem.

LEAH THE NAMER ADDS: This detested spot appropriately inspired the Hebrew name for hell: *Gehinnom*—that is, Valley of Hinnom.

OUR MOTHERS CONCLUDE: Today we have renamed this place Auschwitz.

THE LAW OF FOREIGN NATIONS

OUR DAUGHTERS ASK: Why does the Torah command us to be different from our neighbors? As it is written: "YOU SHALL NOT FOLLOW THE PRACTICES OF THE NATION THAT I AM DRIVING OUT BEFORE YOU" (20:23). Being different from our neighbors has usually gotten us into trouble.

THE RABBIS ANSWER: This law is designed to keep Jews from assimilating into the cultures in which they have lived. To that end, we long ago developed the principle known as *Hukkat Ha-Goi*, "Law of the [Foreign] Nation," based on this verse from Leviticus. Traditionally, we have shown our differences from other nations by looking or acting as inverse images of our neighbors. Therefore, at various times throughout our history, we have worn distinctive Jewish dress; and at other times, gentiles themselves have imposed such demands upon us—for the very same reason. Yet once we left the confines of the ghetto, most of us took on the dress of our neighbors.

SERAKH BAT ASHER THE HISTORIAN POINTS OUT: And sometimes we've held on to distinctive Jewish costume long after gentile styles or restrictions have changed. Then we set ourselves apart not only from other peoples but even from most of our own.

31. EMOR:
Separateness

(LEVITICUS 21:1–24:23)

ORAH TEACHES: This parasha sets out elaborate details about the role and obligations of the priests. Following these are laws concerning the observance of holy days, including the Sabbath and the New Moon, as well as laws concerning the sacred oil and breads used in the Tabernacle. The parasha concludes with an incident involving a blasphemer, who curses God's name and is punished by divine decree.

MAKING BREAD

BERURIAH THE SCHOLAR TEACHES: In the desert Sanctuary and later in the Jerusalem Temple, bread played a vital part in cult ritual. Each week, twelve special loaves, called *lekhem panim*, "showbreads"—literally, "bread of the face"—were baked and displayed on a table in the Sanctuary, then later eaten by the priests. One of the principal sacrifices was the *minhah*, consisting of unleavened cakes (since leaven was forbidden on the altar), made of fine wheat or barley flour mixed with oil and frankincense, then baked, pan fried or deep fried, and salted. Leavened breads were presented to the priests on other occasions.

THE SAGES IN OUR OWN TIME ELABORATE: In the ancient Near East, bread, *lekhem*, consisted of baked wheat or barley (and probably spelt) cakes. Barley was usually eaten in early summer, since it ripened earlier than wheat. Leavened bread was called *hametz*; unleavened bread, *matzah*. Choicer bread was sometimes made of semolina, the hard inner heart of wheat grains. The kneaded dough was baked on coals or in ovens, in the kitchen or in portable field ovens (during harvest seasons). It is likely that the Israelites learned how to make leavened bread from the Egyptians, who were great bakers (as well as brewers).

SARAH THE ANCIENT ONE RECOUNTS: When three unannounced guests appeared at my door, I prepared for them *ugot*, "cakes" made of fine flour baked directly on coals or heated stones and covered with ashes.

THE RABBIS ADD: That is why the Book of Proverbs praises the "GOOD WIFE," *eshet hayil,* because she "DOES NOT EAT THE BREAD OF IDLENESS" (31:27).

SARAH ADDS: Of course not—she's too busy baking!

HOW HARD IT IS TO BE A PRIEST

MIRIAM THE PROPHET DECLARES: It's hard enough to be a Levite, following the strict rules of holiness—but to be a *kohen* is twice as hard! For a priest is forbidden to come in contact with death, except for his *immediate* family . . .

THE SAGES IN OUR OWN TIME INTERRUPT: A taboo probably designed to distance the Israelite priesthood from the cults of death worship, so prevalent in the ancient world, especially in Egypt . . .

MIRIAM CONTINUES: And high priests can't attend *any* funerals. And so, when our father, Amram, died not long after we left Egypt, my poor brother Aaron couldn't even attend his burial, while I, both because I am a woman and because I married into the tribe of Judah, was by my old mother's side to bury him.

THE RABBIS INTERJECT: Even though the Torah forbids a *kohen* to bury anyone who is not a *blood* relative, even his own wife, we have had compassion on *kohanim* and have overruled this taboo. For in some cases, a husband may be his wife's only close relative and so must be allowed to attend to her burial. Of course, we have not gone so far as to overturn the Torah's rules on which women a priest may marry, since we recognize that holy men must have holy wives. So we have continued to bar them from marrying harlots and divorcées.

OUR MOTHERS OBJECT: This rule is no longer valid, because a divorced woman is no longer by definition an unfaithful wife. You yourselves have greatly expanded the grounds for divorce beyond a wife's infidelity.

THE RABBIS COUNTER: But if we overrule all laws that are no longer valid, nothing holy will remain!

DINAH THE WOUNDED ONE CHALLENGES: But how can the Torah call holy the treatment of a priest's daughter who trespasses sexually? For it is written: "WHEN THE DAUGHTER OF A PRIEST DEGRADES HERSELF THROUGH HARLOTRY, IT IS HER FATHER WHOM SHE DEGRADES; SHE SHALL BE PUT TO THE FIRE" (21:9). How is this any different from Molech worship?

THE SAGES IN OUR OWN TIME EXPLAIN: In most traditional cultures, a daughter is the most protected—and accordingly the most restricted—member of a family. Because she represents part of her father's estate, he would rather forfeit his property than surrender it to another. And because she also represents her father's honor, something especially precious to priests, he hopes to regain that honor by sacrificing her, thereby exorcising his own shame.

DINAH RETORTS: I rest my case!

MOTHER LOVE AMONG THE FLOCKS

OUR DAUGHTERS ASK: Why are we commanded not to kill a young animal until it's eight days old? As it is written: "IT SHALL STAY SEVEN DAYS WITH ITS MOTHER" (22:27). What difference does that make to the dead animal or its mother?

THE RABBIS ANSWER: Many of the Torah's laws about the treatment of animals are ethical "object lessons" for us. Thus we are not to consume blood, so that we learn to sanctify life; we are not to eat certain animals that scavenge or kill for food, so that we shun such behavior; we are not to tear food from living animals, so that we avoid inflicting unnecessary pain; we are not to eat from food that has not been tithed or shared with the needy, so that we acknowledge the true Source of our sustenance and act justly. And in this parasha, we are commanded that "NO ANIMAL FROM THE HERD OR FROM THE FLOCK SHALL BE SLAUGHTERED ON THE SAME DAY WITH ITS YOUNG" (22:28).

MOTHER RACHEL ADDS: From the days of the Garden of Eden until Noah's generation, human beings did not eat animal flesh, but after the Great Flood, our lust for meat grew so great that God permitted us to kill and eat other creatures, but only if we did so with mindfulness and discipline. Since animal mothers, like human ones, love their young, we should spare them unnecessary distress by taking away their young too soon after birth or by allowing the mothers to see them die. Two other laws—the prohibition against seething a kid in its mother's milk and the commandment to send away a mother bird before taking her eggs—are likewise intended as models of compassionate behavior.

THE BLASPHEMING SON OF SHELOMIT

OUR DAUGHTERS ASK: In the middle of this extensive list of ritual laws, we unexpectedly encounter a grisly story: A "half Israelite" (his father is

Egyptian) gets into a fight with another Israelite and "PRONOUNCES THE NAME IN BLASPHEMY" (24:11). God sentences the offender—and anyone else who blasphemes—to death by stoning, to be carried out by the community outside the camp. Why is the blasphemer identified only by his mother's name: "THE SON OF SHELOMIT THE DAUGHTER OF DIBRI OF THE TRIBE OF DAN" (24:11)? Why do both he and his father remain nameless?

THE RABBIS ANSWER: The blasphemer's father was none other than the Egyptian taskmaster whom Moses had killed for beating a Hebrew slave. The name of the dead slave's wife was Shelomit. The night before her husband died, Shelomit had been raped by this same Egyptian. Her bastard son's sin of blasphemy is her fault, because her very name reveals that she was a harlot who greeted all men with open arms and a warm greeting of "Shalom."

LEAH THE NAMER COUNTERS: Utterly preposterous! Her name means "Woman of Peace," the daughter of "Divri," a version of the "Word of God." You yourselves acknowledge that she was raped.

DINAH THE WOUNDED ONE CRIES: Don't blame the victim!

THE SAGES IN OUR OWN TIME SUGGEST: That the priestly book of Leviticus identifies her as a Danite may reflect the fact that in later centuries, the temple of Dan in northern Israel was one of the sites of a rival cult, where a golden calf was set up by the rebel king Jeroboam.

32. BEHAR:
Community

(LEVITICUS 25:1–26:2)

TORAH TEACHES: This parasha presents the laws concerning the observance of the sabbatical and jubilee years. The Israelites are commanded to give their fields and vineyards "A COMPLETE REST" every seventh year, eating only what grows from the uncultivated ground. After seven sabbaticals—that is, in the fiftieth year—the Israelites are commanded to "PROCLAIM LIBERTY THROUGHOUT THE LAND FOR ALL ITS INHABITANTS." On Yom Kippur of that year, the shofar is to be sounded, announcing the jubilee "year of release," during which all tribal lands are to return to their original borders and all slaves are to go free.

SABBATICALS AND JUBILEES

OUR DAUGHTERS ASK: Are sabbatical and jubilee years intended for Israelite women as well as men?

HULDAH THE PREACHER ANSWERS: Yes, God addresses both men and women concerning these laws. *Every* Israelite is to observe them, as it is written: "YOU, YOUR MALE AND FEMALE SLAVES" (25:6). During the sabbatical year, all Israelites are to cease cultivating their fields and vineyards in order to allow "A YEAR OF COMPLETE REST FOR THE LAND" (25:4).

BERURIAH THE SCHOLAR ELABORATES: What's especially remarkable about Israelite sabbatical law is its progressive *social framework*. We can see this most clearly in the laws governing the jubilee, the *seventh* sabbatical year. Every fiftieth year, all of Israelite society is to return to its original tribal borders, and no Israelite is to remain indentured or in debt.

LEAH THE NAMER ADDS: The term "jubilee" comes from the Hebrew word *yovel*, meaning ram's horn, since blasts of the ram's horn were to inaugurate this special year.

OUR DAUGHTERS ASK: But are women supposed to be included in the redistribution of wealth? Or does God address only the men this time, as it is written: "EACH MAN [*ish*] SHALL RETURN TO HIS HOLDING" (25:10)?

THE SAGES IN OUR OWN TIME ANSWER: For the most part, the mechanism of the sabbatical and jubilee years merely restored the *status quo ante.* Since women didn't tend to own property, they couldn't regain what was never theirs to lose. But women did participate actively in the economic life of the country, so they certainly benefited from the year off from agricultural labor, as well as from the jubilee year's release from personal or family debt.

OUR BUBBES OBJECT: But how could they ever enjoy time off? Who else was going to take care of the children, prepare the meals, weave the clothing, tend the house, and deliver babies?

OUR DAUGHTERS ADD: Think of all the untapped potential still remaining in this ancient model of social reengineering!

THE GIFT OF SEVEN YEARS

OUR MOTHERS TEACH: We are all responsible for each other—those who have for those who have not, those who own for those who are owned, those who gain for those who lose. As it is told:

Once, a rich man lost all that he had. To support his family, he became a day laborer, working hard from dawn until dusk. One day, Elijah appeared to him disguised as an Arab and told him that he was destined to be blessed with a gift of seven prosperous years. "Do you want them now or at the end of your life?" Elijah asked him.

"I will ask my wife for advice," the man replied. And he ran home and told his wife what had happened.

"Ask for them now," his wife said, "for if we ask for them at the end of our lives, we will know that we have but seven years to live." And he did exactly what his wife advised.

That day, his children uncovered a chest of gold coins while they were digging in their yard.

"Let us use this gift wisely," advised his wife. And so they shared their good fortune generously with those less fortunate.

At the end of seven years, Elijah returned to take back his gift.

"When you first appeared," the man told Elijah, "I asked my wife for advice, and I would like to do the same again before returning the gift to you."

And when he asked his wife what he should do, she said, "Tell him that if he can find another couple who have used such a gift more wisely than we have, he can have his treasure back."

And though Elijah traveled from one end of the earth to the other, he failed to find two more generous people. And so he never reclaimed his gift, and the couple lived to a ripe old age, opening their hands to all in need until the day they died.

SLAVERY

OUR DAUGHTERS ASK: How can the Torah condone slavery when we ourselves were once slaves? Although God warns the people not to enslave permanently any other Israelite, "FOR THEY ARE MY SERVANTS, WHOM I FREED FROM THE LAND OF EGYPT" (25:42), the Torah voices no such scruples about *non-Israelite* slaves. As it is written: "IT IS FROM THE NATIONS ROUND ABOUT YOU THAT YOU MAY ACQUIRE MALE AND FEMALE SLAVES" (25:44). Isn't this hypocritical?

HAGAR THE EGYPTIAN SLAVE ANSWERS: Indeed it is! When it came to slavery, the Israelites were no different than any of their neighbors. They regarded slaves like me as nothing but property, to be bought, sold, and passed down to their children.

SERAKH BAT ASHER THE HISTORIAN ADDS: Long after Israel lay in ruins, its people exiled to strange lands, where they were sometimes no better off than slaves; and long after Christianity had abandoned much of Jewish law, this "peculiar institution" of slavery remained in the legal inventory of Western cultural institutions. How quickly we forget where we came from.

33. BEKHUKOTAI:

Among the Ruins of History

(LEVITICUS 26:3–27:34)

ORAH TEACHES: After presenting these last ten chapters of communal laws, known collectively as the "Holiness Code," Leviticus concludes with a promise and a threat: If Israel obeys these laws, God will bring peace and prosperity to the land and its inhabitants. But if Israel fails to uphold God's commandments, disaster will follow: famine, disease, wild beasts, wholesale devastation, and exile. Then the land will at last enjoy the sabbaths denied it by its people, and the repentant people will return to God, who will renew the ancient covenant with them.

FORESHADOWING THE DESTRUCTION

OUR DAUGHTERS ASK: Moses warns the people that terrible things will happen if they fail to uphold God's laws of holiness: They'll face ruin and destruction, and the nations of the world will crush them between the millstones of history. As it is written: "TEN WOMEN SHALL BAKE YOUR BREAD IN A SINGLE OVEN AND DOLE IT OUT BY WEIGHT" (26:26), yet even such measures will fail to satisfy the people's hunger. Where do these horrific images come from? And what kind of God inflicts them?

THE SAGES IN OUR OWN TIME ANSWER: Because this image and others in this curse so closely parallel eyewitness accounts reported by Isaiah, Jeremiah, and Ezekiel in the wake of later national catastrophes, it's likely that this Levitical section was composed *after* the Babylonian exile, in the sixth century B.C.E. We can also hear echoes of Lamentations: "WE GET OUR BREAD AT THE PERIL OF OUR LIVES, BECAUSE OF THE SWORD OF THE WILDERNESS. OUR SKIN GLOWS LIKE AN OVEN, WITH THE FEVER OF FAMINE" (5:9–10).

OUR MOTHERS ADD: Such images also recall our recent near destruction, when even one hundred women could not fill a single oven with bread but instead entered the ovens themselves and fed the hungry flames.

LILITH THE REBEL CRIES: But it was not our failure that led to the Holocaust. It was God's! Where was God when we were suffering?

MOTHER RACHEL ADDS: And where was the rest of the world?

THE MIRACLE OF FRESH BREAD

OUR MOTHERS RECOUNT: During the nightmare years of World War II, the specter of famine continuously stalked the death camps. Even those who survived never forgot the "fever of famine" and the lack of bread. As Yaffa Eliach recounts about one Auschwitz survivor, Tula Friedman:

"A waiter came to the table with a basket of assorted breads. Tula closed her eyes and inhaled the aroma of freshly baked bread as one inhales the sweet smells of a bouquet of freshly cut flowers. She passed the basket to me without taking any. 'Thank you,' she told the waiter, 'but I am on a diet.' She then turned to me. 'You know, in camp I used to dream that one day I would marry a baker and in our house there would always be an abundance of bread.'

" 'For this basket of bread,' another woman across the table said, 'you could buy in camp all the jewelry you see at this Bar Mitzvah. Once in Bergen-Belsen, I exchanged a diamond ring for a thin slice of white bread.'

"The bread on the table was still untouched. The waiter came again to the table. 'Ladies, I see that you are not hungry today.'

" 'Not today,' replied Tula, 'and not ever again.'

"The waiter was about to remove the bread. 'Leave it on the table,' said another woman. 'There is nothing more reassuring in this world than having a basket of freshly baked bread on the table in front of you.' "

THE HIDDEN FACE OF GOD

ESTHER THE HIDDEN ONE PRAYS: How long, O God, how long will you hide your face from us? How mysterious are your ways, how measureless your silence! When will you shine your face upon us once more, O Shekhinah-Who-Dwells-in-This-World? When will you lift us up from darkness into light? Why does your prophet Isaiah declare: "FOR YOUR CRIMES, YOUR MOTHER WAS SENT AWAY" (50:1)?

THE HOLY ZOHAR EXPLAINS:

The Blessed Holy One said:
You have made Me homeless as well as yourselves,
for the Queen has left the palace along with you.
Everything is ruined, My palace and yours!
For a palace is worthless to a king unless he can enter with his queen.
A king is only happy when he enters the queen's palace
And finds her with her son;
they all rejoice as one.
Now neither the son nor the queen is present;
the palace is totally desolate.
What can I do?
I Myself will be with you!

MIRIAM THE PROPHET ADDS: As will I. And together we will work
toward redemption!

NUMBERS

במדבר

Leadership

34. BAMIDBAR:

Inclusion

(NUMBERS 1:1–4:20)

TORAH TEACHES: The Book of Numbers takes its English name from its initial recorded event: the first census of the Israelites a year after their exodus from Egypt. After the census, God delineates the arrangement of the twelve tribes that will surround the central Tent of Meeting on all four sides. The population of the Levites is not recorded in the general census but is recorded separately. The Levites are assigned special duties and rights because of their unique status as God's priests. And among the Levitical families, Aaron's ancestral house is charged with the special duties of maintaining the Tabernacle.

NUMBERS

OUR DAUGHTERS ASK: What a quarrelsome book Numbers is! It's filled with rebellions: Eldad and Medad prophesying without official sanction; Miriam and Aaron challenging their brother, Moses; the spies backing off from the conquest of Canaan; Korakh trying to take over the priesthood; the five daughters of Zelophekhad bucking patriarchal inheritance laws. What's going on here?

THE SAGES IN OUR OWN TIME ANSWER: Numbers is an alternative version of Leviticus, probably edited by the priests in later times. The two books share the same preoccupation with lineage, authority, and ritual propriety. Numbers presents several dramatic object lessons about the dangers of rebellion and heresy. It warns its readers that a house divided and unruly cannot stand.

LILITH THE REBEL COUNTERS: Nor can a house which relegates women to the sidelines! Thank God that Miriam and the daughters of Zelophekhad had the courage to speak up!

THE CENSUS, OR, WHO COUNTS?

OUR DAUGHTERS ASK: Who is counted—and not counted—in the first census of the Israelites?

SERAKH BAT ASHER THE HISTORIAN ANSWERS: The explicit reason for this census is to identify "ALL THOSE IN ISRAEL WHO ARE ABLE TO BEAR ARMS" (1:3). In other words, the census is designed to transform Israel from a slave people into a military force. The total number of men of fighting age—twenty and up—comes to 603,550. So central is this event considered in Israel's national history that it provides the English name for this fourth book of the Torah: Numbers.

LEAH THE NAMER ADDS: But its Hebrew name, as with the other four books, is taken from its first word, *bamidbar*, "in the desert."

BERURIAH THE SCHOLAR EXPLAINS: So not everyone is included in this number. The women, the children under twenty, and probably those too old or unfit for service (although, significantly, no upper age limit or physical condition is set for fighting men) are left out. In addition, nothing is said here about the *erev rav*, the mixed multitude that accompanies the Israelites out of Egypt. As for the Levites, they are not included in this counting but are subject to a separate census of "ALL THE MALES FROM THE AGE OF ONE MONTH UP" (3:15). These total 22,000 men.

LILITH THE REBEL COMMENTS: As a result of this census, the women now disappear from view, uncounted—like their children and the mixed multitude. Although the actual population of Israelites—fighting men, Levites, and everyone else—must have amounted to several million people, the Rabbis almost always talk about the "600,000 who stood at Sinai," not acknowledging that they are including only the men numbered in this census. The rest of us are still waiting to be counted.

35. NASO:

Jealousy

(NUMBERS 4:21–7:89)

TORAH TEACHES: This parasha describes a ritual involving a woman suspected of adultery. This is the only example in Judaism of "trial by ordeal"—that is, a procedure for judging an individual's innocence or guilt by subjecting her to a physical test.

The parasha also contains the laws of the Nazirite, an individual who chooses to take a vow of abstinence and separation from the community. Following this section is the Blessing of the Priests, *Birkat Kohanim*, to be conferred on the people by Aaron and his sons.

The parasha concludes with the consecration of the Tabernacle, celebrated for twelve days with gift giving by all the tribes.

RESPONSIBILITY FOR SIN

OUR DAUGHTERS ASK: Although the Torah often excuses women from responsibility—for example, for being personally obligated for their own vows—here they're regarded as obligated equally with men, as it is written: "WHEN A MAN OR WOMAN COMMITS ANY WRONG TOWARD A FELLOW [Israelite], THUS BREAKING FAITH WITH YHVH, AND THAT PERSON REALIZES HER GUILT, SHE SHALL CONFESS THE WRONG THAT SHE HAS DONE. SHE SHALL MAKE RESTITUTION IN THE PRINCIPAL AMOUNT AND ADD ONE-FIFTH TO IT, GIVING IT TO HER WHOM SHE HAS WRONGED" (5:5–7). Why are women responsible in this case?

HULDAH THE PREACHER ANSWERS: This law proves that women sometimes did control property, and that with such control, they assumed some of the same rights and obligations as men. So if they wronged another person, it was their own responsibility—not their husbands' or fathers'—not only to confess but also to compensate those they had wronged, including an additional twenty percent penalty. Through this law, the Torah, acknowledging that adulthood carries with it both moral and economic accountability, conferred that social status upon women.

TRIAL BY ORDEAL

OUR DAUGHTERS ASK: How can the Torah prescribe the primitive "trial by ordeal" as a means of divining truth? Is this quasi-magical ritual any different from medieval autos-da-fé or some of the other diabolical methods practiced by the Spanish Inquisition? And don't such practices go against the grain of Judaism?

WILY REBECCA ANSWERS: If we examine this ritual more closely, we discover profound psychological insight behind it—if we judge it within the context of the Torah's own time and place. Because as much as we fittingly condemn this practice for humiliating the woman and exonerating the man, we have to acknowledge also its primary purpose as an *exorcism of jealousy,* which, if left to fester, might have led the woman's husband to abuse, abandon, or banish his wife, leaving her economically destitute and socially outcast.

THE RABBIS EXPLAIN: Furthermore, when this law was first commanded, the people's moral conduct was more praiseworthy, more in keeping with God's ways, than it was in our time. In the Torah's time, if a man justly accused his wife of adultery, this ritual, which we later called the ritual of the *sotah,* "the woman who strays," served its divine function of exposing the sinner to public view and ridding the camp of impurity. But later, after the Temple had been destroyed, we realized the people's moral nature had so deteriorated that men were just as likely to be guilty of adultery as women, and so we were forced to outlaw this practice.

OUR DAUGHTERS REPLY: If you think things were bad then, just look at them now. We need a ritual for a whole society that strays.

A FIT OF JEALOUSY

BERURIAH THE SCHOLAR EXPLAINS: The Torah sets down specific preconditions that entitle a suspicious husband to impose this ritual on his wife. The first is *secrecy:* "IF ANY MAN'S WIFE HAS GONE ASTRAY AND BROKEN FAITH WITH HIM IN THAT A MAN HAS HAD CARNAL RELATIONS WITH HER UNBEKNOWNST TO HER HUSBAND, AND SHE KEEPS SECRET THE FACT THAT SHE HAS DEFILED HERSELF WITHOUT BEING FORCED, AND THERE IS NO WITNESS AGAINST HER . . ." (5:12–13). This criterion excludes cases of rape, open promiscuity, accusation by a fellow Israelite, and confession of infidelity by the wife herself. (Each of these situations has its own set of laws and consequences.) What is most significant in this case is that the husband *has no way of proving* that his wife has "BROKEN FAITH WITH HIM."

OUR DAUGHTERS ASK: But the Torah doesn't say, "If a man *suspects* that his wife" but rather says, "IF ANY MAN'S WIFE *HAS GONE ASTRAY*..." How does the narrator know this if there are no witnesses?

WILY REBECCA ANSWERS: The narrator adopts this posture in order to appease the jealous husband, to make him feel vindicated as he plays out his suspicions. This way the husband can preserve his honor so that his wife can save hers.

OUR DAUGHTERS ASK: What about *her* feelings? Does the ritual take them into account?

BERURIAH ANSWERS: Here we discover another clue about the Torah's perspective. For it is written of the husband: "BUT [IF] A FIT OF JEALOUSY COMES OVER HIM AND HE IS WROUGHT UP ABOUT THE WIFE WHO HAS DEFILED HERSELF; OR IF A FIT OF JEALOUSY COMES OVER ONE AND HE IS WROUGHT UP ABOUT HIS WIFE *AL-THOUGH SHE HAS NOT DEFILED HERSELF*—THE MAN SHALL BRING HIS WIFE TO THE PRIEST" (5:14–15). In this special case, the focus is on the husband's *feelings*, but in other cases of moral offense, the Torah addresses an individual's or the community's *purity status:* whether ritual contamination, requiring purification, has occurred. Here, the husband brings "FOR HER" an offering of barley flour, but he is not to pour on it the oil and frankincense normally required for meal offerings. For it is designated as "A MEAL OFFERING OF JEALOUSY," a *minhat zikaron mazkeret avon*—that is, an "OFFERING OF REMEMBRANCE WHICH RECALLS WRONG-DOING" (5:15).

ESTHER THE HIDDEN ONE SUGGESTS: During the ritual, the priest places the husband's offering upon his wife's hands, so that the woman herself *becomes* the altar. It is at her expense, through her agency, that her husband is offering up this memorial to his own distrust.

WILY REBECCA EXPLAINS: In other words, the husband brings only a make-believe sacrifice, a simulation of a sin offering, although to him it is real enough. What he's purging from his consciousness is not his wife's sin but the memory of his own suspicion of that sin. What the ritual is addressing is not his wife's passions but his own.

ABBAYE'S SUSPICIONS

THE RABBIS RECOUNT: Once, Rabbi Abbaye overheard a man ask a woman if he could accompany her as they walked through the forest. Suspecting that the man planned to seduce her, Abbaye followed them. But no foul play occurred, and when the couple reached the other side of the forest, they went their separate ways.

"It was not *their* evil inclination but *my own* that was whispering in my ear!" said Abbaye to himself. "Had I been with that woman, I would surely have seduced her!"

Filled with shame, Abbaye went to the riverbank to throw himself in. But an old man suddenly appeared and said to him, "The greater the man, the greater his evil inclination."

And so Abbaye returned home in peace.

MUDDYING THE WATERS

OUR DAUGHTERS ASK: What a bizarre ritual! Why is it so loaded with symbolism and theatricality, more the stuff of melodrama than sacred drama? Why does the priest take "SACRAL WATER IN AN EARTHEN VESSEL AND, TAKING SOME OF THE EARTH THAT IS ON THE FLOOR OF THE TABERNACLE, . . . PUT IT IN THE WATER" (5:17)? Why this use of *earthly* materials in contrast to the gold, silver, and bronze implements normally associated with priestly ritual? And what's the religious significance of dirt?

THE RABBIS ANSWER: All these things are intended to symbolize the woman's shame, whether deserved or simply experienced during this ritual.

HULDAH THE PREACHER DISAGREES: No, they represent the Torah's own disdain for this husband who would subject his wife to such public dishonor. After all, how could the priests treat seriously a ritual performed with clay pots and dirt?

OUR DAUGHTERS ASK: If this ritual is intended as a psychological exorcism, how can we justify the next part of it, as it is written: "AFTER HE HAS MADE THE WOMAN STAND BEFORE YHVH, THE PRIEST SHALL BARE THE WOMAN'S HEAD" (5:18)? What could be more humiliating in that society than to bare a married woman's hair in front of other men? Could there be any possible reason to do so besides shaming her?

BERURIAH THE SCHOLAR ANSWERS: Let's remember the primary function of this ritual: to exorcise a husband's unsubstantiated jealousy. The first part of the ritual addresses his suspicion of her guilt: he brings a mock sin offering and then watches the priest prepare a potion of dirty water—perhaps evoking his more vengeful feelings. Then the ritual begins to appeal to other sentiments: all see his wife's hair, normally a sight he alone is privy to. Perhaps he then feels attracted to her, even remembers that he still loves her . . .

DINAH THE WOUNDED ONE ADDS: Or perhaps he feels pity . . .

LILITH THE REBEL COUNTERS: Or maybe he enjoys humiliating her! Only after that is he willing to take her back.

OUR DAUGHTERS ASK: Is drinking "THE WATER OF BITTERNESS THAT INDUCES THE SPELL" (5:18) also meant to humiliate her? After all, the priest makes her swallow a potion made of water, dirt from the Tabernacle floor, and ink dissolved from the curse written by the priest. The woman's physiological reactions to this foul-tasting brew are supposed to vindicate or doom her.

MIRIAM THE PROPHET REPLIES: It's hard to avoid associations here with me, whose very name means "sea of bitterness." Midrash and folklore have long connected me with water, sometimes bitter, other times sweet and redemptive. I am the quintessential symbol of Jewish women's paradoxical lot— on the one hand, guardian, leader, prophet, and sage; on the other, critic, victim, and mute.

DINAH THE WOUNDED ONE EXCLAIMS: No wonder the waters are bitter!

HOW TO CAST A SPELL

OUR DAUGHTERS ASK: How did Israelite priests justify casting spells, as they do in this ritual? Doesn't this go against the Torah's own ban on magic?

BERURIAH THE SCHOLAR ANSWERS: Surprisingly, the priests' actions do remind us of classical fairy tales, in which sorcerers and witches cast magic spells. For before giving the woman the potion to drink, the priest explains to her: If you are innocent of your husband's charges, nothing will happen to you. But if you're guilty, "MAY YHVH MAKE YOU A CURSE AND AN IMPRECATION AMONG YOUR PEOPLE, AS YHVH CAUSES YOUR THIGH TO SAG AND YOUR BELLY TO DISTEND; MAY THIS WATER THAT INDUCES THE SPELL ENTER YOUR BODY, CAUSING THE BELLY TO DISTEND AND THE THIGH TO SAG" (5:21–22). The Torah calls this part of the formula "THE CURSE OF ADJURATION" (5:21).

THE SAGES IN OUR OWN TIME TEACH: More than a prediction, this curse is what linguists call *performative* language—that is, in pronouncing these words, the priest is enacting the curse, so that if the woman is indeed an adulteress, the curse will come true.

OUR DAUGHTERS ASK: What kind of curse is this, when "the belly distends and the thigh sags"? What's supposed to happen to her?

THE RABBIS EXPLAIN: If the woman was indeed guilty of straying, her body would reveal her guilt in a physical malady, such as a miscarriage, a prolapsed uterus, or a hysterical pregnancy, the ultimate effect being the inability to bear children. Thus the guilty woman would be punished precisely where she had sinned—that is, measure for measure. And if nothing happened, she would be declared innocent and would be welcomed back into her household and community with honor.

WILY REBECCA RETORTS: There's no record that this curse *ever* worked! But that's because what really matters here is that the *husband hears* the curse and *imagines its effect.*

OUR DAUGHTERS ASK: But if such is the case, why does the priest make the accused woman sanction her own curse? As it is written: "AND THE WOMAN SHALL SAY, 'AMEN, AMEN!'" (5:22) Enough is enough already!

LEAH THE NAMER ANSWERS: The Hebrew word *amen* is related to *emet,* meaning "truth." So when the accused woman says, "Amen, amen!" in response to the priest's curse, she's actually joining with him in affirming his words. Her acquiescence invests the ritual with additional force: because if she's proven guilty, she's forfeited her right to appeal; but if she's cleared, she can point to God's own ruling in the case.

OUR DAUGHTERS ASK: Why does the priest end his part of the ritual by erasing what he's just written down? As it is written: "THE PRIEST SHALL PUT THESE CURSES DOWN AND RUB IT OFF INTO THE WATER OF BITTERNESS" (5:23). Doesn't this action cancel the curse?

THE SAGES IN OUR OWN TIME ANSWER: The figurative English expression "I'll make you eat your words," meaning "I'll have my revenge," loosely parallels this step in the *sotah* ritual. After speaking the curse, the priest writes it down and then dissolves the ink into the earthen bowl already muddied with dirt from the Tabernacle floor. Anthropologists call this practice sympathetic magic, the belief that physically acting upon a talisman or another symbolic token—here words on parchment—by eating, drinking, burning, puncturing, burying, or handling it, can bring about magical results. By drinking the curse she's already verbally assented to, the accused woman takes it in and lets it work its magic on her body, punishing her for or freeing her from her husband's accusation.

OUR MOTHERS MUSE: Today we practice our own kind of sympathetic magic in our lives, cherishing mementos and memories, good luck charms, and other fragments of our vanished past.

DOUBLE STANDARDS

OUR DAUGHTERS DECLARE: This ritual is appallingly unfair to the woman! Because even if she's proven innocent after going through this whole awful ordeal, the Torah still lets her husband off the hook, as it's written: "THE MAN SHALL BE CLEAR OF GUILT." But if she's proven guilty, "THAT WOMAN SHALL SUFFER FOR HER GUILT" (5:31). Why does she have to suffer if she's sinned, while her husband faces no penalty if he's falsely accused her? And what if a wife suspects her husband of going astray, or what if she's simply overcome by a fit of jealousy? Shouldn't there be a comparable ritual to exorcise her feelings? Surely the Torah does not exempt men from infidelity or suggest that women are immune to feelings of jealousy—think of Rachel and Leah! Isn't the Torah here guilty of a double standard?

THE RABBIS ANSWER: We too were so troubled by these obvious inequities that we sanctioned this ritual only in cases where the husband himself was first cleared of sexual impropriety. And Rabbi Yohanan ben Zakkai finally outlawed the ritual even while the Temple still stood. He evidently recognized how destructive marital jealousy could be for the disenfranchised Jewish people, whose only solace and hope against the imperial Roman war machine was a stable, enduring family.

THE PATH OF THE NAZIRITE

OUR DAUGHTERS ASK: We've always been taught that Jews do not renounce the body in favor of the soul, that Judaism is a this-worldly religion. So is the Nazirite an exception to this rule, an ascetic who withdraws herself from the world?

BERURIAH THE SCHOLAR ANSWERS: Although the Torah doesn't promote celibacy or monastic communities, it does permit individuals—men and women—to take upon themselves for a predetermined period of time (and in rare cases, as with Samson and Samuel, for a lifetime) a *Nazirite vow*, during which time they swear to renounce all intoxicants, abstain from eating anything derived from grapes, shun contact with corpses, and refrain from cutting their hair. Yet despite these restrictions—the same as those applying to priests, except for the additional ban on haircuts—Nazirites were otherwise integrated into society, allowed to marry, conduct business, and observe all the commandments. The individual signaled the end of the Nazirite term by shaving off the consecrated hair in front of the Tabernacle and offering the locks up to God upon the sacrificial altar.

OUR DAUGHTERS ASK: Why would someone take upon herself such a vow?

THE RABBIS ANSWER: "TO SET [her] SELF APART [*le-hazir*] FOR GOD" (6:2). According to both the Mishnah and the Jewish historian Josephus, many Israelite women took upon themselves Nazirite vows, especially in Roman times, including two royal figures, the convert Queen Helena of Adiabene and Berenice, sister of King Agrippa II, who became a Nazirite—*nezirah*—after recovering from illness.

THE NAZIRITES QUEEN HELENA AND BERENICE

SERAKH BAT ASHER THE HISTORIAN RECOUNTS: When the righteous convert Queen Helena of Adiabene sent her son off to war, she vowed to become a Nazirite for seven years if he returned home safely. He did return unharmed, and she fulfilled her vow. But when she came to settle in the land of Israel, the Rabbis ruled that the first seven years were invalid and required her to remain a Nazirite for seven more. At the end of these fourteen years, she happened by chance to become ritually impure. Some say she continued her vow for yet another seven years; others, for only thirty days.

Berenice, the sister of Agrippa II, king of Chalcis (southern Lebanon)—and some say his lover—also took upon herself a Nazirite vow when she recovered from illness. When the Romans marched on Jerusalem, she and her brother defected to the Roman camp and from there watched the destruction of the city and the Temple. She ended her days in Rome, out of favor with Titus as well as her own people.

36. BEHA'ALOTKHA:

Spiritual Leadership

(NUMBERS 8:1–12:16)

TORAH TEACHES: This parasha opens with various laws concerning the Levites and the celebration of Passover. Then the Torah describes the divine cloud that constantly hovers over the Tabernacle, guiding the people. This is followed by a detailed description of the marching formation of the Israelite camp.

When the people now complain bitterly of hunger and cry out for meat, Moses despairs and asks God to end his life. God instructs him to share the burden of leadership with seventy elders.

Following God's instructions, Moses appoints seventy elders, who surround the Tabernacle, where, possessed by *ruakh*, the spirit drawn from Moses, they begin speaking in tongues. Two other elders, Eldad and Medad, who remain elsewhere in the camp, also receive the spirit and speak in tongues. Alarmed by what he takes as an act of defiance, Joshua demands that these two renegades be restrained. But Moses disagrees, declaring: "WOULD THAT ALL GOD'S PEOPLE WERE PROPHETS, THAT GOD PUT THE DIVINE SPIRIT UPON THEM!" (12:29) Then God sends quail to the people upon a wind sweeping in from the sea, followed by a severe plague.

Miriam and Aaron speak out against Moses, and God strikes Miriam with leprosy. For the next seven days, Miriam is isolated outside the camp, and the people wait for her return before traveling on.

MOTHERING THE CHILDREN OF ISRAEL

OUR DAUGHTERS ASK: For forty years, Moses puts up with endless complaints from the people: Why did you take us out of Egypt to die in the desert? What will we eat? Where can we find water to drink? Why are you taking us to a land ruled by giants who will devour us? Mark our words, Moses—we'll find our graves here in the wilderness! How does he deal with such unrelenting negativity?

MOTHER RACHEL ANSWERS: Moses reserves his own grumbling for God's ear. In turn, God is patient with Moses, supplying the people's wants and at times disciplining them. And even when the object of Moses' criticism, God remains patient and listens.

OUR DAUGHTERS OBJECT: But even the most long-suffering parent has limits! Doesn't Moses sometimes lose his patience?

MOTHER RACHEL ANSWERS: Of course he does! Here, for instance, when the people claim that life was better for them back in Egypt, Moses vents his frustration to God, comparing himself to a mother and a nurse, as it is written: "WHY HAVE YOU DEALT ILL WITH YOUR SERVANT, AND WHY HAVE I NOT ENJOYED YOUR FAVOR, THAT YOU HAVE LAID THE BURDEN OF ALL THIS PEOPLE UPON ME? DID I CONCEIVE THIS PEOPLE, DID I BEAR THEM, THAT YOU SHOULD SAY TO ME, 'CARRY THEM IN YOUR BOSOM AS A NURSE CARRIES AN INFANT,' TO THE LAND THAT YOU HAVE PROMISED ON OATH TO THEIR FATHERS?" (11:11–12)

LEAH THE NAMER ADDS: The Hebrew word that Moses uses for nurse, *omen*, refers to a *male* caretaker. For not only mothers and nurses commit themselves to caring so selflessly for their children. Fathers, too, lovingly tend their children.

SARAH THE ANCIENT ONE EXPLAINS: Here Moses is distinguishing himself from *all* caretakers, male and female, biological parents and adoptive ones. Compared to these, Moses feels himself at a remove—or wishes he were. In recommending that Moses ease his burdens by convening a council of seventy elders, God is acknowledging to him that sometimes even parents need to share their burdens.

OUR BUBBES ADD: Sometimes only grandparents can summon up enough patience to love children, *no matter what they do.*

WOULD THAT ALL GOD'S PEOPLE WERE PROPHETS

OUR DAUGHTERS ASK: Does Moses mean what he says when he declares: "WOULD THAT ALL GOD'S PEOPLE WERE PROPHETS, THAT GOD PUT THE DIVINE SPIRIT UPON THEM!" (11:29)? Is he really willing to share his spiritual leadership with "all God's people"?

MIRIAM THE PROPHET ANSWERS: Judging from how he reacted when Aaron and I challenged his authority shortly after this declaration, I would have to say no. He got carried away in the excitement of the moment.

ESTHER THE HIDDEN ONE PROCLAIMS: If only his words were true! If only all of us—men and women, Jew and gentile, high and low, gifted and flawed—were seekers and seers of holiness. That would truly signal the dawn of the messianic age.

SIBLING REBELLION

MIRIAM THE PROPHET TEACHES: Even though the Torah states that both "MIRIAM AND AARON SPOKE AGAINST MOSES" (12:1), only I am singled out by the narrator and by God for punishment.

LEAH THE NAMER POINTS OUT: Note that the verb *va-tedaber*— "spoke against"—is in the feminine singular, though both Aaron and Miriam are its subject.

THE RABBIS ADD: And note also that Miriam's name is listed first, reversing the usual order in the Torah, and that only Miriam is stricken with leprosy, while Aaron remains untouched, proving that she is the instigator of this challenge to Moses.

LILITH THE REBEL PROTESTS: No, it only proves that she's taken the rap.

OUR DAUGHTERS ASK: But what motivates Miriam to speak up against her younger brother Moses? Is it really because of "THE CUSHITE WOMAN HE HAD MARRIED" (12:1)? Who is she? And what has she done wrong?

THE RABBIS ANSWER: She is an Ethiopian queen—"Cush" being the biblical name for Ethiopia—whom Moses marries after fleeing Egypt but before reaching Midian. Others teach that she is Moses' Midianite wife, Zipporah. In this second interpretation, "Cush" refers to either her native country or her beauty.

OUR DAUGHTERS ASK: Why does Miriam speak against her to Moses?

THE RABBIS ANSWER: Some say that Miriam's complaint is racially motivated: she objects to her brother's marriage to a black woman.

HAGAR THE STRANGER OBJECTS: I doubt that! We know that the ancient Near East, especially the North African region of the Nile Delta, was a melting pot of ethnic groups, so this kind of racial bias seems unlikely.

THE RABBIS SUGGEST: Another view is that Miriam is rebuking her brother for refusing to sleep with his wife once he has returned from Mount Sinai, newly "dedicated" to God. So Miriam is speaking not *against* the Cushite woman but on her behalf.

BERURIAH COMMENTS: How often is the wife of a great leader widowed because of his career demands! Therefore to all of Miriam's other merits we should add: defender and guardian of women's sexual rights.

HIYYA AND THE POMEGRANATE

THE RABBIS RECOUNT: Rabbi Hiyya was so afraid of his own evil in-clination that he did not sleep with his wife for several years. Frustrated, his wife disguised herself as a prostitute and came to Hiyya where he was studying in his garden. Hiyya desired her and asked her fee.

"That pomegranate at the top of that tree," she said.

Hiyya quickly clambered up the tree and plucked the fruit. Then the two lay together, and Hiyya rose up, full of remorse, and went off to weep. When he came home, he found his wife kindling fire to make dinner. He jumped into the oven and was consumed by the flames kindled by his own wife.

GOD'S HEARING

OUR DAUGHTERS ASK: Miriam and Aaron present not one but two challenges to Moses, as it is written: "A CUSHITE WOMAN WHOM HE HAD MAR-RIED!" (12:1) and also, "HAS YHVH SPOKEN ONLY THROUGH MOSES? HAS HE NOT SPOKEN THROUGH US AS WELL?" (12:2) To the first complaint—"He married a Cushite woman!"—God says nothing. But to the second charge—"Has God not spoken through us as well?"—the Torah declares: "GOD HEARD IT" (12:2). Why does God respond only to Miriam and Aaron's second challenge?

WILY REBECCA ANSWERS: The whole business with the Cushite woman is a red herring, a pretense to contest their brother's authority—and neither Moses nor God takes the bait. But when Miriam and Aaron throw down their real gauntlet—their demand for shared power—God then hears them loud and clear and reacts with anger.

EVE THE MOTHER OF LIFE ADDS: Similarly, Adam's and my orig-inal sin is not the gaining of sexual knowledge but the rebelling against God's authority.

AND OUR BUBBES CHIME IN: As we say, You don't play around with God. First, it's not allowed, and second, God won't let you.

MIRIAM AS TARGET

OUR DAUGHTERS ASK: Throughout this incident, God addresses *both* Miriam and Aaron, as it is written: "AND [God] CALLED OUT, 'AARON AND

MIRIAM!'" (12:5) Aaron even admits his complicity, pleading with Moses after Miriam is punished: "ACCOUNT NOT TO *US* THE SIN WHICH *WE* COMMITTED IN *OUR* FOLLY" (12:11). Why then is only Miriam stricken with leprosy?

THE RABBIS ANSWER: No, Aaron is punished too, but it is through the mental suffering caused by the shame brought upon his priesthood by Miriam's leprosy.

SARAH THE ANCIENT ONE DISAGREES: No, Miriam is singled out because Aaron has already suffered enough through the earlier deaths of his two sons.

GOD'S HOUSEHOLD

OUR DAUGHTERS ASK: When speaking up in defense of Moses, God characterizes him as "MY SERVANT MOSES . . . TRUSTED THROUGHOUT MY HOUSEHOLD" (12:7). What exactly does the Torah mean by God's "household"?

THE SAGES IN OUR OWN TIME ANSWER: Anthropologists use the term "domestic religion" to describe the spiritual practices particular to women's experience. Women's lives until quite recently have traditionally been circumscribed by home, family, and the demands of daily sustenance. Their connections with the sacred—stories, symbols, songs, rituals, customs, prayers, religious imagery—have typically found expression in these idioms. Men's religious lives, on the other hand, have been primarily public, played out in communal spaces and spectacles. In this parasha, we get a rare glimpse of God's own concept of domestic religion. In contrast to the oracular "visions" and "dreams" through which God communicates with all other prophets, Moses "IS TRUSTED THROUGHOUT MY HOUSEHOLD. WITH HIM I SPEAK MOUTH TO MOUTH, PLAINLY AND NOT IN RIDDLES" (12:7–8).

LEAH THE NAMER EXPLAINS: The word "household"—*bayti*—has been interpreted by some to refer to the *house* of Israel, that is, the Jewish people, or to God's divine house in the heavens.

OUR BUBBES BREAK IN: It's a good thing that God's house is *up there!* Because, as we say: If God lived on earth, all his windows would be broken!

OUR MOTHERS COMMENT: It's also possible to imagine God's house as a more humble affair, a kitchen perhaps, filled with warm smells and prattling children, two steaming cups of tea on the table, and an empty chair, waiting.

AARON AS MIRIAM'S MOUTHPIECE

OUR DAUGHTERS ASK: After Miriam is stricken with leprosy, why does Aaron speak *for* her? As it is written: "AND AARON SAID TO MOSES, 'O MY LORD, ACCOUNT NOT TO US THE SIN WHICH WE COMMITTED IN OUR FOLLY. LET HER NOT BE AS ONE DEAD'" (12:11–12). Why doesn't Miriam speak for herself? In fact, why doesn't she speak a single word throughout this entire episode? Why does Aaron serve as her mouthpiece, as he did for Moses before Pharaoh?

MIRIAM THE PROPHET ANSWERS: Women rarely speak in the Torah, especially after the Book of Genesis. Clearly, this silence reflects our subordinate status in ancient Near Eastern society: to be seen—and even then, behind a veil—and not heard. And unlike the matriarchs who were so instrumental in managing the first families of the clan—often even more so than the men—we women who came out of Egypt were no longer a shaping force among our people. Not even I, matriarch of the ruling family, was granted a powerful voice. For here, in my bold bid for such a role, I was slapped down, whitened out, and silenced. In fact, my only solo moment in the entire Torah is at the Sea of Reeds, when I *echo* a single verse of my brother's song, and even then I "chant *for* the women," not for myself. After my challenge to Moses, I appear only once more in the Torah—at my death. Even then, according to the Torah, the people pass over my death in silence. But the women heard my words—even though the Torah failed to record them. Let them live again through you, my descendants.

MIRIAM'S LEPROSY

OUR DAUGHTERS ASK: The Torah describes Miriam as "STRICKEN WITH SNOW-WHITE SCALES" (12:10). What exactly happens to her?

THE RABBIS ANSWER: Miriam is punished for slandering Moses. For if we regard the Hebrew word for leprosy, *metzora*, as an acronym, it becomes *motzi shem ra*—that is, an act of character defamation.

THE SAGES IN OUR OWN TIME DISAGREE: No, Miriam's crime is impiety, since that was considered an offense punishable by leprosy in the ancient Near East.

MOTHER RACHEL SUGGESTS: We can also read this scene (12:10–13) as God's rebuke of *all three* of them. Two previous verses in the parasha set the stage: First, in response to Miriam and Aaron's complaints against Moses, God reacts like a parent frustrated by her children's bickering: "COME OUT, YOU THREE, TO THE TENT OF MEETING!" (12:4) Then, after dressing down the older two siblings for picking on their younger brother, God withdraws, "STILL INCENSED WITH THEM!" (12:9).

HULDAH THE PREACHER CONTINUES: And what follows are the material consequences of their squabble: Miriam the healer loses her health, becoming—according to the Septuagint (the Greek version of the Tanakh, the "Old Testament")—"like an abortion," or, as Aaron puts it, like a stillborn baby "WHO EMERGES FROM HIS MOTHER'S WOMB WITH HALF HIS FLESH EATEN AWAY" (12:12). And so the woman whom Jewish legend identifies as one of the Hebrew midwives in Egypt becomes her own opposite. Likewise with Aaron: The man whom God once designated as a "mouth" to Moses must turn now to his tongue-tied younger brother and plead with him to pray on Miriam's behalf. And Moses himself is reprimanded: God rebuffs his brief prayer on behalf of his sister, banishing her for seven days outside the camp.

OUR MOTHERS REMARK: We can almost hear the three of them yelling, as God's final words fade out, "Come back! We didn't mean it!"

MOSES' PRAYER FOR HEALING

LEAH THE NAMER TEACHES: Moses' prayer on behalf of his sister is remarkably brief: "O GOD, PLEASE HEAL HER!" (12:13) It's in fact the shortest prayer in the Torah. In Hebrew, it reads almost like an incantation: *"El na refa na la."* And though it's been suggested that the prayer's brevity reflects either Moses' impartiality or his reluctance, we might interpret it instead as evidence of spontaneous feeling.

DINAH THE WOUNDED ONE EXPLAINS: For when those we love are stricken suddenly, the most we can sometimes do is cry out. And sometimes even that cry is wordless.

SPITTING

OUR DAUGHTERS ASK: Responding to Moses' prayer for Miriam's healing, God declares: "IF HER FATHER SPAT IN HER FACE, WOULD SHE NOT BEAR HER SHAME FOR SEVEN DAYS?" (12:14) Why this strange response? Why would a father spit on his daughter?

THE SAGES IN OUR OWN TIME ANSWER: In the ancient Near East, spitting was often incorporated into healing and exorcism rituals. It was also a gesture of contempt and humiliation.

THE RABBIS RECOUNT: There once was a certain woman who was in the habit of going every Sabbath evening to the study house to hear Rabbi Meir teach. One Sabbath evening, her husband came home early to find the house empty and the table unset. Enraged, he swore to bar his wife from home until she spat in her teacher Meir's eye. Hearing of the husband's harsh oath and wishing to help the poor woman, Meir sought her out and asked her to spit not once but seven times in his eyes, claiming that this was the only remedy that would heal them from disease. Although initially reluctant, the woman finally did what he asked, and she was readmitted by her husband into her home.

WILY REBECCA CHALLENGES: Is God up to the same tricks?

WAITING FOR MIRIAM

MIRIAM THE PROPHET COMMENTS: It's difficult to tell from the Torah's words exactly how the people felt about me. For nowhere is their attitude recorded. One of the most telling clues can be gleaned from this parasha. It is revealed that the people did not move on while I remained quarantined outside the camp. As it is written: "AND THE PEOPLE DID NOT MARCH ON UNTIL MIRIAM WAS READMITTED" (12:15).

OUR DAUGHTERS ASK: Whose idea was it to wait for her?

THE RABBIS ANSWER: Some say that God made the people wait for her, just as she waited besides the Nile until her baby brother was rescued. Others teach that God punished the entire nation for Miriam's sin, delaying their arrival in Israel by one extra week. Still others teach that the people themselves, out of respect for Miriam, refused to travel until she was healed.

LILITH THE REBEL SUGGESTS: Perhaps God was punishing her for her bravado. So dependent had the people and her two brothers become upon her resuscitative powers that she grew too proud and had to be humbled. The people gave her time to regain her dignity before reentering the camp.

MIRIAM CONCLUDES: All these interpretations agree on one thing: To God and to the people, I was indeed someone to be reckoned with!

37. SHELAKH LEKHA:
Faith

(NUMBERS 13:1–15:41)

TORAH TEACHES: Moses appoints twelve men, one from each tribe, to scout out the land of Canaan before the Israelites attempt to conquer it. Forty days later, the twelve spies return, reporting that the land is indeed "FLOWING WITH MILK AND HONEY" but that its people are too mighty to conquer. Two of the spies, Caleb and Joshua, disagree, claiming that with God's help, the land will surely fall into their hands. Persuaded by the alarming report of the other ten spies, the people rise up in mutiny against Moses and Aaron, demanding to return to Egypt.

Angered by the people's lack of faith, God threatens to destroy them and begin over again with Moses, but Moses calms God's wrath. God then commutes the rebels' death sentence to forty years of wandering in the wilderness, until all the men who had been slaves in Egypt have died. Of that entire generation, only Caleb and Joshua will be allowed to enter the Promised Land. Too late, the people defy God's verdict and resolve to press on into Canaan, but they are routed by the Canaanites and forced to withdraw.

The parasha ends with laws concerning sacrifices to be offered once the people have settled in the land as well as the commandment to attach fringes to the corners of their garments to remind them of their allegiance to God's law.

SOME HOMESPUN LESSONS FROM THE INCIDENT OF THE TWELVE SPIES

OUR BUBBES TEACH: So much we can learn from the mistakes made by those spies! For instance:

The cat likes fish, but she doesn't want to wet her paws.
The way you look at someone, so that person appears to you.
The smoothest way is full of stones.

THE DOOM OF THE SPIES

OUR DAUGHTERS ASK: Why are *all* the people punished because ten of the twelve spies have brought back an unfavorable report? As it is written: "NONE OF THE MEN WHO HAVE SEEN MY PRESENCE AND THE SIGNS THAT I HAVE PERFORMED IN EGYPT AND IN THE WILDERNESS, AND WHO HAVE TRIED ME THESE MANY TIMES AND HAVE DISOBEYED ME, SHALL SEE THE LAND THAT I PROMISED ON OATH TO THEIR FATHERS" (14:22–23). Why should everyone suffer for the sins of these few?

THE RABBIS ANSWER: All the Israelite *men*—excepting Joshua and Caleb—lose heart after hearing the ten spies' disheartening report. All the men confront Moses and Aaron, protesting that "OUR WIVES AND CHILDREN WILL BE CARRIED OFF" (14:3) if the Israelites try to fight the people of Canaan. So all the men deserve God's stern judgment. But *every one* of the women takes heart and prepares herself without any qualms to enter the land. To reward the women for their faith as well as for their earlier refusal to contribute their earrings to make the Golden Calf, God grants all the women the privilege of entering the Promised Land.

MIRIAM THE PROPHET INTERJECTS: All the women, that is, except me. But unlike my brothers Moses and Aaron, I was not told why I was doomed to die in the wilderness. I can only conclude that I was a strong enough leader to have earned my stripes as they did.

THE TALE OF RAHAB AND THE SPIES

OUR DAUGHTERS ASK: When the people are finally ready to enter the Promised Land after forty years of wandering in the desert, Joshua sends two spies to the walled city of Jericho. But what kind of spies does he end up sending! Instead of scouting out the enemy's fortifications and arms, they instead go straight to a prostitute's house and "LIE THERE" (2:1), presumably with her. At no time do they ask her any questions, nor do they ever leave her quarters "IN THE ACTUAL WALL" (1:15) to gather strategic information for Joshua. Rahab *volunteers* information to them about her own people's morale and tells them about an escape route. Why does the Torah choose this foreign woman—a prostitute, no less!—as the heroine of this tale?

THE RABBIS ANSWER: We chose this story as the traditional haftorah for this parasha because of its obvious connection to the story of the Twelve Spies, but we also did so because we consider Rahab a model of the righteous convert. For although she began life as an idolater, she later embraced belief in one God, as it is written: "FOR YHVH YOUR GOD IS THE ONLY GOD IN HEAVEN ABOVE AND ON EARTH BELOW" (Joshua 2:11). And though she began as a prostitute, she later became Joshua's wife. And though she began as an enemy of Israel, she is the ancestor of many of Israel's kings and prophets, including Huldah.

LEAH THE NAMER ADDS: Her very name tells her story, for *rahav* means "wide," and that is how she greets the new conquerors of her land. She opens wide her house . . .

LILITH THE REBEL BREAKS IN: And her legs!

ESTHER THE HIDDEN ONE REVEALS: Rahab is Israel's shadow, a mirror of Jewish history. For just as the Israelites escape the Angel of Death by smearing blood on their doorposts, so Rahab dooms her people with a crimson cord (2:18). And just as the Israelites leave *mitzraim* (Egypt), a "narrow place," so they come at last to *merhav*, a wide land of freedom. And just as the ten spies who first scout out the land regard themselves as grasshoppers next to the giants of Canaan, so Rahab reports that her own people quake before the approaching Israelites. In Rahab, we meet both a *havera*, a friend, and a *herev*, an enemy—literally, "sword." And we must choose—*vahar*—between them.

WILY REBECCA QUIPS: Rahab proves that walls are only as strong as their weakest stone—and a society only as strong as its most marginal citizen.

FOLLOWING YOUR HEART AND EYES

THE RABBIS TEACH: God commands "THE ISRAELITE PEOPLE . . . TO MAKE FOR THEMSELVES FRINGES ON THE CORNERS OF THEIR GARMENTS" (15:38), to remind them not to stray from the right path. These fringes, originally incorporated as part of a man's daily clothing, in time evolved into the *tallit*, a man's traditional Jewish prayer shawl.

OUR DAUGHTERS ASK: Since women—until very recently and still only in liberal Jewish communities—have traditionally been exempted (and conventionally forbidden) from wearing a tallit, how are we supposed to respond to these verses, recited twice a day as part of the traditional liturgy? If we're forbidden to look upon these fringes, how are we supposed to remind ourselves "TO BE HOLY TO OUR GOD" instead of yielding to our own impulses? Is the Torah implying that we women have no "lustful urge" for our hearts and eyes to follow?

LILITH THE REBEL JUMPS IN: Which is, of course, utterly ridiculous! We all need spiritual compasses to keep our bearings.

MIRIAM THE PROPHET EXPLAINS: The tallit provides a wonderful opportunity for women's spiritual expression. Into it we can weave our dreams, our visions, our prayers, and our secrets for Shekhinah's ears alone.

ESTHER THE HIDDEN ONE TEACHES: Rabbinic tradition has already invested the tallit, especially the *tzitzit*, the fringes, with mystical symbolism. Women can now embroider our own symbols into the knots and windings, the colors, shape, and design, and the *atarah* (decorative collar). And there, under the sheltering canopy of our tallit, we can encounter the Holy-One-Who-Dwells-Within.

THE SYMBOLISM OF KNOTS

OUR DAUGHTERS ASK: As one of our reminders to keep the faith, we're commanded to wear fringes—*tzitzit*—on the corners of our garments. As it is written: "THAT SHALL BE YOUR FRINGE; LOOK AT IT AND RECALL ALL THE COMMANDMENTS OF YHVH AND OBSERVE THEM" (15:39). Why do we also tie knots in the fringes of our tallit?

OUR BUBBES ANSWER: Knots contain powerful magic. By tying a person's hair or clothing, we can gain control over that person's soul or trap that soul inside the body. That's why pious midwives untie knots when they attend a woman's labor—to prevent knots in the umbilical cord and to let the newborn's soul go free. We also loosen the knots in shrouds to let out the departing soul.

BERURIAH THE SCHOLAR EXPLAINS: In the Bible, "loosening knots" is mentioned as one of the magician's arts. In the Talmud, magic itself is sometimes called "binding and loosening." And a post-Talmudic spell against demons includes the incantation: "Bound, bound, bound!"

ESTHER THE HIDDEN ONE REVEALS: But it is different in the case of the knots in the *tzitzit*. For the five knots in each bundle of eight strings symbolize our sacred bond with the One-Whose-Presence-Dwells-Among-Us. They also represent the five senses, the five books of the Torah, and the first five words of the *Shema*, in which we declare our faith in God's unity. The eight strings and five knots added together equal thirteen, the numerical value of the final word of the Shema, *ehad*, meaning "one." So when we look upon the fringes, we are reminded of the unity of God and all that is holy.

A PRAYER FOR TAKING HALLAH

OUR MOTHERS TEACH: The Torah commands us: "WHEN YOU ENTER THE LAND TO WHICH I AM TAKING YOU, AND YOU EAT OF THE BREAD OF THE LAND, YOU SHALL SET SOME ASIDE AS A GIFT TO YHVH: AS THE FIRST YIELD OF YOUR BAK-ING, YOU SHALL SET ASIDE A LOAF AS A GIFT" (15:18–20). And so we pray, recit-ing the uplifting words of the pious Sore bas Toyvim:

"You should remove a portion of the first dough that you knead, and by virtue of this, 'God will fill your storehouses to the brim' (Proverbs 8:21). . . . In the past, the *koyen* [priest] would take the heave offering and the *leyvi* [Levite] would take a tithe. The pauper would take the pauper's tithe and there would also be a second tithe at other appointed times. But now, because of our many sins, the *beys hamikdesh* [Holy Temple] has been destroyed, and all sacrifices have been annulled except for the *mitsve* of *khale* [hallah], which has remained.

"Therefore, *riboyne shel oylem* [Master of the Universe], we beseech You to ac-cept this *mitsve* of *khale* and to send us many blessings, wherever we may turn. May our children not become estranged from us, for many years to come. May the *mitsve* of *khale* be accepted as equivalent to the 613 *mitsves* of the holy *toyre* [Torah]."

38. KORAKH:
Rebellion

(NUMBERS 16:1–18:32)

ORAH TEACHES: On several occasions as they wander through the wilderness, the Israelites challenge the exclusive authority of Moses. In this parasha, it is Korakh, son of Moses' first cousin Izhar, who leads a mutiny, enlisting as allies the Reubenites Datan and Abiram (two of the Rabbis' favorite villains) and On, as well as two hundred fifty chieftains. Their indictment of Moses and Aaron: "YOU HAVE GONE TOO FAR! FOR ALL THE COMMUNITY ARE HOLY, ALL OF THEM, AND GOD IS IN THEIR MIDST. WHY THEN DO YOU RAISE YOURSELVES ABOVE YHVH'S CONGREGATION?"

MOSES ANSWERS THEM WITH HIS OWN CHALLENGE: "THE MAN WHOM YHVH CHOOSES, HE SHALL BE THE HOLY ONE. YOU HAVE GONE TOO FAR, SONS OF LEVI!" Instructing the rebels to bring their fire pans to the Tabernacle, he declares: "IF THESE MEN DIE AS ALL MEN DO . . . IT WAS NOT GOD WHO SENT ME. BUT IF GOD BRINGS ABOUT SOMETHING UNHEARD OF, SO THAT THE GROUND OPENS ITS MOUTH AND SWALLOWS THEM UP WITH ALL THAT BELONGS TO THEM, YOU SHALL KNOW THAT THESE MEN HAVE SPURNED GOD." And so—in dramatic detail—Moses' prophecy comes to pass.

The parasha ends with an inventory of priestly entitlements and the story of the miraculous flowering of Aaron's rod.

THE REBELLION OF KORAKH

OUR DAUGHTERS ASK: Do these men who challenge Moses deserve such a cruel and unusual punishment? Isn't Moses playing the tyrant here, using God as his executioner, in order to suppress legitimate dissent? Even if we take into account the realpolitik of the times, isn't the rebels' punishment—the deaths of "ALL KORAKH'S PEOPLE" (16:32), including wives and children—unnecessarily vindictive?

THE RABBIS ANSWER: No, Korakh's offense is so monstrous that even though the heavenly court does not normally punish children under twenty, the rule was suspended in this case because of the seriousness of Korakh's sin.

Our daughters ask: But even if Korakh and his followers do deserve what they get, why are innocent women and children swallowed up along with the guilty?

Dinah the Wounded One answers: The Torah gives no reason why they are punished for what only the men have done. Earlier in the chapter, in fact, God threatens to annihilate *all* the Israelites, but Moses and Aaron appeal for more selective punishment: "when one man sins, will you be wrathful with the whole community?" (16:22) Yet even though God accedes to their pleas, innocent women and children die with the guilty. Indeed, women and children have always been victims in war, even holy ones.

Sarah the Ancient One remarks: Sometimes there's just no telling what God is up to. After all, when God called Abraham to take my beloved Isaac up to the mountain, did God truly intend to take the life of an innocent boy? Or was it only a trick to test how well Abraham understood the ways of this strange new God? Maybe the rebellion of Korakh was just such a test—to see whether these so-called priests could work out their religious differences unlike those who had come before them, without resorting to threats and violence.

Lilith the Rebel retorts: In which case, they fail. It turns into a typical case of male brinksmanship, drawing lines in the sand: You've gone too far! . . . No, *you've* gone too far—and I'll call upon my god to prove it! If women had been in charge, we certainly would have handled the situation more sensibly.

AARON'S ANCESTRAL HOUSE

Huldah the Preacher teaches: After the disastrous death of Korakh and his confederates, followed by a plague that kills an additional fourteen thousand Israelites, God makes clear that only Aaron and his direct descendants are to manage the sacred duties associated with God's house: "any outsider who encroaches shall be put to death" (18:7). However, this privilege brings with it a burden: "you with your sons and the ancestral house under your charge shall bear any guilt connected with the sanctuary; you and your sons alone shall bear any guilt connected with your priesthood" (18:1).

Our daughters ask: Are only men included in Aaron's ancestral line? What about Aaron's direct female descendants? Are they considered outsiders, under the ban of death for encroaching on holy ground, or do they also inherit the privilege of entering the Sanctuary, and with it the burden of priestly guilt?

SERAKH BAT ASHER THE HISTORIAN ANSWERS: The Torah does not say—and Aaron's house is no more.

PRIESTLY PERKS

BERURIAH THE SCHOLAR TEACHES: Because Levites are banned from owning land—they lived scattered among the twelve tribes (except for the priestly cult that resided in Jerusalem)—the rest of the Israelites are required to supply their material needs through taxes (tithes, redemption of firstborn males and animals, firstfruits), donations, and gifts. These offerings are divided into two categories: "most holy" (*kodesh kodashim*) and "holy" (*kodashim*).

OUR DAUGHTERS ASK: Who's entitled to eat these holy offerings?

THE RABBIS ANSWER: Only male priests can eat of the former; the other gifts are permitted to all ritually pure members of priestly households, including unmarried women and slaves. But married women and hired workers, who maintain their own households, are excluded. The "most holy" offerings, consisting primarily of the unburned parts of the meal—sin and guilt offerings—are the choicest and are therefore reserved for God's sacred stewards.

OUR MOTHERS COMMENT: But from a nutritional perspective, these animal products—mainly red meat, internal organs, and skin, all of them seasoned with salt—contain dangerously high concentrations of cholesterol, saturated fat, and sodium. So maybe priestly women were not so disadvantaged after all.

A COVENANT OF SALT

OUR DAUGHTERS ASK: Why are these special sacred offerings described as "AN EVERLASTING COVENANT OF SALT BEFORE YHVH" (18:19)? What's the symbolism of salt?

THE SAGES IN OUR OWN TIME ANSWER: In the ancient Near East, salt was the best preservative against decay and therefore served as a symbol of permanence. Covenants were sealed with salt, a practice that continues to this day in Arab communities. In Israel, salt has always been abundant because of the Dead Sea, called in Hebrew the "Salt Sea." It is possible that the story of Lot's wife transformed into a pillar of salt was inspired by the curiously shaped salt deposits in this area.

THE RABBIS EXPLAIN: Salt was required on all Temple sacrifices. It continues to play a vital role in draining blood to "kasher" meat.

SERAKH BAT ASHER THE HISTORIAN ADDS: As a symbol of the tears shed by the Hebrew slaves in Egypt, salt embitters spring greens at the seder table. And to remind us of the Temple sacrifices, Adam's curse to earn bread by his sweaty labor, and our often lachrymose history, we salt our hallah at Sabbath and festival tables.

OUR BUBBES INTERJECT: And salt also protects us from harm, which is why we use it in rituals for risky times like birth, marriage, and death. That's why our mothers in ancient Israel used to rub their newborn babies with salt. It can't hurt.

ESTHER THE HIDDEN ONE OFFERS: Medieval mystics taught that salt drives off evil spirits.

OUR MOTHERS CONCLUDE: Which may explain why, to this day, we bring salt and bread to a new home to symbolize our hopes for permanence and blessing.

39. HUKKAT:

Miriam's Well

(NUMBERS 19:1–22:1)

TORAH TEACHES: This parasha is permeated by death. Chapter 19 describes the puzzling ritual of the Red Heifer that purifies someone contaminated through contact with a corpse. In the following chapter, both Miriam and Aaron die, and Moses hears his own death sentence after he strikes the rock contrary to God's instructions. And in chapter 21, many of the people die from a plague of fiery serpents when they complain about the lack of water.

THE PARADOXICAL RITUAL OF THE RED HEIFER

THE RABBIS TEACH: For millennia, we have considered the ritual of the Red Heifer the most baffling law in the Torah. Even the wise King Solomon confesses that "I succeeded in understanding the whole Torah, but as soon as I reached this chapter about the Red Heifer, I searched, probed, and questioned: 'I said I will get wisdom but it was far from me' (Ecclesiastes 7:23)." The great Yohanan ben Zakkai claimed that God *means* this law to be incomprehensible: "It is a statute [*hukkah*] I have laid down, a decree that I have decreed, and you are not authorized to violate my decree."

And yet some among us have proposed that this paradoxical ritual, which "purifies the defiled" (those contaminated by death) and "defiles the pure" (those who prepare and dispense the ashes of the Red Heifer), served to atone for Israel's collective sin, since the mother cow in this ritual atoned for the sin of her son, the Golden Calf.

STILL OTHERS TEACH: This ritual atoned for whatever unknown sin had led to a particular death, since the red of the cow's ashes and blood, combined with the red hyssop, cedar, and "crimson stuff," fulfilled Isaiah's prophecy: "THOUGH YOUR SINS BE RED AS SCARLET, THEY SHALL TURN AS WHITE AS SNOW" (Isaiah 1:18).

BUT ACCORDING TO OTHERS: The ritual of the Red Heifer discouraged bereaved people from holding on to the bodies or spirits of their beloved dead.

THE RABBIS CONCLUDE: So rare are pure red heifers that only nine were identified from the time of the Torah until the destruction of the Second Temple. The tenth will be located and prepared by the Messiah.

ESTHER THE HIDDEN ONE ADDS: Only then will the mystery of death and beyond also be revealed.

MIRIAM'S DEATH

OUR DAUGHTERS ASK: Why isn't there a period of national mourning when Miriam dies, as there is at Aaron's death? Hasn't she also been a national leader for forty years! And why does the Torah narrate Miriam's death in only a single unadorned sentence: "THE ISRAELITES ARRIVED IN A BODY AT THE WILDERNESS OF ZIN ON THE FIRST NEW MOON, AND THE PEOPLE STAYED AT KADESH. MIRIAM DIED THERE AND WAS BURIED THERE" (20:1), while her brother's death is divinely scripted in elaborate detail later in this same chapter? When Aaron is about to die, the whole people watch from the foot of Mount Hor as his son Eleazar and Moses accompany him up the mountain. There, atop the mountain, Moses strips his brother of his priestly vestments and puts them on Eleazar, and then Aaron dies. Uncle and nephew then descend, and the people "BEWAILED AARON THIRTY DAYS" (20:29). We aren't even told how Miriam dies or when.

THE SAGES IN OUR OWN TIME EXPLAIN: Aaron is the high priest, head of the national religious hierarchy, a position of great power and prestige in the ancient world.

OUR DAUGHTERS ARGUE: But that doesn't explain why Miriam's death receives so little attention. Were women, even national leaders, not mourned like men?

THE RABBIS ANSWER: Miriam does get the death she deserves. She is one of only six people—Abraham, Isaac, and Jacob, and the three children of Amram and Yokheved: Miriam, Aaron, and Moses—who have merited death by the kiss of God. Neither the Angel of Death nor the worms have had any power over these holy souls. Miriam's death occurred on the tenth day of the month of Nisan, forty years to the day after the Israelites first set aside a lamb for their first Passover feast in Egypt, and precisely one year before they crossed the Jordan into the Promised Land. To memorialize her death, this day was long ago established as a fast day for all righteous women, a custom that has fallen into disuse.

MIRIAM THE PROPHET ANSWERS: Perhaps it is time to revive this custom and properly honor my passing.

MIRIAM'S WELL

MIRIAM THE PROPHET SINGS: Hear the ancient legend of Miriam's Well!

THE RABBIS BEGIN: Immediately after Miriam died, the people complained that they lacked water. And so we learn that with her death disappeared the miraculous well that had accompanied the Israelites throughout their desert journey. As long as Miriam was alive, the well sustained the people; but as soon as she died, the well vanished, resurfacing periodically in Jewish legend—most often in the Sea of Galilee (although sightings have been reported as far away as Poland).

SERAKH BAT ASHER THE HISTORIAN ADDS: At twilight on the sixth day of Creation, God created this well, which in time passed to Abraham and from him to Hagar and then on to Isaac. But the well was lost during the Egyptian captivity.

MIRIAM CONTINUES: Because of my merits—my powers of prophecy, my protection of my baby brother Moses, my skillful midwifery among the Hebrew slaves, and my victory song at the Sea of Reeds—this well was restored to the Jewish people and was called by my name.

OUR MOTHERS OFFER: An ancient folk tradition teaches that Miriam's well fills all wells at the end of Shabbat and gives such water miraculous curative powers.

OUR DAUGHTERS DECLARE: In our own day, Miriam's well has become for us a symbol of Jewish women's creativity, spirituality, collective experience, healing, and wisdom.

SONG OF THE WELL

BERURIAH THE SCHOLAR RECOUNTS: Some time after Miriam's death, the people move on to Be'er near the land of Moab. There, at a well—the literal meaning of *Be'er*—they sing the following song:

Spring up, O well—sing to it—
The well which the chieftains dug,
Which the nobles of the people started
With maces, with their own staffs. (21:17–18)

THE RABBIS EXPLAIN: God teaches the Israelites how to summon up water with this incantation after Miriam's Well disappears at her death. In the ancient Temple in Jerusalem, this song was chanted every third Sabbath at the *minhah* sacrifice; Moses' Song at the Sea was sung on the other two Sabbaths.

WOMEN AND WELLS

BERURIAH THE SCHOLAR TEACHES: Women and wells are often linked in the Torah. When Abraham banishes Hagar for the first time, she encounters an angel by a wellspring in the wilderness; the second time, she hears God's voice by a spring. Rebecca meets her beloved by a well, as do Rachel and Zipporah. And the Rabbis tell of a miraculous well associated with Miriam that sustains the Israelites in the desert.

OUR DAUGHTERS ASK: What connects women to wells?

MOTHER RACHEL ANSWERS: Like water bubbling up mysteriously from the earth, nurturing fluids issue forth from women's bodies: menstrual blood to nourish life, the waters of birth, breast milk—and so many tears.

40. BALAK:

Humor and Irony

(NUMBERS 22:2–25:9)

TORAH TEACHES: When the Children of Israel, two million strong, approach King Balak's domain, he summons the pagan prophet Balaam to curse this formidable enemy before they attack. Balaam first refuses to obey, arguing that this people is blessed by God, but he changes his mind when God assures him that his mission has divine sanction. En route to Balak, Balaam's ass balks when she encounters an angel with a drawn sword. Balaam, blind to the angel, beats the ass until she speaks to him, after which the angel makes himself visible to Balaam as well. Arriving at Balak's side, Balaam blesses Israel instead of cursing it—against his own will.

THE TALE OF BALAAM AND HIS ASS

THE SAGES IN OUR OWN TIME EXPLAIN: Most scholars agree that this story, extending from chapter 22 until the end of chapter 24, was probably composed independently and later inserted here, linked to the ongoing narrative by its setting in Moab, where the Israelites are now encamped (22:1). The story is quite different from anything else in the Torah, spiced with humor and a fantastic talking beast; and like the later Book of Esther (likewise regarded by scholars as a fairy tale rather than a historical account), it dramatizes—through comic reversal—the triumph of the Jews over a wicked enemy. This is the only parasha in the last four books of the Torah that makes no mention of Moses.

OUR BUBBES COMMENT: Our favorite part of this story is the one about Balaam and his ass. Of course, it doesn't surprise us that the animal is a *she*-ass. Nor does it surprise us that the *Tzena Urena*—written by a man for us poor illiterate women—saw fit to neuter the ass when she was translated into Yiddish. They couldn't fool us! It's clear that only a female animal would show such wit and wisdom. After all, *she's* not the ass in this story!

THE RABBIS RETORT: That's not the point of this incident. From it we learn that "Man rides, but God holds the reins."

Our bubbes fire back: And women bear the burdens for both of them!

INTERTWINED DESTINIES

Our daughters ask: Balak is the king of Moab. So why does his plot against the Israelites involve both "THE ELDERS OF MOAB AND THE ELDERS OF MIDIAN" (22:7)?

Serakh bat Asher the Historian answers: Both of these nations have a long and complicated history with the Jewish people. Moab is born out of the incestuous union between Lot and his daughters, and his descendants include Ruth, King David, and the messianic line—as well as the characters in this parasha, King Balak and the Moabite people. "THE ELDERS OF MIDIAN, VERSED IN DIVINATION" (22:7), coconspirators in Balak's plot, also trace their roots back to Israelite ancestry: Midian is Abraham's son by Keturah. And Moses himself marries a Midianite woman, Zipporah, whose father is a priest, versed in divination like the Midianites in our tale.

Huldah the Preacher points out: To its credit, the Torah doesn't paper over the cracks and stains of Israel's foundational history. And so Israel's kinsmen are shown as both its enemies and its allies. That's one of the Bible's most uncomfortable and precious truths.

Esther the Hidden One reveals: And in the messianic age, all of Abraham's children—Isaac and Ishmael, Midian and Esau—will be united in the sanctuary of peace. May such peace come soon, and in our days.

KINDNESS TO ANIMALS

Our daughters ask: Jewish tradition teaches us that we should feed our beasts before we feed ourselves. Why should the Rabbis care so much about how we treat our animals?

Huldah the Preacher answers: Because sometimes they take better care of us than we do of them. For example, when Balaam's ass sees the angel with the drawn sword, she risks her life to save her master. Her reward is a beating.

SOOTHSAYING DOGS

OUR MOTHERS RECOUNT: Asses are not the only beasts who speak their minds! As it is told:

An old Jew once met old Father Abraham as he went walking.

"Ask any favor and it will be granted to you," Abraham said to him.

The old man replied, "I wish to understand the language of animals."

"And so you shall," said Abraham, and then he vanished.

When he arrived home, the old man overheard his two dogs, barking to each other. How surprised he was when he found that he could understand them!

"What a feast we will have tomorrow," said one of the dogs, "for tonight our master's cow will die."

Hearing this, the old man immediately took his cow to market and sold her.

The next day, he heard the dogs talking again. "What a feast we will have tomorrow," one said, "for in the morning the house will catch fire, and we can raid the pantry while the old couple try to put out the flames."

So the old man packed up his belongings and sold his house.

But on the third day, the dogs said to each other, "Pity our poor master, for when the sun sets tonight, his wife will die."

Not knowing how to save his wife from the Angel of Death, the old man ran to his rabbi and told him all that had befallen him.

"Rabbi, what can I do?" he cried.

"You old fool!" the rabbi chided him. "You've turned a blessing into a curse! Abraham's gift was meant to save your wife by your sacrificing in her place your cow and house. But you've misunderstood the dogs' message, and now your wife must die."

And so when the sun set, the old man closed his wife's eyes and sat down to mourn.

THE CONSEQUENCES OF TELLING THE TRUTH

DINAH THE WOUNDED ONE TEACHES: Balaam beats his ass for affirming the truth—that there is danger facing them in their path—a truth Balaam himself cannot see. How often does the truth stare us in the face like this—an angel with a drawn sword—and we are beaten for honoring it. How often do women—mothers, wives, and daughters—see this terrible angel and suffer abuse for revealing the sword: alcoholism, incest, neglect, rage. Beaten enough, the victim summons up the courage and strength to speak (if she is still able), as is it written: "WHAT HAVE I DONE TO YOU THAT YOU HAVE BEATEN ME THESE THREE TIMES?" (22:28). And then, if we are fortunate, an angel may appear, and then even a curse may yield to a blessing.

BLESSING AND THE EVIL EYE

OUR DAUGHTERS ASK: Balak summons Balaam to curse Israel, but he ends up blessing them. What happens? Does God take away his free will and turn him into a puppet? And what's the connection between blessings and curses?

OUR BUBBES ANSWER: We Jewish mothers and grandmothers have long known that blessings are even more dangerous than curses. We know that what activates the evil eye, the *ayin ha-ra,* is jealousy. And so a mother worries: If I praise my child—"a beauty, a genius, healthy like a bull"—it's as good as cursing her. Pooh, pooh, pooh—better I should call her ugly, conceal her virtues so that the evil eye stays away and does her no harm. *Keine eyin hore!*

OUR DAUGHTERS ASK: But don't you realize that to withhold praise is also a curse, a crushing blow to a child's pride? It's better to bless than to curse—even at the risk of provoking the evil eye.

BALAAM'S INTIMACY WITH HIS ASS

THE RABBIS EXPLAIN: Balaam knew his ass intimately as a man knows a woman. As she says to him: "LOOK, I AM THE ASS THAT YOU HAVE BEEN RIDING ALL ALONG UNTIL THIS DAY!" (22:30)

DINAH QUIPS: Why else would she have accepted such cruel treatment from his hand? Why else would she have tried to save his life at the peril of her own?

GOD'S LESSONS FOR BALAAM

OUR DAUGHTERS ASK: After beating his poor ass three times, Balaam's at last allowed to see the obstacle in their path: "THE ANGEL OF GOD STANDING IN THE WAY, HIS DRAWN SWORD IN HIS HAND" (22:31). When the angel confronts him and accuses him of treating his ass unfairly, Balaam offers only a lame excuse: "I DID NOT KNOW YOU WERE STANDING IN MY WAY" (22:31). He makes no apologies for beating his innocent beast. But instead of punishing him for his thoughtlessness, God then "UNCOVER[S] BALAAM'S EYES" (22:31). What does God reveal to Balaam if the angel has already made himself visible to him?

WILY REBECCA ANSWERS: Because Balaam shows no remorse for his foolish actions, the angel punishes him by making him continue his journey, forcing him to make an ass of himself before all his neighbors and to discredit himself in their eyes as a seer.

BALAK'S REVENGE

OUR DAUGHTERS ASK: Immediately after Balaam blesses the people he's been sent to curse, the Israelites turn his blessing on its head, cursing the people he's just blessed—namely, themselves. Even though Balaam has predicted that "NO HARM IS IN SIGHT FOR JACOB, NO WOE FOR ISRAEL" (23:21), they bring disaster down on their own heads by acting out sexually and worshiping idols. And these things happen at the invitation of Moabite women—that is, Balak's subjects. As it's written: "THE PEOPLE PROFANED THEMSELVES BY WHORING WITH THE MOABITE WOMEN, WHO INVITED THE PEOPLE TO THE SACRIFICES OF THEIR GOD" (25:1–2). Outraged, God punishes the Israelites with a plague, killing 24,000, and then orders Moses to have their ringleaders publicly impaled. What's happened to Balaam's blessing?

OUR BUBBES EXCLAIM: Like a curse, a blessing is not a telegram; it doesn't arrive so fast!

THE RABBIS REPLY: What the Moabites failed to do from a distance—curse the Israelites—they accomplished by drawing them nearer, sharing first their beds and then their altars. It is well known that cultic prostitution and sexual excess were essential features of many ancient Mediterranean religions, which is why we imposed so many restrictions against intercourse—sexual, economic, social, and cultural—with other nations. We had no choice but to impose such separatist policies, because the Israelite rank and file repeatedly failed to live up to another of Balaam's visions: Israel as "A PEOPLE THAT DWELLS APART, NOT RECKONED AMONG THE NATIONS" (23:9).

HAGAR THE STRANGER QUIPS: And as you can see by looking around at your community today, you Jews continue to have trouble closing your tent flaps completely to strangers.

OUR MOTHERS ANSWER: But many who come in choose to join us and follow our ways, thereby enriching our people immeasurably.

RELIGIOUS ZEAL

OUR DAUGHTERS ASK: This parasha ends with quite a dramatic scene: Aaron's grandson Pinkhas, discovering an Israelite man copulating with a pagan woman, "STABBED BOTH OF THEM, THE ISRAELITE AND THE WOMAN, THROUGH THE BELLY" (25:8). How does the Torah justify such fanaticism?

DINAH THE WOUNDED ONE ANSWERS: Probably no people on earth has suffered more from the evils of religious extremism than the Jews. Victims of crusades, jihads, inquisitions, pogroms, forced conversions, and expulsions, and in our own times the barbarism of modern state religion as well as bitter infighting within the Jewish community, Jews have learned to be wary of those who claim to act in the name of God. Yet here the grandson of a high priest impulsively murders the son of an Israelite chieftain and the daughter of a Midianite tribal leader in a fit of rage. While Moses and the people are weeping over the recent apostasy at Baal-peor, Pinkhas follows the couple into "the chamber". . .

LEAH THE NAMER INTERRUPTS: Interpreted as the Tabernacle, a secondary priestly tent, or a marriage canopy . . .

DINAH FINISHES: And spears them both "through the belly" (*kovatah*).

THE RABBIS EXPLAIN: We also interpret *kovatah* to mean "womb" (related to *nekevah*) or female genitals. Although we cannot condone Pinkhas' rash action, the Torah gives us little wiggle room here. For as a result of Pinkhas' bold deed, the divine plague is checked, and in the next parasha—which even bears Pinkhas' name!—God rewards him for his zeal by designating him as the forebear of the High Priest's line. Because we are committed to revering every jot and tittle of the Torah as the word of God, we can only redeem such a text by reinterpreting or neutralizing it. That is why we have ruled that *"halakha ve'ain morim ken"*: although such religious zeal is permissible, we do not teach people to act this way.

MIRIAM THE PROPHET RETORTS: We could also show our reverence for the Torah by refusing to reinterpret such passages and instead attributing the Torah's excesses and inequities to human fallibility. In this way, we redeem God.

41. PINKHAS:
Women at the Margins

(NUMBERS 25:10–30:1)

TORAH TEACHES: As a reward for Pinkhas' zeal in slaying the two idolaters—Zimri and his Midianite lover, Cozbi—God appoints Aaron's grandson heir to the high priesthood.

In preparation for the Israelites' battle with Midian and their imminent settlement in Canaan, God orders that a second national census be taken, so that tribal lands can be allocated after the conquest. As part of this census, all the tribes and clans are named, according to their ancestry: the twelve sons of Jacob, their sons, and those among their male descendants who have established their own clans. In this list of almost one hundred names, only six women are mentioned: the five daughters of Zelophekhad, and Serakh, daughter of Asher, the only granddaughter of Jacob who is named in the Torah.

When the census is over, Moses finds himself confronted with an anomalous case: Zelophekhad, one of the Manassites, has died without leaving male heirs. His five daughters petition Moses to inherit his land, urging him: "LET NOT OUR FATHER'S NAME BE LOST TO HIS CLAN JUST BECAUSE HE HAD NO SON!" When Moses brings this case before God, the daughters' claim is upheld as "just," and they are given a hereditary holding in their family's land.

At God's bidding, Moses climbs a mountain to view the land that he will not be allowed to enter, and brings Joshua to Eleazar to be appointed Moses' successor. The parasha ends with a detailed description of the daily, Sabbath, new moon, and holiday sacrifices.

COZBI DAUGHTER OF ZUR

OUR DAUGHTERS ASK: Why does the Torah choose to identify the *pagan* woman killed by Pinkhas together with an Israelite man? As it is written: "THE NAME OF THE MIDIANITE WOMAN WHO WAS KILLED WAS COZBI DAUGHTER OF ZUR; HE WAS THE TRIBAL HEAD OF AN ANCESTRAL HOUSE IN MIDIAN" (25:15). Who is Cozbi and why are we given her lineage?

BERURIAH THE SCHOLAR ANSWERS: The three people involved in this incident are not just ordinary folk. Cozbi is a princess, daughter of one of

Midian's tribal leaders. Her lover, Zimri, is the son of a clan chieftain. And Pinkhas is Aaron's grandson, heir to the high priesthood.

THE RABBIS POINT OUT: In killing Zimri, Pinkhas is obeying God's command to impale the ringleaders of the Baal-peor affair.

HAGAR THE STRANGER INTERJECTS: But in killing Cozbi, Pinkhas is in effect declaring war on Midian. In the ensuing war between the Israelites and the Midianites, Cozbi's father, Zur, is one of the chieftains killed.

OUR DAUGHTERS ASK: Why is Cozbi named when so many other biblical women—the wives of Noah, Lot, and Job; the daughters of Pharaoh and Jephthah; the mothers of Abraham and Samson—remain nameless in the Bible?

THE RABBIS ANSWER: Until we name them in the Midrash! As for Cozbi, her name, like so many others in the Bible, is freighted with meaning. The Hebrew root *kozev* means "to deceive" or "to lie." That is because Cozbi *makes a lie* out of her father's teachings—that is, to give herself only to the greatest man in Israel. Others teach: She commands her father: "*Kas be*—'Devour for me' this people." Cozbi's name was originally *Shevilanai*, related to the Arabic word meaning "womb opening"—that is, whore. As a popular proverb puts it: "What business does Shevilanai have by the reeds of the lake? What is she doing among the peeling rushes? Her sins stain even her own mother's name."

LILITH THE REBEL COUNTERS: Vulgar misogynist fantasies!

LEAH THE NAMER SUGGESTS: Maybe not, for the Hebrew name Cozbi may derive from the Akkadian word *kuzabatum*, meaning "voluptuous" or "well developed."

OUR MOTHERS CONCLUDE: Sometimes it's better to remain nameless in the Bible.

THE DAUGHTERS OF ZELOPHEKHAD

THE RABBIS TEACH: Zelophekhad's daughters pursue their claim to their father's inheritance because they believe that "God's love is not like the love of a mortal father; the latter prefers his sons to his daughters, but the One who created the world extends divine love to women as well as to men. 'GOD'S TENDER MERCIES ARE OVER ALL GOD'S WORKS'" (Psalm 145:9). In fact, so wise, pious, and learned are these five daughters that they choose to remain unmarried for forty years because they cannot find suitable partners. As a result of their piety, when they later marry, they all miraculously give birth at 130, like Moses' mother, Yokheved.

THE SAGES IN OUR OWN TIME SUGGEST: No, this story justifies why women were later permitted to inherit land within a patriarchal system.

BERURIAH THE SCHOLAR COUNTERS: Or we can understand this story as a valuable lesson for us all, teaching us that Jewish law has the flexibility to expand and embrace women, giving us increasingly more rights and a fairer share of our common legacy.

SOURCE OF THE BREATH OF ALL FLESH

OUR DAUGHTERS ASK: What is God's real name? How do we name that which is infinite? Can one name contain such vastness? But if we begin to call God by many names, can we ever exhaust the list?

THE RABBIS ANSWER: Judaism has many names for God, foremost among them *YHVH*, the Tetragrammaton, the Four-Letter Name, once pronounced only by the High Priest on Yom Kippur, then silenced altogether after the destruction of the Temple. Other names include status terms such as *Adonai*, "Lord"; *Melekh*, "King"; *Ribono shel Olam*, "Master of the Universe"; and attributes like *Tzur*, "Rock"; *Go'el*, "Redeemer," and *Ha-Makom*, "the Place."

HAGAR THE STRANGER BREAKS IN: Don't forget variations on the name of the ancient Mesopotamian god El, such as *Elohim* and *El Shaddai*.

LILITH THE REBEL PROTESTS: I object to the Rabbis' preference for divine names emphasizing hierarchy and male power, such as King, Master, and Lord. I prefer feminine images of generativity and nurture, such as the ancient name *Ha-Rahaman* (derived from the Hebrew root *rehem*, meaning "womb") and its feminine form, *Rahamema*, as well as new names based on the feminine symbols of water—*Ein*, "Fountain"; *Ma'ayan*, "Spring"; *Be'er*, "Well"; *Mekor*, "Source."

ESTHER THE HIDDEN ONE ADDS: And *Shekhinah*, the indwelling feminine Presence especially beloved to the mystics. The mystics also describe God as *Ein Sof*, the One-Without-End.

MIRIAM THE PROPHET POINTS OUT: Here when Moses appeals to God to appoint a successor, he addresses God as *Elohai ha-rukhot l'khol basar*, "SOURCE OF THE BREATH OF ALL FLESH" (27:16). This too is a nurturing image, for is there anything more intimate and sustaining than our breath?

42. MATTOT:
Vows and Commitments

(NUMBERS 30:2–32:42)

TORAH TEACHES: The first chapter of this parasha details the biblical rules governing vows and oaths. The opening verse addresses Israelite men, charging them to honor the verbal commitments they make. The next fourteen verses apply specifically to women, elaborating in considerable detail the limits of their freedom to commit themselves with their own words. Dependent women—those still living under their father's roof—can fulfill their own vows only if their father does not object; similarly, married women have to have the *tacit* approval of their husbands. If, however, their father or husband objects to their vow *immediately upon learning of it*, the vow is thereby annulled, and the woman bears no responsibility for the commitment she has made. The only women who are permitted to make independent vows are widows and divorcées. The text makes no mention of women who do not marry, presumably because such cases are so rare.

In revenge for Midian's sexual and idolatrous seduction at Baal-peor, the Israelites wage a savage war, killing all male Midianites, among them five kings (including Cozbi's father, Zur) and the pagan prophet Balaam; burning down all their cities and encampments; and taking all the women, children, cattle, and property as spoils of war. Moses is enraged that the Israelite fighters have spared "every female"—women are the ones responsible for the earlier plague—and orders the men to kill "every woman who has known a man carnally," as well as all the male children (presumably because they might one day form a fifth column in Israel's midst). But the Israelite soldiers are instructed to spare all the virgins—that is, the men are free to appropriate them as wives or slaves.

THE LIMITS OF A WOMAN'S WORD

THE RABBIS TEACH: We Jews have always regarded taking a vow quite seriously. The third commandment warns us not to take God's name in vain. We have always urged people to avoid taking vows whenever possible, since the consequences of failing to fulfill them can provoke God's wrath. Although Jews no longer generally regard vows within such a theological framework, we still recall their authority each Yom Kippur when we symbolically annul them in the Kol Nidrei prayer. Of course, we vow our allegiance to God every day when we acknowledge God's unity in our prayers.

OUR DAUGHTERS ASK: If vows were once so vitally important, why does the Torah forbid dependent daughters and married women to take vows upon themselves?

SERAKH BAT ASHER THE HISTORIAN ANSWERS: In "those days," women were generally subordinate to men's authority and possessed little or no economic power. Thus a woman could not give away what did not belong to her—her father's or husband's property—or even take an oath to restrict her own already limited freedom—by becoming a Nazirite, for instance.

LILITH THE REBEL COMMENTS: How many women "these days" still live as though such patriarchal principles were still in effect!

TALES ABOUT VOWS

OUR MOTHERS POINT OUT: Although the Torah allows men to annul women's oaths, it doesn't work the other way around. And unfortunately, if men make foolish vows or fail to fulfill solemn ones, it is often women who suffer the consequences, as we can see in the following stories.

JEPHTHAH'S DAUGHTER

JEPHTHAH'S DAUGHTER SHE'ILAH, THE ONE-WHO-IS-DEMANDED, RECOUNTS: When my father, Jephthah, prepared to go into battle against our bitter enemies, the Ammonites, he rashly vowed to sacrifice "WHATEVER COMES OUT OF THE DOOR OF MY HOUSE" (Judges 11:31) should he have the good fortune to win the war. But when he returned home in victory, it was I, not some dumb beast, who joyfully ran out to greet him. Thus it was I, his virgin daughter, who offered herself up on the altar of his folly so that he could fulfill his sacred vow. And so I died, still in the bloom of my youth.

THE RABBIS INTERJECT: Jephthah was not the only one to blame for this senseless death. Pinkhas, who was the High Priest at that time, should have known better than to allow it. But Pinkhas was too proud, too offended by

Jephthah's low social status, to involve himself in She'ilah's desperate plight—and thus his silence cut short her young life as surely as did her father's reckless vow.

OUR MOTHERS RECOUNT: And so She'ilah went with her companions to the hills for two months, to bewail her lost maidenhood. Then she returned home and submitted to her father's will. In ancient days, her death was remembered by all the women of the land, as it is written: "SO IT BECAME A CUSTOM IN ISRAEL FOR THE MAIDENS OF ISRAEL TO GO EVERY YEAR, FOR FOUR DAYS IN THE YEAR, AND CHANT DIRGES FOR THE DAUGHTER OF JEPHTHAH THE GILEADITE" (Judges 11:39–40).

OUR MOTHERS OFFER: Perhaps we might revive this custom in our own day, to lament those of our daughters who die young, never knowing a woman's full joy.

RABBI YOSEF WOSK SUGGESTS: The proper season for observing these "Four Days of Jephthah's Daughter," *arba'at yamim Bat Yiftakh*, would be early summer. For we can hear in the story recounted in Judges precise verbal echoes of Miriam's similar victory celebration centuries earlier at the Sea of Reeds. Both women are described as going out to dance with "DRUMS AND CYMBALS" (Judges 11:34; Exodus 15:20). Since Miriam—and by analogy, She'ilah—sang their songs on the twenty-first of Nisan, we should then add two months to cover the period when She'ilah prepared for her death, bringing us to the twenty-first of Sivan as the date of her tragic sacrifice. Her death would therefore have been mourned in ancient times from the twenty-first to the twenty-fourth day of Sivan, and so we might observe these days again. To commemorate this event, women might choose to study and observe new rituals, to visit and bring comfort to modern-day victims of violence, or to take time for retreat and meditation. In this way, we might "act in some small measure in partnership with the Creator *letakein et haolam*—to repair a wounded world."

THE WEASEL AND THE WELL

THE RABBIS RECOUNT: Once upon a time, a young woman fell into a well and was pulled out by a young man who heard her cries as he passed by. The young woman suggested that they betroth themselves to each other, calling as the two witnesses to their vow the well into which the woman had fallen and a weasel who just then scampered by. Then they parted ways and lost touch with each other. Although the young woman no longer knew where the young man lived or what had become of him, she nonetheless stayed true to her oath, refusing all suitors who came to seek her hand in marriage. In time she went mad, and her parents abandoned all hope of her marrying.

The young man, on the other hand, forsook his oath and forgot all about his first love. He married another woman, but their first child was strangled by a weasel, and their second drowned in a well. Suspecting a supernatural hand at work, his wife pressed him until he confessed to his earlier vow. She then ordered him to divorce her and seek out the woman he had first betrothed. After searching far and wide, he at last found her and asked her distraught parents for her hand. But as he approached the madwoman, she lunged at him, her long nails outstretched like claws. Desperately he cried out, "Weasel and well!" Instantly, she recovered her sanity and agreed to marry her erstwhile suitor, who had betrothed her long ago by the well. And they lived happily ever after.

Therefore beware of betraying matches, for they are as hard to achieve as splitting the Red Sea, and they are even harder to break.

THE UNPAID PLEDGE

OUR BUBBES TEACH: Shame on anyone who makes a vow intending *not* to fulfill it! Such a false promise will cost you much more in the end. As it is told:

A rich miser once went to the Lemberger Rav and asked him to curse his wife so she would die.

"Make a pledge for charity," advised the Rav, "and don't pay it. The Talmud teaches that your wife will die as a punishment."

So the miser went to shul that Shabbos and made a generous pledge for *tzedakah*. Immediately after sundown, everyone demanded that he pay. He refused.

From that day on, his wife only grew stronger. He went back to the Rav to complain.

"She didn't die," explained the rabbi, "because it wouldn't be a punishment for you. But if you treat her kindly so you begin to love her, then she'll die."

And so the miser bought his wife gifts and spoke nicely to her. And to his great surprise, he fell in love with her. But then his wife became deathly ill.

The man ran back to the Rav. "Now I don't want her to die! I love her!"

"Then pay," ordered the Rav.

THE SPOILS AND SPOILED OF WAR

OUR DAUGHTERS ASK: How can the Torah sanction the murder of every Midianite woman and child, except female virgins? As it is written: "NOW, THEREFORE, SLAY EVERY MALE AMONG THE CHILDREN, AND SLAY ALSO EVERY WOMAN WHO HAS KNOWN A MAN CARNALLY; BUT SPARE EVERY YOUNG WOMAN WHO HAS NOT HAD CARNAL RELATIONS WITH A MAN" (31:17).

HAGAR THE STRANGER INTERJECTS: Not only sanction but command!

THE RABBIS ANSWER: But it was the Midianite women who led the Israelites into sin! As it is written: "THEY ARE THE VERY ONES WHO, AT THE BIDDING OF BALAAM, INDUCED THE ISRAELITES TO TRESPASS AGAINST YHVH IN THE MATTER OF PEOR, SO THAT YHVH'S COMMUNITY WAS STRUCK BY THE PLAGUE" (31:16). So how can the Torah permit the Midianite virgins to live and marry Israelite men? Fortunately, such unions were finally outlawed after the Jews returned from Babylonian exile.

OUR DAUGHTERS ASK: Why are you *not* troubled by the genocide brutally perpetrated against Midian—the slaughter of all men (including noncombatants), all male children, and most of the women—as well as the enslavement and forced marriage of the surviving women?

SERAKH BAT ASHER THE HISTORIAN ANSWERS: After three thousand years on the receiving end of history, we find that what now outrages and vexes us in this text is different from what once troubled the Rabbis—but we should recognize that today our rabbis are rather different too.

43. MASSEI:

Strangers

(NUMBERS 33:1–36:13)

ORAH TEACHES: This last parasha in the Book of Numbers begins with a review of the Israelites' itinerary from Egypt to the east bank of the Jordan River, where they now encamp within view of the Promised Land. God instructs Moses to assign tribal leaders and land allotments, and to designate forty-eight towns for the Levites, including six cities of refuge for people fleeing because they have committed involuntary manslaughter. This section is followed by laws concerning homicide.

The parasha concludes by revisiting the case of Zelophekhad's daughters, who are to inherit their father's land in Canaan since he has died without any male heirs.

STINGS AND THORNS

OUR DAUGHTERS ASK: If we're not supposed to marry people from other nations, follow their ways, or worship their gods, how are we supposed to relate to them? Are we supposed to isolate ourselves in ghettos—or isolate them? There's never been a time in Jewish history when we didn't have non-Jewish neighbors.

DINAH THE WOUNDED ONE ANSWERS: One of the most persistent motifs in the Torah is xenophobia, fear of strangers. Many of the laws are framed with the express purpose of remaining separate from outsiders, as it is written: "YOU SHALL NOT FOLLOW THE PRACTICES OF THE NATIONS THAT I AM DRIVING OUT BEFORE YOU . . . YOU SHALL BE HOLY TO ME, FOR I, GOD, AM HOLY, AND I HAVE SET YOU APART FROM OTHER PEOPLES TO BE MINE" (Leviticus 20:23, 26). The Israelites are warned not to become intimate with their neighbors, lest they "whore" after their gods. In fact, the Torah considers no sin more heinous than idolatry, with its attendant rituals—licentiousness, death worship, child sacrifice, and moral pollution. The carnage chronicled in the subsequent books of Joshua, Judges, and Kings represents the Israelites' attempt to rid the land of all other inhabitants so that they won't remain as "STINGS IN YOUR EYES AND THORNS IN YOUR SIDES" (33:55).

HAGAR THE STRANGER RETORTS: Yet all that bloodshed did not wipe us out or banish our gods, and Israel continues to be stung and pricked by our presence in its midst. Indeed, modern Israel is still reaping this legacy.

OUR DAUGHTERS ASK: Isn't there any other way to protect ourselves from the stings and thorns of our neighbors?

OUR BUBBES PIPE UP: As we say, When your enemy falls, don't rejoice; but don't pick him up, either.

MIRIAM THE PROPHET ANSWERS: If we truly remain "holy to God" and resist the temptations of our own inner demons, we do not have to demonize others and profane their faith. We need every ally we can find to overcome the real villains in this world.

ALL IN THE FAMILY

OUR DAUGHTERS ASK: Although the daughters of Zelophekhad are allowed to inherit their father's portion in the land, they're required to marry men within their father's clan. The five daughters marry their first cousins from the tribe of Manasseh, "AND SO THEIR SHARE REMAINED IN THE TRIBE OF THEIR FATHER'S CLAN" (36:12). But how relevant is all this now? After two thousand years of being exiled from Israel, what's the point of discussing tribal shares? Are such distinctions still necessary—or even possible?

BERURIAH THE SCHOLAR ANSWERS: Anthropologists define a tribe as a social group sharing a number of common features: language, land, culture, religion, ancestry, political organization, and economy. The original twelve tribes of ancient Israel are no more: ten tribes were "lost" in the Assyrian conquest of northern Israel in 722 B.C.E., and the remaining two tribes, Judah and Benjamin, together with a number of Levitical and priestly families, have wandered the earth for centuries without a permanent home, until 1948. Only the surviving remnant of the tribe of Levi—Levites and *kohanim*—have retained their tribal identities, although ironically they were never granted any portion in the land.

OUR MOTHERS COMMENT: Yet despite this history of exile, we Jews still largely behave in tribal ways. Although today we inhabit many lands, languages, and cultures, we still orient ourselves—symbolically and literally—to a common homeland and act *as if* we lived there, even if only in "virtual reality."

MIRIAM THE PROPHET CONCLUDES: Not an unreasonable way to keep one's bearings in the sprawling global village we call home.

DEUTERONOMY

דברים

Memory

44. DEVARIM:
Eldering

(DEUTERONOMY 1:1–3:22)

TORAH TEACHES: On the east side of the Jordan, in view of the Promised Land, Moses speaks to the people for the last time. In this first of three long addresses, Moses reviews their forty-year journey in the wilderness, from Mount Horeb—that is, Sinai— until the present time. He highlights the Israelites' military defeats—most notably their failure of nerve soon after leaving Egypt, when the spies brought back an unfavorable report, followed by the military debacle at Hormah at the hands of the Amorites—as well as their triumphs, culminating in their recent conquest of the Amorite kings Sihon and the giant Og.

GOD AS NURSE

MIRIAM THE PROPHET TEACHES: As the people prepare to enter the land without him, Moses seeks to bolster their spirits for the trials ahead. Knowing that they will face fierce combat, he reminds them that God "WILL FIGHT FOR YOU, JUST AS HE DID FOR YOU IN EGYPT BEFORE YOUR VERY EYES" (1:30).

MOTHER RACHEL ADDS: But after forty years leading this "stiff-necked people," Moses has also learned that a warrior God cannot sustain them all the time. The desert has introduced them to other adversaries besides human ones: hunger and thirst, sickness, scorpions, and, perhaps most dangerous of all, the inner demons of despair and rebellion. And so, to brace them to combat these enemies, Moses reminds them that in the wilderness, "YOU SAW HOW YHVH YOUR GOD CARRIED YOU, AS A MAN CARRIES HIS SON, ALL THE WAY THAT YOU TRAVELED UNTIL YOU CAME TO THIS PLACE" (1:31).

OUR MOTHERS ADD: Or as a mother carries her children until they are old enough to walk on their own.

FEMININE IMAGES OF GOD

ESTHER THE HIDDEN ONE TEACHES: The mystics called God *Ein Sof,* the One-Without-End. And no wonder. So many names, so many faces. Shekhinah is as boundless as our imagination and beyond our imagination!

OUR DAUGHTERS EXCLAIM: But almost always the God we encounter is portrayed as male—King, Man of War, Mighty One, the Superhero of Superheroes. Always *He,* never She!

BERURIAH THE SCHOLAR RESPONDS: Our tradition does contain many images of the feminine aspects of God, but for the most part, these have been left in the shadows. Only the kabbalists creatively explored this dimension of God's "personality," primarily the Shekhinah, the immanent divine presence closest to our own experience.

SARAH THE ANCIENT ONE POINTS OUT: But if we look in the Bible, we find ample testimony to God's maternal qualities. The prophet Isaiah reassures us that we will not be forgotten in our times of national catastrophe. For God promises that "AS ONE WHOM HIS MOTHER COMFORTS, SO WILL I COMFORT YOU" (Isaiah 66:13).

MOTHER RACHEL ADDS: And for those of us who have suffered the intimate sorrow of barrenness, God offers the sympathy flowing from Her own womb. As it is written: "TRULY, EPHRAIM IS A DEAR SON TO ME, A CHILD THAT IS DANDLED! WHENEVER I HAVE TURNED AGAINST HIM, MY THOUGHTS WOULD DWELL ON HIM STILL. THAT IS WHY MY WOMB [*me-ay*] TREMBLES FOR HIM. I WILL TRULY SHOW MOTHERLY COMPASSION [*rahem arahamenu*] UPON HIM" (Jeremiah 31:20).

WILY REBECCA INTERJECTS: And just as I cried out in the agony of my labor, so God cries out every time Her people struggle to break the bonds of oppression and breathe free. As it is written: "I HAVE BEEN SILENT FAR TOO LONG, KEPT STILL AND RESTRAINED MYSELF; NOW I WILL SCREAM LIKE A WOMAN IN LABOR, I WILL PANT AND I WILL GASP" (Isaiah 42:14).

SHIFRA AND PUAH PROCLAIM: And just as we braved death to help new life emerge from the killing fields of Egypt, so God midwives us all as we ford the perilous straits of birth. As David declared: "YOU DREW ME FROM THE WOMB, MADE ME SECURE AT MY MOTHER'S BREAST" (Psalm 22:10).

LILITH THE REBEL QUIPS: And don't forget one of God's favorite names, *El Shaddai*—literally, "God of Breasts"!

OUR BUBBES MUSE: And when we disappoint ourselves and those we care about, God acts as our grandmother, always forgiving us and taking us back in love.

PRIESTLY RETIREMENT

OUR DAUGHTERS ASK: What roles did elder priests play in the life of the people? Surely they must have been a great spiritual resource.

BERURIAH THE SCHOLAR REPLIES: Male Levites began their service at twenty-five or thirty and were retired from active duty at fifty. Retired priests could "ASSIST THEIR BROTHER LEVITES AT THE TENT OF MEETING BY STANDING GUARD, BUT THEY SHALL PERFORM NO LABOR" (Leviticus 8:26).

OUR DAUGHTERS ASK: Why were they made to retire so young?

SARAH THE ANCIENT ONE ANSWERS: Fifty was old at that time. Very few lived to 127, as I did.

THE RABBIS ADD: It was physically too taxing for older priests to continue disassembling, transporting, and reassembling the portable Tabernacle.

OUR DAUGHTERS ASK: What about the female Levites? Presumably they didn't participate in the physical work of transporting the Sanctuary. What were their priestly duties? And what happened to them when they reached fifty?

THE SAGES IN OUR OWN TIME ANSWER: We know very little about the roles played by female Levites in priestly life. We suspect that they later participated in sacred musical performances in the Temple. Other than that, their lives are lost to us.

SARAH THE ANCIENT ONE SUGGESTS: In a previous parasha, God tells Moses to appoint seventy elders to assist him in his leadership duties. Perhaps retired priests, male and female, turned to such spiritual "eldering" as a second career. Then, as now, there is much to learn from the wisdom of age.

ELDERING AND THE ROLE OF THE CRONE

SARAH THE ANCIENT ONE TEACHES: How much wisdom one gathers in a lifetime! By the time I reached ninety, I had seen much of my world—the fabulous city of Ur, the harsh desert, the monuments of Egypt! And I had lost even more than I had gained—my family, my language, my faith, my homeland. Out of this wonder and this loss, I built a life alongside my husband, with my only son. And when I died, Abraham paid me homage by buying a field from our neighbors, and there he buried me, in a cave facing my beloved grove in Mamre.

SERAKH BAT ASHER THE HISTORIAN CONTINUES: Our people have been blessed with many wise women like Sarah: the widow Naomi, Deborah the Judge, the Wise Woman of Tekoa, Huldah the Prophet, and I myself, who have witnessed our people's struggles throughout the centuries. If only we celebrated our collective wisdom! If only we rejoiced to have such living treasures in our midst!

OUR MOTHERS RESPOND: In recent years, we have begun to recognize the valuable role elders can play in guiding the younger generations. Among women, such awareness has led to the creation of "crone" ceremonies, often called Simkhat Hokhmah—literally, "joy of wisdom"—celebrating the mature wisdom of older women. Such ceremonies can include rituals—*hakafot* (circles or processions), songs, teachings, gifts, poems, masks, a process-of-life review, and special prayers—shared within a circle of several generations of women.

OUR DAUGHTERS ASK: And what if age has mastered a woman so that her wisdom has departed before she could pass it on?

THE RABBIS ANSWER: We must respect age as if we were welcoming the Shekhinah. And Rabbi Judah taught: Be careful to honor the old who have forgotten their learning because of age, for both the second tablets and the fragments of the first were placed together in the ark.

45. VA-ETKHANAN:
Mindfulness
(DEUTERONOMY 3:23–7:11)

TORAH TEACHES: In his second discourse, Moses continues his review of the people's forty years in the wilderness, bringing them back to the awesome events on Mount Horeb, where they received the Law in the form of Ten Commandments and encountered God's presence in natural signs and wonders. Moses reminds them of their sacred covenant with God and of the dire consequences that will follow if they violate it. He exhorts them not to abandon their faith in one God and to beware the seductions of their new land.

This parasha contains the central declaration of Jewish faith, the *Shema:* "Hear, O Israel! YHVH is our God, YHVH is one," and the *Ve-Ahavta*, the charge to love God and adhere to the commandments. Included in this charge are the commandments of tefillin and mezzuzah.

YOU SHALL NOT ADD ANYTHING OR TAKE ANYTHING AWAY

OUR DAUGHTERS ASK: Why are future generations forbidden to modify the words of the Torah? As it is written: "YOU SHALL NOT ADD ANYTHING TO WHAT I COMMAND YOU OR TAKE ANYTHING AWAY FROM IT" (4:2). What about rabbinic interpretation, the oral tradition, the folk Torah? What about *our* voices?

SARAH THE ANCIENT ONE ANSWERS: No culture, no matter how traditional, ever remains static. Social customs evolve, political power shifts, unforeseen situations pose new questions and demand new responses. Therefore every legal system must master the challenges of historical change—or fail.

BERURIAH THE SCHOLAR REMARKS: Indeed, the Jewish legal system has proven remarkably flexible—despite or perhaps because of its having been forced to adapt to so much upheaval during its three-thousand-year history. Regarding the Torah as the cornerstone of its law, it has erected an elaborate architecture of interpretation—the Mishnah and the Talmud, the medieval codes, collections of Responsa—that reflect the complex experiences of a people in exile.

SERAKH BAT ASHER THE HISTORIAN CONTINUES: But once the Enlightenment broke down the ghetto walls, many Jews quickly embraced the Western freedoms of liberty, equality, and fraternity, eagerly leaving behind their allegiance to rabbinic law and its demands.

MIRIAM THE PROPHET CONCLUDES: So we are now free to take this yoke upon ourselves, not because we are told to, but because we choose to! And we are also free to continue to interpret the Torah with our new understanding of its ancient words.

OUR DAUGHTERS ASK: But the Torah warns us not to "ADD ... OR TAKE AWAY" from any of the "LAWS AND RULES WHICH I AM INSTRUCTING YOU TO OBSERVE" (4:1). How do we reconcile our interpretive freedom with this commandment to refrain from taking such liberties?

THE RABBIS ANSWER: We believe with perfect faith that on Mount Sinai, God gave Moses not only the Written Law—that is, the Torah—but also the Oral Law, including all subsequent *rabbinic* interpretations of the written Torah.

LILITH PROTESTS: And what about all of God's words that have echoed beyond the range of the Rabbis' ears?

MIRIAM THE PROPHET ANSWERS: Surely God will be pleased to see them restored to their proper place in the Torah.

IMMANENCE

THE SAGES IN OUR OWN TIME TEACH: Theologians speak of two dimensions of the divine: transcendence and immanence. Ancient gods were believed to inhabit an intermediate realm between these two dimensions— transcendent yet limited, immanent yet not intimate.

MIRIAM THE PROPHET ELABORATES: The God of the Torah expands both these boundaries. YHVH is both Ruler of the Universe and "CLOSE AT HAND ... WHENEVER WE CALL" (4:7). To speak about God as transcendent is to point beyond human experience: God as Creator of heaven and earth, vaster than time and space, beyond our imagination. To speak about the divine as immanent is to meet God "face-to-face": in nature, in godly people, and in our own hearts.

THE DANGERS OF FORM

HULDAH THE PREACHER TEACHES: Surrounded by idolatrous cultures, the Israelites are constantly tempted to imitate them. The Torah repeatedly reminds the people that God is invisible to human eyes. As it is written: "BE MOST CAREFUL—SINCE YOU SAW NO SHAPE WHEN YHVH SPOKE TO YOU AT HOREB OUT OF THE FIRE" (4:15). Therefore they are forbidden to represent God in any physical form—"THE FORM OF A MAN OR A WOMAN" (4:16); beasts of the land, sky, or sea; or a heavenly body—lest they be lured into worshiping it.

LEAH THE NAMER ADDS: The Hebrew word *nidahta*, "lured," comes from a root meaning both "to draw toward" and its opposite, "to cast out." Both consequences await those who try to imprison God inside an idol's image.

THE PORTION ALLOTTED TO OTHER PEOPLES

OUR DAUGHTERS ASK: Although the Torah is constantly warning the Israelites not to worship idols, here in this verse the Torah seems to approve idol worship among "OTHER PEOPLES EVERYWHERE UNDER HEAVEN" (4:19). Only Israel, freed from the "IRON BLAST FURNACE . . . TO BE GOD'S VERY OWN PEOPLE" (4:20), must remain absolutely faithful to one God. So is idolatry "bad for the Jews" only? Is the idolatry of other nations part of the divine plan? As it is written: "THESE YHVH YOUR GOD ALLOTTED TO THE OTHER PEOPLES" (4:19). Doesn't the Torah elsewhere regard pagan practices as "abominations" and "abhorrences"?

THE RABBIS ANSWER: Idolaters who act ethically, according to the seven universal "Laws of Noah," are only "follow[ing] the customs of their fathers" and are therefore not to be condemned. It is only when they act immorally—sacrificing children, engaging in sexual depravity, committing acts of violence—that they are to be despised. But the righteous among them "will have a share in the world to come."

THE DIVINE ATTRIBUTE OF MERCY

MOTHER RACHEL TEACHES: Like any parent, God alternates between offering carrots and sticks. Usually the threats of punishment outweigh—both in words and in drama—the promises of blessing. Perhaps this fact reflects—in hindsight—the reality of later Israelite history or, simply, the way of the world. Moses warns the people that in their new land, they will prove faithless to God and turn to idolatry. And as punishment, God will exile them from the land; but when at long last they repent, God will remember the ancient covenant and redeem them. As it is written: "FOR YHVH YOUR GOD IS A COMPASSIONATE GOD" (4:31).

LEAH THE NAMER EXPLAINS: This God of redemption is described here as *rahum*, from *rehem*, meaning "womb." Other words derived from this Hebrew root include *rahamim*, usually translated as mercy; *rahem*, to have compassion; *Ha-Rahaman*, the Merciful One; and, curiously, *raham*, a species of vulture, perhaps an acknowledgment that even its assigned role in nature derives from God's compassion.

ESTHER THE HIDDEN ONE REVEALS: To the Rabbis, Compassion, *Rahamim*, is the divine attribute that balances God's other major aspect, Judgment, *Din*, or Power, *Gevurah*. Drawing upon this tradition, some contemporary feminists have begun using the divine name *Rahamema*—the feminine form of *Ha-Rahaman*—in prayer and song.

THE COVENANT AT SINAI

OUR DAUGHTERS ASK: It's often quoted to us that the covenant enacted between God and Israel at Horeb transcended that historical moment, as it is written: "IT IS NOT WITH OUR FATHERS THAT GOD MADE THIS COVENANT"; rather, the covenant is made "WITH US, THE LIVING, EVERY ONE OF US WHO IS HERE TODAY" (5:3). To whom is Moses speaking? Are *we* included in the *us?*

THE RABBIS ANSWER: With the exception of Moses, Joshua, and Caleb, every other male Israelite who was present at that awesome event when God "SPOKE OUT OF THE FIRE" (5:4) is now dead. Moses is speaking to the next generation, who will renew the covenant and pass it on.

MIRIAM CONCLUDES: So that means us, the living, every one of us who is here today!

THE EMPATHIC POWER OF THE SABBATH

OUR DAUGHTERS ASK: The fourth commandment as it's repeated here differs from the version in Exodus (20:8–11) in several ways. First of all, instead of "Remember" (*zakhor*), the Torah here says "Observe" (*shamor*). What's the difference?

THE RABBIS ANSWER: This deliberate discrepancy conveys several important lessons: that keeping the Sabbath requires *doing* as well as refraining from doing certain things; that only God can speak two words simultaneously; that at a forty-year distance from the original events, Moses needs stronger language to motivate the people.

BERURIAH THE SCHOLAR POINTS OUT: The *reasons* given for observing the Sabbath are also different in the two versions. In Exodus, we are told that our own weekly rest recalls God's original pause from labor on the seventh day of Creation. But here we are told the Sabbath reminds us that we were once slaves who had no respite from toil. We must therefore rest not only ourselves but also our servants, guests, and animals.

HULDAH THE PREACHER ADDS: It would be good to carry this lesson into our weekdays as well.

THE ROOTS OF DESIRE

BERURIAH THE SCHOLAR TEACHES: In the Exodus account, the tenth commandment forbids coveting a neighbor's house, wife, slaves, beasts, or "ANYTHING THAT IS YOUR NEIGHBOR'S" (20:14). But this second version places "YOUR NEIGHBOR'S WIFE" before his house and adds to the list "HIS FIELD" (5:18).

LEAH THE NAMER ELABORATES: Even more significant is the use here of two different Hebrew words for "covet": in Exodus, only one verb—*takhmod*—is used. But in Deuteronomy, this verb applies only to a neighbor's wife; a second verb—*titaveh*—applies to everything else. Normally, *takhmod* refers to desire stimulated by the eyes; *titaveh*, by the appetites, principally sexual lust and hunger.

HULDAH THE PREACHER POINTS OUT: In the Bible, both words occur for the first time—and together—in the story of Eve and the serpent: "WHEN THE WOMAN SAW THAT THE TREE WAS GOOD FOR EATING AND A DELIGHT (*ta'avah*) TO THE EYES, AND THAT THE TREE WAS DESIRABLE (*nekhmad*) AS A SOURCE OF WISDOM, SHE TOOK OF ITS FRUIT AND ATE" (Genesis 3:6).

DINAH THE WOUNDED ONE CONCLUDES: In other words, when a man covets his neighbor's property, he's seeking material pleasure, but when he lusts after his neighbor's wife, he's seeking to satisfy his heart and mind. Either way, he's setting himself up for a fall.

THE REVERENCE OF DAUGHTERS

OUR DAUGHTERS ASK: After reviewing the awesome events at Sinai, Moses directs the people to observe all of God's laws so that future generations will follow their example and "LONG ENDURE" (5:30). But his charge—"SO THAT YOU, YOUR SON, AND YOUR SON'S SON MAY REVERE GOD" (6:2)—is framed in the masculine singular. What about daughters?

OUR MOTHERS ANSWER: It has always been Jewish women—as mothers, aunts, grandmothers, and honorary "bubbes"—who have raised and shaped each generation, both through example and through "folk Torah" (proverbial wisdom, custom, songs, stories, memories, and rebuke). How much stronger we can be as a people now that men *and* women are being given both Torahs to teach!

THE ORANGE ON THE SEDER PLATE

OUR DAUGHTERS ASK: Are women commanded to retell the story of the Exodus? Why is it written that "WHEN IN TIME TO COME YOUR SON ASKS YOU, 'WHAT MEAN THE DECREES, LAWS, AND RULES . . .'" (6:20)? What about if *we* ask?

THE RABBIS EXPLAIN: Taking this verse together with three others in the Torah, we created the section in the Passover Haggadah traditionally known as "The Four Sons." This particular verse we've rewritten and placed in the mouth of the wise son, who seeks to know what these laws mean to us *(otanu)*, thus including himself within the fold; the wicked child, in contrast, writes himself out by asking what these laws mean "to *you*."

BERURIAH THE SCHOLAR POINTS OUT: But look at this verse in its original context! It addresses *you (etkhem)*, not "us," suggesting that it's not always easy to tell the insiders from the outsiders.

LILITH THE REBEL JUMPS IN: Exactly! And we've recently underscored this rabbinic muddle by adding something new to the seder plate: an orange.

OUR DAUGHTERS ASK: Why an orange?

LILITH REPLIES: I'm glad you asked! It seems that a number of years ago, feminist scholar Susannah Heschel was challenged about a woman's right to rabbinic ordination: "A woman belongs on the bimah," jeered a man in the audience, "as much as an orange belongs on the seder plate." Hence the orange. We can thus ask: What does this orange mean to *you*—or to *us?*

AMULETS

OUR DAUGHTERS ASK: Aren't tefillin and mezzuzah simply superstitious amulets used to ward off the evil eye and demons? Why do we need them anymore?

THE SAGES IN OUR OWN TIME ANSWER: Every culture invests certain objects with potent magical powers. These charms, talismans, and amulets protect individuals against the equally potent forces of evil that threaten to harm them. The Hebrew word for amulet is *kame'a*, deriving from either the Hebrew root for "to bind" or the Arabic for "to hang," since amulets are usually either worn or displayed. From earliest times, amulets—in the form of written texts or objects such as herbs, animal tails, stones, and crafted artifacts—have played an important role in Jewish folk custom. They've been especially popular to effect cures, to ensure good health and fertility, to protect pregnant women, and to ward off the evil eye.

THE RABBIS COMMENT: Although we've been wary of the magical powers associated with amulets, we have to acknowledge that they do sometimes work. So we permit carrying one even on the Sabbath—which would normally be forbidden—but *only if* the amulet has proven effective by curing illness three times.

46. EKEV:
Chosenness

(DEUTERONOMY 7:12–11:25)

ORAH TEACHES: Moses reminds the people that God has chosen this nation for a special purpose—to root out idolatry and to live as a holy people according to God's commandments. Blessing will be the reward of faithfulness; ruin and desolation the wages of sin. As they prepare to conquer their promised land, they must always be mindful that it is God's favor, not their own might, that guarantees them victory.

Then Moses recalls the shameful incident of the Golden Calf, when God came close to destroying the people and starting over again with Moses. He reminds them that only through Moses' intercession did God forgive the people and confer a second set of tablets to replace those Moses had smashed in his own anger over the people's apostasy. Moses also reminds them of their responsibilities toward the weak and helpless among them.

The parasha concludes with a passage that constitutes the second paragraph of the *Shema:* "IF, THEN, YOU OBEY THE COMMANDMENTS," these are the blessings that will grace your new land; if you do not, these are the curses that will doom you.

THE BLESSINGS OF FERTILITY

THE SAGES IN OUR TIME EXPLAIN: As Moses prepares to bid farewell to his people, he offers them a blessing: that God will "LOVE YOU AND BLESS YOU AND MULTIPLY YOU . . . YOU SHALL BE BLESSED ABOVE ALL OTHER PEOPLES: THERE SHALL BE NO STERILE MALE OR FEMALE AMONG YOU OR AMONG YOUR LIVESTOCK" (7:13–14). Because we live today in a world so threatened by overpopulation, we forget that this same world once faced the opposite threat, depopulation due to plague, famine, warfare, and limited medical resources. In Iron Age Israel, for instance, the average life span for men was forty; for women, thirty (due to a high death rate in childbirth). Half of the children died by the age of eighteen; as many as one-third before age five. In addition, a pioneer agricultural society such as Israel's was even more labor-intensive than settled communities, requiring women to bear larger families *and* contribute more hours to the household economy. Set against this background, it is no wonder that fertility was so desirable—and barrenness so dreaded.

TRIAL BY ORDEAL

SARAH THE ANCIENT ONE TEACHES: Throughout the Torah, God tests human mettle by way of trials of faith—Adam and Eve in the Garden, my Abraham on Mount Moriah, Jacob in his struggle with the Angel, the Hebrew midwives in Goshen, Yokheved by the banks of the Nile, Moses and Aaron in Pharaoh's court, and the accused adulteress before her jealous husband. Here, in his final speech, Moses sees the entire wilderness experience as just such a test of faith, as it is written: "THAT GOD MIGHT TEST YOU BY HARDSHIPS TO LEARN WHAT WAS IN YOUR HEARTS: WHETHER YOU WOULD KEEP HIS COMMANDMENTS OR NOT" (8:2). What a demanding examiner, and what a dangerous examination!

THE MIXED BLESSING OF CHOSENNESS

THE RABBIS TEACH: Today as in the past, we Jews continue to regard ourselves as God's "Chosen People." As the Torah states: "[God] CHOSE YOU, THEIR LINEAL DESCENDANTS, FROM AMONG ALL PEOPLES" (10:15). Our broken world still needs God's Torah as its repair manual. That's why the traditional blessing for an *aliyah* still echoes this biblical verse, proclaiming that God "chose us from among all the peoples and gave us the Torah."

OUR DAUGHTERS OBJECT: But many of us no longer feel comfortable with the notion of Jewish *chosenness*. How often has our claim to being special singled us out for persecution and censure, or, at the very least, resentment and envy. By what right do we hold ourselves above and apart from other peoples?

THE RABBIS ANSWER: Many of us share your discomfort, and have devised various ways to address this issue. And so some contemporary prayer books reinterpret the traditional Torah blessing by retranslating the English phrase *"and* gave us the Torah" as *"by* giving us the Torah," which makes the Jewish people special only in its possession of the Torah. Others have gone one step further, setting other spiritual traditions on a par with Judaism by replacing the phrase "who chose us from among all peoples" with "who brings us near to God's service."

SERAKH BAT ASHER THE HISTORIAN POINTS OUT: Some of the early Zionists also rejected the special burden of chosenness in suggesting that the antidote to anti-Semitism was for Jews to renounce chosenness altogether, becoming "a nation like all other nations" in their own land.

MIRIAM THE PROPHET COUNTERS: But many of those who settled in Israel reappropriated for themselves the biblical prophets' legacy of *ethical* vocation, a variation of chosenness. In our own ways, each of us must choose how to serve as chosen advocates of God's teachings.

47. RE'EH:
Feasts of Joy

(DEUTERONOMY 11:26–16:17)

ORAH TEACHES: Moses prepares the people to enter the land by instructing them to perform a ritual drama of blessing and curse as soon as they cross the Jordan.

What follows next is a series of laws concerning sacrifice, diet, and restrictions regarding religious behavior, especially taboos against imitating many of the pagan practices of the peoples around them. The people are reminded of their obligations toward the Levites and the less fortunate, including the poor and the slave.

Then follow laws concerning the three pilgrimage festivals of Passover, Shavuot and Sukkot, during which every resident of the land is commanded to rejoice.

PAGAN NATURE CULTS

THE SAGES IN OUR OWN TIME TEACH: In the ancient world, trees were revered as the *Axis Mundi*, the world axis, connecting heaven and earth. Regarded as imbued with living spirits, they were universally worshiped, often in specially planted sacred groves identified with Asherah, a Canaanite sea goddess, and Astarte, a fertility goddess. Popular among the Israelite common folk, the groves were expressly forbidden by the Torah and ordered destroyed, as the Torah states: "YOU MUST DESTROY ALL THE SITES AT WHICH THE NATIONS YOU ARE TO DISPOSSESS WORSHIPED THEIR GODS, WHETHER ON LOFTY MOUNTAINS AND ON HILLS OR UNDER ANY LUXURIANT TREE" (12:2). Yet despite this directive, sacred trees reappeared periodically in Israelite worship—even within the king's own family—and had to be stamped out again.

OUR MOTHERS COMMENT: We can understand why trees have been so attractive for worship. They're natural symbols of divinity: they grow taller and live longer than human beings; provide shelter, shade, and food; and often grow in the most inhospitable environments.

BERURIAH THE SCHOLAR ELABORATES: Within Jewish tradition itself, trees have proved a rich source of metaphor and imagery. Like many other cultures, Jews have represented family genealogy through trees. In ancient times, Jewish tombstones represented death by a broken tree. The Tree of Life has long adorned Jewish sacred architecture: the pillars of the Temple, crowned by ornamental pomegranates, simulated tree trunks; later, models of these pillars flanked Torah arks. Similarly, the wooden rods anchoring the Torah scroll are called *atzei hayyim*, "trees of life," a name also applied to the Torah itself. And in modern times, the state of Israel has focused on reforestation as a concrete demonstration of national rebirth.

ESTHER THE HIDDEN ONE REMARKS: The mystical *sefirot* of the kabbalists are represented by an inverted tree, whose roots are planted in the heavens and whose emanations flow like sap into our world. Each of us has our own personal root in the heavens above us, or in the God-spark deep within us.

OUR DAUGHTERS WONDER: Perhaps Judaism's incorporation of tree motifs in sacred architecture, ceremonial art, and literary imagery is our way of domesticating the wild spirits of the sacred groves.

THE LURE OF FOREIGN GODS

OUR DAUGHTERS ASK: Why does Moses warn the Israelites not to "INQUIRE ABOUT THEIR GODS, SAYING, 'HOW DID THOSE NATIONS WORSHIP THEIR GODS'" (13:30)? Why "HOW" and not "WHY"? What leads someone to abandon one spiritual path and take up another?

OUR MOTHERS ANSWER: *Practicing* a new faith usually precedes *believing* in its gods. So as his people prepare to face the idol worshipers of Canaan, Moses warns them not to follow the idolaters' ways. For he understands that the concreteness of *doing* wins converts more readily than the abstraction of doctrine.

TITHES AS COLLATERAL FOR PROSPERITY

HULDAH THE PREACHER TEACHES: We are commanded to take care of those who have less than we do—the priest, the widow, the stranger, the fatherless—by donating a tenth part of our harvest, a tithe, for their support. As it is written: "FOR THERE WILL NEVER CEASE TO BE NEEDY ONES IN YOUR LAND,

WHICH IS WHY I COMMAND YOU: OPEN YOUR HAND TO THE POOR AND NEEDY KINS-
MAN IN YOUR LAND" (15:11).

AKIVA, HUSBAND OF RACHEL, TEACHES: Tradition is a fence for
the Torah. Tithes protect wealth, vows protect abstinence, silence protects wisdom.

THE RABBIS RECOUNT: In Israel long ago, there lived a pious farmer
who owned a large field. Every year, the farmer set aside one-tenth of his yield
as a tithe for the poor and the priests. When the man was about die, he instructed his son: "Be sure to tithe your harvest each year, for that is the secret
of the land's fruitfulness."

But after his father's death, the son began reducing the portion he set aside
as a tithe. And each year, the field produced less, until the harvest dwindled to
one-tenth its former yield.

To the son's annoyance, his relatives came to visit him, dressed in holiday
clothes and filled with good cheer. "I deserve compassion, not mockery!" he re-
proached them.

"You should rejoice," they replied. "For before, you were the landlord, and
God was the priest. Now God is the landlord, granting you your tithe as priest."

That year, the son tithed a full tenth of his crop, and the land soon returned
to its former fruitfulness.

COMMUNAL RESPONSIBILITY FOR THE WIDOW

THE RABBIS TEACH: We are commanded to care for the widow in our
midst. As it is written: "AND THE WIDOW IN YOUR SETTLEMENTS SHALL COME AND
EAT [her] FILL" (14:29). We learn from the following story:

Once upon a time, the two sons of a widow went to glean corn in a nearby
field, but the landowner stopped them. Disappointed, the two returned home
empty-handed, hoping that their mother had been luckier in obtaining food.
But she had had no more success than they. The sons laid their heads upon
their mother's knees, and mother and children died that same day. And so God
warns us: "Just as you have taken their lives, I will surely take your lives from
you, as it is written: 'Do not rob the wretched because he is wretched, nor crush
the poor in the gate, for God will take up their cause and despoil those who despoil them of life'" (Proverbs 22:22–23).

THE LOT OF THE FEMALE SLAVE

Serakh bat Asher the Historian teaches: So central to Israelite culture was the legacy of its slave past—"remember that you were slaves in the land of egypt" (15:15)—that it was woven into the very fabric of its moral code. Although slavery remained part of Israelite society—indeed, it was universal in the ancient world—the Torah mandated that all male and female Hebrew slaves . . .

Hagar the Egyptian Slave interrupts: But not foreign slaves!

Serakh replies: No, unfortunately not. Israelite culture was enlightened—but only for its time. And so only Hebrew slaves were to be freed after six years of service, and they were to be provided with sufficient means to make a new start in life. But if a slave refused to leave, protesting, "'i do not want to leave you'—for he loves you and your household and is happy with you—you shall take an awl and put it through his ear into the door, and he shall become your slave in perpetuity" (15:16–17). To prefer slavery to freedom was considered so shameful that the Torah ordered such a slave branded for life.

The Rabbis explain: Female slaves did not have this option; rather, they had no choice but to accept their freedom. For we interpret the phrase immediately following the above passage—"do the same with your female slave" (15:17)—as referring only to the master's obligation to *provision* his freed female slave, not to pierce her ear if she refused to leave.

Hagar comments: Given the lot of female slaves in the ancient world, what woman would consent to remain a slave if she was free to leave? Even a life of exile is preferable to bondage.

THE COMMANDMENT TO REJOICE

Our mothers teach: The Torah commands us to rejoice, as it is written: "you shall rejoice . . . with your son and daughter, your male and female slave, the levite in your communities, and the stranger, the orphan, and the widow in your midst" (12:12, 16:11). And how are we to fulfill this commandment? God has promised us that "If you make my four poor folk happy—the Levite, the stranger, the orphan, and the widow—I shall make your four happy—your son, your daughter, your male and female slave."

HULDAH THE PREACHER COMMENTS: One of the most satisfying duties required of an adult Jew is "TO REJOICE BEFORE YHVH YOUR GOD" (16:11) during Jewish holidays. This commandment is repeated several times in the Torah; its observance is especially praiseworthy during Sukkot, when we are told that "YOU SHALL HAVE NOTHING BUT JOY" (*ve-hayeeta akh same'akh*) (16:15).

THE RABBIS ELABORATE: In ancient times, all adult Jewish males were commanded to make a pilgrimage three times a year—during the harvest festivals of Pesach, Shavuot, and Sukkot—to "THE PLACE WHERE YHVH WILL CHOOSE"—the Temple in Jerusalem—and offer sacrifices there to God. As it is written: "THREE TIMES A YEAR . . . ALL YOUR MALES SHALL APPEAR" (16:16).

OUR DAUGHTERS ASK: And were women included in these sacred pilgrimages?

THE RABBIS ANSWER: Although women were not bound to go— since their maternal duties exempted them—and were banned from entering the inner courts of the Temple, they often accompanied their husbands to Jerusalem, participating with them in the national thanksgiving celebrations there. In addition to women, the following individuals were exempt from obligation: deaf-mutes; the mentally deficient; children; sexually abnormal people, either of unknown sex (a *tumtum*, with genitals that are undeveloped or not visible) or of double sex (an androgyne, possessing sexual organs belonging to both genders); slaves; and the physically impaired—those who are lame, blind (even if only in one eye), sick, elderly, or too frail to make the trip.

LILITH THE REBEL RETORTS: Of course, women didn't have to go. They had their hands full taking care of all those dependents the men had left behind!

MOTHER RACHEL ADDS: And in so doing, they too were hallowing God's name and commandments.

THE STORY OF THE PROPHET HULDAH

THE RABBIS TEACH: As the haftorah for this parasha, we have chosen the dramatic story found in the second book of Kings, narrating the rediscovery of the lost Book of Deuteronomy. When the young king Josiah read this book, he realized that the people had long neglected the law, and so he commanded them to observe the Passover according to what was written in the recovered scroll. Such a Passover festival had not been celebrated for many decades in Jerusalem.

Huldah the Prophet recounts: But before Josiah issued his decree, he first came to me to authenticate the book that had been found. Then the word of YHVH came to me, and I sent the terrible prophecy back to the king: "I am going to bring disaster upon this place and its inhabitants, in accordance with all the words of the scroll which the king of Judah has read." But I also told Josiah that "because your heart was softened and you humbled yourself before YHVH . . . I will gather you to your fathers and you will be laid in your tomb in peace. Your eyes shall not see all the disaster which I will bring upon this place" (2 Kings 22:16–20). And so it came to pass—thirty-five years later, the evil Nebuchadnezzar, king of Babylon, swept down upon Judah, destroyed the Temple, and carried our people to his own land, where they wept in exile until God redeemed them through the hand of Cyrus of Persia. But as I foresaw, Josiah died before this tragedy befell our people, and he slept in peace in his tomb.

48. SHOFETIM:
Magic and Superstition

(DEUTERONOMY 16:18–21:9)

TORAH TEACHES: Moses continues his second address, instructing the people to appoint judges—*shofetim*—and to pursue justice vigilantly. He warns them about the excesses of monarchy and instructs them to guard against such excesses by holding their kings accountable to God's law.

Next are laws concerning the rights and privileges of the priests, prohibitions against magical practices, and the definition of valid prophecy. Then follow instructions to create six cities of refuge to protect people guilty of involuntary manslaughter from blood avengers; laws concerning legal testimony; and the laws of warfare. The parasha concludes with the case of an unidentified corpse discovered in the no-man's-land between two inhabited towns and the ritual to be performed to absolve the nearest town of the unassigned blood guilt.

THE PERILS OF POLYGAMY

BERURIAH THE SCHOLAR TEACHES: In biblical times, monogamy was considered the social ideal and a metaphor of religious fidelity. Marrying more than one wife was discouraged. Most biblical men had only one wife, although several had concubines. No prophet was married to more than one woman. Kings, however, had the means and the political incentives to acquire many wives, among them idol worshipers, who introduced pagan practices into the Israelite court and Temple. That's why the Torah decrees that "[the king] SHALL NOT HAVE MANY WIVES, LEST HIS HEART GO ASTRAY" (17:17). The great King Solomon was reputed to have a thousand consorts—seven hundred wives and three hundred concubines.

THE RABBIS INTERJECT: But we later ruled that kings should restrict themselves to eighteen, twenty-four, or forty-eight wives.

SERAKH BAT ASHER THE HISTORIAN EXPLAINS: Jewish law did not officially outlaw polygamy until the year 1000 C.E., when Rabbi Gershom ben Judah, known as the "Light of the Exile," banned this practice in northern France and Germany. Although still legal in the Jewish communities of Spain, Italy, northern Africa, and the Middle East, polygamy was nonetheless rare—mostly because it cost too much to maintain more than one wife. Eventually polygamy disappeared among Jews (although immigrants to modern Israel from Islamic countries have occasionally brought two wives along with them).

OUR DAUGHTERS QUIP: With the divorce rate climbing ever higher, polygamy today is making a comeback, only now the spouses marry each other serially instead of simultaneously.

SEDUCTIONS OF THE OCCULT

OUR DAUGHTERS ASK: Why is the Torah so uncompromising about occult practices? As it is written: "LET NO ONE BE FOUND AMONG YOU . . . WHO IS AN AUGUR, A SOOTHSAYER, A SORCERER, ONE WHO CASTS SPELLS, OR ONE WHO CONSULTS GHOSTS OR FAMILIAR SPIRITS, OR ONE WHO INQUIRES OF THE DEAD" (18:10). What real harm is there in such activities? Besides, isn't it possible that some people actually do have special magical powers beyond our own?

THE RABBIS ANSWER: If someone truly *believes* in the power of occult rituals to influence nature, that person is guilty of sorcery and deserves punishment. But if a conjurer is simply trying to create an illusion, such practice is not a sin. What is most important in determining guilt is intent. We have ruled that only witchcraft and conjuring the dead by using human bones are punishable by death; other forms of sorcery—communicating with and on behalf of the dead without contact with human remains; divination based on certain events or circumstances; fortune-telling with sand, stones, and other objects; astrological forecasts; and casting spells for healing or magical purposes—are punishable by flogging.

OUR MOTHERS MUSE: How distant are we from the practices described in this parasha? Three thousand years after the Torah pronounced this warning, our "modern" world still abounds in witchcraft and magic—fortune-tellers, astrologers, mediums, crystals, and scores of superstitions, as well as a multibillion-dollar "Halloween industry" of movies, books, paraphernalia, and "new age" merchandise that capitalizes on our abiding fascination with the occult.

OUR DAUGHTERS COMMENT: Which proves that even with our advanced technology and hardheaded reason, we're still vulnerable to the three demons that have always threatened people: scarcity, evil, and death. As much as we might want to confine our religious beliefs to the ethical monotheism of the Torah and Jewish tradition, we have to admit that that's not enough for us. It's too abstract, too removed from our own daily lives and losses, too intangible.

LILITH THE REBEL INTERRUPTS: And too much the creation of men.

OUR DAUGHTERS REMARK: The truth is that we crave experiences that engage our senses, our hands and eyes, our feelings. We don't want to be reassured or preached at—we want to be enchanted!

WAR AND WOMEN

OUR DAUGHTERS CHALLENGE: After killing all the adult men of an enemy city, Israelite soldiers are permitted to take the women, children, livestock, and "EVERYTHING IN THE TOWN" (20:14) as booty and "enjoy"—literally, "eat"—it. Five verses later, these same soldiers are commanded to spare the fruit trees surrounding an enemy town, for "ARE TREES OF THE FIELD HUMAN TO WITHDRAW BEFORE YOU INTO THE BESIEGED CITY? ONLY TREES THAT YOU KNOW DO NOT YIELD FOOD MAY BE DESTROYED" (20:19–20). But aren't unarmed women and children human? Do they have any way of withdrawing before a hostile army?

DINAH THE WOUNDED ONE EXPLAINS: Protection of an enemy's fruit trees demonstrates neither the Torah's ecological sensitivity nor its inverted morality. No, this law only reflects the reality that fruit trees are more valuable to the victors if left planted in their home soil than uprooted from it; the reverse is true of women, children, and livestock. What might be labeled "rape" or "theft" in peacetime is called the "spoils of victory" in war.

ALEXANDER AND THE FAIR JUDGMENT

OUR MOTHERS RECOUNT: Not only men make good judges. As it is told:

Once, Alexander came to a faraway land ruled only by women. He wanted to conquer them, but they mocked him: "If you defeat us, what dishonor! And if we defeat you, what shame!" So he made peace with them.

Then he said, "Show me your justice."

So they brought him to the court, where one of the women sat in judgment. Two men came before her, each accusing the other of foul play.

"I bought land from this man," said one of them, "and I found a treasure buried in my field, which I had not agreed to buy. But when I ordered the seller to take the treasure back, he refused." The other protested, "When I sold my land to this man, I sold him what was above and below it as well. If I take back the treasure, I will be a thief!"

The judge asked the two men if they had children of marriageable age. They told her that one of them had a daughter, the other a son.

"I order them to marry each other," ruled the judge, "and share the treasure between them."

When he heard the judge's ruling, Alexander laughed. "In my kingdom," he said, "I would have ordered both men killed, and I would have kept the treasure for myself!"

"Do you have sheep, goats, and cows in your country?" the women asked him.

"Of course!" answered Alexander.

"Then it is for their sake that the sun shines and the land yields its bounty, for the people clearly do not deserve such blessing."

And when Alexander departed from this land, he left behind an inscription on the gates: "A fool was I until I came here to learn wisdom from the women."

49. KI TETZE:
Safety Nets
(DEUTERONOMY 21:10—25:19)

ORAH TEACHES: This parasha contains a lengthy list of laws for maintaining a just society. Among the topics covered are treatment of women captured in war, birthrights, punishment of a disobedient son, disposal of the corpse of an executed capital offender, handling of lost property, cross-dressing, robbing a bird's nest, the taboo of mixed species, the accused virgin, adultery, rape, those excluded from membership in Israel, cult prostitution, interest, vows, divorce, loans, treatment of vulnerable members of society, levirate marriage, a woman who seizes a man's genitals, and honest weights and measures.

The parasha concludes with the commandment not to forget Amalek, who attacked the Israelites' rear soon after they left Egypt.

THE WOMAN CAPTIVE

BERURIAH THE SCHOLAR TEACHES: If, in the course of battle, an Israelite soldier captures a beautiful woman and wants to marry her (ugly women presumably would be desirable only as slaves), he first has to conduct her through a special ritual: "YOU SHALL BRING HER INTO YOUR HOUSE, AND SHE SHALL TRIM HER HAIR, PARE HER NAILS [or: LET HER NAILS GROW LONG], AND DISCARD HER CAPTIVE'S GARB" (21:12). Afterward, he must leave her alone for a month to mourn her parents and everything else she's lost. Only after this period can the soldier marry her, through an act of "possession"—that is, by sleeping with her.

THE RABBIS INTERJECT: He must also wait to make sure that she wasn't pregnant when he took her captive.

OUR DAUGHTERS ASK: And what if he's changed his mind in the meantime and no longer wants her as his wife?

BERURIAH ANSWERS: He can't keep her as a slave or sell her to another man but must let her go free.

THE RABBIS ELABORATE: Her shorn hair, long nails, and reddened eyes will make her so unattractive that he will want to send her away rather than marry her.

OUR DAUGHTERS ASK: But only fifteen verses earlier, the Torah permits Israelite soldiers to take foreign women as "PREY" and to "EAT THE SPOILS OF YOUR ENEMY" (20:14)! Aren't these two laws in conflict?

HULDAH THE PREACHER EXPLAINS: The crucial difference is the man's *intent.* If he views the woman as an *object* from the outset—his slave, the spoils of war—so she remains. But if he treats her as a person, as his betrothed, he owes her the honor shown a wife. She has in effect "converted" to marry him, shearing off her prior identity and mourning her old life. To cast her out after that would be tantamount to murder.

REVERSING THE LEGACY OF GENESIS

OUR DAUGHTERS ASK: In the Genesis stories, the firstborn son in a family is not automatically guaranteed the birthright; in fact, he generally loses it to a younger brother. Is this pattern meant to be an ideal for the Jewish family?

THE SAGES IN OUR OWN TIME ANSWER: The term "firstborn" in ancient Near Eastern law designated an heir's legal status, not his birth order. A father was free to appoint *any* of his sons (but not his daughters, of course) as his primary heir, entitled to a double portion of the inheritance and control of the household gods. However, such uncertainty about who would inherit almost guaranteed jealousy and subversiveness among the children in the next generation. To stabilize and humanize Israelite society, the Torah here abolishes a father's prerogative to name his "firstborn," especially if he does so primarily out of favoritism toward a beloved wife at the expense of an unloved one. As it is written: "HE MAY NOT TREAT AS FIRSTBORN THE SON OF THE LOVED ONE IN DISREGARD OF THE SON OF THE UNLOVED ONE WHO IS OLDER" (21:16). No matter how he feels about his oldest son or the boy's mother, "HE MUST ACCEPT THE FIRSTBORN . . . SINCE HE IS THE FIRST FRUIT OF HIS VIGOR, THE BIRTHRIGHT IS HIS DUE" (21:17).

LEAH COMMENTS: If we reexamine my family's stories in light of this background, we can understand that Ishmael and my own sons had legitimate reason to fear being dispossessed by their younger brothers. For in their case, their father chose his heir to please his wife, his favored wife, the one he loved.

A WAYWARD AND DEFIANT SON

OUR DAUGHTERS ASK: The Torah mandates death to a "WAYWARD AND DEFIANT SON WHO DOES NOT HEED HIS FATHER OR MOTHER" (21:18). What about daughters? Weren't they ever wayward and defiant?

DINAH THE WOUNDED ONE ANSWERS: They had little opportunity for such rebellion back then (nor do they today in most traditional cultures). No, the only crimes counted against them in the Torah are sexual: if they're not yet betrothed, their sexual indiscretion represents an economic loss to their father; if they're already betrothed, their sin constitutes adultery, punishable by death, the same punishment facing a rebellious son.

HULDAH THE PREACHER COMMENTS: In both cases, although the father brings the accusation against his children, only the community— through the council of elders—can execute judgment.

DINAH RETORTS: If only there had been such law and order in my time!

THE BAN ON CROSS-DRESSING

OUR DAUGHTERS ASK: In our modern Western culture, the lines between what's appropriate for men and women to wear are often blurred. Some people, like pop stars and transvestites, cross these lines deliberately. On certain occasions, like Halloween, Purim, costume parties, and Mardi Gras, it's acceptable in many circles to dress in drag. So why does the Torah label cross-dressing "abhorrent"? As it is written: "A WOMAN MUST NOT PUT ON MAN'S APPAREL, NOR SHALL A MAN WEAR WOMAN'S CLOTHING" (22:5). What's the big deal?

THE SAGES IN OUR OWN TIME ANSWER: Cross-dressing was part of the mythology and ritual of the Near Eastern goddess cults of Inanna, Anat, and Ishtar. Like their Hellenistic counterparts, Diana and Artemis, these goddesses embodied certain antithetical aspects: they were characterized as both chaste and promiscuous, motherly and bloodthirsty. The Egyptians described Anat as "the goddess, the victorious, a woman acting as a man, clad as a male, and girt as a female."

LILITH QUIPS: So today we're witnessing what one Jewish teacher has called the "return of the repressed"!

THE BIRD'S NEST: A MODEL OF MERCY

THE RABBIS TEACH: How extraordinary is the principle of *kan zippor*, the "bird's nest"! As it is written: "IF, ALONG THE ROAD, YOU CHANCE UPON A BIRD'S NEST, IN ANY TREE OR ON THE GROUND, WITH FLEDGLINGS OR EGGS AND THE MOTHER SITTING OVER THE FLEDGLINGS OR ON THE EGGS, DO NOT TAKE THE MOTHER TOGETHER WITH HER YOUNG. LET THE MOTHER GO, AND TAKE ONLY THE YOUNG, IN ORDER THAT YOU MAY FARE WELL AND HAVE A LONG LIFE" (22:6–7). This commandment is a model not only of kindness toward animals but also of how we should treat each other. For if we learn to extend mercy toward God's creatures, we will thereby prepare ourselves for even greater acts of loving-kindness. And the reward for sending away the mother bird—"length of days"—is precisely the same reward promised for honoring one's parents.

BERURIAH THE SCHOLAR INTERJECTS: But rewards don't always turn out as promised. Ironically, one of the most famous episodes of rabbinic apostasy—that of Elisha ben Abuyah, who was my husband Meir's beloved teacher and my great friend—was precipitated when this principle failed to deliver its promise. For it happened that once Elisha saw a young boy fall to his death from a tree as he honored his father's request to send away a mother bird before taking her eggs. Horrified that this boy had died when he should have been doubly blessed with long life, Elisha lost his faith. From that moment on, he was known in the Talmud simply as "Aher," the Other One.

ESTHER THE HIDDEN ONE REVEALS: Faith always requires a leap, sometimes far beyond reason.

THE LAWS OF MARRIAGE AND DIVORCE

THE SAGES IN OUR OWN TIME TEACH: In biblical times, marriage meant different things at different times, depending upon one's gender, family status, and prevailing local custom. In *matrilocal* families such as Rachel's and Leah's, a husband joined his *wife's* family when they married. For the wife's father, his daughter's marriage promised income from the *mohar* (the bride-price) paid by the suitor, as well as the addition of an extra male worker. For the husband's father, on the other hand, his son's marriage represented a loss: the cost of the bride-price as well as that son's labor. The reverse was true in *patrilocal* families like Ruth's, to which a bride brought not only her own labor but also the economic benefits of her offspring. And if her husband happened to be the firstborn, her own son would provide the clan with a male heir. And every marriage could potentially enhance a father's political, social, and economic prestige through connection with another family and clan.

LEAH INTERJECTS: Although a mother could share with her husband the pleasure of seeing her children married and their futures secure, the only material benefit she received was security for her old age, mostly through the support of her daughters-in-law (as Naomi receives from Ruth), and the honor shown her by her sons and grandchildren. And mothers often helped arrange their children's marriages.

MOTHER RACHEL ADDS: But neither bridegrooms nor brides had much of a voice in choosing their life partners. Betrothals were arranged while we were quite young, and they usually served our parents' social and economic needs. On occasion, however, young men made their own decisions: sometimes motivated by love, as in the case of Jacob and Moses; sometimes by lust, as with Shechem and some Israelite soldiers at war; and other times by a political agenda, as with Israelite kings. We women, on the other hand, had little say in our choice of partners. For the most part, it was our father (or, if he was dead, our brothers or uncles) who decided whom we married. Our father could even decide to sell us as slave-wives. And in certain cases—a family of daughters, Levite households, or widows with no male heirs—the Torah limited our options for marriage even further.

OUR DAUGHTERS ASK: And what happened when a husband died?

BERURIAH THE SCHOLAR ANSWERS: Then the woman was powerless to look after her own interests. Property passed to her husband's heirs—specifically the sons, unless he had none, in which case the daughters inherited. If the couple was childless, the man's brothers inherited. In no case did the widow receive a share. That's why the Torah requires that the entire community take responsibility for maintaining the widow.

OUR DAUGHTERS ASK: And if the marriage ended in divorce?

HULDAH THE PREACHER ANSWERS: The Torah provides for no such "safety net" in that case. If a man divorced his wife—and only men could initiate divorce—the husband had no obligation to support his ex-wife.

THE RABBIS POINT OUT: But we corrected this inequity by instituting certain legal changes that provided a safety net for widows and divorcées: women now receive a *ketubah*, a marriage contract, that guarantees them certain economic benefits if the husband dies or the marriage dissolves; in the latter case, they are also entitled to a *get*, a divorce writ, which frees them to remarry.

And in the Middle Ages, Rabbenu Gershom (who also outlawed polygamy) required that a woman's consent be obtained for a divorce.

OUR DAUGHTERS ASK: On what grounds can a man initiate a divorce?

THE RABBIS ANSWER: Because divorce threatened such dire economic consequences for women, the Torah protects them from arbitrary or impulsive divorces by ruling that only infidelity should be considered reasonable grounds to end a marriage. The school of Shammai later reaffirmed this teaching, but the school of Hillel liberalized the law considerably, ruling that divorce could be justified whenever the wife did *anything* offensive to her husband, even just ruining his food. Akiva even allowed divorce if the husband found a more attractive woman. Jewish law sides, as usual, with Hillel but also throws a bone to Shammai: though a man *may* divorce his wife for any cause, he *must* do so if she has been unfaithful.

OUR DAUGHTERS ASK: But are the Rabbis' rulings better or worse for women?

LILITH THE REBEL ANSWERS: They never asked us—but now that we're pulling up a chair at their table, we can make up our own minds.

THE ACCUSED BRIDE: THE STEEP PRICE OF SEXUAL ORDER

OUR DAUGHTERS ASK: In parashat "Naso," we're told what happens if a man suspects his wife is an adulteress. But now we learn that he can accuse her even before he sleeps with her if he has doubts about her chastity. As it is written: "HE TAKES AN AVERSION TO HER AND MAKES UP CHARGES AGAINST HER AND DEFAMES HER [literally: brings upon her an evil name], SAYING, 'I MARRIED THIS WOMAN; BUT WHEN I APPROACHED HER, I FOUND THAT SHE WAS NOT A VIRGIN'" (22:13–14). Does she have to go through the same kind of trial by ordeal?

HULDAH THE PREACHER ANSWERS: No, this time the burden of proving her innocence falls upon her father, since he's responsible for controlling her behavior while she lives under his roof. So if he can produce "THE EVIDENCE OF THE GIRL'S VIRGINITY" (22:15)—that is, the bloodstained sheet from her wedding night—then the elders of the city punish the husband: flogging him, making him pay his father-in-law a steep fine, and "sentencing" him to irrevocable marriage with his new wife. But if the bride's father cannot produce evidence of her virginity, then the men of the city stone her "AT THE ENTRANCE TO HER FATHER'S HOUSE" (22:21).

DINAH THE WOUNDED ONE COMMENTS: Either way, the woman loses: if she's falsely accused, she remains married forever to a man who hates her; if proven guilty, she dies. But the two men—her father and her husband—face considerably better odds: for even though the husband, if proved guilty of perjury, risks losing money, honor, and his right to leave the marriage, at least he doesn't risk losing his life. And if his accusation sticks, he regains his bride-price and the freedom to remarry. As for the bride's father, if his daughter is proven guilty, he loses his daughter and his name, but if she's acquitted, he gains as much as double the usual bride-price. Like his new son-in-law and unlike his own daughter, he faces no death sentence.

THE SAGES IN OUR OWN TIME EXPLAIN: Because a father would be highly motivated to "fake" a bloodstained sheet to protect his daughter, the Torah assigns the council of elders the right to render final judgment.

OUR MOTHERS CRY: We can only imagine how the bride's mother must have suffered! Like her daughter, she too loses in either case.

THE BLOODY SHEET

OUR DAUGHTERS ASK: As in many other traditional cultures, biblical law demands that a bride's parents produce "evidence" of her virginity—a bloodstained sheet—to prove that the groom has not been cheated by being sold "damaged goods." But what if her hymen has broken naturally before marriage or if she's born without one? Does the Torah always presume "unchastity" unless proven otherwise?

THE RABBIS ANSWER: Because a woman convicted of adultery faces such severe penalties, we've gone to great lengths in interpreting this law to exonerate women of sexual indiscretion. So, for example, if she claims (or according to a more strict opinion, can prove) that her hymen ruptured through an injury, we consider her still a virgin. And if she has intercourse before the age of three, we consider her still a virgin . . .

DINAH THE WOUNDED ONE INTERRUPTS: How thoughtful! Making allowances for the violation of a two-year-old girl!

THE RABBIS EXPLAIN: We compare it to "poking a finger in the eye," because we believe that the hymen will grow back. Even the mere fact that her wedding is celebrated with customs reserved for virgins—the bridal litter, a veil, unbound hair, a certain bridal song, roasted corn for the guests—shows that we agree that there is sufficient proof that she is truly a virgin bride.

OUR DAUGHTERS RESPOND: In other words, don't ask, don't tell!

A LIFE SENTENCE OF MATRIMONY

OUR DAUGHTERS ASK: If a man's accusation against his new wife proves false, he faces three penalties: flogging, a steep fine, and the forfeit of his right ever to divorce his wife. Although it's clear that all three punishments injure him, doesn't the last also hurt his wife, by chaining her forever to a man who hates her?

BERURIAH THE SCHOLAR ANSWERS: We can make sense of this last penalty only if we consider it in its historical context: in biblical society, the husband alone had the right to initiate a divorce. And if he chose, he could send his wife away without her consent—and penniless. But in the case of a false accusation, he became his wife's equal.

OUR MOTHERS ADD: Yes, they were equally miserable!

THE LAWS OF ADULTERY

BERURIAH THE SCHOLAR EXPLAINS: The Jewish definition of adultery does not correspond to the norms of modern Western society. In Jewish law, adultery occurs only if a *married* woman (including a betrothed woman still living in her father's house) has sexual intercourse with a man who is not her husband. But if a man—whether married or single—sleeps with an *unmarried* woman, such behavior is not considered adulterous.

DINAH THE WOUNDED ONE RETORTS: In fact, for centuries sexual intercourse was considered one of three legitimate ways for a man to betroth an unmarried woman. Even worse, a woman who was raped was not only betrothed to her violator; he was forbidden ever to divorce her.

HAGAR THE STRANGER BREAKS IN: And men could take multiple wives and concubines, as well as visit prostitutes, while women were permitted merely one husband. Only in the Middle Ages were some Jewish men restricted to a single wife.

HULDAH THE PREACHER ELABORATES: In biblical times, a convicted adulterer was sentenced to death by stoning. But in time the penalty was lessened: a husband had no choice but to divorce an adulterous wife, but if the husband was the adulterer, he could remain married to his wife. Furthermore, an adulterous wife was forbidden to marry her lover, which left her outcast from family life and security. In some communities, adulterous couples were flogged, excommunicated, exiled, or paraded through the town with shaven heads. The child of an adulterous union was branded a *mamzer* (bastard) and forbidden to marry anyone but other *mamzerim* for ten generations.

THE RAPE OF A BETROTHED VIRGIN

BERURIAH THE SCHOLAR TEACHES: A betrothed woman who has never been married—that is, a virgin—occupies a unique legal niche, with its own set of laws. In most respects, she's regarded as though she were married.

OUR DAUGHTERS ASK: So if she sleeps with another man before her wedding, is she considered an adulteress?

BERURIAH ANSWERS: The Torah's ruling in this case reveals a lot about the social realities of town and country during biblical times. For if a woman and her lover sleep together within the city limits, the Torah orders them both executed as adulterers: "THE YOUNG WOMAN BECAUSE SHE DID NOT CRY FOR HELP IN THE TOWN, AND THE MAN BECAUSE HE VIOLATED HIS NEIGHBOR'S WIFE" (22:24). The Torah assumes that if the woman had cried out, the citizens of the town would have rushed to her aid. So her silence can only be interpreted as consent on her part. But if she has intercourse with a man in a rural area, he is condemned to death and she is presumed innocent, since no one could have heard her cries for help. The text compares this to a case of unwitnessed murder.

THE RABBIS INTERJECT: But because we realize that human nature is much more complicated than these two clear-cut cases, we gradually expanded the definition of rape and seduction to cover *any* sexual acts forced upon a woman, and fined the rapist for damage done not only to her father but to the victim as well.

OUR MOTHERS COMMENT: How different things are today! For if a woman is sexually assaulted in a city, we know only too well that her cries, if heard at all, will likely go unheeded; or she may be silenced by her assailant before she can even cry out. And as for the case of extramarital sex in a field or forest, we've long scripted romantic comedy from just such trysts. In these settings, the young woman may sometimes be an all too willing partner.

THE RAPIST-HUSBAND—JUST DESERTS OR CRUELTY?

OUR DAUGHTERS ASK: The Torah decrees that a man who forces himself upon an *unattached* virgin—that is, rapes her—has to pay her father fifty shekels (the usual bride-price for a virgin) and to marry her, without the option of divorce. The fine is supposed to compensate her father for his lost income. But what about the rape victim? How could this marriage possibly compensate her for what she's lost? What does it mean for her to spend her entire life married to a man who's raped her? How can economic security be worth such a steep price?

THE RABBIS ANSWER: We too consider the notion of forced marriage under such circumstances so distasteful, so abhorrent, that we modified this law considerably. And so we ruled that the rapist must marry his victim *only if* she desires the marriage; however, if she or her father is unwilling, they may refuse. And we levied fines upon the offender not only to compensate the woman's father for his lost income and sullied honor but also to compensate the victim herself for "pain, indignity, and blemish." In fact, so intent are we to protect women from sexual coercion that we're willing to consider cases of rape even *within marriage.* Indeed, any sexual act that begins through force does violence to a woman. As it is told:

Once, when a woman came to Rabbi Yohanan with a claim that she had been raped, he challenged her: "And didn't you enjoy it?" She said to him: "And if a man dipped his finger in honey and stuck it in your mouth on Yom Kippur, is it not bad for you yet enjoyable by the end?" And he accepted her claim.

DINAH THE WOUNDED ONE RETORTS: How timeless and universal are men's fantasies about women's sexual nature!

HONOR YOUR FATHER'S WIFE

THE SAGES IN OUR OWN TIME TEACH: It was customary in ancient Near Eastern culture for sons to inherit their father's wives along with the rest of their property. The Torah, however, forbids a son to sleep with his father's wives, not only while they are married to him but even after he is dead.

OUR MOTHERS COMMENT: Once a son, always a son; once a mother, even a stepmother, always a mother.

SACRED PROSTITUTION

WILY REBECCA EXPLAINS: The Torah does not outlaw prostitution. That's why when my grandson Judah hired his daughter-in-law, Tamar, disguised as a roadside prostitute, after his wife's death, the incident is reported without censure.

THE RABBIS CONTINUE: And why the Jericho harlot Rahab, who shields the two spies sent by Joshua, is spared by the Israelite army during their conquest of the city. In fact, we consider her a righteous convert, who marries Joshua and becomes the ancestor of the prophets Jeremiah and Huldah.

BERURIAH THE SCHOLAR INTERJECTS: But prostitution is proscribed within two very specific contexts: pagan cults and the Temple. In contrast to pagan worship, where the sexual and the sacred are intertwined, Judaism demands that they be radically separate during worship.

LEAH THE NAMER ADDS: Israelites are therefore forbidden to become *kedeshim* (male) or *kedeshot* (female), usually translated as "cult prostitutes" (from the root *k-d-sh*, meaning "holy" or "consecrated"). In pagan cultures, such religious functionaries presided over temple rituals, among which were fertility rites. And the Torah forbids male and female prostitutes to bring their wages to the Temple in fulfillment of vows. Because their wages are "tainted," they can't be used for sacred service. The word used here (23:19) for male prostitute is *kelev*—literally, "dog"—indicating how low a rung such men occupied on the social ladder.

HULDAH THE PREACHER RECOUNTS: During my time, King Josiah expelled from the Temple *kedeshot* who were quartered there. These women wove clothing for the pagan goddess Asherah, whose statue was itself enshrined within the holy sanctuary.

OUR MOTHERS COMMENT: And not so long ago, thousands of young Jewish girls, naive new immigrants coming to America in search of a better life, fell prey to ruthless pimps who sold them into prostitution. Their stories remain largely untold in sentimentalized portraits of the "world of our fathers."

A SPECIAL CASE OF REMARRIAGE

THE RABBIS TEACH: If a man divorces his wife because he finds her "obnoxious" (*ervat davar*, a term usually designating sexual transgression) and, therefore, sends her away empty-handed, he is forbidden to remarry her if she is widowed or divorced after a second marriage. As it is written: "THEN THE FIRST HUSBAND WHO DIVORCED HER SHALL NOT TAKE HER TO WIFE AGAIN, SINCE SHE HAS BEEN DEFILED" (24:4).

OUR DAUGHTERS ASK: If he's willing to overlook her previous sexual misconduct, isn't it his decision to make? He's the one who will have to live with it.

THE RABBIS ANSWER: We question the first husband's motives for wanting her back. He may be a swindler, first cheating his wife out of her legal property by divorcing her "for cause" and then trying to rob her again, by claiming possession of her second husband's property through remarriage.

OUR DAUGHTERS ASK: But what if he really has had a change of heart and wants to remarry the wife of his youth?

THE RABBIS REPLY: Once a woman has entered another man's bed, she can never "go home again."

THE MARITAL OBLIGATIONS OF HUSBANDS

THE RABBIS TEACH: The Torah exempts a man from military service during his first year of marriage, in order to "GIVE HAPPINESS TO THE WOMAN HE HAS MARRIED" (24:5). We've defined the commandment "give happiness to one's wife" quite precisely, including in this definition the quality and frequency of a wife's conjugal rights. Specifically, a husband is obligated to satisfy his wife sexually—or else divorce her. Of course, we do make allowances for the demands of various professionals. So we prescribe the following schedule of marital relations: every day for "men of independence"; twice a week for laborers; once a week for ass drivers; once in thirty days for camel drivers; once every six months for sailors. And students may leave their wives for up to a month without the women's permission; some say for up to three years. We also urge husbands to give their wives sexual pleasure when they are pregnant, nursing, or acting especially seductive; and when the man is to take a journey. Some of us have even argued that a woman's sexual desire exceeds a man's. And so when God curses Eve, telling her that "YOUR URGE SHALL BE FOR YOUR HUSBAND, AND HE SHALL RULE OVER YOU" (3:16), the real curse is in the second half of the verse—that is, women will be forced to wait upon men's sexual *initiative* to satisfy their desire.

LILITH THE REBEL RETORTS: Which is precisely why I walked out!

THE MEMORY OF MIRIAM: A REPRISE

OUR DAUGHTERS ASK: This parasha contains the only mention of Miriam in the entire book of Deuteronomy. When Moses comes to the laws concerning leprosy, he warns: "REMEMBER WHAT YHVH YOUR GOD DID TO MIRIAM" (24:9). Otherwise he erases his sister from his lengthy review of the past forty years in the wilderness. Why does he bring her up at this moment?

THE RABBIS ANSWER: Moses is only drawing a logical connection: Just as Miriam was punished with leprosy for speaking out against her brother, so will the people be punished.

OUR DAUGHTERS ASK: But for what sin are they being punished?

THE RABBIS ANSWER: Some say slander; others rebellion.

OUR DAUGHTERS ASK: But why isn't any such incident specified?

BERURIAH THE SCHOLAR ANSWERS: To understand what's going on, we need to widen our lens to take in all of chapter 24 of Deuteronomy. The first four verses discuss the case of a man who sends away his wife because he finds her "obnoxious" but then wants her back, which is forbidden by law. The fifth verse instructs a man to "GIVE HAPPINESS TO THE WOMAN HE HAS MARRIED." Both cases might apply to Moses himself: In Exodus, we're told that Jethro brought Zipporah and her two sons back to Moses "AFTER SHE HAD BEEN SENT HOME" (18:2); no reason is given for her having been sent away.

LEAH THE UNLOVED WIFE EXPLAINS: The Midrash claims that Moses stopped sleeping with his wife after he came down from Sinai; Miriam criticized him and was stricken with leprosy. And so now, as Moses reminds the Israelite men of their obligation to make their wives happy, he recalls his own failures on this score. And when he pronounces the word "leprosy," it triggers the memory of his sister's rebuke. He counters this painful memory by warning the people to remember her punishment, then quickly turns away from his pain by reeling off a string of laws about social justice. And he reminds the people about their redemption from Egyptian bondage, a past event about which he feels considerably more comfortable.

REFUSING THE LEGACY OF GUILT

OUR DAUGHTERS ASK: In the Ten Commandments, God promises to visit the guilt of parents upon their children for three or four generations (5:9). How does guilt "visit" children?

OUR MOTHERS ANSWER: Behavior modeled by parents usually repeats in the next several generations. So do parents' beliefs, their family myths, and their emotional responses to the world. In this parasha, we're warned not to make things worse by legislating intergenerational guilt. As it is written: "A PERSON SHALL BE PUT TO DEATH ONLY FOR HIS OWN CRIME" (24:16). We're advised to leave such visits to God.

THE LEVIRATE MARRIAGE

BERURIAH THE SCHOLAR TEACHES: The institution of levirate marriage is one of Judaism's oldest and oddest institutions. When a woman is widowed without children, the Torah requires her to marry her dead husband's brother, the *levir* (Latin for "brother-in-law"), in order to produce a male heir to inherit her husband's property and name. It is the eldest brother's duty to marry his brother's widow, the *yevamah*; if he refuses, other brothers (if there are any) can oblige. If all refuse, the eldest brother must perform *halitzah*, the ceremony described in this parasha: the widow pulls off the brother's sandal, spits in his face, and sends him off as "THE FAMILY OF THE UNSANDALED ONE" (25:10).

TAMAR POINTS OUT: But as you saw in my case, if the *levir* didn't want to perform his duty toward his brother's widow, he sometimes refused to release the widow to remarry, condemning her to considerable hardship.

THE RABBIS ADD: Which is why we later modified this law. We ruled that if the *levir* didn't want to marry the widow, he couldn't make her wait until a younger brother reached thirteen but instead had to release her immediately through *halitzah*. And if the *levir* refused to perform *halitzah*, a rabbinic court could compel him to do so by imprisoning him.

OUR MOTHERS PROTEST: But you didn't go far enough! Because even with these rabbinic changes, Orthodox Jewish women still face problems because of this ancient law! If the *levir* himself is underage, mentally incompetent, obstinate, or missing, the widow remains "chained" *(agunah)*, forbidden to remarry, as is also the case with the woman whose husband has disappeared. Rabbinic law has yet to abolish the institution of levirate marriage.

SERAKH BAT ASHER THE HISTORIAN ADDS: How extraordinary, then, that from the sixteenth century on, the Jewish community of Safed forbade its women to marry refugees whose brothers had been left behind on the Iberian peninsula after the Spanish expulsion. They wanted to make sure that their future widows would not be left chained.

SEIZED BY THE GENITALS

BERURIAH THE SCHOLAR TEACHES: The Bible mandates *mutilation* as a punishment when a pregnant woman is accidentally injured while two men are fighting; and when a woman comes to her husband's aid during a fight by grabbing his opponent's genitals. What the two cases share is a woman's becoming embroiled in a fight between two men. Where they differ is in their sense of justice.

THE RABBIS EXPLAIN: When a man injures a pregnant woman whose only crime is being in the wrong place at the wrong time, he is assessed damages *to her husband's property:* if she miscarries or if she herself is injured, he pays for the damage through monetary compensation: "EYE FOR EYE . . . WOUND FOR WOUND, BRUISE FOR BRUISE" (21:24–25). Thus, measure for measure, the accidental damage is undone.

DINAH THE WOUNDED ONE OBJECTS: Not in this world!

HULDAH THE PREACHER COMMENTS: However, the case is radically different if a woman *deliberately* intervenes in a fight between men. Although she's acted to support her husband, her action violates a boundary even more sacred than marriage: a man's own sexual property.

LEAH THE NAMER ADDS: What today some affectionately call the "family jewels."

THE RABBIS JUMP IN: And for this sacrilege . . .

LILITH INTERRUPTS: *Whether or not any permanent damage is sustained.*

THE RABBIS PICK UP AGAIN: The court is to "SHOW NO PITY" (25:12) but is to cut off the offending hand. In so doing, the insult to male pride is undone.

DINAH CONCLUDES: Maybe in this world, but not in the next!

50. KI TAVO:
The Sin of Gloom
(DEUTERONOMY 26:1–29:8)

TORAH TEACHES: Moses continues his review of the laws that are to govern Israelite society in the new land. When they cross over the Jordan, the people are to perform a ritual drama on two mountains, dividing the twelve tribes into two choruses, facing each other. They are then to declaim in vivid detail the various blessings and curses that will befall the people according to their adherence to God's laws.

At the end of this parasha, Moses begins his third and final address to the people.

THE RITUAL ON THE TWO MOUNTAINS

BERURIAH THE SCHOLAR TEACHES: When the people enter and claim their new land, their first act must be to offer thanks for a successful journey and the fulfillment of God's promise. Moses therefore instructs them to set up—as soon as they cross the Jordan—an altar on Mount Ebal and inscribe upon plastered stones "THE WORDS OF THIS TEACHING" (literally, "Torah") (27:3). They're also commanded to perform a dramatic ritual, dividing themselves by tribes into two facing choruses, half on Mount Gerizim, the other half on Mount Ebal.

MOTHER RACHEL ELABORATES: The six tribes on the first mountain—Leah's middle four sons and my own two sons—will bless the nation; the other six—our handmaids' four sons and Leah's youngest and oldest sons—will curse them. Blessings and curses are both framed in conditional terms: If you observe God's laws, such will be your reward; but if you disobey, such will be your punishment. As usual, the curses far outweigh the blessings.

HULDAH THE PREACHER EXPLAINS: The list of laws that must be obeyed comprises a rather odd assortment of taboos: *religious*—making idolatrous images and setting them up in secret; *familial*—insulting one's parents; men sleeping with their sister, mother-in-law, or father's wife; and *social*—cheating on land boundaries; misdirecting the blind; subverting the rights of strangers, widows, and orphans; committing murder in secret or offering bribes in cases of murder; and bestiality.

WILY REBECCA POINTS OUT: What these taboos have in common is that they can all be carried out with relative impunity, either because the victims are powerless or because the deeds are done in private. And so Moses tells the people that they're to respond "Amen" when they hear the curses—because he wants them to recognize that only God and their own conscience will enforce these laws. As it is written: "CONCEALED ACTS CONCERN YHVH OUR GOD; BUT WITH OVERT ACTS IT IS FOR US AND OUR CHILDREN EVER TO APPLY ALL THE PROVISIONS OF THIS TEACHING" (29:28).

THE CURSE OF BARRENNESS

OUR MOTHERS TEACH: Moses warns the people that if they disobey God's laws, "CURSED SHALL BE THE ISSUE OF YOUR WOMB" (28:18). Infertility—in the form of barrenness or miscarriage or stillbirth—has traditionally been viewed as a curse, often as punishment for some wrongdoing. Through the centuries, women have responded to their own infertility in a variety of ways, such as praying for divine intervention and devising various folk remedies to open up their wombs. Many of these customs and rituals—some dating back to biblical times—are still in use today.

LEAH THE NAMER ELABORATES: Among the most effective remedies for barrenness are the following:

CHICKPEAS: Known by many names—*nahit, arbes, himtza, bub, ceci, kara,* and *garbanzos*—these legumes have long been a staple in the Jewish diet. Wise women have long believed that eating chickpeas promotes fertility. Chickpeas should also be eaten on the Sabbath after the birth of a son.

ETROG: A yellow citrus fruit similar in size and taste to a lemon, the etrog, or citron, is unique among fruits because its female organ, the *pittam* (stem), through which it is fertilized, does not drop off when the fruit is ripe, and because the tree bears fruit throughout the year. In addition, the etrog, shaped like a woman's uterus and cervix, symbolizes female fertility and generativity. Some say that this so-called apple of Paradise was the forbidden fruit eaten by Adam and Eve in the Garden of Eden, because "etrog" sounds so much like *ragag,* a Hebrew verb meaning "to desire." Because Eve's punishment for eating this fruit was to bear children in pain, pregnant women should eat an etrog to ease the pain of childbirth. Some women bite off the *pittam* after Sukkot to place under the pillow of a woman experiencing difficult labor. The Rabbis teach that a pregnant woman who eats an etrog will produce "fragrant children."

AMULETS: In Europe, amulets called *kimpetbriefel* were often used to protect pregnant women and their unborn children against miscarriage and the demon Lilith, and to protect women during childbirth. Some of these amulets bear the names "Senoy, Sansenoy, and Semangelof," the three angels sent by God to fetch back the rebellious Lilith to Eden, as well as the incantation: "Adam and Eve, barring Lilith."

IRON: As in many other cultures, Jewish folklore has long regarded iron as powerful protection against demons, since it can cut through rock, under or within which evil spirits live. Some teach that iron's antidemonic power comes from its Hebrew name, *barzel*, which is an acronym for "Bilhah, Rachel, Zilpah, and Leah," Jacob's four wives, whose spiritual merits protect against evil spirits. For centuries, a piece of iron—a knife, a sword, or a synagogue key—was placed under the pillow of a pregnant or childbearing woman, in a child's cradle, near a sick or dying person, or in a nest of chicks during a thunderstorm, to protect them from harm.

MOTHER RACHEL ADDS: And if none of these remedies bring children out of your womb, you can open up your heart and let children in—by adopting them, or nurturing others' children.

THE WAGES OF NEGATIVE THINKING

OUR DAUGHTERS ASK: The Torah demands of us not only right action but also right *feeling*. We're commanded to *love* God, to *suppress* jealousy, to *abhor* idolatry, to support the needy with *willing hearts*, to *renounce* grudges. And we're also commanded to *rejoice*, especially during festivals. And if we don't?

OUR MOTHERS ANSWER: The consequence of refusing to "SERVE YHVH YOUR GOD IN JOY AND GLADNESS OVER THE ABUNDANCE OF EVERYTHING" (28:47) is to be forced to serve one's enemies "IN HUNGER AND THIRST, NAKED AND LACKING EVERYTHING" (28:48). For the twin offenses of gloom and ingratitude, God "WILL PUT AN IRON YOKE UPON YOUR NECK" (28:48).

ESTHER THE HIDDEN ONE reveals in the name of CO-
LETTE, SAGE OF JERUSALEM: Grief is pure, emerging from the depths
of feeling and then disappearing when exhausted. Sadness, on the other hand,
is different. A person must cultivate it so as to be interesting to herself. Sadness
is like a stone weighing one down. To be free, one must cast it off.

SARAH THE ANCIENT ONE remarks: What a precise description
of depression!

THE GREAT POWER OF PSALMS

OUR BUBBES TEACH: You can never worry too much about the future!
It can't hurt!

OUR DAUGHTERS PROTEST: But it doesn't usually help, either. How
often do we brood about the troubles waiting for us in the future, instead of
looking forward to the joys. How often do we torment ourselves about
tragedies that never even happen. If we could only count our blessings as reli-
giously as we count our curses!

OUR MOTHERS REPLY: You're right—and *you're* right too! As it is
told:

In the legendary city of Chelm, there once lived a lovely young woman by
the name of Teltza. One day as she was sweeping the floor, she began to fanta-
size about her rosy future:

"Today I'm fifteen years old, young and carefree. In a year or two, Papa will
marry me to a fine young scholar, and all of Chelm will dance at our wedding.
A year later, I'll give birth to a beautiful baby boy, and everyone will rejoice at
the bris. He'll grow up, bright and handsome, and then he'll have a bar mitzvah—but oh, what if he suddenly becomes ill and dies?"

And with that, Teltza began to wail and weep at the top of her lungs. Her
mother heard her and came running, and was soon wailing bitterly next to her
daughter. Then her father and grandmother joined them, and before long, the
house filled up with loud cries.

Word of the calamity spread rapidly throughout Chelm, and in no time, all
the townspeople had gathered at Teltza's house to mourn with the grief-
stricken family.

Then the rabbi of Chelm appeared and announced: "We must all chant
psalms to avert whatever disaster is endangering this family." And so they all
began to chant psalms.

Along came the miller, who was the only person not born in Chelm. When he asked people what had happened, no one seemed to know. So he sought out Teltza herself and asked her.

Sobbing, she told him her tale of woe.

The miller laughed. "What a foolish young girl you are! Your sadness is based on four 'if's—if you marry, if you give birth to a son, if he becomes ill on his bar mitzvah, and if he dies. But none of these events has yet taken place!"

Immediately, Teltza dried her tears and smiled. Others followed her lead, and soon everyone was laughing and dancing with joy.

"You see," pronounced the rabbi, "nothing works in evil times like chanting psalms. It never fails!"

EMBLEMS OF DESOLATION

BERURIAH THE SCHOLAR TEACHES: The catalog of punishments assigned to the chorus on Mount Ebal predicts especially gruesome ordeals for city dwellers, because they lack access to food and water in the event of siege. In such times, the "MOST TENDER AND DAINTY [mother] . . . SHALL BEGRUDGE THE HUSBAND OF HER BOSOM, AND HER SON AND HER DAUGHTER, THE AFTERBIRTH THAT ISSUES FROM BETWEEN HER LEGS AND THE BABIES SHE BEARS; SHE SHALL EAT THEM SECRETLY, BECAUSE OF UTTER WANT" (28:56–57).

SERAKH BAT ASHER THE HISTORIAN EXPLAINS: Unfortunately, this image all too accurately reflects historical reality. During the two sieges of Jerusalem, in 586 B.C.E. and 70 C.E.; during the First Crusade in the Rhineland, in 1096; and, most recently, during the Holocaust, in our own century, desperate measures were sometimes the only means of survival for Jews.

JEWISH WOMEN DURING THE HOLOCAUST

OUR MOTHERS LAMENT: Crueler even than the sting of death were the unimaginable choices that faced our people during the dark night of the Shoah: Forced to choose who would live, who would die. Choosing to share food that could not even sustain a single mouth, or to hoard food that could save another. Choosing to entrust one's children to strangers, or not to trust one's own friends. How cruel to be a mother during such times!

As it is told: In Auschwitz, Livia Bitton Jackson was once forced to work for twenty-four hours without food or water. When she returned to the barracks, her sick mother insisted that Livia eat the bowl of soup she had saved for her, or she would spill it on the ground. When Livia refused, her mother spilled the soup, and the two women wept together all night, their hearts breaking with grief.

As it is also told: Once, when Rabbi Israel Spira was sawing wood as part of a forced labor detail at the Janowska Road Camp, a woman ran up and demanded a knife from the Jews working there. When the German in charge of the prisoners questioned her, she made the same demand of him, and he handed her his pocket knife. Bending down and picking up her newborn baby, swaddled at her feet in rags, she circumcised him and recited the Hebrew blessing. Then she handed the bloody knife and the baby to the German. Said Rabbi Spira at that moment: "Next to Abraham on Mount Moriah, where can you find a greater act of faith than this Jewish mother's?"

51. NITZAVIM:
Empowerment
(DEUTERONOMY 29:9–30:20)

TORAH TEACHES: In this parasha, Moses concludes his final address to the people, reiterating the mutual obligations of Israel and God. He tells the people that in the future they will be unfaithful to God and will be punished severely for their infidelities. But he also assures them that God will forgive them and bring them back from exile. Before them lies a choice. Moses exhorts them: Choose life!

A HIERARCHY OF LISTENERS

HULDAH THE PREACHER TEACHES: In his final discourse before his farewell elegy in the next parasha, Moses addresses and inventories his vast congregation: "YOU STAND THIS DAY, ALL OF YOU, BEFORE YHVH, YOUR GOD—YOUR TRIBAL HEADS, YOUR ELDERS AND YOUR OFFICIALS, ALL THE MEN OF ISRAEL, YOUR CHILDREN, YOUR WIVES, EVEN THE STRANGER WITHIN YOUR CAMP, FROM WOODCHOPPER TO WATERDRAWER" (29:9–10). Just as a speaker follows a conventional order in addressing an audience, starting with the most important guests and concluding with the generic "ladies and gentlemen," so Moses here follows a descending order (although significantly he excludes the Levites from this list). The women come after the leaders, the men, and the children, but before strangers and menial laborers. They are also not directly addressed; only the men of Israel are included in the initial "you." All others are "attached" to the men through the possessive pronoun "your."

MIRIAM THE PROPHET POINTS OUT: And yet, intentionally or inadvertently, Moses leaves open the possibility that the circle of address will be expanded in the future, for he states that God's covenant applies not only to the patriarchs and to their male descendants standing "HERE WITH US THIS DAY" but also to those "WHO ARE NOT HERE WITH US TODAY" (29:14). In the Hebrew original, the word *et* (meaning "to" in this case) is not followed as it usually is by a direct object but instead leaves a suggestive vacancy. We can fill it in with our own names.

THE GOD OF LOVE

OUR DAUGHTERS ASK: Throughout the Torah, we've encountered many faces of God: the Judge, the One-Who-Exacts-Vengeance, the Redeemer, the One-Who-Keeps-Faith-with-Israel, the Source of Life. But rarely do we meet the One-Who-Loves-Us. Is this only a Christian idea?

HULDAH THE PREACHER ANSWERS: Because we've lived in Christian cultures for so many centuries, many of us have written off some legitimately Jewish ideas simply because they've been adopted by our daughter faith. As a threatened minority, we've often defined ourselves *reactively* in relation to our host culture: whatever *they* believe, we believe the opposite. As much as such reverse psychology builds group identity, it also narrows the range of religious choice. Among the ideas that we've written off at various times are messianism, heaven, hell, the afterlife—and the notion that "God loves us," which is solidly embedded in traditional Jewish liturgy but rarely voiced as part of a Jew's personal belief system. As it is written here in the Torah: "THEN YHVH YOUR GOD WILL RESTORE YOUR FORTUNES AND TAKE YOU BACK IN LOVE" (30:3).

THE SAGES IN OUR OWN TIME OFFER: The modern German Jewish philosopher Franz Rosenzweig placed God's love at the heart of Judaism and regarded a belief in that love as the Jew's only effective defense against existential despair, which he calls the "Everlasting No." As he writes in his own magnificent love song to Judaism, *The Star of Redemption:* "The soul is at peace in the love of God, like a child in the arms of its mother, and now it can reach beyond 'the uttermost parts of the sea' and to the portals of the grave—and is yet ever with [God]."

THE STORY OF SKOTSL

OUR DAUGHTERS ASK: As he prepares to die, Moses assures his people that the Torah is not in the heavens or across the sea but "VERY CLOSE TO YOU, IN YOUR MOUTH AND IN YOUR HEART" (30:14). Is that still true? For isn't it also written: "WHO AMONG US CAN GO UP TO THE HEAVENS AND GET IT FOR US" (30:12)? What are we supposed to do now that we no longer have a superhuman champion like Moses to intercede with God on our behalf?

OUR MOTHERS ANSWER: Once upon a time, there lived in Russia a community of women who reached just such a point of despair when the Russian army came and marched off all their men. Because the women themselves had no direct access to the Torah, neither to its words nor to the performance of many of its *mitzvot,* their Jewish lives came to a standstill. There were no men to perform a bris, slaughter kosher meat, lead prayers, read from the Torah, or conduct a funeral. Finally, one young woman, named Skotsl, suggested that they build a human ladder to heaven and ask God what to do. Because it was her idea, Skotsl was elected to be their spokeswoman.

But just as Skotsl reached the top of the wobbling tower, the woman at the bottom sneezed, and the whole pillar of women collapsed. After they had picked themselves up and made sure no bones were broken, they looked around for Skotsl—but she was nowhere to be found. And since that day, she has never been seen again. Did she reach heaven and become stranded there? Or did she fall to earth somewhere so distant that she could not find her way back home? Or did she die in the fall?

To this day, when some Jewish women greet each other, they announce, *"Skotsl kumt!"*—"Skotsl comes!"—hoping that at last Skotsl has returned with answers from heaven and beyond the sea.

CHOOSE LIFE

OUR DAUGHTERS ASK: How often is the following line quoted to us as one of the central principles of Judaism: "I HAVE PUT BEFORE YOU LIFE AND DEATH, BLESSING AND CURSE. CHOOSE LIFE" (30:19–20). But it's not always so simple to "choose life"! The choices are not always so clear.

SARAH THE ANCIENT ONE ANSWERS: Read on! The Torah explains further what it means: "IF YOU AND YOUR OFFSPRING WOULD LIVE" (30:19)—that is, you must choose to foster new life to bring forth the next generation; "BY LOVING YHVH YOUR GOD"—the choice demands that you follow a path of devotion; "[by] HEEDING GOD'S COMMANDS"—the choice also demands that you follow a path of spiritual and moral discipline; "AND [by] HOLDING FAST TO GOD" (30:20)—and you must follow a path of faithfulness.

OUR MOTHERS ADD: What a sublime recipe for happiness!

52. VAYELEKH:
The Hidden Face

(DEUTERONOMY 31:1–31:30)

TORAH TEACHES: As he contemplates his approaching death, Moses assures the people that Joshua will lead them ably, under God's guidance. He then lays his hands upon Joshua and appoints him his successor. Moses writes down his Teaching and hands it over to the priests, instructing them to read it to the people every sabbatical year, during the festival of Sukkot.

Then God appears to Moses and Joshua at the Tent of Meeting in a pillar of cloud. God tells Moses that after his death, the people will forsake the Torah, and God's face will then become hidden to them. God instructs Moses to recite a poem before the people to bear witness to their fate, their perfidy, and their ultimate redemption.

THE HIDDEN FACE OF GOD

OUR DAUGHTERS ASK: God's face is often hidden from us, just as the Torah predicts: "YET I WILL KEEP MY COUNTENANCE HIDDEN ON THAT DAY, BE-CAUSE OF ALL THE EVIL THEY HAVE DONE IN TURNING TO OTHER GODS" (31:18). How can we find God at such times?

ESTHER THE HIDDEN ONE ANSWERS: When God withholds favor from us, our tradition speaks of *hester panim*, the hiding of God's face . . .

LEAH THE NAMER INTERRUPTS: Which is a form of your own name! *Esther* means "I will hide," for you are the One-Who-Hid-in-the-Palace in order to save her people from destruction.

ESTHER CONTINUES: Yes, hiding is sometimes as much a sign of love as revelation. When God shows favor, we say that the divine face shines upon the people. The Priestly Blessing, which channels divine favor to the people through the *kohen's* outstretched fingers, invokes the radiance of God's face as a sign of grace and peace.

DINAH THE WOUNDED ONE OBJECTS: After Auschwitz, many of us reject as indefensible any effort to justify God's silence as *hester panim*. A God whose face remained hidden when the world was so dark no longer deserves our allegiance. Martin Buber characterizes God's hiddenness during this period as an "eclipse." Richard Rubenstein calls it the "death of God."

MOTHER RACHEL ADDS: But Abraham Joshua Heschel imagines God as suffering with all victims, waiting until humanity turns its own face back toward God. Indeed, at the height of her suffering, Etty Hillesum, a young Dutch Jew who perished in Auschwitz, reached out toward God, declaring, "We must help You to help ourselves . . . to safeguard that little piece of You, God, in ourselves." And Kalonymus Kalman Shapiro, rabbi of the Warsaw Ghetto, who likewise lost his life in the Holocaust, affirms: "The weeping that the person does together with God—that strengthens him. . . . It is hard to rise, time and again, above the sufferings; but when one summons the courage—stretching the mind to engage in Torah and divine service—then he enters the inner chambers where God is to be found."

THE MAID OF LUDOMIR

OUR MOTHERS TEACH: For women, God's face has often been hidden by those who have jealously veiled the secrets of Torah from our gaze. Nonetheless, we have continued to seek out God's Countenance throughout the centuries and have felt it shining upon us. Occasionally, there have been women especially gifted in such holy quests, who have inspired us and taught us how to seek for ourselves.

SERAKH BAT ASHER THE HISTORIAN ADDS: In ancient times, such women served as matriarchs and judges, prophets and healers, and, occasionally, scholars and mystics. In more recent times, women have also become rabbinic leaders and decisors. One of the first of this rare breed was Hannah Rachel Werbermacher, known as the Maid of Ludomir, the only female hasidic "rebbe" in Europe.

HANNAH RACHEL RECOUNTS: I was an only child, the apple of my parents' eyes. Everyone in Ludomir knew my strange ways, how I would *daven* with such fervor that some claimed I was possessed by a dybbuk or the spirit of the she-demon Lilith. But it was only my love for God that filled me, like a seedpod ready to burst. My father, may his name be for a blessing, taught me from his holy books—not *gemara*, of course, but midrash, aggadah, and *musar*. I know that in his heart he still prayed for a son, but he never made me feel second best. And my beloved mother, may she find eternal rest in the arms of the

Shekhinah—how I ached when the Holy One took her from me. So deep was my grief that I became gravely ill—but then God healed my broken heart with a vision, and I received a new and sublime soul. From that moment on, I took upon myself the *mitzvos* of a man—tallis, tefillin, even reciting *kaddish* for my holy father when he passed on. Rather than mock me, the dear people of Ludomir, God bless them, honored me as their *rebbe*, building me a shul with my own apartment, from which I taught them Torah every *shalus sheudis*—through a doorway so the men shouldn't see my face. But it proved too much for the rabbis that I should be so respected and so free—so when the *zaddik* of Chernobyl proposed a good match, I had no choice but to agree. From that moment on, I was no longer the rebbe of Ludomir, just a scholar's wife. So I left for the Holy Land to study kabbalah and hasten the coming of *Mashiakh*, praying for a time when women like me could study and teach Torah with pride and honor.

MIRIAM THE PROPHET ADDS: To honor the memory of Hannah Rachel and all the hidden seekers who came before her, let us all strive to recognize God's face wherever it shines!

53. HA'AZINU:
Ethical Wills

(DEUTERONOMY 32:1–52)

TORAH TEACHES: Moses recites God's prophetic poem before the people, extolling the divine might and favor that have blessed Israel to this day. The poem foretells Israel's betrayal of the covenant and God's terrible vengeance.

Then God instructs Moses to ascend Mount Nebo, to view the land of Canaan before he dies.

THE VOCABULARY OF FAREWELL

BERURIAH THE SCHOLAR TEACHES: Moses ends his life by declaiming two long poems: the first, a farewell ode; the second, an ethical will in the form of a blessing, similar to the one delivered by Jacob on his deathbed. In the first poem, Moses assumes the role of thundering prophet, foretelling Israel's doom and subsequent redemption. Delivered in the divine persona, it constitutes a *theodicy*, a justification of the ways of God to humankind. Like most ancient poetry, "Ha'azinu" is filled with imagery drawn from the natural world. Many of these images derive from public contexts of power and violence; others, from more private realms of generativity and nurture.

MOTHER RACHEL ELABORATES: God is imaged here as the One who conceived and bore Israel. As it is written: "IS NOT HE THE FATHER WHO CREATED YOU, [who] FASHIONED YOU AND MADE YOU ENDURE!" (32:6). In a second, unusual birth image, God is characterized as "THE ROCK THAT BEGOT YOU" (32:18). And God not only has given birth to Israel but has also raised the people as a loving parent raises children: "LIKE AN EAGLE WHO ROUSES HIS NESTLINGS, GLIDING DOWN TO HIS YOUNG, SO DID [God] SPREAD [the divine] WINGS AND TAKE [Israel], BEAR HIM ALONG ON [God's] PINIONS" (32:11).

DINAH THE WOUNDED ONE POINTS OUT: Yet despite these images of life and nurture, the dominant tone of the poem is one of death and destruction, first as God punishes Israel for its infidelities, and then as God avenges them upon their enemies.

ESTHER THE HIDDEN ONE RESPONDS: So must it be within the uncompromising terms of monotheism: "THERE IS NO GOD BESIDES ME. I DEAL DEATH AND GIVE LIFE; I WOUNDED AND I WILL HEAL: NONE CAN DELIVER FROM MY HAND" (32:39).

OUR MOTHERS COMMENT: And on a more limited scale, so must it be with human parents as well. For at first, when all the power is ours, we shape our children and in the process, often unconsciously and certainly unwittingly, both wound and heal them. Then we send them off to cross the Jordan, where they will have to muddle through on their own.

ETHICAL WILLS

OUR DAUGHTERS ASK: In his farewell addresses, Moses bequeaths to future generations teachings, laws, admonitions, blessings, and the inspiring example of his life. What can we leave behind for our children that can possibly compare with that legacy?

OUR MOTHERS ANSWER: One of the most extraordinary legacies we have is the tradition of the ethical will, a document in which we pass on to our children our own "Torah," the wisdom and advice of a lifetime. Many women throughout the ages have written such ethical wills for their children. Others have transmitted their "Torah" in the form of memoirs. One of the most famous of these memoirs was written by Gluckel of Hameln (1646–1724), a twice-widowed mother of thirteen whose business aptitude supported her family while she was alive and whose sage advice continues to inspire us after her death.

GLUCKEL RECOUNTS: "A bird once set out to cross the windy sea with its three fledglings. The sea was so wide and the wind so strong, the father bird was forced to carry his young, one by one, in his strong claws. When he was halfway across with the first fledgling, the wind turned to a gale, and he said, 'My child, look how I am struggling and risking my life on your behalf. When you are grown up, will you do as much for me and provide for my old age?' The fledgling replied, 'Only bring me to safety, and when you are old I shall do everything you ask of me.' Whereat the father bird dropped his child into the sea, and it drowned, and he said, 'So shall it be done to such a liar as you.' Then the father bird returned to shore, set forth with his second fledgling, asked the same question, and, receiving the same answer, drowned the second child, with the cry, 'You too are a liar!' Finally, he set out with the third fledgling, and when he asked the same question, the third and last fledgling replied, 'My dear father, it is true you are struggling mightily and risking your life in my behalf, and I shall be wrong not to repay you when you are old, but I cannot bind myself. This, though, I can promise: when I am grown up and have children of my own, I shall do as much for them as you have done for me.' Whereupon the father bird said, 'Well spoken, my child, and wisely; your life I will spare and carry you to shore in safety.'"

THE SILENCE SURROUNDING MIRIAM'S DEATH

OUR DAUGHTERS ASK: When Moses finishes reciting his song, God instructs him to ascend Mount Nebo, where he will die, "AS YOUR BROTHER AARON DIED ON MOUNT HOR AND WAS GATHERED TO HIS KIN" (32:50). Why is there no mention of Miriam's death?

THE RABBIS ANSWER: All three leaders—Aaron, Miriam, and Moses—died by the "kiss of God." All three deaths were decreed by God during the same month, and they were assigned to die within the same year: first Miriam, on the first of Nisan; then Aaron, four months later; and finally Moses, on the seventh of Adar.

OUR DAUGHTERS ASK: But why doesn't God remind Moses here of his sister's death as well as Aaron's? Is it because she dies in the wilderness, while Moses, like his brother, will die on a mountain?

MIRIAM THE PROPHET ANSWERS: Perhaps the next verse provides a clue, for here God reminds Moses of the sin—striking the rock at Meribah—that has cost him *and his brother*—"you" here is in the plural—entry into the Promised Land. My own sin—speaking out against Moses—is mentioned earlier, although then only in reference to the proper observance of the laws of leprosy, not in reference to any punishment.

THE SAGES IN OUR OWN TIME SUGGEST: Either the editors of Deuteronomy had no access to what feminist scholars call the "Miriam tradition" or they deliberately chose to censor it out of the text.

MIRIAM QUIPS: Luckily, the Midrash was more generous!

54. VEZOT HA-BERAKHAH:
Letting Go
(DEUTERONOMY 33:1–34:12)

ORAH TEACHES: Just before he dies, Moses recites a farewell song, blessing each tribe and recalling details of its history. Then he ascends to the top of Mount Nebo, where God shows him the land he will not be allowed to enter. Moses dies, and God buries him in a secret grave. And the people mourn their beloved leader's death for forty days.

RETURNING TO HIS MOTHER'S ARMS

MOTHER RACHEL TEACHES: Among Moses' final words in his elegiac Song of Blessing is an image of homecoming. As it is written: "THE ANCIENT GOD IS A REFUGE, A SUPPORT ARE THE ARMS EVERLASTING" (53:27). After all the violent metaphors—God as fire-breathing dragon, as bloody swordsman and archer, as wrathful Avenger and Judge—this depiction of God as embracing parent is particularly moving.

OUR MOTHERS COMMENT: As Robert Frost once put it: "Home is the place where, when you have to go there, / They have to take you in."

PASSING ON THE MANTLE

THE RABBIS TEACH: Moses not only appoints Joshua as his political successor but also asks him to serve as the guardian of his surviving family: to comfort and support his elderly mother, Yokheved, "who has the terrible misfortune of losing all her children in her lifetime"; to protect his wife, Zipporah, a "poor proselyte"; and to provide for his two orphaned sons, "to whom it was not granted to be my successors."

MOTHER RACHEL EXCLAIMS: What a poignant last request from Israel's greatest leader!

THE BRIDE WHO SAVED HER HUSBAND
FROM THE ANGEL OF DEATH

MIRIAM THE PROPHET DECLARES: How terrible is the day of our death, for on that day each of us stands alone before an Angel who is not accustomed to being refused! But sometimes even this Angel yields to the power of tears. As it is told:

The prophet Elijah once informed a young man that he was destined to die on his wedding day. Sure enough, on that day, an uninvited guest arrived at the wedding feast, an old man, dirty and unkempt. To the other guests' amazement, the groom invited the guest to his own table and paid him great honor.

The old man said to the bridegroom, "I have come to take your soul, as you have been forewarned."

When the young man's father heard these terrible words, he pleaded with the Angel of Death—for that was who this was—to take his life instead of his son's. But when he saw the Angel's dreadful face, he drew back. The same thing happened with the bridegroom's mother.

Then the young bride bravely stepped forward and challenged the Angel: "Does it not say in the Torah that a new groom shall rejoice with his bride for a whole year? And does it not also say, 'a life for a life'? Therefore take my life, and let my husband live!"

The Angel of Death raised his sword to slay her, but he was overcome with pity, and a tear fell from his eye. He flew to heaven and pleaded for mercy before the Throne of Glory. God granted his petition, and the couple lived happily until a ripe old age.

SECRET GRAVES

THE RABBIS TEACH: The site of Moses' grave still remains a secret, as it is written: "AND NO ONE KNOWS HIS BURIAL PLACE TO THIS DAY" (34:6). For even God worried that Moses might become a cult figure after his death. That's why God buries Moses secretly, in a grave that was created at twilight on the sixth day of Creation. This hidden grave, where his body lies still untouched by decay, is connected by a subterranean passage to the Cave of Makhpelah, where the Patriarchs and Matriarchs (excepting Rachel, Bilhah, and Zilpah) lie buried. For the same reason, Aaron's grave on Mount Hor is also not marked. Legend has it that it vanished as soon as Moses left the cave where Aaron died.

OUR DAUGHTERS ASK: And Miriam's grave?

MIRIAM THE PROPHET ANSWERS: No such legends recount the whereabouts of my grave or explain why it remains unmarked. It is likely that the Rabbis never worried about the emergence of a Miriam cult.

LILITH THE REBEL QUIPS: Until now!

YOKHEVED'S TEARS

OUR DAUGHTERS ASK: According to the Midrash, Yokheved lives to enter the Promised Land—although that makes her 250 years old! How does she react to the death of her last child?

THE RABBIS ANSWER: Like that of other bereft mothers in Jewish legend—Sarah, whose heart bursts joyfully upon her learning that Isaac has been spared from Abraham's knife; and Rachel, who forever weeps for her exiled children—Yokheved's mourning for her son is of epic proportions. Refusing to believe that Moses is really dead, she retraces his forty-year journey, looking for him, returning to Egypt, where she questions the Nile and the Red Sea, and then inquiring of the desert, Mount Sinai, and the rock that Moses struck in anger. Each protests that it hasn't seen her son since Moses performed miracles upon it. Joshua follows a similar course, until God chides him: "How long will you continue to seek Moses in vain? He is dead, but indeed it is I that have lost him, and not you."

MIRIAM THE PROPHET DECLARES: And so I now chide you as God once chided the Children of Israel: How long will you continue to seek me in vain? I am not in the heavens or across the sea, but I am very close to you, in your mouth and in your heart. Indeed, it is you who have lost me, but if you seek me, I will show myself to you. And together we will choose life!

BE STRONG, BE STRONG, AND TOGETHER LET US BE STRENGTHENED!

IRIAM THE PROPHET SINGS: The world is so much in need
of healing. So many suffer, so many stumble forward in ignorance, so many lose hope. So often we despair, convinced that
the Holy One has been shackled and blinded by the minions of
the Other Side. Yet despite our discouragements, still we struggle on, knowing
that together we can redeem the world. Know that when things seem most
bleak, the One-Who-Dwells-in-This-World is always nearby to help you. I always offer you succor: the healing waters of my well. Drink deep of its nour-
ishing waters and be renewed!

OUR DAUGHTERS SING:

MIRIAM HANEVI'AH / מִרְיָם הַנְּבִיאָה

מִרְיָם הַנְּבִיאָה עֹז וְזִמְרָה בְּיָדָהּ
מִרְיָם תִּרְקוֹד אִתָּנוּ לְהַגְדִּיל זִמְרַת עוֹלָם
מִרְיָם תִּרְקוֹד אִתָּנוּ לְתַקֵּן אֶת־הָעוֹלָם:
בִּמְהֵרָה בְיָמֵינוּ הִיא תְּבִיאֵנוּ
אֶל מֵי הַיְשׁוּעָה:

Miryam hanevi'ah, oz vezimrah beyadah.
Miryam, tirkod itanu lehagdil zimrat olam.
Miryam, tirkod itanu letaken et ha-olam.
Bimiherah veyamenu he tevi'eynu
el mey hayeshua, el mey hayeshua.

Miriam the Prophet,
strength and song are in her hand.
Miriam will dance with us
to swell earth's song.
Miriam will dance with us
to redeem the world.

Soon, in our day,
she will bring us
to the waters of redemption.

Epigraph: "We All Stood Together," by Merle Feld. Used by permission of the author.

GENESIS

1. BERESHIT

The Creation of Souls: Louis Ginzberg, *Legends of the Jews* (Philadelphia: The Jewish Publication Society, 1909–38), I, 55–59.

Isha of my ish: B. Sotah 17a.

Lilith: Ginzberg, *Legends of the Jews* I, 65–66.

Put a fence around the Torah: Pirke Avot 1:1.

We have compared the Jewish People to an apple tree: B. Shabbat 88a.

An orchard of holy apples: Zohar 2:88a.

Maligning woman's nature (as the Rabbis later do): Genesis Rabbah 8:2.

2. NOAH

Naamah: Genesis Rabbah 23:3.

Abraham and I were brother and sister: See Genesis 20:12.

The daughter of Enheduanna: Enheduanna, the daughter of the Akkadian king Sargon, was a priestess and the composer of a number of famous hymns. I have taken the liberty of imagining Enheduanna as Sarah's mother.

"Whatever Sarai tells you, do as she says": See Genesis 21:12.

Amitlai: Ginzberg, *Legends of the Jews* I, 186–93.

3. LEKH LEKHA

"And the persons that they had acquired": Genesis Rabbah 40:14.

Sarah's beauty is legendary: Ginzberg, *Legends of the Jews* I, 221–22.

An invisible angel saves her: Ibid., 223–24.

The Israelites' status as a pioneer culture: For a discussion of the economic and social conditions prevailing in Iron Age Israel, see Carol Meyers, *Discovering Eve: Ancient Israelite Women in Context* (Oxford: Oxford University Press, 1988), chap. 3: "Setting the Scene: The Highland Environment of Ancient Israel," 47–71.

Pharaoh gave me to Sarah: Genesis Rabbah 45:2.

4. Vayera

This third daughter was named Paltit: Ginzberg, *Legends of the Jews* I, 249–50.

Lot's wife brings this fate upon herself: Ibid., 254–55.

Abraham knows all along that God will intervene: B. Baba Kamma 92a.

Abraham and Sarah hold two great feasts: Ginzberg, *Legends of the Jews* I, 262–63.

Ishmael "plays" with Isaac: Ibid., V, 246, n. 211.

When Ishmael calls out: Genesis Rabbah 53:14.

Sarah goes to Hebron: Ginzberg, *Legends of the Jews* I, 286–87.

5. Hayei Sarah

God as matchmaker: Genesis Rabbah 68:4.

She falls off her camel: Ginzberg, *Legends of the Jews* V, 263, n. 301.

Sarah's tent: Ibid., I, 297.

6. Toldot

Woman's suffering is greater than man's: B. Niddah 30a.

Red lentil soup: I owe this recipe to Betsy Platkin Teutsch, who explains that "I make this soup for Shabbat Toldot, which, mysteriously, always seems to come at the perfect seasonal moment to shift to hot soup on Friday night in the Northeast where I live. Esau thought this was soup to die for (Genesis 25:30–34). (I imagine it's one of the few times men cooked in the Bible!) At any rate, it's a luscious color and easily prepared for low-fat, delicious fare."

"As lowly as a lentil": J. Sanhedrin 2:5.

"The lentil has no mouth": B. Baba Batra 16b.

Middle Eastern Lamb and Rice Pilaf: Adapted from Gloria Kaufer Greene, *The Jewish Holiday Cookbook* (New York: Times Books, 1985), 82.

7. Vayetze

Jacob's ladder: Genesis Rabbah 68:4, 12–14.

An eye for an eye: See parashat "Mishpatim."

The Torah later proscribes: See parashat "Akharei Mot."

I hid myself under their bed: Lamentations Rabbah, Proem 24. The Austrian Jewish writer Stefan Zweig created a story based on this Midrash, "Rachel Arraigns with God," in *Jewish Legends* (New York: Markus Wiener, 1987), 147–64.

It was revealed to me that God had betrothed me to Esau: Genesis Rabbah 70:16; 71:2.

Through the meanings I divined: The etymologies of these names are based upon the notes to the 1985 JPS translation of TANAKH.

I was also honoring the Divine Lady Asherah: Interpretation suggested by Raphael Patai in *The Hebrew Goddess* (New York: Ktav, 1967), 280–81, n. 15.

Bilhah's sons: These etymologies are based upon the notes to the 1985 JPS translation of TANAKH.

What Rachel never found out was that it was I who originally carried Joseph: Torah Shelemah, Genesis 30:21.

8. VAYISHLAKH

Oni: I owe this reading to Rachael Turkienicz, who points out that Onkelos, the Septuagint, and Rashi all translate *oni* as "pain" in Genesis 35:18 but as "strength" or "power" in Genesis 49:3. The medieval commentator Nachmanides Ramban claims that Rachel intends the word to mean "sorrow," but that Jacob translates it as "strength" (*yamin*), thus turning a negative name into a positive one. Ramban admits that this is the only time a mother's choice of names is overturned, but gives no reason for this exception. Though Ramban does tie Jacob's interpretation to his own blessing of Reuben in Genesis 49:3, he refuses to consider that Rachel might have deliberately chosen this meaning herself in naming her son. Turkienicz's original insight (in an unpublished essay) is to redeem Rachel's act as a testimony to her great love for Jacob as well as their child.

Dinah is mentioned only once more: Genesis 46:15.

Asnat: For the story of Asnat, see parashat "Miketz."

Timna: In chapter 38 of Genesis, Judah goes down to the city of Timna for the sheep shearing. There he meets his daughter-in-law, Tamar, disguised as a roadside prostitute.

Amalek: Amalek plays a central role in Israel's history, first as an enemy that attacks the Israelites from the rear soon after they leave Egypt (see parashat "Beshallakh") and later as an adversary of King Saul (I Samuel 15). Because of their cowardly assault on the vulnerable rear guard of the Israelite ranks, Amalek is cursed for eternity. According to the Book of Esther, Haman descends from this villainous line.

9. VAYESHEV

The Fable of the Ape and the Leopard: Adapted from *Tales of the Jewish Aesop: From the Fox Fables of Berechiah HaNakdan* by Moses Hadas (New York: Columbia University Press, 1967), no. 61.

Tamar's pedigree: According to some biblical scholars, the story of Judah and Tamar was set down at the time of Judah's dominance among the tribes. David's capital of Jerusalem was in the kingdom of Judah; his lineage stems from this tribe. See 2 Samuel 13, for the story of another Tamar, one of David's daughters, who is raped by her half-brother Amnon.

Levirate marriage: See parashat "Ki Tetze."

Jephthah's daughter: In the tragic story of Jephthah's daughter, found in the Book of Judges, the Israelite general Jephthah foolishly vows to sacrifice "whatever comes out of the door of my house to meet me on my safe return" (11:31), not expecting to be greeted by his only daughter, "with timbrel and dance" (11:34). Father and daughter both agree to fulfill Jephthah's rash vow, but only after the young woman has "bewailed her maidenhood upon the hills" (11:58) with her companions. Although she is nameless in the Bible, the Midrash identifies her as She'ilah, the One-Who-Is-Demanded. Her story is read as the traditional haftorah for parashat "Hukkat." For Jacob's vow, see parashat "Vayetze."

The ultimate reunion of all of Abraham's children: This claim is an extrapolation derived from a structuralist reading of the kinship structure in the Book of Ruth. See Harold Fisch, "Ruth and the Structure of Covenant History," *Vetus Testamentum* XXXII, no. 4 (1982), 425–437.

Potiphar's wife Zuleika: Ginzberg, *Legends of the Jews* II, 44–58. The story of Zuleika and Joseph has captured the imaginations of Jewish, Christian, and Muslim writers for centuries. For other literary treatments of this tale, see Michael McGaha, *Coat of Many Cultures: The Joseph Story in Spanish Literature, 1200–1492* (Philadelphia: The Jewish Publication Society, 1996).

10. MIKETZ

Asnat: Ginzberg, *Legends of the Jews,* II, 170–74.

Praying for a good dream: This represents only the first part of a longer prayer, the rest of which consists largely of biblical citations. The origin of this prayer is in the Talmud, B. Berakhot 55b. This particular formulation is taken from *The Complete Artscroll Siddur,* ed. Nosson Scherman (New York: Mesorah Publications, 1985), 968.

11. VAYIGGASH

Mother of Asnat, mother-in-law of Joseph: See parashat "Vayiggash."

Serakh bat Asher: This biblical figure has been the subject of numerous legends and commentaries. For a complete discussion of these sources, see Judith Antonelli, *In the Image of God: A Feminist Commentary on the Torah* (Northvale, NJ: Jason Aronson, 1995), 123–26; and Leila Leah Bronner, *From Eve to Esther: Rabbinic Reconstructions of Biblical Women* (Louisville: Westminster/John Knox, 1994), 42–56. See also parashat "Pinkhas."

Seventy descendants: There is some discrepancy between the count given here and a similar count given in Exodus 1:1–7. The Rabbis, as always, try to reconcile this discrepancy in the Midrash. See Ginzberg, *Legends of the Jews* V, 359, n. 321.

12. VAYEKHI

For the next four hundred years, the Israelites lived as an enslaved people: Both traditional commentators and modern scholars have debated the duration of Israelite slavery. In the first divine covenant with Abraham (Genesis 15:13), God reveals to Abraham that his descendants will be slaves in Egypt for four hundred years, a period described as lasting only four generations (15:16). Exodus 6:13–30 lists four generations between Jacob and Moses, but I Chronicles 7:20–27 lists ten generations between Jacob and Joshua. One traditional way to reconcile this discrepancy is to understand that the "four hundred years" refers to the period extending from the Abrahamic covenant (or from Abraham's and Sarah's first sojourn in Egypt) to the Exodus, whereas the actual period of national slavery was actually considerably shorter—210 or 230 years. For additional discussion and sources regarding this subject, see Gunther Plaut's commentary and notes on Exodus 12:40, *The Torah: A Modern Commentary,* ed. Gunther Plaut (New York: UAHC Press, 1981), 462–63.

The Testament of Jacob: Modern biblical scholars have proposed numerous theories about the authorship, editing, and dating of the biblical canon. But though they disagree about the details, there is a general consensus that the single work we now call the Tanakh (what Christians call the "Old Testament") is actually an edited anthology of texts that evolved over many centuries.

Until their divided house collapsed: The united kingdom under David, consisting of all twelve tribes, lasted only one more generation, under the rule of David's son Solomon (10th c. B.C.E.). Under Solomon's son Rehoboam, the kingdom split in two: the southern kingdom of Judah, made up of the two tribes of Judah and Benjamin, ruled by the Davidic line centered in Jerusalem; and the breakaway northern kingdom of Israel, consisting of the other ten tribes, with their own capital and religious shrines. The northern kingdom was conquered and dispersed in 722 B.C.E. by Assyria; Judah was conquered first by Babylonia in 586 B.C.E. and then again by Rome in 70 C.E., which marked the end of Jewish sovereignty in the land until the establishment of the modern state of Israel in this century.

So greatly does Jacob love Rachel: Genesis Rabbah 98:25.

Everything depended upon Rachel: Ibid., 71:2.

Bilhah and Zilpah: Book of Jubilees, 132, cited in Alfred Edersheim, *Sketches of Jewish Social Life*, updated edition (Peabody, MA: Hendrickson, 1994), 59.

EXODUS

13. SHEMOT

Shifra and Puah: These are not Israelite names but rather common northwest Semitic names. Shifra means "beautiful one" and Puah simply "girl." Ginzberg, *Legends of the Jews* II, 250–54. See also Exodus Rabbah 1:13. The Israeli Bible scholar Yair Zakovitch contends that the textual evidence strongly points toward the conclusion that these two women were not *Hebrew* midwives but rather midwives *of the Hebrew women (meyaldot ha-ivri'ot)*. That the Torah takes the trouble to point out that these women "feared God" (a fact that presumably would have been self-evident of the Hebrews themselves) and that they served other populations besides the Hebrew slaves—for they claim that "the Hebrew women are not like the Egyptian women" (1:19)—proves that they were not Israelites, but were either Egyptian or members of some other Mesopotamian group, as their western Semitic names would suggest. See Yair Zakovitch, *And You Shall Tell Your Son: The Concept of the Exodus in the Bible* (Jerusalem: Magnes Press, 1991), 125–26.

When my brother Moses was born: Ginzberg, *Legends of the Jews* II, 264.

Aaron, Moses' older brother: The three children of Amram and Yokheved—Aaron, Miriam, and Moses—rarely appear together in the Torah, strong evidence that several different story traditions circulated among the ancient Israelites. Here, in the first appearance of this family, neither Moses nor Miriam is identified by name, and an older brother is not even mentioned. Aaron does not appear until after Moses encounters the Burning Bush, and even there is referred to only as a fellow Levite, not Moses' brother. Miriam first receives her name after the crossing of the Sea of Reeds. See also parashat "Beshallakh."

To divorce their wives: Ginzberg, *Legends of the Jews* II, 258–59, 262.

Among these non-Jewish heroes are several women: For the story of Yael, see Judges 4:17–22; 5:24–30. The story of Rahab can be found in Joshua 2:1–24; 6:22–25. The Rabbis saw fit to give these gentile heroines further recognition by assigning their stories as haftarot in the yearly Torah cycle: the story of Yael (along with that of Deborah) for parashat "Beshallakh" and the story of Rahab for parashat "Shelakh Lekha."

Princess Batyah: Ginzberg, *Legends of the Jews* II, 266–72; III, 30. Batyah's privilege to enter Paradise alive was shared by the antediluvian Enoch, "who walked with God"; the prophet Elijah, who ascended to heaven in a fiery chariot; and Jacob's granddaughter Serakh bat Asher. See parshiyot "Vayishlakh" and "Pinkhas."

Gives him a royal Egyptian name: Although the Torah claims that Pharaoh's daughter bases Moses' name upon the Hebrew root *mosheh*, "draws out," because she draws him out of the Nile, scholars have suggested that his name actually derives from the Egyptian *mses*, meaning "son of," as in Ramses, "son of Ra."

They devise a test for the child: Ginzberg, *Legends of the Jews* II, 272–75.

The Torah itself later names: As is typical in Hebrew, these women's names all carry meaning: *Yokheved* means "honor of God"; *Miriam*, "bitter sea"; *Batyah*, "daughter of God." No etymology is proposed in the Torah for Yokheved and Miriam, pivotal figures in the life of Moses. And in the case of Pharaoh's daughter, neither an Egyptian nor a Hebrew name is mentioned; she is simply an instrument in the story, like her father, the unnamed Pharaoh.

The courtship of Moses and Zipporah: Ginzberg, *Legends of the Jews* II, 291–94.

Gershom: See parashat "Lekh Lekha" for a discussion of Hagar's name.

The attacker is none other than God's satanic messenger: Ginzberg, *Legends of the Jews* II, 328.

Bridegroom of Blood: This brief passage has been the subject of extensive controversy among biblical and feminist scholars. Of the many feminist critics who have written about this episode, Ilana Pardes, in her chapter in *Counter-Traditions in the Bible* (Cambridge, MA: Harvard University Press, 1992), 79–97, presents one of the most comprehensive treatments. Pardes cites Moshe Greenberg's interpretation of this incident as foreshadowing the tenth plague (80), and Shemaryahu Talmon's notion of this passage as a symbolic covenant (86). She agrees with Daniel Boyarin's suggestion that this biblical incident reveals "a faultline between ideologies"—that is, between monotheism and polytheism.

14. VA-ERA

Serakh bat Asher: See parashat "Vayiggash."

Miriam marries Caleb: Ginzberg, *Legends of the Jews* II, 253.

The identities of Aaron, Miriam, and Moses: Miriam appears only five times in the Torah: Exodus 15; Numbers 12:1–15, 20:1, 26:59; and Deuteronomy 24:8–9. (The first time she appears, chapter 1 of Exodus, she is nameless.) Mentioned only twice more in the Bible—in 1 Chronicles 5:29 and Micah 6:4—she is simply listed together with her two brothers in family genealogies.

15. Bo

The origin of this ritual and text: And also in parashat "Va-Etkhanan."

"Each of us must feel as if she herself was redeemed": Adapted from traditional text of the Passover Haggadah. In recent years, numerous feminist and egalitarian Haggadot have been developed that broaden the inclusiveness of the traditional text.

When Jacob goes down to Egypt: But see note above on Genesis 46, especially verses 26–27 in parashat "Vayiggash."

Altogether number two million: Ginzberg, *Legends of the Jews* V, 439, n. 246.

16. Beshallakh

Disinterring bodies and reburying them: Solomon Ganzfried, *Code of Jewish Law* ("Kitzur Shulkhan Arukh"), transl. Hyman Goldin, rev. ed. (New York: Hebrew Publishing Company, 1963), chap. 199:11, 105.

The songs of the judge Deborah: Excerpts from the stories of Deborah and Yael (chapters 4–5 in Judges) have appropriately been chosen as the traditional haftorah for this parasha.

Female prophets: For the story of Huldah, see 2 Kings 22, 2 Chronicles 34:22–28, and parashat "Re'eh"; for Noadiah, see Nehemiah 6:14.

Women's performance tradition: On the drum-dance-song tradition in ancient biblical and east Mediterranean cultures, see Carol Meyers, "Miriam the Musician," in *A Feminist Companion to Exodus-Deuteronomy,* ed. Athalya Brenner (Sheffield, England: Sheffield Academic Press, 1994), 207–30.

Kol isha: Orthodox rabbinical authorities have ruled that a woman's voice should not be heard by men when they pray lest they be distracted from holy thoughts. As a result, women have been isolated into special women's sections in Orthodox synagogues. See Susan Grossman and Rivka Haut, *Daughters of the King: Women and the Synagogue* (Philadelphia: The Jewish Publication Society, 1992), which contains several essays touching on this issue.

Joyful song and dance: Cited in Yitzhak Buxbaum, *Jewish Spiritual Practices* (Northvale, NJ: Jason Aronson, 1990), 487, 24:12:1.

Hannah, who prayed so hard: I Samuel 1:9–19. The Rabbis of the Talmud cite her prayer as a prime example of sincere worship, B. Berakhot 31a–b.

Tekhines: Although scholars disagree about precisely how many of these *tekhines* were written by women, there is general consensus that women did write most of them. Numerous collections of Yiddish *tekhines* have been published since the sixteenth century, and today they are being made available in English translation. An English version (together with the original Yiddish) of the *tekhine* of Sora bas Toyvim mentioning "miryem hanviye" can be found in *The Merit of Our Mothers: A Bilingual Anthology of Jewish Women's Prayers,* compiled and introduced by Tracy Guren Klirs; translated by Tracy Guren Klirs, Ida Cohen Selavan, and Gella Schweid Fishman; annotated by Faedra Lazar Weiss and Barbara Selya (Cincinnati: Hebrew Union College Press, 1992), 36–37.

When at last I rose up with Aaron: See parashat "Beha'alotkha."

Miriam's names: For the Egyptian etymology of Miriam's name, see *The Women's Bible Commentary,* ed. Carol Newsome and Sharon Ringe (Louisville: Westminster/John Knox, 1992), 32; for rabbinic etymology, see Exodus Rabbah 1:17.

Manna: Ginzberg, *Legends of the Jews* III, 41–50.

Kol yisrael arevim zeh-la-zeh: B. Shevuot 39a.

Amalek within: Levi Yitzhak of Berditchev, in Martin Buber, *Tales of the Hasidim: Early Masters* (New York: Schocken, 1947), 227–28.

17. Yitro

He takes me with him, together with our two sons: Exodus 4:20.

After being chided by his brother: Ginzberg, *Legends of the Jews* II, 327.

Moses deliberately changes the audience: One of the most influential articles in modern Jewish feminist history was published by Rachel Adler in *Response* magazine in 1973, under the title "The Jew Who Wasn't There," and reprinted in *On Being a Jewish Feminist,* ed. Susannah Heschel (New York: Schocken, 1983), 12–18. Adler's title alludes to this verse in Exodus, where Moses effectively writes women out of the Revelation at Sinai. She maintains that even twenty-five centuries later, many Jewish men are still warning each other: "Do not go near a woman." See also Athalya Brenner, "An Afterword: The Decalogue—Am I an Addressee?" in *A Feminist Companion to Exodus-Deuteronomy,* 255–58.

To read with greater suspicion: Feminist critics talk about reading texts using a "hermeneutics of suspicion." That is, they recommend that we approach written documents always on the lookout for "subtexts," hidden agendas below the surface of an author's prose. As for "translating with greater sympathy," vigorous efforts are being made today to create "gender-neutral" (also called "gender-sensitive") prose, in both original compositions and translations. Nowhere is this effort more controversial than in the realm of sacred texts, that is, the Bible and liturgy. In the Jewish community, all three liberal movements—Conservative, Reform, and Reconstructionist—have altered their prayer books to differing extents to reflect these concerns. Jewish translations of the Tanakh, however, have not yet addressed these concerns.

We have rejected this notion of "father's guilt": The Thirteen Attributes can be found in Exodus 34:6–7.

Because children are naturally more inclined: Mekhilta VII: 28–36. See also Rashi on *"ish aviv ve'et imo tira'u."*

18. Mishpatim

Biblical law: The reader interested in pursuing this subject further should turn to relevant primary sources, such as rabbinic literature, Responsa, and codes, as well as secondary sources such as Menahem Elon's magisterial four-volume *Jewish Law* (Philadelphia: The Jewish Publication Society, 1994); topical articles in the *Encyclopedia Judaica;* and the work of feminist scholars such as Rachel Biale, Judith Wegner, Judith Hauptman, Rachel Adler, and Judith Plaskow. Also recommended are the essays on Exodus, Numbers, and Deuteronomy in *The Women's Bible Commentary.*

Her conjugal rights: See parashat "Ki Tetze."

The laws of rape: Ibid.

Beruriah and Meir: The story of Beruriah's seduction is first found in Rashi's comment to B. Avodah Zara 18b. Significantly, the Talmud itself does not tell of Beruriah's shameful fall and suicide. It is possible that the medieval commentator Rashi felt the need to discredit Beruriah to prove his loyalty to patriarchal tradition, since his own daughters, like Beruriah, were bold women who studied Torah and even wore tefillin, scandalous behavior even in today's Orthodox community. The story of Meir's seduction is found in "Midrash Aseret HaDibrot," collected in *Beit HaMidrash,* ed. Adolph Jellinek. See Rachel Adler's article "The Virgin in the Brothel and Other Anomalies: Character and Context in the Legend of Beruriah," in *Tikkun,* November/December 1988, 28–32, 102–5.

In ancient Israel, "witchcraft" was widespread: The Bible and Talmud report repeated attempts to stamp out witchcraft, which suggest that such occult practices were common—and irrepressible. One of the most famous incidents involved King Saul, who secretly consulted the Witch of Endor, after he himself had decreed a ban on such meetings (I Samuel 28). See also parashat "Kedoshim" for more discussion about sorcery and the occult.

"The more women, the more witchcraft": Pirke Avot 2:7.

Shimon ben Shetakh: J. Hagigah 2:2, 77d; Rashi on B. Sanhedrin 44b. Shimon ben Shetakh was a first-century B.C.E. Palestinian sage who was reputed to have destroyed these eighty witches to fulfill a pledge he made when he was elevated to his position as Nasi.

"The daughters of Israel were addicted": B. Eruvin 64b. Shimon bar Yohai was a second-century sage in Palestine who is traditionally credited with authorship of the Zohar, the classic work of Jewish mysticism.

"Although there is no divination, there are signs": J. Shabbat 8c. See also parashat "Shofetim."

During the days when the Temple stood in Jerusalem: With the conquest of Jerusalem by David in 996 B.C.E., the people became united under a centralized monarchy, a unity that was reaffirmed three times each year through the festival pilgrimages. When the Second Temple was destroyed by the Romans in 70 C.E., this unity came to an end, as the people were scattered in exile. From that moment on, these pilgrimages have been celebrated only symbolically, through the special liturgy unique to these festivals, which to this day are known as *shalosh regalim,* the three "on-foot days," from the Hebrew word meaning "foot."

Neighbors' pagan rites: For a long time, scholars subscribed to this explanation of the taboo on mixing milk and meat. However, in recent times, this view has been largely discredited.

To keep life and death apart: In her groundbreaking book, *Purity and Danger* (London: Routledge and Kegan Paul, 1966), anthropologist Mary Douglas explores this idea in considerable depth.

To sensitize us to an animal's feelings: Commentary of Nachmanides.

To discipline our eating: B. Yoma 39a.

The numerical value of halav: Drawing a correlation between Hebrew words based on their numerical equivalence is a traditional technique known as *gematria,* derived from either the Greek word for "geometry" or *gamma tria*—that is, the third letter of the alphabet equals three.

God is not a person: The medieval Spanish philosopher Maimonides, also known as the Rambam, argued that "God speaks in the language of men," that is, any biblical reference to God's body—hands, face, eyes, ears—is purely metaphorical, a concession to limited human understanding.

Angels: Until modern times (and even to this day), angels have been "unofficially" included in Jewish tradition, especially in folklore and folk practice. Discredited by the rationalist bias of modern Judaism, they have recently been enjoying a comeback. Books about angels regularly top the best-seller list; angel cards and amulets fill New Age shops and homes, rituals invoke angels for healing and blessing.

A Prayer for the Angel of Justice: A *tekhine* written by Rochel-Esther Bas Avi-chayil of Jerusalem, c. 1930, cited in *A Book of Jewish Women's Prayers,* translated, selected, and with commentary by Norman Tarnor (Northvale, NJ: Jason Aronson, 1995), 87–88.

19. TERUMAH

Cherubim: B. Baba Batra 99a; B. Yoma 54a. See also the chapter on this subject in Raphael Patai, *The Hebrew Goddess* (New York: Ktav, 1967), 59–98.

When the Jerusalem Temple replaced the Mishkan: See 1 Kings 6:23–36.

The Sabbath Loaves: This story is attributed to Rabbi Isaac Luria, also known as the ARI (Hebrew for "lion" and also an acronym of his name), the dominant figure of sixteenth-century Jewish mysticism in Safed. The version here is based directly on the original tale; later versions often "sanitized" the ending, changing the rabbi's death to rehabilitation. The version offered here, adapted from Micha Joseph Bin Gorion, *Mimekor Yisrael: Classical Jewish Folktales* I (Bloomington: Indiana University Press, 1976), 524–27, is based on the original version found in "Shivhei Ha-Ari," an ancient collection of stories surrounding the life of Isaac Luria. *Conversos* were those Jews who converted to Catholicism rather than face expulsion or execution by the Spanish Inquisition. In Spain, Portugal, and their territories in the New World, *conversos* practiced a unique blend of public Catholicism and clandestine Judaism; once free of the Inquisition's reach, many chose to re-embrace Judaism, but usually they had lost most of the most basic knowledge of their ancestors' faith. The term *Marrano,* another name for these forced converts, has fallen out of favor, since the word derives from the Spanish word for "swine."

The mystical Community of Israel: Adapted from *Zohar: The Book of Enlightenment,* transl. Daniel Matt (New York: Paulist Press, 1983), 36.

"Not 'I will dwell below'": Joseph Gikatilla, *Gates of Light* ("Sha'are Orah") transl. Avi Weinstein (New York: HarperCollins, 1994), 25. Gikatilla was a thirteenth-century Spanish kabbalist who developed a systematic approach to the complex system of Kabbalah.

20. TETZAVEH

Tekhine on the Ner Tamid: From "The Rules for Lighting Candles," in "Tekhine of the Three Gates," *The Merit of Our Mothers, A Bilingual Anthology of Jewish Women's Prayers,* compiled and introduced by Tracy Guren Klirs, translated by Tracy Guren Klirs, Ida Cohen Selavan, and Gella Schweid Fishman, annotated by Faedra Lazar Weiss and Barbara Selya (Cincinnati: Hebrew Union College, 1992), 20. The author of this *tekhine* identifies herself as *"rebetsn sore,"* daughter of Rabbi *"mordkhe,"* grandson of Rabbi *"mordkhe,"* who was head of the *"bez-din"* of the holy congregation of Brisk.

Priestly vestments: See Aryeh Kaplan's notes to this parasha in *The Living Torah* (New York: Maznaim Publishing Company, 1981).

Women have been the primary weavers: The most comprehensive study of women's role in the history of weaving is Elizabeth Wayland Barber, *Women's Work: The First 20,000 Years* (New York: W. W. Norton, 1994).

How the Hoopoe Got Its Crest: Arab folktale, adapted from Hayyim Nahman Bialik, *And It Came to Pass* (New York: Hebrew Publishing Company, 1938), 97–101.

Song of the Seamstress: "*Tog Azoy Vi Nacht*" ("Day the Same as Night"), cited in Susan A. Glenn, *Daughters of the Shtetl: Life and Labor in the Immigrant Generation* (Ithaca: Cornell University Press, 1990), 28; "Weaving a Shroud for the Czar," 36.

21. KI TISSA

The women's jewelry: Ginzberg, *Legends of the Jews* III, 121–22. In recent years, Rosh Hodesh has regained its former popularity as a "women's holiday," inspiring many Jewish women to gather at the beginning of each Jewish month to celebrate newly created rituals, share songs and stories, study, and enjoy one another's company.

Elijah's Cup: Eastern European tale, adapted from Annette and Eugene Labovitz, *Time for My Soul* (Northvale, NJ: Jason Aronson, 1987), 350–52.

The Levites hung their harps upon the willows: This image comes from Psalm 137.

The image of a genderless God: This issue is explored in considerable depth in Howard Eilberg-Schwartz, *God's Phallus and Other Problems for Men and Monotheism* (Boston: Beacon Press, 1994).

The cult of Asherah: Modern archaeologists and biblical historians have uncovered extensive evidence of goddess worship in ancient Israel. One especially significant find has been an inscription from Kuntillet Arjud in the Negev, which reads: YHVH ve'asherato ("YHVH and his asherah"). See Mark S. Smith, *The Early History of God: Yahweh and the Other Deities in Ancient Israel* (San Francisco: HarperCollins, 1990), 85–88.

Like Rachel's teraphim: See parashat "Vayetze."

When they first settled the land: Not all scholars subscribe to the notion that the Israelites were foreigners to Canaan. Another theory contends that some of the Israelite tribes may have already been dwelling in the land and eventually merged with the newcomers to form the Jewish people.

King Ahab and his foreign queen: Appropriately, the Rabbis chose the story of Jezebel's pagan influence in the royal court of Israel and the prophet Elijah's triumph over her idolatrous priests as the haftorah for this parasha (I Kings 18:1–9).

Asa, Yehoshafat, Hezekiah, and Josiah: For the stories of Israel's monarchy and its involvement with idolatry and foreign influences, see the biblical books of Kings and Chronicles.

Feminism's intellectual flirtation with the goddess: One of the most controversial aspects of Jewish (as well as Christian) feminism—and a source of tension among feminists themselves—is the subject of pagan elements within monotheistic religion. Some feminists have been attracted to the pagan antecedents of Western religion, including goddess worship, folk practices (including white and black magic), astrology and necromancy, and a host of other practices, banished or abandoned by monotheism. See parashat "Kedoshim" for more extensive comments on this subject.

Surely temptation has never had trouble: See parashat "Mishpatim" for the story of Beruriah's seduction.

22. VAYAKHEL

They spun the wool while it was still on the goats: Ginzberg, *Legends of the Jews* III, 174.

Women's mirrors: Ibid., 174–75.

The Mirror and the Glass: Adapted from Louis Newman, *Hasidic Anthology* (Northvale, NJ: Jason Aronson, 1987), 425–26.

Queen Helene and the Golden Candlestick: adapted from Zev Vilnay, *Legends of Jerusalem* (Philadelphia: The Jewish Publication Society, 1995), 83–84. See also parashat "Naso."

Rabbi Hanina and the Table Leg: B. Taanit 25a.

23. PIKUDEI

The Stone of Weaving: Vilnay, *Legends of Jerusalem*, 15. *Shulhan Arukh*, Orah Hayyim, 551:8.

Making cloth has been primarily women's work: See also parshiyot "Tetzaveh" and "Terumah."

Remember the poor girls: The Triangle Fire was an infamous incident that brought to public attention the dangerous and inhumane working conditions in the New York sweatshops at the turn of the century. This tragedy galvanized the early union movement in the garment industry. In the 1911 fire, 146 young workers, mostly Jewish and Italian women immigrants, lost their lives.

Introduced colored wool garments into Egypt: Barber, *Women's Work*, 252–55.

"She looks for wool and flax": This poem, the final chapter of the Book of Proverbs, is traditionally sung by Jewish husbands to their wives at the beginning of the Friday night meal. Although some women today object to its depiction of woman as "superhousewife," others point to the breadth and scope of duties ascribed to the mistress of the household, including major economic and leadership roles.

LEVITICUS

24. VAYIKRA

The Torah of the Priests: For an excellent introduction to Leviticus from a feminist point of view, see Judith Romney Wegner's essay in *The Women's Bible Commentary*, 36–44. Traditionally, a Jewish boy begins his formal Jewish education at age five by studying the book of Leviticus, because he is still so pure that it is appropriate for him to study the laws of purity. It is hard to imagine a less compelling entry into Jewish study!

Purification Offering: In most English commentaries, the Hebrew term *hattat* is mistakenly translated as "sin offering," based on the root *hayt*, the common Hebrew word for "sin" (literally, "to miss the mark"). Bible commentators Baruch Levine and Jacob Milgrom object to this translation, preferring "purification offering," since the *hattat* sacrifice served to *purify* ritual impurity rather than to *expiate* wrongdoing. See Baruch Levine, *The JPS Torah Commentary on Leviticus* (Philadelphia: The Jewish Publication Society, 1989), and Jacob Milgrom, *The JPS Torah Commentary on Numbers* (Philadelphia: The Jewish Publication Society, 1990).

Korban, from the root: The Hebrew root is *k-r-v*, which is the root of numerous other Hebrew words, such as "relative" (one who is close); "soon" (a time that is close); "to bring near" (to welcome or befriend); "to approach sexually"; and, somewhat paradoxically, "to approach with hostility" (the noun form means "conflict" or "battle").

Served the same function that psychotherapy serves today: On the therapeutic function of sacrifice and psalms, see Herbert Levine, *Sing unto God a New Song: Contemporary Readings of the Psalms* (Bloomington: Indiana University Press, 1995), 48–61.

Only gentle animals: This is the explanation offered by the *Tzena Urena* on this parasha. (See explanation of *Tzena Urena* in notes to parashat "Balak.") According to the Torah, only *kosher* animals could be sacrificed.

"Donah, Donah": B. Baba Metzia 85a. The song "Donah, Donah" was composed by Sholom Secunda for the Yiddish musical theater in 1940; the Yiddish words were written by Aaron Zeitlin. The English lyrics were written by the composer's son, Sheldon Secunda, Teddi Schwartz, and Arthur Kevess. Used by permission.

Miriam and her seven sons: Psalms 113:9; B. Gittin 27b; Seder Eliyahu Rabbah 151–53. There also exists a more familiar version of this story, "Hannah and Her Seven Sons," which is customarily linked to Hanukkah and the Hadrianic persecutions.

25. TZAV

Levite women sang and performed: Although not all scholars are in agreement about this, recent archaeological and documentary evidence points to the participation of women in public and Temple ritual involving music and dance. Carol Meyers maintains that Israelite women had a long tradition of musical leadership, both inside and outside "official" religion. "Miriam the Musician," in *A Feminist Companion to Exodus-Deuteronomy*, 207–30.

Domestic religion: See also parashat "Ki Tissa."

Blood: See parshiyot "Tazria" and "Metzora" for fuller discussions of these laws.

26. Shemini

Like Sarah at the Akedah: See parashat "Va-era."

"All the house of Israel shall bewail": See Leviticus 10:6–8.

The Two Jewels: Midrash Mishle 31:10.

The laws of kashrut: Other dietary laws appear elsewhere in the Torah. See Exodus 23:19, 34:26; and Deuteronomy 14. See also Baruch Levine's essay "The Meaning of the Dietary Laws," in his commentary on Leviticus, *The JPS Torah Commentary* (Philadelphia: The Jewish Publication Society, 1989), 243–48.

And what is the meaning of these statutes, laws, and rules: This question, a direct quote from Deuteronomy 6:20, is found in "The Four Children" section of the Passover Haggadah. Although the Haggadah places this question in the mouth of the wicked child, the Torah attributes it to all children who inquire about the meaning of Passover.

To sensitize our hearts: See notes to parashat "Mishpatim."

27. Tazria

The Torah compares this period: See comment on Leviticus 15:33 below.

The physical differences between the genders: Most notably Nachmanides, also known as the Ramban.

"Bears seed and gives birth": Some commentators interpret this phrase as referring both to conception and to childbirth; others, only to birth itself.

In the case of the Red Heifer: See parashat "Hukkat."

Mistranslation of the Hebrew ḥattat: See earlier comment in endnote for parashat "Vayikra."

Prayer to Be Recited at the Hour of Childbirth: Excerpted from *Out of the Depths I Call to You: A Book of Prayers for the Married Jewish Woman,* ed. and transl. Nina Beth Cardin (Northvale, NJ: Jason Aronson, 1992), 100. Originally published in Italy, 1786.

28. Metzora

When something transgresses the body's threshold: This threshold is what anthropologists call "liminal" space—the boundary between life cycle stages, between public and private space, between health and sickness, life and death. See the writings of anthropologists Victor Turner, Clifford Geertz, and Mary Douglas, especially the latter's *Purity and Danger* (London: Routledge and Kegan Paul, 1966), which deals specifically with ritual purity in the Bible.

How to manage our fear ritually: In recent years, healing has become a central issue in the Jewish community. Jewish healing centers have opened in several major cities, and new resources—prayers, readings, traditional teachings, as well as programs—have become more widely available. In some communities, Miriam's Well has become a symbol of healing.

Niddah: This word is usually translated as "family purity," but it is used elsewhere in the Bible to mean "impurity." The laws that govern a married couple's behavior during and after a woman's period are so complex and extensive that rabbinic law has devoted several tractates of the Mishnah and the Talmud to the subject, as well as considerable legal commentary. Since the Enlightenment, however, many Jewish women have abandoned regular monthly visits to the *mikvah* (ritual bath) after their periods and at other times of ritual impurity.

Most societies have cordoned off women: Until the Ethiopian Jewish community was airlifted en masse to Israel in 1991, the women in this community would isolate themselves in special "women's houses" during their menstrual periods and after giving birth, while their husbands would tend the house, fields, and animals, as well as the children, who could visit their mothers whenever they wanted. Thus, for much of their adult lives, these women resided in a separate society of women. The practice has been discontinued in Israel, requiring considerable social adjustment in this community.

Menarche Ritual: Adapted from Phyllis Berman, "Enter: A Woman," *Menorah*, November/December 1985. Other examples of this kind of new life cycle ritual have been collected by Rabbi Debra Orenstein in *Lifecycles*, vol. I: *Jewish Women on Life Passages and Personal Milestones* (Woodstock, VT: Jewish Lights, 1994).

The Clever Wife: Iraqi Jewish folktale, collected in Dov Noy, *Folktales of Israel* (Chicago: University of Chicago Press, 1963), no. 47.

29. AKHAREI MOT

Holiness Code: Scholars believe that this material represents the contributions of a new school of priestly writers of the Torah, a branch of the so-called P tradition.

Karet: This penalty can be compared to the practice of shunning among the Amish or the status of the Untouchable caste in India. See also parashat "Kedoshim."

These marriages are permitted: B. Sotah 20a.

Mamzer: To this day, this definition of "bastard" applies in the traditional Jewish community, and it has serious consequences in Israel as well as in the diaspora. So, for instance, the children of divorced Jews who remarry without first obtaining a Jewish divorce *(get)* are considered bastards by more traditional Jewish authorities and thus forbidden to marry any Jew except another *mamzer.*

Homosexuality: B. Sanhedrin 54a. This is one of the most controversial issues facing the contemporary Jewish community. Although the Reconstructionist and Reform movements have openly welcomed gays to the rabbinate and synagogue membership, the Conservative movement is hotly debating how open it wishes to be toward gays. And the Orthodox movement maintains the traditional taboos, although even within that community there are those who advocate a stance of compassion rather than censure.

Lesbianism: For a discussion of this topic in Jewish law, see Rachel Biale, *Women and Jewish Law* (New York: Schocken, 1984), 192–97.

Who was engendering whom: Today the technique of artificial insemination has allowed lesbian couples to give birth and raise children, introducing new wrinkles into this ancient law.

Addressed to women as well as men: Significantly, although this sexual taboo is addressed to both sexes, the grammatical form of the verb *ta'amod*—third-person feminine imperfect instead of masculine imperative, like all the other laws in this section—suggests that the Torah is communicating this ruling only to men, who will then relay it to women.

It is forbidden to mix together: The Torah characterizes bestiality as *tevel*, translated as "perversion" (18:23). The word derives from the Hebrew root *b-l-l,* "to mix up." This concept of forbidden mixtures is called *sha'atnez,* and it is still observed by many Orthodox Jews, especially in the manufacture of clothing. See parashat "Kedoshim."

The Mouse Seeks a Wife: Adapted from Hadas, *Tales of a Jewish Aesop,* no. 28. This fable was written by Berechiah ben Natronai HaNakdan, known also as Benedictus le Pointeur ("Blessed the Punctuator") in twelfth-century France. Berechiah adapted and translated into Hebrew many of the popular fables of Aesop, Romulus and Remus, and Marie de France, often incorporating within his versions biblical quotations and allusions and concluding his fables with a Jewish moral. This particular fable can be found in the folktales of many other cultures.

30. KEDOSHIM

So comprehensive and central is this parasha: Leviticus Rabbah 24.

Adultery, incest, male homosexuality, bestiality: See parashat "Akharei Mot."

Intercourse with a menstruating woman: See parashat "Metzora."

From her poor father: See also parashat "Mishpatim."

The Witch of Endor: I Samuel 28:3–25.

Manasseh, Amon, Josiah: The story of Manasseh's reign can be found in 2 Kings 21:1–18 and 2 Chronicles 33:1–20; of Amon in 2 Kings 21:19–26 and 2 Chronicles 33:21–25; of Josiah in 2 Kings 22:1–23:30 and 2 Chronicles 34–35.

Hukkat Ha-Goi: For a fuller discussion of this law and its historical repercussions, see the article on this topic in the *Encyclopedia Judaica.* See also parashat "Balak."

31. EMOR

When three unannounced guests: See parashat "Vayera."

Kohen: According to the Torah, the *kohanim* (plural of *kohen*) were direct descendants of Aaron's family and thus members of the tribe of Levi. They attended to the sacrifices in the Sanctuary; the Levites were their assistants. During the time that the Temple stood in Jerusalem, the *kohanim* remained within the Temple precincts, while the Levites mostly lived among the people, except when they were serving their two-week rotation in the Temple.

A priest is forbidden: Immediate family is defined as mother, father, son, daughter, brother, and unmarried sister. If a *kohen's* sister is married, he is forbidden to attend her burial. See also parashat "Shemini."

Because I am a woman and because I married: The mourning taboos did not apply to female *kohanim.* And if they married outside the tribe of Levi, they then belonged to their husband's clan. See also parashat "Beshallakh" on the marriage of Miriam to Caleb.

The Torah's rules on which women: Just as priests are banned from defiling themselves through contact with corpses, so they are forbidden to marry certain women—"harlots" and divorcées. The ideal priest's wife is a virgin from a Levitical family. But other women are also appropriate—widows as well as virgins from other tribes.

The grounds for divorce: Divorcées are forbidden to *kohanim* because biblical law assumes only one ground for divorce: infidelity. Therefore a divorced woman was considered morally unfit to marry a priest. Although the house of Hillel later allowed other grounds for divorce, the ban on a *kohen* marrying a divorced woman remains in effect for Orthodox Jews to this day.

A priest's daughter: The only member of a Levitical family whose status ever changes is a priest's daughter. If she marries, even within the priestly clan, her brother may not bury her when she dies. If she marries a layman, she is barred from eating certain priestly foods derived from community sacrifices and donations. (Although Levitical men who are either born with or acquire physical defects lose their right to officiate at the altar, they are never barred from eating priestly foods.) But if she is divorced or widowed, she regains her former status by returning to her father's house. For since she cannot inherit from her husband, she has no other means of support. Although divorcées originally had no financial claim upon their husbands, the Rabbis later altered this inequitable situation by introducing the institution of the *ketubah.* But if the priest's daughter had children, then she is forever barred from the priestly entitlements, and must rely upon her children to support her. Obviously, priestly daughters had considerable incentive either to marry within the clan— or not to marry at all.

Torah's laws about the treatment of animals: See parashat "Shemini."

From the days of the Garden of Eden: Ginzberg, *Legends of the Jews* I, 166–67.

Seething a kid in its mother's milk: See comment on Exodus 23:19; this law is repeated in Exodus 34:26 and Deuteronomy 14:21.

The commandment to send away a mother bird: See comment on Deuteronomy 22:6–7.

The blasphemer's father: Exodus Rabbah 1:28.

The Temple of Dan: See I Kings 25:25–31. There was also a priestly group in Dan claiming descent from Moses. Thus the Aaronide priests had an additional reason to paint Dan negatively.

32. BEHAR

Sabbatical and jubilee years: Although comparative documents from neighboring cultures and archaeological evidence confirm the common practice of rotating crops in this region, scholars cannot determine how many of the sabbatical laws—if any—were actually followed in ancient Israel. To this day, however, numerous Jews in Israel observe many of the sabbatical laws concerning the use of agricultural produce every seventh year.

Its progressive social framework: Whether or not these institutions actually operated in ancient Israel, their articulation must have served a particular ideological need. Perhaps they emerged at a time when many people had been dispossessed from their land and wanted to retrieve it—for instance, when the people of Judah were returning from Babylonian exile in the early sixth century B.C.E. After living away from the land for fifty years, these urban expatriates had no doubt lost touch with agricultural realities and were presenting an idealized vision of pastoral life.

Women didn't tend to own property: However, they did own the *principal* that constituted their bride-price (see parashat "Vayiggash") and occasionally even inherited their father's land (see parashat "Pinkhas").

The Gift of Seven Years: Midrash Zuta Ruth 4:11.

"Peculiar institution" of slavery: When the slave owners of the American South wished to justify slavery, they turned to the Bible; so did the abolitionists, who found justification for their views in the same Good Book, teaching us that texts are remarkably malleable.

33. BEKHUKOTAI

The "Holiness Code": See notes to parashat "Akharei Mot."

Where was God when we were suffering?: The issue of theodicy—"justifying God's justice," or "Why do the good suffer and the evil prosper?"—has been a central concern of most religions. The Jewish literature on this subject is vast, stretching from the biblical Book of Job to recent books such as Harold Kushner's best-seller, *When Bad Things Happen to Good People.* A number of challenging theological works have been written in the fifty years since the Holocaust, trying to respond to this event within the framework of traditional Jewish theology.

The Miracle of Fresh Bread: Excerpted from "To Marry a Baker," in Yaffa Eliach, *Hasidic Tales of the Holocaust* (New York: Oxford University Press, 1982), 206–207.

How long will you hide your face: The concept of *hester panim,* the "hiding of God's face," has long been part of Jewish theology. Confronted with the presence of evil in the world, biblical writers, especially the Psalmists and several of the prophets, explain suffering as resulting from God's hiding the divine face. See parashat "Vayelekh" for a fuller discussion.

The holy Zohar explains: From *Zohar: The Book of Enlightenment,* translated and annotated by Daniel Matt (New York: Paulist Press, 1983), 160–61. The Zohar, composed in the thirteenth century, is the central text of Kabbalah, Jewish mysticism. In the theosophy of Kabbalah, the feminine aspect of God, known as *Shekhinah* or *Malkhut,* has gone into exile along with Israel, suffering with the people until both She and they will one day be redeemed. The King symbolizes the transcendent dimension of God. The Palace symbolizes the world. The parable ends with the transcendent aspect proclaiming that it is immanent—that is, with us always.

NUMBERS

34. BAMIDBAR

The Book of Numbers: In her recent book on Numbers, *In the Wilderness: The Doctrine of Defilement in the Book of Numbers,* JSOT Supplement Series, 158 (Sheffield, England: Sheffield Academic Press, 1993), anthropologist Mary Douglas suggests that the book is allegorical, casting the women within its narratives as stand-ins for Israel as God's bride. For an overview of Numbers from a feminist perspective, see Katherine Doob Sakenfeld's essay in *The Feminist Bible Commentary*, 45–51.

Erev rav: Ginzberg, *Legends of the Jews* V, 439, nn. 245, 246.

The "600,000": Throughout rabbinic writings, the formulaic number "600,000" is frequently cited as the total population of the people of Israel, especially in reference to the events at Mount Sinai. Rarely is mention made of the fact that this number includes only the Numbers' count of men of fighting age.

35. Naso

"Commits any wrong toward a fellow": The term used here for "breaking faith"—*lim'ol ma'al*—has a specialized meaning in the Book of Leviticus: to commit an offense against the Sanctuary.

After the Temple had been destroyed: Mishnah Sotah goes to great lengths to make it unlikely that this ritual could ever be practiced. Talmud Sotah (11a–b) contains several stories about heroic women who were faced with an accusation of being a *sotah*, suggesting that the Rabbis were proto-feminists when it came to this issue.

Abbaye's Suspicions: B. Shabbat 31a.

A married woman's hair: See also parashat "Ki Tetze."

"Sea of bitterness": Exodus Rabbah 26:1.

The Torah's ban on magic: See also parshiyot "Mishpatim" and "Kedoshim."

Performative language: The concept of performative language has been the focus of many linguists and philosophers in this century. One of the earliest and clearest discussions of the topic can be found in British philosopher J. L. Austin's *How to Do Things with Words*, ed. J. O. Urmson (New York: Oxford University Press, 1962).

Her body would reveal her guilt: See discussion of the *sotah* in Biale, *Women and Jewish Law*, 183–89.

We sanctioned this ritual: Numbers Rabbah 9:44. Yohanan ben Zakkai's ruling can be found in Mishnah Sotah 9:9.

The Nazirite: The ban on cutting their hair set Nazirites apart from all other Israelites, even from the Levitical priests, whose hair could be neither long and unkempt nor completely shaven. During the term of the Nazirite's vow, no razor was to be used, and the untrimmed hair was to be regarded as consecrated to God. So holy was this hair that it could not come in contact with death, not even if the Nazirite's parents or siblings should die.

Samson: The traditional haftorah for this parasha appropriately recounts the birth of Samson, an event announced to Samson's mother—nameless in the Book of Judges (chapter 13) but named "Hezlalponit" in the Midrash (Ginzberg, *Legends of the Jews* VI, 204–5, n. 111)—by an angel. His mother vows to raise him as a Nazirite in gratitude for his birth.

Refrain from cutting their hair: In biblical times, a woman's hair was considered a vital part of her beauty. Thus it seems likely that *all* Israelite women grew their hair long. If that was the case, then only two of the Nazirite laws—the bans on consuming grape products and intoxicants, and on approaching a dead body—applied to female Nazirites. Although at one point Israelite men shaved their heads as a sign of mourning, women *never* did (unlike some of their sisters in neighboring pagan cults). A shaven head would thus clearly mark women, even more than men, as former Nazirites, although such women probably uncovered their heads only in private. Nonetheless, to go about with her head bald, even if covered, must have represented a significant sacrifice for these women, a sign of exceptional religious devotion.

According to both the Mishnah and the Jewish historian Josephus: Mishnah Nazir 3:6, 6:11; Josephus, *Wars* 2:15:1. It is interesting to compare the ascetic practices of the Nazirites with those of the Essenes and the Dead Sea community at Qumran, who similarly subjected themselves to dietary and dress restrictions. See chapter on "Women" in Lawrence Schiffman, *Reclaiming the Dead Sea Scrolls* (Philadelphia: The Jewish Publication Society, 1994).

Many Israelite women took upon themselves: With their father's or husband's tacit consent—see Numbers 30:3–16.

Queen Helena of Adiabene: The story of the first-century C.E. queen can be found in Mishnah Nazir 3:6. See also parashat "Vayakhel."

Berenice: A member of the Jewish aristocracy in Israel (first century C.E.), Berenice was married three times—twice to foreign kings—and came close to marrying Titus, the Roman conqueror of her own people, but this marriage was blocked by his father, Vespasian, and the Roman ruling elite.

36. BEHA'ALOTKHA

The verb va-tedaber: Sifre Numbers 99; Avot de Rabbi Natan 9, 39.

She is the instigator of this challenge: Despite all the ambiguities in this account, some commentators unequivocally "blame the victim," deducing Miriam's crime from her punishment. See Naomi Graetz's article "Did Miriam Talk Too Much" in Brenner, *Feminist Companion to Exodus-Deuteronomy*, 231–42.

The Cushite woman: See Jacob Milgrom's comment on this verse in *The JPS Torah Commentary*, "Numbers," 93.

Refusing to sleep with his wife: Ginzberg, *Legends of the Jews* III, 256. According to the Midrash, Miriam as a young child had similarly rebuked her own father, Amram, when he decided to stop sleeping with his wife and advised the other male Israelite slaves to stop sleeping with theirs in order to rob Pharaoh of more Hebrew babies to kill. See notes to parashat "Shemot."

Women's sexual rights: See parashat "Ki Tetze."

Hiyya and the Pomegranate: B. Kiddushin 81b.

The whole business with the Cushite woman: See Phyllis Trible's article "Bringing Miriam out of the Shadows," in Brenner, *Feminist Companion to Exodus-Deuteronomy*, 174–79.

The mental suffering caused by the shame: See Gunther Plaut, ed., *The Torah: A Modern Commentary* (New York: Union of American Hebrew Congregations, 1981), 1101.

Aaron has already suffered enough: See parashat "Shemini," which recounts the death of Aaron's sons, Nadab and Abihu. Some commentators assign equal responsibility to Aaron in this challenge to Moses' authority but explain that Aaron has already suffered enough through the death of his sons.

"Plainly and not in riddles": According to the Rabbis, Moses was unique among the prophets, the only one granted unmediated access to God, unlike all others, who had to divine God's will through dreams and riddles. Moses alone was able to view God through a single lens, a "specularium," whereas others only saw "darkly," through as many as nine lenses. Leviticus Rabbah I, 4.

Bayti has been interpreted: Ginzberg, *Legends of the Jews* VI, 91, n. 493.

I will appear only once more in the Torah: See parashat "Hukkat."

Miriam is punished for slandering Moses: Ginzberg, *Legends of the Jews* III, 259.

Like a parent frustrated by her children's bickering: Later on, in verse 14, the analogy to human family dynamics is made even more explicit.

According to the Septuagint: Translating the Torah into Greek became necessary because the Jews of ancient Egypt became so Hellenized that most could no longer read the Torah in the original Hebrew. A famous rabbinic legend about this translation recounts that when seventy-two (in some versions, seventy) Jewish sages from Israel were sequestered on an island in seventy-two separate rooms, so faithful were they to every letter of the holy scroll that every single translation was identical. B. Megillah 9a–b.

"El na refa na lah": This scene reminds us of a similar moment in Exodus, when Moses himself is stricken with leprosy—the phrases in Exodus 4:6 and Numbers 12:10 are identical—then miraculously healed. See also parashat "Metzora."

Spat in Meir's eye: J. Sotah I, 16d.

Miraculous well: See parashat "Hukkat."

Waiting for Miriam: Ginzberg, *Legends of the Jews* III, 261.

37. SHELAKH LEKHA

To reward the women for their faith: Rashi. See also parashat "Ki Tissa."

Unlike my brothers Moses and Aaron: Numbers 20:24.

I was doomed to die in the wilderness: Miriam's death is recounted in parashat "Hukkat."

Rahab: The story of Rahab and the two Israelite spies whom she hides in Jericho (Joshua 2:1–24) is the traditional haftorah for this parasha.

She later became Joshua's wife: Ginzberg, *Legends of the Jews* IV, 5.

Haver, herev, vahar: All of these words are anagrams of *Rahav*, Rahab's name (unvocalized) in Hebrew.

Mystical symbolism: See Aryeh Kaplan's *Tzitzith: A Thread of Life* (New York: National Council of Synagogue Youth/Orthodox Union, 1984). In recent years, there has been an explosion of creative tallitot, many of them handmade. One interesting pattern is the "rainbow tallit," designed by Zalman Schachter-Shalomi and distributed by the P'nai Or Religious Fellowship. The colors of this tallit represent the *sefirot* (emanations) of Kabbalah. Women's tallitot often diverge even more radically from the striped rectangular pattern and materials of the traditional tallit. The *atarah*—literally, "crown"—is the decorative band sewn at the top edge of the tallit, forming a kind of collar at the wearer's neck. Although not prescribed, the *atarah* has become a standard feature of the tallit. On a traditional man's tallit, the band is usually white and often has the Hebrew blessing for donning the tallit embroidered on it. In contemporary versions of the *atarah*, on both men's and women's tallitot, this decorative element has expanded its role, offering opportunities for individual expression. *Atarot* can vary in color, material, design, and inscription.

"Loosing knots": Daniel, 5:12, 16.

Taking hallah: From "Tkhine of Three Gates" by Sore bas Toyvim (seventeenth century, Ukraine), in *The Merit of Our Mothers*, 14.

38. KORAKH

The rebellion of Korakh: According to biblical scholars, this narrative represents a fusion of three story traditions, each offering a different account of a rebellion against Moses.

Korakh's offense is so monstrous: Ginzberg, *Legends of the Jews* III, 300.

Why are innocent women and children swallowed up: The question of theodicy—why do the innocent suffer—recurs frequently in the Torah, most notably in parashat "Vayera," where God tells Abraham to sacrifice his son Isaac and where Abraham argues with God over the destruction of Sodom and Gomorrah. See also the note to parashat "Bekhukotai."

And I'll call upon my god to prove it: One of the most famous episodes of dueling holy men can be found in I Kings 18, where the prophet Elijah takes on the priests of Baal in a competition between Israel's God and theirs. Fittingly, this story was chosen as the traditional haftorah for parashat "Ki Tissa," the episode of the Golden Calf, to serve as yet another instance of Israel's rebellion against Moses and God.

Aaron's house is no more: Although the institution of the priestly cult—the *kohanim* with their attendants, the Levites—effectively ended with the destruction of the Second Temple in 70 C.E., a vestige of this institution has survived in a few ritual practices: Jews who claim descent from the *kohanim*—Aaron's line—receive the first honor during the Torah service, and *levi'im*—descendants of the Levites—receive the second; in those communities where the special ceremony called *dukhanen* is observed on the pilgrimage festivals (and daily in Jerusalem), *kohanim* and *levi'im* play a special role; in the *pidyon ha-ben* ceremony—the redemption of a firstborn—a *kohen* receives the symbolic redemption price from the parents in exchange for releasing the child from Temple service. In some Jewish communities, these hierarchical distinctions have been dropped in favor of more egalitarian practices.

The symbolism of salt: See also the story of Lot's wife in parashat "Vayera."

39. HUKKAT

Even the wise King Solomon confesses: Yalkut Shimoni 759. Rabbinic tradition attributes to Solomon the authorship of the book of Ecclesiastes, together with the Song of Songs (also known as Song of Solomon) and Proverbs.

The great Yohanan ben Zakkai: Pesikta de Rav Kahana 4:7; Numbers Rabbah 19:8. Yohanan ben Zakkai was a first-century rabbi who is credited with establishing a rabbinic academy at Yavneh in the wake of the Roman defeat of Jerusalem.

Served to atone for Israel's collective sin: Pesikta Rabbati 14:14.

So rare are pure red heifers: Mishnah Parah 3:5.

Aaron's death: Ginzberg, *Legends of the Jews* III, 320–34. According to biblical scholars, this incident is yet more evidence of the hidden hand of the Aaronide priests, Aaron's descendants, in creating the final text of the Torah.

Death by the kiss of God: B. Baba Batra 17a.

The Fast of Miriam: Eliyahu Kitov, *The Book of Our Heritage* II (New York: Feldheim, 1978), 157–61. Although most traditional commentators agree that Miriam died on the tenth of Nisan, a few place her death on the first of this month. See Aryeh Kaplan, *The Living Torah* (New York: Maznaim Publishing, 1981), commentary on Numbers 20:1.

Legend of Miriam's Well: Ginzberg, *Legends of the Jews* III, 50–54.

Miriam's well fills all wells: Eliyahu Kitov, *The Book of Our Heritage,* rev. ed. (New York: Feldheim, 1978), 2:162.

Song of the Well: Ginzberg, *Legends of the Jews* III, 53. See also Milgrom's excursus on this topic in *The JPS Torah Commentary,* "Numbers," 460–62.

40. BALAK

Probably composed independently: This tale, like many other parts of the Torah, began as an independent composition, and was only later anthologized into the canon of the Pentateuch. See Milgrom's excursus on this story in *The JPS Torah Commentary,* "Numbers," 468–76.

Tzena Urena: A Yiddish Torah commentary composed by Rabbi Yaakov ben Yitzhak Askenazi in the seventeenth century especially for ignorant women who couldn't read Hebrew (some couldn't read at all) and who had no access to rabbinic lore and interpretation. It was immensely popular and has gone through over 200 printings since its publication. It is now available in English as *The Weekly Midrash: Tz'enah Ur'enah,* transl. Miriam Stark Zakon (New York: Mesorah Publications, 1983).

Incestuous union of Lot and his daughters: See parashat "Vayera."

Midian is Abraham's son: Genesis 25:1; see parashat "Hayei Sarah."

We should feed our beasts: B. Gittin 62a.

Soothsaying Dogs: Lithuanian Jewish folktale. Adapted from Dov Noy, *Folktales of Israel,* no. 25. (Chicago: University of Chicago Press, 1963).

The evil eye: The Yiddish expression *keine eyin hore* means "against the evil eye," or, in Hebrew, *beli ayin ha-ra.*

Balaam knew his ass intimately: Ginzberg, *Legends of the Jews* III, 365.

Why we imposed so many restrictions: For a fuller discussion of this principle, known as *hukkat hagoi,* and its historical repercussions, see the article on this topic in the *Encyclopedia Judaica.* See also parashat "Kedoshim."

Kovatah: Numbers Rabbah 20:29. See also Antonelli, *In the Image of God,* 374–76.

Halakha ve'ain morim ken: B. Sanhedrin 39a.

41. PINKHAS

The Israelites' battle with Midian: See parashat "Balak" for the beginning of this story and parashat "Mattot" for its conclusion.

Serakh: See parashat "Vayiggash" for the legends of Serakh bat Asher.

Daughters of Zelophekhad: B. Baba Batra 119a. See parashat "Massei" for further discussion of this topic.

Cozbi's name: B. Sanhedrin 82a–b.

Names for God: See "God, Names of," in the *Encyclopedia Judaica* for a comprehensive survey of this subject. In mystical tradition especially, the names of God have served as a focus of meditation, complex numerological theories, and "practical kabbalah" in the form of amulets, incantations, spells, a contemplative mandala called a *mizrakh* (literally "east," after its function to orient the user toward Jerusalem), and folk remedies. New feminist liturgies have coined new terms and phrases, often drawing upon ancient sources.

42. MATTOT

The Kol Nidrei prayer: This solemn prayer, chanted on the evening of Yom Kippur, literally means "all vows." Its origin probably goes back to the Spanish Inquisition, when Jews who were forced to convert to Christianity would secretly renounce these vows in order to remain true to their Jewish beliefs.

Nazirite: See parashat "Naso."

Jephthah's Daughter: This story, found in Judges 11, is traditionally read as the haftorah for parashat "Hukkat," to parallel the death of Miriam. It more appropriately belongs here, since it is Jephthah's foolish vow that results in his daughter's death.

Pinkhas was too proud: Ginzberg, *Legends of the Jews* IV, 46. See also parashat "Pinkhas."

Four Days of Jephthah's Daughter: These suggestions were offered by Rabbi Yosef Wosk in his article "The Four Days: A Proposal for the Annual Observance of Bat-Yiftach" in *Neshama,* Winter 1991, a Jewish feminist quarterly published in Boston.

The Weasel and the Well: B. Taanit 8a.

The Unpaid Pledge: Oral tale of the Klausenberg Hasidim, cited in Jerome Mintz, *Legends of the Hasidim* (Chicago: University of Chicago, 1968), 381–83.

After the Jews returned from Babylonian exile: When Persia conquered Babylonia in the sixth century B.C.E., Cyrus the Great granted the Jews permission to return home after fifty years of exile. The scribe Ezra spearheaded a move to break up intermarriages by persuading Israelites to divorce their foreign wives. See Ezra 9–10.

43. MASSEI

The original twelve tribes: Although the number is based upon the twelve sons of Jacob, the count is somewhat more complicated than that. The Levites did not inherit land, bringing the number down to eleven, but Joseph received a double portion through his two sons, Ephraim and Manasseh, who constituted two of the tribes, thus bringing the number back up to twelve.

Jews still largely behave in tribal ways: Even today, Jews sometimes humorously refer to themselves as "members of the tribe." Despite the loss of tribal distinctions and their connection to specific landholdings, the feeling of belonging to a tribe persists.

DEUTERONOMY

44. DEVARIM

"That is why my womb trembles for him": The translation is that of Phyllis Trible, who points to many parallels in this chapter of Jeremiah between God and Rachel. *God and the Rhetoric of Sexuality* (Philadelphia: Fortress Press, 1978), 45. See also parashat "Pinkhas" on names of God.

Began their service at twenty-five or thirty: Twenty-five, according to Numbers 8:24; thirty, according to Numbers 4:3.

Physically too taxing: The upper age limit was lifted in the Jerusalem Temple, where the priestly duties required less physical strength.

Sacred musical performances: See parashat "Beshallakh."

Spiritual "eldering": The notion of spiritual eldering has recently been brought to public attention by Rabbi Zalman Schachter-Shalomi, founding father of the Jewish Renewal movement. He addresses this topic in *From Age-ing to Sage-ing* (New York: Time Warner Books, 1995). See also parashat "Beha'alotkha" on retirement of the priests.

The Wise Woman of Tekoa: See 2 Samuel 14.

"Crone" ceremonies: Several of these ceremonies have been gathered by Irene Fine in *Midlife: A Rite of Passage and The Wise Woman: A Celebration* (San Diego: Women's Institute of Continuing Education, 1988). Other ceremonies and reflections about women and aging can be found in Orenstein, *Lifecycles*, vol. I, 307–34.

We must respect age: Genesis Rabbah 63:6.

Be careful to honor the old: B. Berakhot 8b.

45. VA-ETKHANAN

Events on Mount Horeb. See also parashat "Yitro."

Enlightenment broke down the ghetto walls: When Napoleon swept through Europe in the early nineteenth century, he left behind the new ideas spawned by the French Revolution: individual freedom, universal citizenship, the liberating influence of arts and letters, the power of reason. Many of the Jewish communities who came in contact with the French army were excited by these ideas and sought out ways to enter the modern secular world. As a result, many Jews rejected the strictures of traditional Judaism and chose to become free citizens of their countries. Lacking no autonomous authority, Jewish religious leaders had no means of enforcing practice or punishing those who violated their rulings.

Also the Oral Law: To Orthodox rabbinite Jews (and before the Enlightenment, there were no other kinds), the Torah that Moses received on Mount Sinai contained not only the Ten Commandments, not only every word of the Pentateuch (including the description of Moses' own death), but also all *future* interpretations of those words by rabbinic authorities through the ages. One of the major breaks with Orthodoxy came when Reform and Conservative Jews began to take seriously what has come to be called the "Documentary Hypothesis," the theory that the Torah is an edited anthology comprising texts written by different authors or schools at different periods. Despite revisionist claims to the contrary by many Orthodox Jews today, it is clear that over the centuries, even some rabbinic commentators recognized a variety of signatures in the biblical text.

Nidahta: Later in Deuteronomy (22:1), this root appears as a noun, *nidahim,* and means "those who are lost," as an animal that has lost its way.

"Laws of Noah": See parashat "Noah."

"Follow[ing] the customs of their fathers": B. Hullin 13b.

"Will have a share in the world to come": J. Sanhedrin 13:2.

God will exile them: Scholars believe that this "prophecy" was written in hindsight, *after* Assyria had conquered the Northern Kingdom of Israel and exiled the ten tribes to the corners of its empire.

Rahamim: One of the names of the Canaanite goddess Astarte, according to Patai, *The Hebrew Goddess,* 46.

The reasons given are also different: One of the major differences between the books of Exodus and Deuteronomy is that the former emphasizes ritual; the latter, ethics. Because the Book of Deuteronomy is fundamentally a document of Levitical *preaching,* the laws are frequently justified by a moral rationale, whereas in Exodus, as well as Leviticus and Numbers, the laws are simply prescribed, often in minute detail. Purity and contamination are the primary concern of the middle three books; morality and justice, of Deuteronomy.

This verse together with three others: Exodus 12:26, 13:14, 13:8.

What these laws mean "to you": Exodus 12:26.

Orange on the seder plate: This anecdote has become part of the folk Torah and has generated various liturgical supplements to feminist Haggadot.

Amulets: Amulets have always been popular among Jewish women, especially in connection with pregnancy, childbirth, and illness. In recent years, amulets have been designed and collected by many Jewish women, as folk art as well as remedies and talismans.

Carrying one even on the Sabbath: B. Shabbat 61a.

46. EKEV

Iron Age Israel: That is, the premonarchy period, 1200–1000 B.C.E. For a good overview of what women's lives were like during this time, see Meyers, *Discovering Eve;* and Karel Van Der Toorn, *From Her Cradle to Her Grave: The Role of Religion in the Life of the Israelite and the Babylonian Woman,* transl. Sara J. Denning-Bolle (Sheffield, England: Sheffield Academic Press, 1994).

Aliyah: Literally, "going up." This term refers to the honor of reciting blessings before and after the ritual chanting of a passage from the Torah scroll, as well as to a journey to Jerusalem or (in the diaspora) to the land of Israel. In modern times, *aliyah* is synonymous with immigration to Israel.

Contemporary prayer books: The Hebrew conjunction *vav* can be interpreted several ways. To translate it as "by" is the solution adopted by both the Conservative and the Reform movements. The Reconstructionist Sabbath prayer book has not only *retranslated* the traditional Hebrew, as is the case in both Conservative and Reform prayer books, but has actually *changed* the Hebrew, substituting the new formulation *asher kervanu l'avodato,* "who brings us near to God's service." The latest Reconstructionist prayer book, *Kol Haneshama,* has made numerous other changes in both Hebrew and English, reflecting its rejection of chosenness as a principle of Jewish peoplehood. New feminist liturgies are also experimenting with retranslation of Hebrew prayers to reflect a more egalitarian approach.

47. RE'EH

Expressly forbidden by the Torah: See also Deuteronomy 7:5; 16:21.

There lived a pious farmer: Tanhuma Re'eh 10.

Two sons of a widow went to glean: Avot de Rabbi Natan 38, 57a.

The master's obligation to provision: B. Kiddushin 18a–b.

"If you make my four poor folk happy": Tzena U'rena, "Re'eh."

Their maternal duties exempted them: Jewish law excuses women from most time-bound positive commandments so that they can be free to attend to their family responsibilities, especially taking care of children. In modern times, many women have questioned the continued appropriateness of this principle, since so many years of a woman's religious adulthood—from thirteen until she dies—are not defined by domestic demands.

The following individuals were exempt: Mishnah Hagigah 1:1.

Lost Book of Deuteronomy: This story is found in 2 Kings 22:14–23, 25. The Rabbis chose this selection because of its connection to the celebration of the pilgrimage festivals, including Passover, described in this parasha.

48. SHOFETIM

Kings should restrict themselves: B. Sanhedrin 21a.

Rabbi Gershom ben Judah: Known in Hebrew as *Me'or ha-Golah,* the Light of the Exile (960–1028). Besides this famous ruling in favor of monogamy, Rabbi Gershom decreed that a man had to give his wife a writ of divorce, a *get,* if he wished to dissolve the marriage, which had the effect of securing economic protection for the woman. Both measures bettered the condition of Jewish women within the Ashkenazic (northern and eastern European) lands.

We have ruled that only witchcraft: The Hebrew terms for occult practices are rather technical, suggesting that the biblical authors were quite familiar with such practices: witchcraft (*kishuf*) and conjuring the dead by using human bones (*ov* and *yidoni*); communicating with and on behalf of the dead without contact with human remains (*doresh el ha-metim*); divination based on certain events or circumstances (*nikhush,* from *nahkash,* "serpent"); fortune-telling with sand, stones, and other objects (*kesem*); astrological forecasts (*onanut*); and casting spells for healing or magical purposes (*hever*). See also parashat "Kedoshim."

Scarcity, evil, and death: Erwin Goodenough, in *Jewish Symbols in Greco-Roman Times* (Princeton: Princeton University Press, 1988), points to these three fears as the primary motivation behind the religious beliefs of the ancient world.

Alexander and the Fair Judgment: Jewish folklore contains many legends about Alexander the Great, who is reputed to have bypassed Israel on his way to conquer the world, due to a prophecy of doom that came to him in a dream. To thank him for sparing the Jewish people, the High Priest of the Temple in Jerusalem promised Alexander that all Jewish boys born that year would bear his name. The Alexander legends are collected in a medieval work entitled *Alexander Ha-Makedon,* "Alexander the Macedonian." For an excellent selection of these tales in English translation, see Bin Gorion, *Mimekor Yisrael* III, 1423–1450.

49. KI TETZE

He will want to send her away: Rashi, Rambam, Ibn Ezra.

The term "firstborn" in ancient Near Eastern law: For an excellent discussion of Deuteronomy's attitudes toward women, especially as expressed in its legal rulings, see Tikva Frymer-Kensky's essay in *The Women's Bible Commentary,* 52–62.

"Wayward and defiant son": See also parashat "Mishpatim."

They had little opportunity for such rebellion: In most traditional societies today, a daughter's sexual trespasses are severely punished, sometimes even by death.

Cross-dressing: Cited in Patai, *The Hebrew Goddess,* 53.

The bird's nest: There is an extensive rabbinic literature on this topic, focused around this verse and the Talmudic story of Elisha ben Abuyah's apostasy. Milton Steinberg fictionalized the incident in his historical novel *As a Driven Leaf* (New York: Behrman, 1939).

A safety net for divorcées: The *ketubah* is still the centerpiece of the Jewish wedding ceremony. Written in Aramaic and often elaborately decorated, it details the husband's contractual obligations to his wife (and in certain egalitarian ceremonies, of the wife to her husband) and has evolved into a cherished Jewish art form. For Rabbenu Gershom, see note to parashat "Shofetim."

The school of Shammai: The rabbinic schools of Hillel and Shammai, named after two great Sages of the Mishnah in the first century B.C.E., often appear in tension with each other on matters of Jewish law and custom. Shammai represents the more exacting interpretation of the law; Hillel the more lenient. Tradition almost always sides with Hillel, although the minority opinions of Shammai and his followers are included in the discussion and presented respectfully.

Akiva even allowed: B. Gittin 90a.

Are the Rabbis' rulings better or worse: In the three liberal movements in America—Conservative, Reform, and Reconstructionist—changes have already been instituted in Jewish marital law, affecting the wording of the *ketubah*, the procedures for divorce, the rituals of the wedding ceremony, and the conditions for remarriage. Only the Reconstructionist movement currently allows a wife to initiate a divorce and sanctions commitment ceremonies between gay Jews, although the Reform movement is moving in these directions. Although the Orthodox still adhere strictly to traditional law, many women and some men have been clamoring for changes in the treatment of the *agunah* (literally, "the chained woman"), who is forbidden to remarry unless she can prove that her previous husband is either dead or has given her a *get*. In some cases, husbands refuse to grant their wives a divorce unless they receive considerable sums of money. Although Jewish courts in Israel often threaten these recalcitrant husbands with prison sentences, they sometimes prefer to go to jail rather than free their wives to remarry. See Jack Nusan Porter, *The Agunah* (Northvale, NJ: Jason Aronson, 1995).

Her hymen had ruptured: M. Ketubbot 1:7.

"Poking a finger in the eye": M. Niddah 5:4. The possibility that a man would have intercourse with a girl under the age of three has enraged many feminists and has become a flashpoint for their condemnation of Talmudic law.

One of three legitimate ways: The Rabbis in effect outlawed this method by punishing the would-be husband with flogging. J. Kiddushin 1:1; B. Kiddushin 12b; Maimonides, Mishneh Torah, Seder Nashim, Hilkhot Ishut 3:21–22.

He was forbidden ever to divorce her: See comment below on Deuteronomy 22:28.

Jewish men restricted to a single wife: Specifically, "Ashkenazi" Jews, who lived in Europe north of the Mediterranean coastal nations. See notes to parashat "Shofetim."

The penalty was lessened: For a comprehensive discussion of Jewish divorce law, especially as it affects women, see Rachel Biale's chapter on the subject in *Women and Jewish Law,* 70–101.

Mamzer: In English, the word "bastard" refers to an out-of-wedlock child. But in Hebrew, the term technically refers only to children born of an *illegitimate* union—an adulterous liaison, marriage to a woman who has not secured a *get* (and is therefore still legally married to her first husband), marriage between a *kohen* and a divorcée, or marriage to another *mamzer.*

We modified this law: Shulkhan Arukh, Even Ha-Ezer, 177:4.

Rape even within marriage: B. Eruvin 100b.

Once, when a woman came to Rabbi Yohanan: J. Sotah 4:4.

Forbids a son to sleep with his father's wives: Several tales in the Bible revolve around violations of this law. Reuben sleeps with his father Jacob's concubine Bilhah (Genesis 35:22), and David's sons Absalom and Adonijah both sleep with their father's concubines in bids for power (2 Samuel 16:22; I Kings 2:17–25).

Judah and Tamar: See parashat "Vayeshev."

The Jericho harlot Rahab: See parashat "Shelakh Lekha."

Josiah expelled from the Temple: 2 Kings 23:6–7.

Conjugal duties of husbands: See Biale's chapter on "Sexuality and Marital Relations," in *Women and Jewish Law,* 121–46. See also parashat "Beha'alotkha."

Some say slander: See notes to parashat "Beha'alotkha."

Levirate marriage: See parashat "Vayeshev" for the story of Judah and Tamar (Genesis 38) as well as the Book of Ruth, especially chapters 3 and 4. See also Biale, *Women and Jewish Law,* 113–20. The medieval commentator and rabbinic authority Rashi ruled that *halitzah* was always preferable to levirate marriage—*yibum*—unless it could be proven that the *levir* was marrying his sister-in-law purely to fulfill the divine commandment. Ashkenazi tradition—and in recent times the Israeli rabbinate—follows his opinion. Sephardi tradition, on the other hand, follows Maimonides' ruling that *yibum* is always preferable to *halitzah,* although modern laws against polygamy have effectively abolished this alternative tradition.

Jewish community of Safed: Biale, *Women and Jewish Law,* 118–19.

"Eye for eye": See parashat "Mishpatim" for a discussion of this biblical principle, known as *lex talionis.*

50. Ki Tavo

The forbidden fruit: Nahmanides on Leviticus 23:40.

"Fragrant children": B. Menahot 27a.

Barzel: Cited in Trachtenberg, *Jewish Magic and Superstition,* 313, n. 14.

Colette, Sage of Jerusalem: Colette Muscat is an Algerian Jewish mystic, now in her eighties, who holds a "salon" for select "devotees" on Jewish holidays in her Jerusalem home. I was privileged to hear her teachings on "sadness and grief" on Tisha B'Av 1995.

The Great Power of Psalms: Yiddish folktale, cited in S. Simon, *More Wise Men of Chelm* (New York: Behrman House, 1965), 54–62.

Two sieges of Jerusalem: The Babylonians under Nebuchadnezzar besieged and conquered Jerusalem in the sixth century B.C.E.; the Jews returned fifty years later, when Babylonia was conquered by Cyrus of Persia. In the first century C.E., the Romans under Titus besieged and destroyed Jerusalem for a second time and exiled its inhabitants throughout the Roman Empire. In both sieges, the inhabitants of Jerusalem were reduced to desperate straits as their supplies of food and water dwindled to starvation levels. When Jerusalem was under Roman siege, the Jewish zealots within the city walls intentionally burned the city's food supplies to force the Jews inside to fight the Romans rather than hold out longer.

First Crusade in the Rhineland: En route to the Holy Land, many of the Crusaders sacked Jewish communities in Germany, massacring thousands and looting their possessions. In several cases, Jews chose martyrdom rather than face rape and the Crusaders' swords. See Robert Chazan's recent book, *In the Year 1096: The Jews and the First Crusade* (Philadelphia: The Jewish Publication Society, 1996).

Jewish women during the Holocaust: Adapted from Yaffa Eliach's *Hasidic Tales of the Holocaust* (New York: Oxford University Press, 1982), 95–99; 151–53.

51. NITZAVIM

"The soul is at peace": Franz Rosenzweig, *The Star of Redemption* (Notre Dame, IN: Notre Dame University Press, 1985), 171.

Skotsl kumt: Adapted from Beatrice Weinreich, *Yiddish Folktales* (New York: Pantheon Books, 1988).

52. VAYELEKH

Hester panim: See, for example, Isaiah 54:8; Psalms 13:2, 27:8–9, 102:3, 143:7.

The Priestly Blessing: Numbers 6:24–26.

After Auschwitz: See Martin Buber, *Eclipse of God* (New York: Harper and Row, 1952); Richard Rubenstein, *After Auschwitz: Radical Theology and Contemporary Judaism* (Indianapolis: Bobbs Merrill, 1966); Abraham Joshua Heschel, *God in Search of Man* (Philadelphia: The Jewish Publication Society, 1955). Two of the most moving spiritual testimonies to emerge from the midst of the Holocaust are Etty Hillesum's memoir, *An Interrupted Life* (New York: Pantheon, 1983), and *Esh Kodesh*, the theological reflections of Kalonymus Kalman Shapira, the rabbi of the Warsaw Ghetto, published in English as *Holy Fire*, translated and with an introduction by Nehemiah Polen (Northvale, NJ: Jason Aronson, 1994).

Matriarchs and judges, prophets and healers: The matriarchs include Sarah, Rebecca, Rachel, and Leah (and some would add Zilpah and Bilhah). The only female judge named in the Bible is Deborah (Judges 4–5). There are three female prophets: Huldah (2 Kings 22), Noadiah

(Nehemiah 6:14), and the nameless female prophet of Isaiah 8:3. The most noted healer is Miriam. Although not cast in a position of religious or political leadership, Hannah has been recognized as a spiritual role model. The Rabbis name her as the composer of the first prayer (B. Berakhot 31a–b). Although the only scholar recognized in Talmudic tradition is Beruriah, other women have been acknowledged as rabbinic scholars, including Rashi's daughters, who were reputed to have worn tefillin and studied texts, the Ba'al Shem Tov's daughter, and, early in our own century, Henrietta Szold, who studied with male rabbinical students at the Jewish Theological Seminary and served as the first editor of the Jewish Publication Society. Often these women were the daughters of rabbinic scholars who had no sons, and so they inherited their father's "Torah" by default. Women mystics have generally not been noted in the annals of Jewish history, although legend has it that Doña Gracia, the great financier and political leader of the Sephardic Jewish community in the wake of the Spanish Expulsion, studied with the spiritual head of the Safed mystics, Isaac Luria. Folklore includes stories about many women who functioned unofficially as spiritual leaders of their local communities. To this day, a handful of women, in Israel and the Diaspora, continue to attract followers who seek out their special gifts as spiritual guides and healers.

Hannah Rachel of Ludomir: Hannah Rachel, the only child of Monesh Werbermacher, lived in Ludomir (in the Ukraine) from 1805 to 1892. She is the subject of Y. Twersky's 1949 Hebrew novel, *Ha-Betulah me-Ludomir* (The Maid of Ludomir) and has recently been rediscovered as a role model of hasidic piety and learning. See Ada Rapoport Albert, "On Women and Hasidism: S. A. Horodecky and the Maid of Ludomir Tradition," in Ada Rapoport Albert and S. Zipperstein, eds., *Jewish History: Essays in Honor of Chimen Abramsky* (London: P. Halban, 1988), 495–525.

53. HA'AZINU

Gluckel recounts: From *The Memoirs of Gluckel of Hameln,* transl. Marvin Lowenthal (New York: Schocken, 1977), 2–3.

Died by the "kiss of God": See also parashat "Hukkat."

Striking the rock at Meribah: Numbers 20:1–13.

My own sin: Deuteronomy 24:9. See parashat "Ki Tetze."

54. VEZOT HA-BERAKHAH

As Robert Frost once put it: In his poem "The Death of the Hired Man."

Guardian of his surviving family: Ginzberg, *Legends of the Jews* VI, 153, n. 909.

The Bride Who Saved Her Husband: Cited in Moses Gaster, *The Maaseh Book: Book of Jewish Tales and Legends* (Philadelphia: The Jewish Publication Society, 1981), no. 195.

Buries Moses secretly: Ginzberg, *Legends of the Jews* III, 473. So afraid were the Rabbis that Moses would become a cult figure that they excluded his name from the Passover Haggadah, since Moses might have competed there with God for star billing.

Yokheved lives to enter the Promised Land: Ginzberg, *Legends of the Jews* III, 393.

"I am not in the heavens": Paraphrase of Deuteronomy 31:12–14.

Epilogue

Miryam hanevi'ah: Conceived by Rabbi Leila Gal Berner and Dr. Arthur Waskow; Hebrew by Leila Gal Berner. This song originally appeared in *Or Chadash*, a Shabbat morning siddur published by P'nai Or Religious Fellowship, and has since been reprinted in liturgies, Haggadot, and songbooks. Used by permission of the author.

WHO'S WHO: WOMEN WITH NAMES

ADAH: wife of Lamech, mother of Jabal, ancestor of nomads, and of Jubal, ancestor of musicians (Genesis 4:19–20; 23)

ADAH: wife of Esau, daughter of Elon the Hittite (Genesis 36:2); mother of Eliphaz (Genesis 36:4); grandmother of Teman, Omar, Zepho, Gatam, Kenaz (Genesis 36:11); grandmother of Amalek by Timna, concubine of Eliphaz (Genesis 36:12)

ASNAT: daughter of Poti-phera, priest of On; wife of Joseph; according to the Midrash, daughter of Dinah and Shechem, adopted daughter of Potiphar and Zuleika

BASEMATH: wife of Esau, daughter of Elon the Hittite (Genesis 26:34); wife of Esau, daughter of Ishmael, sister of Nebaioth (Genesis 36:3); mother of Reuel (Genesis 36:4); grandmother of Nahath, Zerah, Shammah, Mizzah

BILHAH: maidservant of Rachel, concubine of Jacob, mother of Dan and Naphtali

COZBI: Midianite, daughter of Zur, tribal head of Midianite ancestral house; killed by Pinkhas while making love with Israelite Zimri, son of Salu, chieftain of Simeonite ancestral house (Numbers 25:8, 15)

DEBORAH: Rebecca's nurse

DINAH: daughter of Leah and Jacob; sister of Reuben, Simeon, Levi, Judah, Issachar, and Zebulun; raped by Shechem; according to Midrash, mother of Asnat and mother-in-law of Joseph

ELISHEVA: wife of Aaron; daughter of Amminadab; sister of Nakhshon; mother of Nadab, Abihu, Eleazar, and Itamar

EVE: first woman (Genesis 2–3)

HAGAR: Abraham's Egyptian concubine, mother of Ishmael (Genesis 16; 21:9–21)

HOGLAH: daughter of Zelophekhad, descendant of Manasseh

JUDITH: daughter of Beeri the Hittite, wife of Esau (Genesis 26:34)

KETURAH: second wife of Abraham; mother of Zimran, Jokshan, Medan, Midian, Ishbak, and Shuah

LEAH: oldest daughter of Laban; niece of Rebecca; first wife of Jacob; mother of Reuben, Simeon, Levi, Judah, Issachar, Zebulun, and Dinah

MAHALATH: daughter of Ishmael, wife of Esau, sister of Nebaioth (Genesis 28:9)

MAHLAH: daughter of Zelophekhad, descendant of Manasseh

MEHETABEL: wife of Hadar, king of Edom; daughter of Matred; daughter of Me-Zahav (Genesis 36:39)

MILCAH: wife of Nahor, sister-in-law and niece of Sarah and Abraham (Genesis 11:29), grandmother of Rebecca

MILCAH: daughter of Zelophekhad, descendant of Manasseh

MIRIAM: oldest child of Yokheved and Amram, sister of Aaron and Moses; according to the Midrash, wife of Caleb ben Yefuneh, mother of Bezalel

NAAMAH: sister of Tubal-Cain (Genesis 4:22)

NOAH: daughter of Zelophekhad, descendant of Manasseh

OHOLIBAMAH: wife of Esau, daughter of Anah, daughter of Zibeon the Hivite (Genesis 36:2); grandmother of Jeush, Jalam, and Korah (Genesis 36:14); clan of Esau/Edom

PUAH: one of two midwives who saved Hebrew babies

RACHEL: younger daughter of Laban, niece of Rebecca, sister of Leah, second wife of Jacob, mother of Joseph and Benjamin

REBECCA: daughter of Bethuel, granddaughter of Nahor and Milcah, sister of Laban, wife of Isaac, mother of Jacob and Esau

SARAI/SARAH: wife and half-sister of Abraham; mother. of Isaac; grandmother of Jacob and Esau; great-grandmother of Jacob's twelve sons, Dinah, and of Esau's children

SERAKH: daughter of Asher, granddaughter of Zilpah and Jacob

SHELOMIT: mother of the blasphemer in Leviticus 24, daughter of Dibri of the tribe of Dan

SHIFRA: one of two midwives who saved Hebrew babies

TAMAR: wife of Judah's son Er, mother of Perez and Zerah by Judah (Genesis 38:30), ancestor of King David

TIMNA: concubine of Eliphaz, son of Esau and Adah, mother of Amalek (Genesis 36:12); sister of Lotan, son of Seir the Horite (Genesis 36:22); clan of Esau/Edom (Genesis 36:40)

TIRTZAH: daughter of Zelophekhad, descendant of Manasseh

YOKHEVED: daughter of Levi; wife and aunt of Amram; mother of Miriam, Aaron, and Moses

ZILLAH: mother of Tubal-Cain, forger of copper and iron implements, and Naamah (Genesis 4:19, 22-23)

ZILPAH: maidservant of Leah, concubine of Jacob, mother of Gad and Asher

ZIPPORAH: daughter of Jethro, priest of Midian (also called Reuel, Exodus 2), wife of Moses, mother of Gershom and Eliezer

WHO'S NOT WHO: THE NAMELESS WOMEN

NOAH'S WIFE: Naamah (Midrash)

LOT'S WIFE: Edith (Heb. Idit, Midrash)

LOT'S DAUGHTERS: Paltit, who dies because she offers hospitality to strangers (Midrash), and two others, who bear children by their father—the older, Moab; the younger, Ben-Ammi

JUDAH'S WIFE: "daughter of a certain Canaanite"; mother of Er, Onan, and Shelah

PHARAOH'S DAUGHTER: Thermutis (Egyptian), Batyah (Hebrew, Midrash); adoptive mother of Moses

PHARAOH'S WIFE: Alfar'anit (Midrash)

POTIPHAR'S WIFE: Zuleika (Midrash)

For a complete list of the sources consulted, see bibliographic references in the endnotes. The following is a selected list of recent publications written by, for, and about Jewish women. This list is not meant to be exhaustive but rather to point the way for further study and creative exploration.

BIBLE

Antonelli, Judith. *In the Image of God: A Feminist Commentary on the Torah.* Northvale, NJ: Jason Aronson, 1995.

Brenner, Athalya, ed. *A Feminist Companion to Exodus-Deuteronomy.* Sheffield, England: Sheffield Academic Press, 1994.

————. *A Feminist Companion to Genesis.* Sheffield, England: Sheffield Academic Press, 1994.

Buchmann, Christina, and Celina Spiegel, eds. *Out of the Garden: Women Writers on the Bible.* New York: Ballantine Books, 1994.

Bundesen, Lynne. *The Women's Guide to the Bible.* New York: Crossroad, 1993.

Dennis, Trevor. *Sarah Laughed: Women's Voices in the Old Testament.* Nashville: Abingdon Press, 1994.

Dresner, Samuel H. *Rachel.* Minneapolis: Fortress Press, 1994.

Frymer-Kensky, Tikva. *In the Wake of the Goddesses: Women, Culture, and the Biblical Transformation of Pagan Myth.* New York: Free Press, 1992.

Jeansonne, Sharon Pace. *The Women of Genesis: From Sarah to Potiphar's Wife.* Minneapolis: Fortress Press, 1990.

Laffey, Alice L. *An Introduction to the Old Testament: A Feminist Perspective.* Philadelphia: Fortress Press, 1988.

Newsom, Carol, and Sharon Ringe, eds. *The Women's Bible Commentary.* Louisville, KY: Westminster/John Knox, 1992.

Pardes, Ilana. *Counter-Traditions in the Bible: A Feminist Approach.* Cambridge, MA: Harvard University Press, 1992.

Stanton, Elizabeth Cady. *The Women's Bible.* Boston: Northeastern University Press, 1993. First published in 1885.

Teubal, Savina. *Hagar the Egyptian: The Lost Tradition of the Matriarchs.* New York: Harper and Row, 1990.

―――. *Sarah the Priestess: The First Matriarch of Genesis.* Athens, OH: Swallow Press/Ohio University Press, 1984.

Trible, Phyllis. *Texts of Terror: Literary-Feminist Readings of Biblical Narratives.* Philadelphia: Fortress Press, 1984.

Zornberg, Avivah. *Genesis: The Beginning of Desire.* Philadelphia: The Jewish Publication Society, 1995.

CONTEMPORARY LIFE AND PRACTICE

Adelman, Penina. *Miriam's Well: Rituals for Jewish Women Around the Year.* New York: Biblio Press, 1986.

Fine, Irene, ed. *Midlife: A Rite of Passage and the Wise Woman: A Celebration.* San Diego: Women's Institute of Continuing Education, 1988.

Heschel, Susannah, ed. *On Being a Jewish Feminist.* New York: Schocken, 1983.

Lefkovitz, Lori Hope. "Eavesdropping on Angels and Laughing at God: Theorizing a Subversive Matriarchy," in *Gender and Judaism: The Transformation of Tradition,* ed. T. M. Rudavsky, 157–67. New York: New York University Press, 1995.

Levine, Elizabeth Resnick, ed. *A Ceremonies Sampler: New Rites, Celebrations and Observations of Jewish Women.* San Diego: Women's Institute for Continuing Education, 1988.

Orenstein, Debra, *Lifecycles,* volume I: *Jewish Women on Life Passages and Personal Milestones.* Woodstock, VT: Jewish Lights, 1994.

HISTORY, SOCIAL SCIENCE, AND THEORY

Aberbach, Moshe. *Labor, Crafts and Commerce in Ancient Israel.* Jerusalem: Magnes Press, 1994.

Barber, Elizabeth Wayland. *Women's Work: The First 20,000 Years.* New York: W. W. Norton, 1994.

Douglas, Mary. *Purity and Danger.* London: Routledge and Kegan Paul, 1966.

Edersheim, Alfred. *Sketches of Jewish Social Life,* revised edition. Peabody, MA: Hendrickson, 1994.

Eilberg-Schwartz, Howard. *God's Phallus and Other Problems for Men and Monotheism.* Boston: Beacon Press, 1994.

Glenn, Susan A. *Daughters of the Shtetl: Life and Labor in the Immigrant Generation.* Ithaca: Cornell University Press, 1990.

Meyers, Carol. *Discovering Eve: Ancient Israelite Women in Context.* Oxford: Oxford University Press, 1988.

Patai, Raphael. *The Hebrew Goddess.* New York: Ktav, 1967.

Schiffman, Lawrence. *Reclaiming the Dead Sea Scrolls: The History of Judaism, the Background of Christianity, and the Lost Library of Qumran.* Philadelphia: The Jewish Publication Society, 1994.

Steinberg, Naomi. *Kinship and Marriage in Genesis: A Household Economics Perspective.* Minneapolis: Fortress Press, 1993.

Trachtenberg, Joshua. *Jewish Magic and Superstition.* New York: Atheneum, 1939.

Trible, Phyllis, *God and the Rhetoric of Sexuality.* Philadelphia: Fortress Press, 1978.

Van Der Toorn, Karel. *From Her Cradle to Her Grave: The Role of Religion in the Life of the Israelite and the Babylonian Woman.* Sheffield, England: JSOT Press, 1994.

Westbrook, Raymond, *Property and Family in Biblical Law.* Sheffield, England: Sheffield Academic Press, 1991.

JEWISH LAW AND PRACTICE

Abrams, Judith Z. *The Women of the Talmud.* Northvale, NJ: Jason Aronson, 1994.

Adler, Rachel. "The Jew Who Wasn't There," first published in *Response* in 1973, 7–11, reprinted in *On Being a Jewish Feminist,* ed. Susannah Heschel. New York: Schocken, 1983, 12–18.

————. "The Virgin in the Brothel and Other Anomalies: Character and Context in the Legend of Beruriah," *Tikkun,* November/December 1988, 28–32, 102–5.

Biale, Rachel. *Women and Jewish Law.* New York: Schocken, 1984.

Bronner, Leila Leah. *From Eve to Esther: Rabbinic Reconstructions of Biblical Women.* Louisville, KY: Westminster/John Knox, 1994.

Grossman, Susan, and Rivka Haut. *Daughters of the King: Women and the Synagogue.* Philadelphia: The Jewish Publication Society, 1992.

LITERATURE AND MODERN MIDRASH

Gold, Doris B., and Lisa Stein. *From the Wise Women of Israel: Folklore and Memoirs.* New York: Biblio Press, 1993.

Kaye-Kantrowitz, Melanie, and Irena Klepfisz. *The Tribe of Dinah: A Jewish Women's Anthology.* Boston: Beacon, 1986.

Lowenthal, Marvin, transl. *The Memoirs of Gluckel of Hameln.* New York: Schocken, 1977.

Piercy, Marge. *Mars and Her Children.* New York: Knopf, 1992.

Rosen, Norma. *Biblical Women Unbound.* Philadelphia: The Jewish Publication Society, 1996.

Rush, Barbara. *The Book of Jewish Women's Tales.* Northvale, NJ: Jason Aronson, 1995.

Umansky, Ellen, and Dianne Ashton. *Four Centuries of Jewish Women's Spirituality.* Boston: Beacon, 1992.

Wenkart, Henny. *Sarah's Daughters Sing: A Sampler of Poems by Jewish Women.* Hoboken, NJ: Ktav, 1990.

Zisquit, Linda. *Ritual Bath.* Seattle: Broken Moon Press, 1993.

Zones, Jane Sprague, ed. *Taking the Fruit: Modern Women's Tales of the Bible.* San Diego: Women's Institute for Continuing Jewish Education, 1981.

LITURGY

Brin, Ruth. *Harvest: Collected Poems and Prayers.* New York: Reconstructionist Press, 1956.

Broner, E. M. *The Telling.* San Francisco: Harper/SanFrancisco, 1993.

Cardin, Nina Beth, ed. and transl. *Out of the Depths I Call to You: A Book of Prayers for the Married Jewish Woman.* Northvale, NJ: Jason Aronson, 1992.

Klirs, Tracy Guren. *Merit of Our Mothers: A Bilingual Anthology of Jewish Women's Prayers.* Translated by Tracy Guren Klirs, Ida Cohen Selavan, and Gella Schweid Fishman; annotated by Faedra Lazar Weiss and Barbara Selya. Cincinnati: Hebrew Union College Press, 1992.

National Federation of Temple Sisterhoods. *Covenant of the Heart: Prayers, Poems, and Meditations from the Women of Reform Judaism.* New York: National Federation of Temple Sisterhoods, 1993.

Spiegel, Marcia Cohn, and Deborah Lipton Kremsdorf. *Women Speak to God: The Prayers and Poems of Jewish Women.* San Diego: Women's Institute for Continuing Education, 1987.

Tarnor, Norman. *A Book of Jewish Women's Prayers.* Translated, selected, and with commentary by Norman Tarnor. Northvale, NJ: Jason Aronson, 1995.

Weissler, Chava. "The Traditional Piety of Ashkenazic Women," in *Jewish Spirituality from the Sixteenth Century Revival to the Present,* Arthur Green, ed., 245–75. New York: Crossroad, 1989.

FOLKLORE AND REFERENCE

Eliach, Yaffa. *Hasidic Tales of the Holocaust.* New York: Oxford University Press, 1982.

Frankel, Ellen. *The Classic Tales: Four Thousand Years of Jewish Lore.* Northvale, NJ: Jason Aronson, 1989.

Frankel, Ellen, and Betsy Platkin Teutsch. *The Encyclopedia of Jewish Symbols.* Northvale, NJ: Jason Aronson, 1992.

Kitov, Eliyahu, *The Book of Our Heritage*, rev. ed. New York: Feldheim, 1978.

Kogos, Fred. *1001 Yiddish Proverbs*. New York: Citadel Press, 1970.

Labovitz, Annette, and Eugene Labovitz. *Time for My Soul*. Northvale, NJ: Jason Aronson, 1987.

McGaha, Michael. *Coat of Many Cultures: The Joseph Story in Spanish Literature, 1200–1492*. Philadelphia: The Jewish Publication Society, 1996.

Montefiore, C. G., and H. Loewe. *Rabbinic Anthology*. New York: Schocken, 1974.

Noy, Dov. *Folktales of Israel*. Chicago: University of Chicago Press, 1963.

Schwartz, Howard, and Anthony Rudolf, eds. *Voices Within the Ark: The Modern Jewish Poets*. New York: Avon, 1980.

Vilnay, Zev. *Legends of Jerusalem*. Philadelphia: The Jewish Publication Society, 1995.

Zweig, Stefan. *Jewish Legends*. New York: Markus Wiener, 1987.

INDEX

Aaron, 102, 105, 115, 309n
  ancestral house of, 56, 103, 221–22, 326n
  death and burial, 225, 300, 302, 327n
  Golden Calf incident, 136, 137
  as High Priest, 133, 136, 199
  Korakh's rebellion, 220–21
  and Miriam, 103–4, 113, 185, 212
  and Moses, xvii, 95, 117, 121, 197, 207, 209,
      210–13, 325n
  sons' deaths, 159–61
  wife Elisheva, xxiv, 104, 159–61, 338
Abba bar Kahana, 12
Abbaye, 201–2
Abel, 3, 10
Abihu, 104, 159, 160
Abimelekh, xxi, 19, 22, 27, 39, 67
Abiram, 220
Abraham, 11, 23, 229, 230
  and Abimelekh, 22, 27, 67
  conversion of souls by, 15–16
  death and burial, 31, 225
  and Hagar, xv, xxi, 15, 17–19, 28–29
  leaving of Ur, 12–13, 14, 15, 84
  remarriage, 31, 37–38
  renaming, 15, 20
  son Isaac, 22–23, 27, 30, 31, 32, 37, 44, 221
  son Ishmael, 20–21, 29
  wife Sarah, xx, 16, 175, 249
Absalom, 334n
Adah (wife of Esau), 338
Adah (wife of Lamech), 338
Adam, xv, xx, 3–10, 287
Adler, Rachel, 312n
Adonijah, 334n
Adoption, 288
Adultery
  as forbidden act, 120, 168, 174, 176
  laws and punishment, 180, 276–79
  trial by ordeal, 199–205, 323n
Agrippa II, 206
Ahab, 140
Akiva, 263, 276
Alexander the Great, 269–70, 332n
Alfar'anit, 341
Amalek, 71, 109, 115, 271, 307n
Amitlai, xxiii, 13, 14

Amminadab, 104
Amnon, 307n
Amon, 182
Amram, xvii, 95, 103, 175, 185, 324n
Amulets, 257, 288, 331n
Anat, 110, 140, 273
Angel of Death, 65, 225, 302
Angel of Justice, 128
Angel of Night (Laylah), 3
Angel of Souls, 3
Angels, 64, 65, 127–28, 130–31, 314n
Animals
  kindness to, 229, 274
  mother's love and, 186
  sacrificing of, 151–53, 173, 317n
  soothsaying dogs, 230
"Ape and the Leopard, The," 74
Aphrodite, 27
Apple, as forbidden fruit, 8, 287
Ark, Noah's, 11–12
Ark of the Covenant, 130, 133
Artemis, 273
Asa, 140
Asher, 49, 55, 57, 73, 85
Asherah, 55, 139–41, 261, 281
Asnat, xxiv, 71, 81, 82–83, 85, 338
Assimilation, 183
Astarte, 261, 330n
Atonement ritual, 172
Azazel, 172

Baal, 140
Baal-hanan, 71
Balaam, xv, 47, 228–32, 237, 327n
Balak, 228, 229, 231, 232–33
Barrenness, 17, 70, 158, 180, 287–88
Basemath, 44, 338
Battle songs, 110–11
Batyah, xxiv, 86, 96–98, 101, 310nn, 341
Beauty, physical, 16
Beeri, 44
Ben-Ammi, 341
Benjamin, 56, 57, 62, 64, 69–70, 81–82, 84, 86
Berechiah ben Natronai HaNakdan, 74, 320n
Berenice, 206, 324n
Beruriah, xxiii, 124, 161, 313n, 335–36n

Bestiality, 174, 177–78, 180, 320*nn*
Bethuel, 31
Bezalel, 103, 136, 142
Bilhah, xxiv, 65, 338
    childbearing, 17, 49, 57, 59–60
    death and burial, 69, 86, 89, 302
    Reuben and, 68, 334*n*
    role as matriarch, 56–57, 335–36*n*
Birthrights, 272
Blame, 19
Blasphemy, 186–87
Blessings, 35–36, 199, 231–32, 258–59, 286, 295
Blood, 157–58, 163–64, 167, 168–69, 173
Boaz, 79
Borrowing, 100
Bread, 114–15, 131–32, 184–85, 192, 219, 223
Bridegroom of Blood, 100–101
"Bridegroom Saved from Angel of Death," 302
Bride-price, 61, 124, 274, 277, 322*n*
Bubbes, xix–xx
Buber, Martin, 296
Burning Bush, 93, 100
Burnt offerings, 151, 163, 165

Cain, 3, 5, 10
Caleb, 103, 113, 215, 216, 254
Canaan, 12–13, 15, 60–61, 64, 215–16, 315*n*
Candle lighting, 133–34
Census, of Israelites, 197, 198, 234, 323*n*
Challah, *See* Hallah
Chastity, 276–77, 333*n*
Chattel, 53, 123
Cherubim, 130–31
Chickpeas, 287
Childbirth, 5, 9, 163–66, 288
Children, 30, 70
    abuse of, 123
    adoption of, 288
    bastards, 176, 279, 319*n*, 334*n*
    blessings versus curses, 231
    defiant, 273, 332*n*
    ethical wills to, 299–300
    favoritism and, 20–21, 42, 62, 65, 74
    firstborn, 108, 272
    guilt visited on, 283–84
    honoring of parents, 120, 123, 180
    orphans, 126, 262
    sacrificing of, 182
"Choose life," 292, 294
Chosenness, 258, 259–60, 331*nn*
Circumcision, 28, 100, 157
Clans, 234, 243, 329*nn*
"Clever Wife," 170–71
Colette, Sage of Jerusalem, 289, 335*n*
Conversion of souls, 15–16
Conversos, 131–32, 314*n*
Cozbi, xxiv, 234–35, 338
Creation, of human race, 3–6

Crones, 249–50
Cross-dressing, 273
Crusades, 290, 335*n*
Curses
    barrenness, 17, 70, 158, 180
    blessings versus, 231, 232
    pain in childbirth, 5, 9, 288
    sexual desire and, 8–9
    two-mountains ritual, 286–87
Cyrus of Persia, 266, 329*n*, 335*n*

"Damaged goods," 68, 124, 180, 277
Dan, 49, 57, 73
Dance, 111–12, 317*n*
Datan, 220
Daughters, xix, 122
    defiant, 273, 332*n*
    of priests, 185–86, 321*n*
    reverence of, 256
David, 27, 56, 79, 229, 248, 307*n*
Death, 3, 10, 185
Death penalty, 180
Deborah, xxiv, 31, 64, 69, 110–11, 250, 335–36*n*,
    338
Delilah, 80
Depression, 289
Desire, 3, 255. *See also* Sexual desire
Desolation, 290, 335*nn*
Deuteronomy, 265–66, 330*n*, 332*n*
Diana, 273
Dietary laws, 127, 157, 159, 161–62, 223, 313*n*,
    317*n*
Dinah, xxi, xxii, 58, 66–67, 88, 338
    daughter Asnat, 82–83, 85
    Hamor's request for, 67–68
    lineage, 49, 55, 103
    rape of, 64, 65, 66, 67, 68
    silence/invisibility, 65–66, 70–71, 85
Divorce, 60, 237, 274–76, 278, 321*n*, 332*n*, 333*nn*
Documentary Hypothesis, 330*n*
Dogs, 230
"Donah, Donah" (song), 153–54, 317*n*
Double standards, 205
Dreams, 83, 308*n*

Eavesdropping, 24, 44–45
Edith, xxiv, 22, 26, 223, 341
El, 140, 236
Eldad, 197, 207
Eldering, 249–50, 329*n*
Eleazar, 104, 160, 225, 234
Eliach, Yaffa, 192
Eliezer (Moses' son), 116, 117
Eliezer (servant), xvi, 31–33, 34, 36, 50, 69
Eliezer ben Jacob, 125
Elijah, 86, 189–90, 302, 310*n*, 316*n*, 326*n*
Elijah's cup, 137–38
Eliphaz, 71

Elisha ben Abuyah, 274, 333*n*
Elisheva, xxiv, 104, 159–61, 338
Elon, 44
Elzaphan, 160
Enheduanna, 13, 305*n*
Enlightenment, 252, 330*n*
Enoch, 310*n*
Ephraim, 56, 57, 71, 81, 87, 89, 248, 329*n*
Er, 72, 75, 76
Esau, xvi, 54, 64, 229, 306*n*
    as favored son, 21, 39, 42, 44–45
    genealogy of, 64, 71
    marriage, 37, 44, 67, 74–75
    mother Rebecca's love, 47–48
Esther, xxiii
Ethical wills, 299–300
Etrog (fruit), 287–88
Eve, xv, xxiii, 3–10, 255, 282, 287–88, 338
Evil eye, 231
Excommunication, 180, 181
Exodus, Book of, 330*n*
Exodus from Egypt, 105–8
"Eye for an eye," 51, 285
Ezekiel, 119, 191
Ezra, 329*n*

Faith, tests of, 259
Family, 9–10, 243, 329*nn*. *See also* Children; Parents
Favoritism, 20–21, 42, 62, 65, 74
Fertility, 54, 58, 128–29, 258–59. *See also* Barrenness
Folk remedies, 57–58, 287–88
Food, 287–88. *See also* Dietary laws; *specific foods*
Forbidden fruit, apple as, 8, 287
Foreign nations, law of, 183
Fringes, on garments, 215, 217–19
Fruitfulness. *See* Fertility

Gabriel, 14, 97
Gad, 49, 55, 57, 73
Generosity, 144–45, 189–90
Genitals, male, 285
Gershom, 93, 99–100, 116, 117
Gershom ben Judah, 267–68, 276, 332*n*
"Gift of Seven Years," 189–90
Gikatilla, 314*n*
Gloom, 288–89
Glueckel of Hameln, 299–300
God
    drawing near to, 152–53
    feminine images of, 248
    as healer, 113–14
    hidden face of, 139, 192–93, 295–96, 322*n*
    household of, 211
    immanence and transcendence of, 252
    justice of, 322*n*
    and love, 293
    mercy of, 253–54
    names for, 236, 328*n*

    as nurse, 247
    physical forms of, 253
    sexuality of, 127–28, 314*n*
    See also Shekhinah
Gods/goddesses. *See* Idols; *specific gods and goddesses*
Golden Calf, 136, 137, 138–39, 258
Gomorrah, destruction of, 22
Gracia, Doña, 335–36*n*
Graves, 89, 109–10, 302–3
Grief, 87–88, 289
Guilt, 119–20, 199, 200–205, 283–84, 323
Guilt offerings, 152

Hadar, 71
Hadorah, 85
Hadrian, 155
Hagar, xv–xvi, xxi, 227, 338
    Sarah and, xv, xxi, 15, 17–19, 22, 28–29
    son Ishmael, 17, 20, 29–30
Haggadah, 106, 256, 311*n*, 318*n*, 331*n*, 336*n*
Hair, 202–3, 205–6, 323–24*nn*
Hallah, 114–15, 131–32, 219, 223
Ham, 11
Haman, 307*n*
Hamor, 64, 66, 67, 68
Hands, women's, 142
Hanina ben Dosa, 144–45
Hannah, 110–11, 311*n*, 335–36*n*
Hannah Rachel. *See* Werbermacher, Hannah Rachel
Ha-Rahaman, 59
Healing, 113–14, 213–14, 318*n*, 335–36*n*
Helena of Adiabene, 144, 206, 324*n*
Heschel, Abraham Joshua, 139, 296
Heschel, Susannah, 256
Hezekiah, 140
Hillel, 276, 333*n*
Hillesum, Etty, 296
Hirah the Adullamite, 78
Hiyya, 210
Hoglah, xxiv, 339
Holiness, 179–80, 191–92
Holocaust, 95, 139, 191–92, 290–91, 295–96,
    322*n*
Homosexuality, 174, 176–77, 180, 319*n*
Hoopoe, 135
Horus, 95
Hoshaya the Elder, 28
Hospitality, 23, 24–25
Households, 34, 61–63, 211
Huldah, xxii–xxiii, 217, 250, 265–66, 281, 335–36*n*
Human race, creation of, 3–6
Hur, 113, 115

Idit. *See* Edith
Idols, 242, 253
    goddess worship, 315*n*, 316*n*
    Golden Calf, 136, 137, 138–39, 258
    household, 61–63

Idols (*cont.*)
  Miriam bat Tanhum's story, 155, 317*n*
  Moses' warning, 262
  physical forms of God, 253
  sexual desire and, 141
  See also specific gods and goddesses
Immanence, 252
Impurity, 167–71, 318–19*n*
Inanna, 101, 273
Incest, 26–27, 168, 174, 175, 176, 180
Infertility. *See* Barrenness
Infidelity. *See* Adultery
Inheritance, 272, 322*n*
  by Leah and Rachel, 61
  levirate marriage and, 284
  widows and, 275
  Zelophekhad's daughters, 197, 234–36, 242–43
Injury, 123, 285
Intermarriage, 44, 48, 67, 74–75, 232–33, 242
Iron, 288
Isaac, xvi, 39–40, 229
  Abimelekh and, 39, 67
  birth, naming, circumcision, 19, 20, 22, 24, 27–28
  death, 64, 225
  mother Sarah, 21, 29, 42
  sacrifice of, 22–23, 27, 30, 37, 182, 221
  son Esau, 39, 42
  son Jacob, 39, 45–46, 47, 51
  wife Rebecca, 31, 32–37, 44, 50
Isaiah, 191, 192, 224, 248
Ishmael, xvi, 20, 229
  adoptive mother Sarah, 17
  banishment, 22, 28–29, 119
  birthright, 19, 20–21, 42, 272
  death, 31
  marriage, 44, 67
  mother Hagar, 17, 29–30
  near-death, 29–30
Ishtar, 101, 110, 273
Isis, 27, 95, 101
Israel, name derivation of, 64
Issachar, 49, 55, 73
Itamar, 104, 160
Izhar, 220

Jackson, Livia Bitton, 291
Jacob, xvi–xvii, xxi, xxii, 85, 89, 307*n*
  adoption of grandsons, 87–88
  daughter Dinah, 66, 68
  death and burial, 87, 225, 298
  deceit of Isaac, 39, 45–47, 51, 119
  extortion by Laban, 34, 49, 52, 53
  "eye for an eye," 51
  favoritism by, 65, 72, 87–88
  marriages, 37, 44, 175, 275
  as Rebecca's favored son, 21, 33, 39, 42, 50

  return to Canaan, 60–61, 64
  son Benjamin's naming, 70
  wife Leah, 49, 52–53, 58
  wife Rachel, 49, 50, 51–54, 56, 61–62, 69
  wrestling with angels, 64, 65
Jacob's ladder, 49–50
Japheth, 11
Jealousy, 18–19, 200–201, 231
Jephthah, 78, 238–39, 307–8*n*, 328*n*
Jeremiah, 191, 281
Jeroboam, 187
Jerusalem, 126, 290, 335*n*
Jethro, xvii, 99, 116, 117, 283
Jewelry, and Golden Calf, 137
Jezebel, 140, 316*n*
Jocasta, 27
Joseph, xxii, 47, 62, 329*n*
  death and burial, 87, 109–10
  dreams, 72, 73
  father Jacob, 42, 65, 72, 87, 89
  mother Rachel, 49, 59–60
  naming, 59, 69
  Potiphar's wife, 72, 80
  selling into slavery, 19, 72
  wife Asnat, 71, 81, 82–83
Josephus, 206
Joshua, 28, 254, 281
  Amalek and, 109, 115
  Moses and, 207, 234, 295, 301, 303
  as spy, 215, 216
Josiah, xxii, 140–41, 182, 265–66, 281
Jubilees, 188–89
Judah, xxiii, 81, 84
  mother Leah, 49, 55, 56, 57, 73
  and Tamar, 72, 74–79, 281, 307*nn*
Judah the Prince (rabbi), 153–54, 250
Judges, women as, 269–70, 335–36*n*
Judith, 44, 339
Justice, 267, 269–70

Kabbalah, 314*n*, 322*n*
Keturah, xxiv, 31, 37–38, 229, 339
Kinship, of women, 175–76
Knots, symbolism of, 218–19
Korakh, 197, 220–21, 326*n*
Kosher. *See* Dietary law

Laban, xvii, 31, 34, 49, 52, 60–63, 69
Ladders, symbolism of, 49–50
Laughter, 20, 23–24
Leadership, 117
Leah, xvii, xxi–xxii, 65, 339
  burial with Jacob, 88, 89
  children of, 17, 49, 54–56
  eyes' weakness, 51, 54
  husband Jacob, 49, 51–53, 60–61, 86
  inheritance from Laban, 61

Jacob's favoritism, 65
  as matriarch, 57, 335–36n
  sister Rachel, 57–60, 62–63
Lentils, 43
Leprosy, 163, 167, 212–13, 283
Lesbianism, 177, 319nn
Levi, 49, 55, 56, 57, 64, 67, 73, 103
Levirate marriage, 75, 77, 284, 334n
Levites. *See* Priests
Lilith, xx, 4–5, 288
Loneliness, 170–71
Lot, 11, 13, 15, 22, 24–27, 79
Love, 51–54, 186, 293
Luria, Isaac, 132, 314n, 335–36n

Maacah, 140
Mahalath, 39, 44, 74–75, 339
Mahlah, 339
Maid of Ludomir. *See* Werbermacher, Hannah Rachel
Maimonides, 128, 314n, 334n
Manasseh, 71, 81, 87, 182, 320n, 329n
Mandrakes, 57–58
Manna, 109, 114–15
Marduk, 27
Marriage
  forbidden partners, 174–75
  to foreign wives, 141
  husbands' obligations, 282
  laws related to, 274–76, 333nn
  levirate, 75, 77, 284, 334n
  polygamy, 267–68
  rape within, 280
  seduction of virgins and, 124
  to sisters, 52, 175
  slaves and, 121–22, 180–81
  veiling of bride, 36
  See also Adultery; Divorce; Intermarriage; Remarriage
Matchmaking, 32
Matriarchs, 57, 335–36n
Matzah, 107–8, 184
"Measure for measure," 51, 285
Medad, 197, 207
Mehetabel, 71, 339
Meir, 124–25, 161, 214
Men
  adultery and, 120, 200–201, 205, 278
  compensation by wife's injurer, 123
  favored children and, 20–21
  guilt and, 119–20
  homosexuality, 174, 176–77, 180, 319n
  honoring of father's wife, 280, 334n
  importance of sons, 54–56, 108
  marital obligations, 282
  nocturnal emissions, 167
  sexual desire and, 9
  as widowers, 77, 86

Menstruation
  blood symbolism and, 157–58
  "Clever Wife" tale, 170–71
  forbidden sexual practices, 174
  impurity and, 167, 168–69, 318–19n
  infirmity and, 169
  menarche ritual, 169–70
  Rachel and taboo of, 63
Mercy, 253–54, 274
Mezzuzah, 251, 257
Midian, 38, 229, 235, 237
Milcah (daughter of Zelophekhad), xxiv, 339
Milcah (wife of Nahor), xxiv, 13, 33, 34, 40, 339
Milham (Phoenix Bird), xv, xvii
Milk, 127, 313n, 314n
Miriam, xvii, xviii, xxii, 160, 309n, 310n, 335–36n, 339
  brother Aaron, 212
  brother Moses, 95, 98, 101, 103–4, 283
  challenging of Moses, 197, 207, 209, 210–13, 324nn
  death and burial, 225, 300, 303, 327n
  husband Caleb, 103, 113
  Israelites' waiting for, 214
  as leprosy victim, 212–13
  lineage, 56, 103–4
  names of, 112–13, 310n
  and Promised Land, 137, 216
  search for, 303
  songs of, 109, 110, 212, 239, 304
  strength of character, 95–96
Miriam bat Tanhum, 155, 317n
Miriam's Well, xv–xviii, 226–27
Mirrors, 143–44
Mishael, 160
Moab, 27, 229, 341
Molech, 172, 180
Moses, xv, xvii, xxii, 126, 208, 234, 267, 309n
  ancestors of, 56, 103
  Batyah's rescue of, 93, 96–98
  as "bridegroom of blood," 100–101
  brother Aaron, 159–60, 225
  covenant at Sinai, 50, 254
  death and burial, 225, 300–302, 336n
  forty years of wandering, 215, 247, 251
  God and, 211, 236, 254, 292, 325n, 330n
  and Golden Calf, 136–37, 258
  hierarchy of listeners to, 292
  Korakh's rebellion, 220–21, 326n
  marital obligations, 283
  misquoting of God's message, 117–18, 312n
  mother Yokheved, 93, 94–95, 98
  mothering of Israelites, 207–8
  naming of, 310n
  parting of sea, 109, 110
  prayer for healing, 213, 325n
  Serakh bat Asher and, 85–86

Moses (*cont.*)
    siblings' challenge, 197, 207, 209–13, 324–25nn
    sister Miriam, 95, 98, 101, 103–4, 283, 300
    son Eliezer, 116, 117
    son Gershom, 99–100, 116, 117
    Tabernacle, 130, 133, 136, 142–43, 146, 159
    Ten Commandments, 116, 136–37, 251
    wife Zipporah, 93, 98–101, 116–17, 209, 229,
        283, 301
Mot, 140
Mothers, xix, 17, 186
Mount Sinai, 50, 116, 254
Mourning, 138–39, 159–61
"Mouse Seeks a Wife," 178, 320n
Musicians, women as, 111, 317n
Mutilation of body, 181

Naamah (sister of Tubal-Cain), 339
Naamah (wife of Noah), xxiii, 11, 12, 341
Nachmanides (Ramban), 307n
Nadab, 104, 159, 160
Nahor, xvi, 13
Nakhshon, 104
Naomi, 250, 275
Naphtali, 49, 57, 73
Napoleon, 330n
Nature cults, 261–62
Nazirite, laws of, 199, 205–6, 323n, 324n
Nebuchadnezzar, 266, 335n
Necromancy, 181–82
Negative thinking, 288–90
Nehemiah, 111
Nightmares, 83
Nimrod, 13, 14
Noadiah, 111, 335–36n
Noah, 11, 12
Noah (daughter of Zelophekhad), xxiv, 339
Nocturnal emissions, 167
Numbers, Book of, 197
Numbers, significance of, 164–65

Oaths. *See* Vows
Occult practices, 268–69, 332nn
Odd numbers, 164–65
Oedipus, 27, 75, 97
Offerings, 151–52, 163, 165, 172, 222, 317n
Og, 28, 247
Oholiab, 136
Oholibamah, 71, 339
On, 220
Onan, 72, 75, 76
Orange, on seder plate, 256
Orphans, 126, 262
Osiris, 27, 101

Paltit, 25, 26, 341
Pardes, Ilana, 101

Parents
    ethical wills, 299–300
    favoritism by, 20–21, 42, 62, 65, 74
    guilt visited on children, 283–84
    honoring of by children, 120, 123
    honoring of father's wife, 280, 334n
    insulting of, 180
    mother's love, 186
Passover, 105, 126, 261, 265–66. *See also* Haggadah;
    Seder
Perez, 72, 79
Performative language, 203, 323n
Pharaoh
    Israelites and, 93–94, 95, 106, 109
    Sarah and, xxi, 15, 16, 18, 19
Phoenix Bird (Milham), xv, xvii
Pilgrimages, 126, 265, 313n, 331n
Pinkhas, 233, 234, 235, 238–39
Plagues, 102, 105, 106–7, 207
Polygamy, 267–68
Potiphar, 72, 82–83
Potiphera, 82
Poverty, 126, 263
Power, 63, 126
Prayer, 112, 128, 165–66, 213, 219, 311n, 325n
Prayer shawl (*tallit*), 217–18, 326n
Pregnancy, 285
Priests, 172, 199, 295
    daughters of, 185–86, 321n
    female Levites, 156–57, 249, 317n
    responsibility for needs of, 222, 262
    retirement of, 249, 329nn
    roles/obligations, 184–86, 320–21nn
    Torah for, 151–52, 317n
    trial-by-ordeal role, 202–4
    vestments, 133, 134–35, 146
Promised Land, 93, 137, 215, 216
Pronouns, generic, 118–19, 312n
Prophets, 208, 335–36n
Prosperity, 262–63
Prostitution, 77–78, 281
Psalms, power of, 289–90
Puah, xxiv, 93–94, 101, 248, 309n, 339
Punishment, 173, 180–81, 285, 319n
Purification offerings, 152, 163, 165, 172, 317n
Purity. *See* Chastity; Impurity

Rabbenu Gershom. *See* Gershom ben Judah
Rabbis, role of, xx
Rachel, xvi–xvii, xxi, 57, 59, 65, 307n, 339
    barrenness, 54, 56
    childbearing, 17, 49, 64, 65
    death and burial, 62, 64, 69–70, 89
    as favored daughter, 62–63
    grave, 70, 302
    inheritance from Laban, 61
    and Jacob, 34, 49–54, 60–61, 65, 86–88

as matriarch, 57, 335–36n
mourning for children, 303
sister Leah, 52–53, 58
son Benjamin, 69–70
son Joseph, 59, 69, 89
theft of idols by, 61–63
wells and, 227
Rahab, 96, 216–17, 281, 310n, 325nn
Ramban. *See* Nachmanides
Rape, 66, 68, 124, 168, 278, 279–80
Raphael, 172
Rashi, 313n, 334n
Rebecca, xvi, xxi, 33, 34, 40, 340
barrenness, 40–41
blessing from mother, 35, 36
childbearing, 17, 41
death, 69
husband Isaac, 31, 32–37, 48, 50
as matriarch, 57, 335–36n
son Esau, 47–48
son Jacob, 39, 42, 45–46, 47–48, 50
wells and, 227
Recipes, 43, 46, 306n
Red (color), 158
Red Heifer ritual, 224–25
Rehoboam, 140, 309n
Rejoicing, 261, 264–65
Religious zeal, 233
Remarriage, 281–82
Restitution, 199
Reuben, 70, 72, 81, 103
Bilhah and, 68, 334n
as favored child, 21, 307n
mother Leah, 49, 55, 58, 73
Ritual contagion, 167, 318n
Romance, 51–52
Rosenzweig, Franz, 293
Rosh Hashanah, 57
Rosh Hodesh, 137, 315n
Rubenstein, Richard, 296
Ruth, 27, 79, 229, 275

Sabbath, observance of, 254–55
"Sabbath Loaves," 131–32, 314n
Sabbaticals, 188–89, 321–22nn
Sacrifice, 151–53, 156–57, 173, 182, 215, 317nn
Sadness, 289
Sages, role of, xx
Salt, 222–23
Samson, 80, 205, 323n
Samuel, 205
Sansenoy, 4, 288
Sarai/Sarah, xv, xx–xi, 14, 40, 37, 175, 340
Abimelekh and, 22, 27
childbearing, 17
conversion of souls by, 15–16
death and burial, 30, 31, 249

Hagar and, xv, xxi, 15, 17, 18–19, 22, 28–29
laughter and, 20, 23–24
leaving of Ur, 11, 13, 84
as matriarch, 57, 335–36n
Pharaoh and, xxi, 15, 16, 18, 19
physical beauty of, 16
renaming, 15, 20
son Isaac, 19, 20, 22, 24, 27–29, 30, 37, 303
Sargon, 95
Satan, 30, 100. *See also* Serpent
Saul, 182, 307n, 313n
Scapegoats, 172–73
Schachter-Shalomi, Zalman, 329n
Seamstresses, 135
Seder, 106, 223, 231, 256
Seduction, 80, 124–25, 201–2
Semangelof, 4, 288
Senoy, 4, 288
Septuagint, 325
Serakh bat Asher, xv, xxii, 103, 234, 340
entry into Paradise, 310n
legend of, 85–86
Serpent, 6, 7, 100, 255
Seth, 101
Sexual desire, 8–9
adultery and, 120
husbands' obligations, 282
idolatry and, 141
mirrors and, 143
prostitution and, 77–78
rape and, 66
seduction and, 124–25, 201–2
of women, 80
Sexual discharges, 167, 168
Sexual practices, 168, 174–76, 180, 232, 319–20nn
Shame, 8, 202
Shammai, 276, 333n
Shapiro, Kalonymus Kalman, 296
Shavuot, 50, 126, 261, 265
Shechem, 58, 64, 65, 66, 67, 68, 275
She'ilah, xxiv, 238–39, 307–8n
Shekhinah, xv, 3, 9, 12, 19, 114, 132, 146
barrenness and, 22, 56
God and, 8, 192, 236, 248, 322n
Shelah, 72, 75, 76, 77
Shelomit, 187, 340
Shem, 11
Shifra, xxiv, 93–94, 101, 248, 309n, 340
Shimon bar Yohai, 125, 313n
Shimon ben Shetakh, 125, 313n
Shokhen Ad, xv
Shua, 72, 75, 341
Sihon, 247
Simeon, 49, 55, 64, 67, 73, 81, 103
Simkhat Hokhmah, 250
Sin, 3, 8, 165, 199, 210, 323n
Sisera, 96, 111

Sisters, marriage to, 52, 175
Skotsl, 293–94
Slaves, 322*n*
    female, 106–7, 180–81, 264
    Israelites as, 190, 308*n*
    married, 121–22
Sodom, 22, 26
Solidarity, 96–97
Solomon, 135, 224, 309*n*, 327*n*
Songs, 110–11, 153–54, 212, 239, 304, 317*n*
Sons, 54–56, 108
Sorceresses, 125, 182
Sorcery, 181–82, 268–69, 313*n*
Souls, 3–4, 15–16
Spells, casting of, 203–4
Spira, Israel, 291
Spitting, 213–14
Strangers, fear of, 242–43
Sukkot, 126, 261, 265, 288, 295
Surrogate motherhood, 17
Szold, Henrietta, 335–36*n*

Tabernacle (*Mishkan*), 146, 172, 197
    building of, 142, 143
    consecration of, 159, 199
    furnishings for, 130, 133, 136
Taboos, 286–87
Talmud, 125, 177, 251
Tamar, xxiv, 72, 74–79, 281, 307*nn*, 340
Tefillin, 251, 257
Ten Commandments, 116, 118–19, 120, 136–37, 251
Terah, 11, 12, 13, 14, 15
Teutsch, Betsy Platkin, 306*n*
Theodicy, 322*n*, 326*n*
Thermutis. *See* Batyah
Tiamat, 27
Timna, 71, 340
Tirtzah, xxiv, 340
Tithes, 262–63
Titus, 324*n*, 335*n*
Torah, xix, 6–7
    modification of, 251–52, 330*n*
    for priests, 151–52, 317*n*
Tower of Babel, 11, 12
Transcendence, 252
Transvestism, 273
Tree of Knowledge, 6–7, 8
Trees, 261–62, 269
Trial by ordeal, 199, 200–201, 202–5, 323*n*
Triangle Fire (1911), 147, 316*n*
Two-mountains ritual, 286–87
Tzena Urena, 228, 327*n*

"Unpaid Pledge," 240
Uzziel, 160

Veils, 36, 77
Vespasian, 324*n*
Vestments, 133, 134–35, 146
Virgins, 124, 180–81, 279
    chastity of, 276–77, 333*n*
    Midianite, 237, 241
Vows, 237–40, 328*n*

War, 110–11, 241, 269, 271–72
"Weasel and the Well, The," 239–40
Weaving, 142, 146–47
Weddings, 36
Wells, xv–xviii, 226–27
Werbermacher, Hannah Rachel, xxv, 296–97, 336*n*
Widowers, 77, 86
Widows, 75, 76, 126, 237, 262, 263, 275
Wisdom, 7, 147–48, 316*n*
Witch of Endor, 182, 313*n*
Witches. *See* Sorceresses
Wosk, Yosef, 239

Yael, 96, 111, 310*n*
Yehoshafat, 140
Yohanan ben Zakkai, 205, 224, 280, 327*n*
Yokheved, xv, xvii, xxiv, 175, 235, 340
    entry into Promised Land, 137, 303
    Joshua as guardian of, 301
    meaning of name, 310*n*
    son Moses, 14, 93–95, 98, 101, 303
Yom Kippur, 50, 173, 188, 238, 328*n*
Yose bar Halafta, 32

Zebulun, 49, 55, 73
Zelophekhad's daughters, 197, 234–36, 242, 243
Zerah, 72
Zeus, 27
Zillah, 340
Zilpah, xxi, xxiv, 65, 103, 340
    childbearing, 17, 49, 55, 59–60
    death and burial, 69, 86, 89, 302
    role as matriarch, 56–57, 335–36*n*
Zimri, 234, 235
Zipporah, xv, xvii, xxiv, 209, 340
    Bridegroom of Blood and, 100–101
    husband Moses, 93, 98–101, 116–17, 229, 283
    Joshua as protector of, 301
    wells and, 98–99, 227
Zohar, 132, 193, 313*n*, 322*n*
Zuleika (Potiphar's wife), xxiv, 72, 80, 341
Zur, 234, 235, 237

Ellen Frankel is the author of many books, including *The Classic Tales: Four Thousand Years of Jewish Lore* and *The Encyclopedia of Jewish Symbols*, and is also a storyteller. Dr. Frankel received her Ph.D. in comparative literature from Princeton University. She is editor in chief of The Jewish Publication Society.